The Founding of the

Kamakura Shogunate

1180-1185

WITH SELECTED TRANSLATIONS

FROM THE AZUMA KAGAMI

By Minoru Shinoda

 New York, 1960

COLUMBIA UNIVERSITY PRESS

The addition to the "Records of Civilization: Sources and Studies" of a group of translations of Oriental historical materials, of which this volume is one, was made possible by funds granted by Carnegie Corporation of New York. That Corporation is not, however, the author, owner, publisher, or proprietor of this publication, and is not to be understood as approving by virtue of its grant any of the statements made or views expressed therein.

Published in Great Britain, India, and Pakistan
by the Oxford University Press
London, Bombay, and Karachi

Library of Congress Catalog Card Number: 59–10433
Manufactured in the United States of America

The Founding of the Kamakura Shogunate

1180-1185

NUMBER LVII
OF THE RECORDS OF CIVILIZATION,
SOURCES AND STUDIES

Preface

In the comparatively brief period—about a century—since the emergence of the Japanese from seclusion, the West has shown a surprising degree of interest in the culture of the Japanese. Far from having lessened this interest, the late war appears to have stimulated in the West a greater interest in things Japanese, particularly in such aspects of Japanese culture as art, architecture, literature, drama, and religion.

Although this interest has resulted in a number of notable studies and translations, the greater part of the vast store of materials which constitute the written legacy of the Japanese remains untranslated and unknown in the West. In the field of history alone, despite an excellent start by Western scholars nearly three quarters of a century ago, resulting in the translation and annotation of the two oldest extant chronicles of the Japanese, literally dozens of works still await the translator's hand and the examination of the Western scholar. Granted that not all of this literature merits serious attention, a more representative list of translations of Japanese historical writing than presently exists is most certainly to be desired.

Something of the magnitude of the task of introducing Japanese historical writing to the West may be seen in the example of this study. It purports to cover but five short years of the history of the Kamakura shogunate which lasted for one hundred and fifty years. The author has found it expedient, if not necessary, to translate several chapters of an indispensable historical work covering these years. But these chapters, five of which pertain to the years under examination, constitute but a fragment of a larger work of fifty-two chapters. The present study, in other words, takes up only one tenth of a single historical work.

Nevertheless, it is hoped that in this small way the Western student of Japanese civilization may be introduced to a little-known period of its history as well as to an important historical work. In order that such a dual purpose might be realized within the covers of a single volume the translations are presented in Part Two of this study.

The work in question is the *Azuma kagami* [Mirror of Eastern Japan] concerning which a detailed explanation is provided in the Introduction. For the moment it is well to point out that the *Azuma kagami* is a compilation made by the Kamakura shogunate itself, and hence this study of the founding of the shogunate proposes to present largely the point of the view of the founders. It makes no claim to a thorough consideration of other points of view, except insofar as they are referred to in the *Azuma kagami*. Nevertheless, it is felt that, however narrow its purpose and scope, the explanation and clarification of the aims of the founders themselves and the circumstances surrounding the founding are ample justification for the study.

To facilitate reference to the Japanese text of the *Azuma kagami* the original Japanese dates and era names have been retained. The Western dates and the corresponding Japanese era designations are as follows:

1180—Jishō 4	1184—Juei 3
1181—Jishō 5	Genreki 1, as of Fourth
Yōwa 1, as of Seventh	Month, 16th day
Month, 14th day	1185—Genreki 2
1182—Yōwa 2	Bunji 1, as of Eighth
Juei 1, as of Fifth	Month, 14th day
Month, 27th day	

Records for Juei 2 (1183) are not extant.

Beginning with Chapter III the footnote citations are, for the most part, to the *Azuma kagami*, and they are given simply as dates. Thus the citation "Jishō 5:2,9" is a reference to the entry in the *Azuma kagami* for that date, which is the Fifth Year of Jishō (1181), Second Month, Ninth Day. So that the reader may locate the translation easily, a key consisting of the era name and the Western year has provided at the top of each page of Part Two.

Although diacritical marks have been placed on most of the Japanese words which appear in these pages, they have been omitted from some of the better-known names and terms, such as Kyoto, Kanto, Honshu, Kyushu, shogun, and the like.

ACKNOWLEDGMENTS

The present work, particularly the middle chapters, represents a substantial revision of the dissertation submitted in January, 1957, to the Faculty of Political Science, Columbia University, in partial fulfillment of the requirements for the degree of Doctor of Philosophy. Errors of fact or interpretation in the original and particularly in this revision are mine and not those of my advisers and friends who have assisted me in various ways in the preparatory stages. I am especially indebted to three teachers and scholars, all lately of Columbia University: Sir George Sansom, under whom I was privileged to study and who first suggested the *Azuma kagami* as an object of study; Mr. Ryusaku Tsunoda, who patiently introduced me to the intricate style and contents of the *Azuma kagami* and who has imparted to me what appreciation of the work I now have; and Dr. Hugh Borton, now President of Haverford College, who, with characteristic patience and understanding, guided me through the final and crucial stages of the undertaking. Others who have read the manuscript in part or in whole and who have made valuable suggestions are: Dr. Martin Wilbur, Dr. Wm. Theodore de Bary, Dr. Donald Keene, Dr. Austin P. Evans, Dr. John H. Mundy, and Dr. James Morley. Dr. Morley has been especially helpful, and I am happy to state that his suggestions, in the main, have been adopted in the present work. To Mr. Howard Linton and Miss Miwa Kai of the East Asiatic Collections for their cooperation over the years in placing the necessary references at my disposal I owe a special vote of thanks. I wish also to acknowledge the generous financial assistance given to me in the past by the American Council of Learned Societies, John Hay Whitney Foundation, Japan Society of New York, Inc., and the History Department of Columbia University, the sponsors of the *Records of Civilization*, of which this volume is a part. Finally, a special word of thanks and appreciation goes to my wife, Emiko, for performing the tedious task of typing every draft of this work from beginning to end.

University of Hawaii   MINORU SHINODA
Honolulu

Contents

Illustrations

Part One

The Founding of the Kamakura Shogunate

Chapter I
Introduction

THE SIGNIFICANCE OF THE SHOGUNATE

The importance to Japanese history of the establishment of a military regime at Kamakura in the late twelfth century can scarcely be overemphasized. It marked the beginning of more than six hundred years of organized feudalism.[1] The *bakufu*, or shogunate, as this regime came to be known, was the first of a succession of such regimes which ruled Japan, almost without interruption, until the last half of the nineteenth century. Its founding signaled the decline in influence of the civilian aristocracy and the rise to power of the warrior class. By the policy it adopted toward the traditional ruling house, the Kamakura shogunate laid the basis for the peculiarly Japanese form of diarchy—the coexistence of a *de jure* sovereign, the emperor, and a *de facto* ruler, the shogun—which has characterized Japan's political system from the twelfth century to modern times. The cultural implications of the rise to power of the provincial warrior class and the shift of the nation's political center from Kyoto in the west, steeped in centuries of Chinese lore and learning, to Kamakura in the east, scarcely touched by the traditions and refinements of her western rival, have been great. It has meant, among other things, the more rapid diffusion of learning, the decline of Chinese influence, and the beginning of a more truly indigenous

---

[1] The term "organized feudalism" is applied to the Kamakura shogunate and subsequent military regimes which were organized on a wide territorial basis but which did not disturb the traditional central government of the imperial court nor the autonomy of the various local lords. The latter, who were vassals of the shogun, owed the shogun allegiance and certain services, but otherwise they were free to run their respective domains. Since the Kamakura shogunate was the first of such organized regimes, and since this study is concerned with its founding, it is hoped that the meaning of the term "organized feudalism" will become apparent in the chapters which follow. As for an explanation of feudalism in Japan, a historical survey is provided in Chapter II.

culture. By its emphasis on martial values the shogunate has wrought an incalculable influence on the thinking and way of life of generations of Japanese.

Yet, curiously, this important event in the evolution of the Japanese nation has received comparatively little attention in the West. It would seem, from the puzzlement and curiosity which the coexistence of emperor and shogun generally aroused among early Western visitors to Japan, that there would be by this late date a series of studies on the founding of the Kamakura shogunate and the beginnings of the system of dual rule. The fact is, however, that to date there has been only one serious monograph in a Western language on the subject.[2] Even this study, for all its excellence, was intended by its author to be merely an introductory paper.

No less curious is the fact that there has been so little Western interest in the source material generally regarded by Japanese historians as invaluable in the study and understanding of the founding and the early history of the shogunate. This is the *Azuma kagami* [Mirror of Eastern Japan], the semiofficial history in diary form of the Kamakura shogunate, covering the eighty-six years from 1180 to 1266. Until a few years ago, when a French study of selected source materials of the Kamakura period was published,[3] only scattered passages and documents from the *Azuma kagami* had been translated into a Western language. True, certain features of the work, such as its great length, its difficult and unorthodox style, and its lack of literary appeal, have made it generally unattractive, even to the Japanese; but these features in no wise diminish its value as an historical source. While the *Azuma kagami*, like any other source material, is not without its shortcomings which the historian must guard against, it remains the largest and, in the opinion of Japanese historians, the most important single source on the Kamakura shogunate.

[2] Kanji Asakawa, "The Founding of the Shogunate by Minamoto No Yoritomo," *Seminarium Kondakovianum*, VI (1933), 109–29.

[3] F. Jouon des Longrais, *Âge de Kamakura, sources* (1150–1333), *archives, chartes japonaises* (*monjo*).

THE EVOLUTIONARY CHARACTER
OF THE FOUNDING

This study, based on the *Azuma kagami,* attempts to explain and analyze the circumstances surrounding the founding of the Kama-kura shogunate. It is limited in scope to the period from 1180, the year when warrior groups of Eastern Japan under the leadership of the Minamoto family raised their standard of revolt against the Taira family—then identified with the government at Kyoto—to 1185, when the former achieved victory and when the shogunate, for all practical purposes, was established. Although the period under examination corresponds to the period of the Gempei[4] War, as this struggle was known, and although the war was an integral part of the founding process, the battles will not be described here at any great length—however stirring they were.[5] Rather, this study is concerned with the many problems—largely administrative and political —raised by the war for the Minamoto, for it was in the process of meeting and solving these problems that the shogunate evolved.

It will be noted that the problems faced by the Minamoto were largely those of securing and maintaining the support, not only of the warrior class, including vassals and non-vassals, but also of all other classes of society. Thus, in these pages the reader will be aware of the prominence given to the relations of the Minamoto with: (1) the imperial court and the Kyoto aristocracy who feared the loss of their ancient prerogatives because of the war and who maneuvered, sometimes with and sometimes against the Minamoto, to preserve them; (2) the religious orders, both Shinto and Buddhist,

---

[4] Gempei, from *gen* and *hei,* the Sinico-Japanese readings, respectively, for Minamoto and Taira. Other renditions of this combination of two proper names are Genpei, Gen-Pei, and Gen-Hei. The two families, it will be noted, were commonly referred to as the Genji and the Heiji (*gen* and *hei* plus *ji,* one of two Sinico-Japanese readings for *uji,* the family or clan). Another popular term for the Taira was Heike, *ke* being the Sinico-Japanese reading for *ie,* meaning house or family.

[5] In fact, the *Azuma kagami* is curiously brief, very matter-of-fact and to the point in its treatment of the battles, including the victories achieved by its sponsors. The historical romances, *Heike monogatari* (Tales of the Heike) and the *Gempei seisui-ki* (The rise and fall of the Gen and the Hei) are far more detailed and descriptive of the wars than the *Azuma kagami.* These romances are discussed more fully in the following section.

whose lands were overrun by warriors and who sought relief and restitution from the Minamoto, while their assistance—spiritual and material—was sought by the Minamoto; and (3) the common people, for whom Yoritomo, the chieftain of the Minamoto, showed a surprising degree of concern, whether for reasons of political expediency or out of sincere regard for their welfare. The measures and practices of the Minamoto with regard to these various elements of Japanese society during the war years were to shape the policies of the shogunate, and their success was to give to the organization at Kamakura a stability and permanence beyond the original expectations of the founders. In this connection it is important to note that many of the activities described in the *Azuma kagami* and discussed in these pages bore no direct relationship to the Gempei War. They were for the most part the routine activities of a feudal family, but they were as important as the war measures and policies of the Minamoto, if not more so, in the formation of the Kamakura shogunate.

One further explanation of the aim and scope of this study remains to be made. The terms "founding" and "shogunate" are used in these pages with certain reservations. Correctly speaking, the shogunate as such was not consciously established by Yoritomo, nor was the designation *bakufu,* or "shogunate," applied to his government until 1190. As claimant to the chieftainship of a group of related and associated families in a feudal society, Yoritomo had as his immediate concern in 1180 the improvement and preservation of the private status and fortunes of the group. When he launched the war to exterminate the enemy, he neither planned for nor envisioned a government with the vast public powers and influence which the shogunate was to enjoy a few years later. Between 1180, when the war was launched and a small military headquarters established at Kamakura, and 1192, when the title of shogun was conferred on Minamoto Yoritomo, a dozen years had elapsed and a whole series of events had taken place. And thus the precise year of the founding has been a controversial—though academic—question with Japanese historians, who still differ widely on their choice of dates. Besides the two extremes of 1180 and 1192, at least six other dates are frequently cited by Japanese historians as the year of the founding of the shogunate. These dates and the arguments in their favor which have been briefly summarized below[6] point out an important feature about the founding of the shogunate—that it was gradual and evolutionary, involving a series of wars and events, and extending over a period of years. However, although the designation *bakufu* was not applied to Yoritomo's government until 1190 and the title of shogun not conferred on him until 1192, it is possible to show, as this study attempts to do, that for all practical purposes, the founding of the shogunate had occurred by the end of 1185. By that time Yoritomo's government was functioning as the *de facto* government for the country; moreover, it had achieved a measure of recognition from the imperial court.

THE AZUMA KAGAMI, THE PRINCIPAL SOURCE

The *Azuma kagami* is the chronological record of the Kamakura shogunate in fifty-two chapters covering a period of eighty-six years, from 1180 to 1266. It assumes the form of a diary and appears to have been written on a day-to-day basis as the events it records took place. It has been shown by a number of scholars, however, that the work in its entirety was written in retrospect and compiled, presumably by shogunate scribes and other officials, sometime after 1266, the last year accounted for in the work. Although scholars differ slightly as to the exact period of its compilation, it is now generally agreed that the *Azuma kagami* was written between 1268 and 1301.[7] This is not surprising in view of the history of the Kamakura shogunate, whose founders were busy fighting for their existence in

[6] These dates and the reasons for their choice are: 1183, the year of the abandonment of Kyoto by the Taira and its flight westward; 1184, the year of the installation of the last of three boards at Kamakura, thus completing the administrative framework of the shogunate which was to last throughout its history; the spring of 1185 when the Minamoto defeated the Taira and achieved its supremacy in Japan; the fall of 1185 when Yoritomo's government was granted certain public powers by the imperial court, thus achieving a measure of formal recognition; 1189, the year of the conquest of Northern Japan by Yoritomo's armies, thus bringing all of Japan under one rule for the first time in its history; and 1190, the year of the conferment on Yoritomo of the rank of captain of the Imperial Guards which, by custom, entitled its holder to maintain a *bakufu*.

[7] Wada, for example, assigned the compilation to the period between 1268 and 1273. Yashiro assigned only the first half of the work to this period, and fixed the compilation of the remainder of the work to the period between 1284 and 1301. See Hidematsu Wada, *Kokushi setsuen*, pp. 325–58, and Kuniji Yashiro, *Azuma kagami no kenkyū*, pp. 15–17.

the early 1180s and who scarcely realized then or for some years after that they were establishing a government which was to last for one hundred and fifty years.

The work obviously was intended by its sponsors to be an official history in the manner of the official histories of the imperial court. There, since the Nara period (710–794), the practice had developed of compiling chronological accounts at the command of the emperor, and by the beginning of the tenth century six such accounts, known collectively as the *Rikkoku-shi,* or the Six National Histories,[8] had been compiled. Emulating the imperial court and perhaps motivated further by the need to give dignity to the young military government and to provide it with a justification for its existence, the rulers at Kamakura ordered the compilation of the *Azuma kagami.* However, because of its heavy reliance on non-shogunate documents and materials, especially for its earlier chapters, the work is generally classified as a semiofficial history.

Although it spans eighty-six years, accounts for ten of the years are missing from extant editions.[9] Moreover, entries for many days and months are missing, or may never have been written. There are, for example, only one hundred and ninety days accounted for in the three-year period between 1201 and 1203 (Chapters 17–19). The records also vary in length and fullness, those between 1201 and 1234 (Chapters 17–29), for example, being conspicuously brief. In fact, entries in this section of the work appear to be mere summaries of longer original accounts. On the other hand, the accounts for the early years with which this study is concerned are comparatively long and detailed.

Except for a few isolated passages and letters, the work is rendered throughout in *kambun,* or Sinico-Japanese, reflecting the desire of its sponsors to clothe the record in the accepted language and style of official histories of the imperial court. However, this *kambun* is highly irregular and unorthodox, containing a large admixture of the vernacular and indicating that members of the warrior class were

---

[8] These histories and the period covered by each are: *Nihon-gi* (from the beginnings to 697), *Shoku-Nihon-gi* (697–792), *Nihon kōki* (792–833), *Shoku-Nihon kōki* (833–858), and *Montoku jitsuroku* (850–858), and *Sandai jitsuroku* (858–887).

[9] These are for the years 1183, 1196–98, 1242, 1249, 1255, 1259, 1262, and 1264.

unfamiliar with this type of writing and lacked experience in using it. Although this "dog-Chinese," as Murdoch calls it,[10] leaves much to be desired as a medium of expression, its significance in the study of the warrior society of twelfth-century Japan should not be over-looked. It contains much that is new and fresh in vocabulary and in expression, pointing to the emergence of new concepts and a new way of life in Eastern Japan.

The *Azuma kagami* is more than a chronology of the activities of the Kamakura shogunate; it is also a record of official documents and papers. It contains the shogun's military and administrative orders, the correspondence exchanged between the shogunate and the imperial court, petitions and grievances addressed to the shogun, and other materials, such as reports and rosters. Even conversations purportedly engaged in by the shogun and other officials are recorded throughout the work. Thus the *Azuma kagami* is at once a history and a source book of the Kamakura shogunate. Moreover, the accounts are not limited to important matters of state. The amusements and social activities of the warriors and even matters as private as the shogun's extramarital affairs are recorded with surprising candor. Consequently, the *Azuma kagami* is a rich source of information on the social and cultural as well as the political life of the warrior society of Eastern Japan.

However, the question of its reliability as source material has been raised by a few historians, particularly with respect to the early chapters, compiled as they were nearly a hundred years after the events which they record had taken place. In this connection, it is reasonable to assume that at the time of compilation shogunate materials for the early chapters had been comparatively meager and that the editors had gone to other sources to supplement the accounts. This assumption, in fact, has been borne out by the careful researches of Yashiro Kuniji, who made textual comparisons with other contemporary sources and discovered that many passages in the *Azuma kagami* were adaptations of or had been taken directly from other works.[11] Yashiro's researches show, first of all, that the editors have tapped the rich resources of the so-called house records of the military families of Eastern Japan, such as those of the

---

[10] James Murdoch, *A History of Japan*, I, 418.
[11] See K. Yashiro, *Azuma kagami no kenkyū*, pp. 81–130.

Kumagaya and Kōno families. They show, further, that the compilers have not overlooked the even richer repositories of the religious orders, such as those of the Tōdai-ji, Enryaku-ji, and the Tsurugaoka Shrine. To augment the accounts about events in Kyoto for which the editors lacked firsthand information, they seem to have gone to the diaries of court nobles, such as the *Gyokuyō* (1164–1200) of Fujiwara Kanezane, and the *Meigekki* (1180–1235) of Fujiwara Sadaie. There is also evidence that the *Kaidō-ki,* a contemporary travelogue of unknown authorship, has served as a source for some of the geographical data found in the work. An anthology, the well-known *Kinkai waka-shū* of Minamoto Sadaie, has been used for the few lines of poetry found in its pages. Finally, it has been shown that the popular war narratives—the *Heike monogatari* and the *Gempei seisui-ki*—have been drawn on for some of the details, particularly of the battles which occurred near Kyoto and in Western Japan.

This latter discovery—that the editors had relied on the less factual, more imaginative war romances—has been the chief objection raised against the *Azuma kagami.* However, the reliance is far from excessive and it is more or less limited to details of the military campaigns and battles fought in Western Japan. Moreover, these historical romances as well as the other works drawn on by the editors were themselves primary sources,[12] and hence their use by the editors to supplement shogunate materials—far from diminishing the reliability of the *Azuma kagami* as a historical source—has enhanced its over-all value, as Yashiro himself agrees. Needless to say, the *Gempei seisui-ki* and the *Heike monogatari,* if recognized as essentially *belles lettres*—like their European counterpart, the *chansons de geste*—can and should serve as a valuable complement to the more strictly historical sources.

Perhaps a more serious charge against the *Azuma kagami* is the presence of bias for the Hōjō family, the successors to the Minamoto and the official sponsors of the work. This bias, detected by scholars as early as the Tokugawa period (1600–1867) when the first serious textual studies of the work began, appears mainly in the form of the

---

[12] For a summary of source materials of the Kamakura period, see Chitoshi Yanaga, "Source Materials in Japanese History: The Kamakura Period, 1192–1333," *Journal of the American Oriental Society,* LIX (1939), 38–55.

deliberate omission of events or of documents, and the substitution of Hōjō family documents for those of the shogunate.[13] Fortunately, this fault is noticeable only in the later chapters of the work, although in reading the *Azuma kagami* due caution should be exercised throughout. That the private life of Yoritomo is exposed to public view in the early chapters, sometimes in a rather unfavorable light, while scarcely a mention of the private life of the Hōjō leaders is made in the later chapters, is an example of the manner in which this bias appears. Thus the early chapters of the work with which this study is concerned are comparatively free of this kind of bias.

In fact, it is indicative of the reliability of the beginning chapters of the *Azuma kagami* that they appear to be a collection of materials put together from shogunate and other sources with a minimum of editing and organization. Thus, for example, to reconstruct the Battle of Dannoura, one must examine not only the entry under the date of its occurrence but also a dozen or so subsequent entries. The latter represent the reports, both oral and written, which were brought to Kamakura by participants of the battle and which were recorded under date of their receipt. The former, recorded under date of the occurrence of the battle, which could not have been known in Kamakura until several days had lapsed, was culled and written from non-shogunate materials such as the *Heike monogatari* and the *Gempei seisui-ki*. To be sure, there is in these chapters much repetition and an occasional difference if not a contradiction of viewpoints regarding particular events, but it is this very feature which points to the relative lack of editorial selection, omission, and correction, and which attests to the greater reliability of the early over the last chapters of the work.

By the same token, the first half of the *Azuma kagami* is more reliable as a historical source than the six national histories mentioned above. The latter were official chronicles and thus they, like the second half of the *Azuma kagami*, suffer from the same defect of excessive editing and organization.

It is also important to emphasize that for the period under con-

[13] For example, the *Azuma kagami* in no way implicates the Hōjō in the assassination of Minamoto Yoriie in 1204, contrary to the accounts of the *Gukan-shō, Shōkyū-ki,* and others. It is also strangely silent on the rebellion in Echigo Province in 1201 to which the shogunate despatched troops under Sasaki Moritsuna.

sideration there is no other source which presents the details of
warrior life in the eastern provinces as fully and as candidly as the
opening chapters of the *Azuma kagami*. It is, after all, a work
largely of the warrior class itself and of Eastern Japan, which until
the establishment of the shogunate was regarded as a frontier region,
backward, uncultured, and provincial, and scarcely worth the attention of the nobles and the educated classes of Kyoto and Western
Japan. As such, it is a more genuine product of the warrior class than
the war narratives mentioned above which, in addition to having a
large imaginative element, appear to have been written by persons
who were more familiar with life in Kyoto than with life in the
provinces. At any rate, modern Japanese historians regard the *Azuma
kagami* as an indispensable source and continue to examine its many
pages in their studies of the Kamakura shogunate.

Finally, by way of summarizing the nature of the *Azuma kagami*,
it is well to point out that a single term, such as "chronicle," "compilation," "narrative," or "official history," does not adequately describe this work. It seems to be a little of everything. It is a chronicle
to the extent that its materials are arranged in chronological order. It
is an "official history" in that the work was begun at the instigation
of the Hōjō family, not merely to preserve the records and achievements of the shogunate but also to provide the *raison d'être* for the
Kamakura government. It is a narrative history in the sense that
events are recounted and described. It is also a compilation in that a
wide variety of documents has been brought together and placed
at appropriate places in the work.

A word remains to be said about the editions of the *Azuma
kagami,* of which there are more than a dozen. These fall generally
into three categories: the Kanazawa Bunko edition, copies of which
circulated in Eastern Japan; the Shimazu edition, copies of which
circulated in Western Japan; and the Kikkawa edition, compiled in
1522 from copies available in Kyoto and Western Japan. This last-
named edition, whose existence was unknown until 1911 when it
was presented to the Historiographical Bureau by the Kikkawa
family, has proved to be a godsend to students of the *Azuma
kagami.*[14] Although it contains only 47 chapters, as against the 52
of the other editions, the accounts are on the whole longer, and it

[14] See K. Yashiro, *Azuma kagami no kenkyū,* pp. 2–5.

includes several hundred daily entries not found in the others. Moreover, the incidence of copying errors is surprisingly small, and thus it has been invaluable in emending and supplementing the older known editions of the work.

The compiler of the Kikkawa edition was Migita Hiroakira (d. 1523) of Yamaguchi, whose patron was the wealthy Ōuchi family. The Ōuchi, aspiring to develop the city of Yamaguchi into a cultural center to rival Kyoto, had sponsored the building of many temples and had invited learned monks to take residence there. Migita, taking advantage of their presence, used their services to collate and to make textual studies of the *Azuma kagami*. He also hired itinerant priests to procure or to make copies of the work wherever they could be found. From Migita's own account we learn that the *Azuma kagami* was in great demand as a manual of government by military lords, and that copies of the work were difficult to obtain by his time.

Most of the extant editions, such as the Hōjō, Kurokawa, and Kyoto Library editions, are copies of the Kanazawa Bunko edition. Of these the Hōjō is the best known because of its close association with Ieyasu, who founded the Tokugawa shogunate in 1603. His love for the work, both as literature and as a guide to government, is legendary. The copy which he treasured and constantly carried with him had passed from the Odawara branch of the Hōjō family to the Kuroda family at the time of the siege of Odawara Castle in 1590 by Toyotomi Hideyoshi, and thence to Hidetada, Ieyasu's son, in 1604. To Ieyasu's patronage we owe the first serious studies of the work, and its first printing. He sponsored learned discussions of the book, on one occasion a comparison of the *Azuma kagami* and the *Gempei seisui-ki*. He ordered the well-known scholar, Hayashi Razan, to compile a table of contents as a guide to the reading of the work. This was the *Azuma kagami yōkō* in two chapters. Besides the first printed edition of the book which he promoted— the so-called Keichō edition of 1605—he ordered a Buddhist scholar to place in the text the *kunten,* the system of marks and numerals to render Chinese into Japanese, in connection with a second printing three years later. Tokugawa vassals, such as Kuroda Nyōsui, whose family had presented the Hōjō copy to the Tokugawa, sent a retainer to read and study the *Azuma kagami* with Hayashi Razan, while

Sakai Takamasa requested of Shunzai, Razan's son, a guide and commentary on the work. Shunzai complied with a brief essay called the *Azuma kagami matsuroku* and a transliteration in a mixture of Chinese and *kana,* i.e., the more simple phonetic syllabary derived from Chinese characters, of a portion of the text covering the last few weeks of 1266. Other printings followed, two in the Kan'ei era (1624–1643) and a *kana* edition during the rule of the fourth shogun, Ietsuna (1651–1680), giving to the book a measure of popularity. Although the *Azuma kagami* never attained the widespread popularity of the more imaginative *Heike monogatari* nor became the object of serious study by outstanding scholars, Ieyasu's initial enthusiasm and continued promotion kept alive a small but sustained interest in the *Azuma kagami* by a number of obscure scholars throughout the Tokugawa period. These studies, which were largely textual, were the forerunners of the more critical modern studies of such specialized scholars as Takakuwa Komakichi, Hoshino Tsune, Hara Katsurō, Wada Hidematsu, Yashiro Kuniji, Ryō Susumu, and Hotta Shōzō whose contributions toward an understanding of the *Azuma kagami* are cited in the Bibliography.

There were other copies of the Hōjō edition, such as the special Tokugawa Ieyasu edition and the Mizutani edition, but these are no longer extant. No copy of the Shimazu edition is known to exist, although it has been established that two works of the Tokugawa period—*Azuma kagami dassan* and *Azuma kagami datsuro*—supplementing the missing chapters of the Hōjō edition were based largely on a manuscript copy of the Shimazu edition originally owned by the Nikaidō family. Other extant copies, such as the Maeda and Fushimi editions, the former containing only a portion of one chapter, and the latter a condensation of portions of the work, are mentioned chiefly for their historical interest. The Maeda edition is also the oldest extant manuscript copy of the work, while the Fushimi edition has the distinction of being preserved in rolls.

Chapter II
The Background

THE RISE OF FEUDAL INSTITUTIONS[1]

There can be no adequate portrayal of the founding of the Kamakura shogunate without reference to the general conditions called "feudal" which obtained in twelfth-century Japan. As in Europe, feudalism in Japan was a complex of political, social, and economic forces based on a system of relationship between lord and vassal arising out of the holding of lands and offices in fief.[2] The establishment of the Kamakura shogunate was an outgrowth of these conditions, which had prevailed throughout Japan some centuries earlier. Thus, for a proper understanding of the subject of our study, it is well to trace the development of Japanese feudalism—at least its more salient features—and to describe it as it existed on the eve of the founding of the shogunate.

For this purpose it is best to go back to the seventh century when the social and political basis of Japanese society was the *uji*, the patriarchal unit or clan, and other similar corporations or groups of

[1] This chapter is intended merely to summarize the complex history of the rise of feudalism in Japan. For a more detailed examination of the subject, the reader is directed to the pioneer and scholarly studies of the late Professor Asakawa of Yale, in particular his "Some Aspects of Japanese Feudal Institutions," *Transactions of the Asiatic Society of Japan* (1st series), XLVI (1918), 76–102, and *The Documents of Iriki, Illustrative of the Development of the Feudal Institutions of Japan.* In addition the student of Japanese feudalism should consult the studies of Miura Shūkō, Nakada Kaoru, Maki Kenji, Ishii Ryōsuke, Imai Rintarō, and others whose works have been cited in the Bibliography. The more general histories of the feudal period by Ryō Susumu, Watanabe Tamotsu, and Tsuji Zennosuke are also useful. Although all of these and other studies listed in the Bibliography have been used in the preparation of this chapter, specific references to them have been kept at a minimum.

[2] A recent book growing out of the Conference on Feudalism at Princeton University is recommended for a survey of the principal feudal systems of the world. See Rushton Coulborn, ed., *Feudalism in History.*

people called the *bé* and the *tomo*. The most influential member and theoretical head of this group of units was the imperial family. In its attempts during the seventh century to maintain its primacy and to check the growing influence of some of the other clans over large segments of the land and the people, the imperial family and its supporters embarked upon a drastic reform of the entire structure of law and administration. The Taika Reform, as this effort was called, was based on Chinese ideals and it sought in general to curtail the power and influence of the various clans by establishing a strong central government under the leadership of the imperial family.[3] Departments of government, divided into bureaus and smaller units, were formed. These were to be staffed by a bureaucracy composed of strictly graded officials. A system of local government to be operated by governors and lesser officials sent out by the central government was also established. Government was to be conducted according to four broad categories of codes—administrative, or *ryō*; penal, or *ritsu*; supplementary, or *kyaku*; and detailed procedure, or *shiki*.[4] All land was to become the property of the state, and the cultivable ricelands were to be distributed to the free citizenry on an equitable basis. These were the so-called allotment lands, or *kubunden*. The proportion of the free citizenry to the unfree was to be increased by freeing as many of the peasantry as possible from the control of chieftains and corporations. For the support of the state three main classes of taxes were established— rice tax, or *so*; tributes of local products, or *chō*; and forced labor or its equivalent in kind, called *yō*. The citizen owed these taxes to the state and was also expected to man a national conscript army when called upon.

This ambitious undertaking begun in 645 was only partially completed by 701 when the so-called Taihō Code, containing the administrative and penal codes was promulgated. The *ritsu-ryō-sei*, or "system of [government by] penal and administrative codes," as this initial effort at reforms was called, was followed in the ensuing

---

[3] For a detailed study of the Reform, which is still the standard work in English on the subject, see Kanji Asakawa, *The Early Institutional Life of Japan: A Study in the Reform of 645 A.D.*, especially pp. 252–333.

[4] For a discussion of these codes and, in particular, the administrative system developed by the Reform, see George Sansom, "Early Japanese Law and Administration," *TASJ* (2nd series), IX (1932), 67–109; XI (1934), 117–149.

years by a series of new laws and revisions, codifications, recodifications, and commentaries on the codes, touching upon every aspect of law and administration.

But even as these efforts to explain and codify the law were being expended in the capital, respect for the authority of the law was rapidly diminishing in the provinces. The reasons were many and complex, but fundamentally the laws themselves, based for the most part on Chinese models, were not readily adaptable in Japan. The ambitious plans of the lawmakers, particularly for land reforms and for the establishment of a national conscript army, were never fully carried out. In place of the *kubunden,* the equitably allotted sustenance land, there arose the *shōen,* the privately held manor, which was to become the economic life blood of feudalism. In place of a national conscript army which would have assured the preservation of law and order and the authority of the central government, there arose the independent local lord, the central figure of feudalism, who provided protection for the people which the central government could not provide, and who replaced the representatives of the central government as the ruling element in the provinces. Thus, in time, the customs and traditions which grew up between lord and lord, lord and vassal, owner and tiller of the *shōen,* and between these local institutions and the representatives of a distant, vague, absentee government produced such institutions recognizable in the West as the fief, subinfeudation, commendation, benefice, and the like. In this development the basic elements were the *shōen* and the local lord, and their growth was attributable in large measure to the failure of the Taika Reform. It would be well, therefore, to see first how the *shōen,* the economic basis of feudalism, came into being.

THE SHŌEN

The land measures of the Taika Reform, intended to abolish private holdings of land, were doomed to almost certain failure from their inception. Although, in theory, all land was nationalized and redistributed on an equitable basis to all,[5] including the nobility, so

[5] The basic unit of allotment was 2 *tan* of land for every male member of the family. (One *tan* was equal to approximately .245 of an acre.) Females received only two thirds of this basic unit.

sweeping a measure could not be carried out in practice. There was, to begin with, the strong opposition of the pre-Taika nobility and the clan chieftains who had owned the lands prior to the Reform. To appease them and win their support for the Reform, the government brought them into the new bureaucracy with offers of position and court rank, and, as salary and recompense, lands were provided for them in addition to allotment land which they received on the same basis as the citizenry. The size of these additional lands, called *shikiden,* or office rice fields, and *iden,* or rank rice fields, depended on the importance of the office and the degree of the rank, ranging from 2 *chō* (1 *chō* was equal to 2.9408 acres, or roughly 3 acres) for the lowest offices to 40 *chō* for the prime minister, and from 8 *chō* for holders of the junior fifth rank to 80 *chō* for holders of the senior first rank.[6] Although these lands were not officially private lands, being subject to the rice tax and to be held by the assignee only during tenure of office, they were, in effect, private lands, for offices tended to be hereditary in certain families. Thus some of the choicest lands were effectively removed from the public domains and from the allotment system and transferred to the private use of the nobility. In this way the pre-Taika nobility, whose growing influence the Reform had intended to check by divesting them of their lands, were permitted in fact to retain and enjoy large portions of their former holdings.

These were by no means the only concessions made to the ruling class. The more illustrious members of the nobility might receive from the emperor *shiden,* or gift rice fields, which the emperor could create simply by issuing an edict. The performance of meritorious service for the state was also cause for the grant of special lands. Such lands, which were called *kōden* or merit rice fields, could be held in perpetuity or passed on to heirs for a specified number of generations according to the class of the grant. There was no limit as to the size of these latter two forms of grants, and they were, as a rule, extensive, such as the *shiden* of the province of Harima given to Prince Shōtoku, and the 100 *chō* of *kōden* given to Kamatari, the prime mover of the Reform and the founder of the Fujiwara family. Another form of lands given special status was the *choku-shiden,* the ricelands opened with imperial sanction and reserved

[6] See Rintarō Imai, *Nihon shōen-sei-ron,* pp. 14–17.

maintain slaves and to count them at the ratio of three slaves to one freeman in applying for allotment lands. Although the number of slaves appears to have been small in proportion to the total population,[7] they were owned by a handful of nobles and the larger religious orders. Thus another element was added to the welter of causes which hastened the collapse of the land reforms and which brought about the concentration of land among a few families and institutions.

There were other weaknesses in the allotment system which produced vast inequities in the size of lands distributed to the citizenry. Since the basis of allocation was the number of individuals in a household,[8] it was not unusual for families to make excessive claims with regard to the number of individuals comprising a household. Land registers, for example, for the year 702 preserved at the Shō-sō-in Museum indicate that the smaller families usually numbered up to 30 members and rarely below 10.[9] In some instances the household exceeded 100 members. In one notable case the membership numbered 124 for which it received 13 *chō*, 6 *tan*, and 20 *bu* (a *bu* was equal to 3.9540 square yards, or approximately 4 square yards) of allotment land.[10] In this and in similar cases the head of the household claimed as members not only his spouse and children, but also his parents, his wife's parents, his mistresses, his brothers and sisters and their wives, husbands, and children, his and his wife's uncles and aunts and their children, as well as his retainers and even his slaves. Thus, contrary to the intent of the land reforms, the wealthier families received more land than the commoners. Moreover, such a practice increased the acute shortage of allotment land which had hampered the system from the very outset.

To remedy the scarcity of allotment land, the government resorted to such expediencies as confiscating lands held by monasteries, or converting merit and rank lands into allotment lands. In 708, for example, the government seized 255 *chō* of land in Harima

---

[7] One slave to twenty freemen during the Nara period, according to Takigawa. See Seijirō Takigawa, *Nihon dorei keizai-shi*, pp. 224, 268.

[8] The *ko*, or household, was the basic unit of local administration. For purposes of taxation and general local administration, households were organized into groups of five.

[9] Imai, *Nihon shōen-sei-ron*, pp. 17–18.

[10] *Ibid.*, p. 18.

for use by members of the imperial family. Of the kinds of l[a]
mentioned above, including the office ricelands and rank ricela[nds]
only the imperial ricelands and the gift ricelands were comple[tely]
tax-free. However, as all members of the nobility were exem[pt]
from payment of the tax in kind and the corvee, it meant that
lands they enjoyed were subject only to the rice tax.

Another category of lands exempted from the application of
land reform laws was that including the *shinden* and the *jiden*,
holdings respectively of the Shinto shrines and the Buddhist temp[les.]
The latter in particular were extensive, for Buddhism, since its in[tro-]
duction in the sixth century, had made great progress among m[em-]
bers of the ruling class, who had been steadily donating tracts [of]
land to the various temples as expressions of their religious pi[ety.]
Furthermore, it was the practice to exempt such lands from taxati[on.]
Thus, by the time of the Taika Reform, the terms *jiden* and *shin[den]*
had come to mean, not simply temple and shrine lands, but tax-f[ree]
lands of temples and shrines. Both this fiscal privilege and [the]
patronage of the ruling class were continued under the reforms; th[us]
extensive tracts of land were continuously removed from the tax r[olls]
and from the reserve of cultivable lands for allocation to the peo[ple.]

It was on the extensive land holdings of the Buddhist orders th[at]
a particular kind of estate called the *shōen* developed. The term [is]
a compound of *shō*, the building or buildings for the manageme[nt]
and storage of the produce of the land, and *en*, the attached gard[en]
land, and thus its literal meaning has no special significance. B[ut]
as the *shōen* was a part of the tax-free private lands of the Buddh[ist]
orders, in time the term *shōen* came to be applied to any land whi[ch]
was private as distinguished from public lands and lands allotted [to]
the free citizenry.

However, the growth of the *shōen* had to await other develo[p-]
ments arising from the Taika Reform. One of these was the scarci[ty]
of lands for allotment and the resulting scarcity of revenues fro[m]
such lands. The reformers, having set aside choice lands for use [by]
the nobles to whom exemption from two of the three principal tax[es]
was provided, and having further granted a tax-free status to th[e]
vast holdings of the religious orders, had reduced the lands ava[il-]
able for allotment and for taxation. This situation was not helpe[d]
by the further generosity of the government in permitting nobles [to]

Province belonging to Shitennō-ji,[11] and again, in 768, it seized lands in Kyushu belonging to Kanzeon-ji.[12] The conversion of merit and rank lands into allotment lands was tried in Awa Province in 767.[13]

But these measures, besides meeting the concerted opposition of the religious bodies and the nobility, could not be expected to solve the problem. Thus, as early as 722, the government decided to open up approximately 1,000,000 *chō* of new lands in the outlying provinces for settlement and cultivation. However, these lands, being virgin land for the most part, could not be used immediately for allotment to the free citizenry, nor did the government have the means to prepare them for settlement. Since the nobility, in addition to the larger religious orders, were the only ones with the means to finance these undertakings, the government offered them various inducements, such as promotion in court rank, if the new lands were cultivated and their annual yield exceeded a certain specified volume.[14]

By the following year it was apparent that the program was not proceeding satisfactorily, for the terms were greatly liberalized. The government now offered these lands, called *konden*, or newly opened rice fields, on a tax-free basis for from one to three generations, depending on whether or not an irrigation system was subsequently introduced by the cultivator.[15] All *konden* would revert to the state at the end of the period, although the original cultivator was given the option of continuing to work the lands upon payment of the usual taxes.

The *konden* policy succeeded in opening up new tracts of land in Kyushu and Honshu, but it did not produce the hoped-for results. Cultivators took advantage of the grace period of three generations,

---

[11] The *Shoku-Nihon-gi*, the second of the Six National Histories, is especially informative as to the various measures taken by the government in connection with the Taika Reform, since it covers the period from 697 to 792. Although there is an English translation of the first part of the chronicle (J. B. Snellen, "Shoku-Nihon-gi Chronicles of Japan, Continued from A.D. 697–791" [Books I–VI], *TASJ* 2nd series, XI [1934], 151–239; 2nd series, XIV [1937], 209–278), the references given here are to the Japanese edition. See Jirō Mochizuki, ed., "Shoku-Nihon-gi," *Kokushi taikei*, II, Chapter 28, p. 484.

[12] *Ibid.*, Chapter 29, p. 497.

[13] *Ibid.*, Chapter 28, p. 485.

[14] *Ibid.*, Chapter 9, pp. 138–39.

[15] *Ibid.*, p. 143.

then abandoned the lands instead of continuing to work them as tax-paying freemen. More damaging to the government was the fact that by far the majority of the cultivators were not independent freemen but peasants from the households of nobles who had been sent out to work the lands for their masters in whose names the lands had been registered. In short, the nobles had financed the opening up of these lands in return for title to them and the privilege of exemption from taxes on such lands for three generations.

In this way vast tracts of land came under the control of the nobility. And it was almost impossible for the government to curb the practice, for its own members—from the higher nobles at the court to its governors in the provinces—were the benefactors. In 743 the government recognized the claims of the nobility to these lands, attempting only to limit their acquisition by the nobles to from 50 to 500 *chō* according to their rank.[16] And thus a fundamental principle of the land reforms started one hundred years earlier—the abolition of private lands—had been virtually abandoned by the government. Some of these private estates, which developed from lands registered in the names of noble houses, were the first to be called *shōen*. As pointed out earlier, it was a term borrowed from the Buddhist estates.

During the eighth and ninth centuries the Buddhist orders had been increasing their lands. In one important respect their activities were far more damaging to the government than those of the nobles, for they claimed tax immunity for their newly acquired lands. Technically, lands acquired by the temples by means other than as gift ricelands were subject to tax. In fact, temples were forbidden to buy or sell land, as a decree of 746 indicates, but despite the prohibition, the Buddhist orders dealt in lands and continued to enlarge their holdings.

One other class of offenders who encroached upon public lands must not be overlooked. This was the group of landowners in the provinces whose ancestors had settled in the outlying regions some generations earlier and had staked out lands for themselves. These lands were called *myōden,* or name ricelands, from the practice of their claimants giving names or designations to their lands, and the owners were called *myōshu,* or "masters of name ricelands."

[16] *Ibid.,* Chapter 15, pp. 246–47.

The average *myōden* was not large, but a few *myōshu* in different localities had acquired control of large tracts of land. These were the forerunners of the later *daimyō,* the great landlords or territorial magnates, who were better known in the pre-Kamakura period as *jūnin,* a term which meant "resident" but which implied that its bearer was the principal resident of the locality. He was distinguished from the *myōshu* not only by the size of his holdings but also by the fact that he maintained an armed following for the protection of his lands and the peasants who cultivated his lands.

The holdings of the *jūnin* were comprised of various kinds of land, which might include parcels handed down in his family and lands seized from other *myōshu* and from the public domains. However, an important part of his holdings were not lands themselves but rather rights to them. These rights took the form of specified shares of the annual yield of lands belonging to others who had sought his protection. In the outlying regions, where the authority of the government was weak or nonexistent, protection was a primary need. Thus for the smaller landowners the customary way of acquiring protection was to commend a part of their cultivated fields or, more correctly, to pledge a specified share of their annual yield to their more powerful neighbors, the *jūnin.* This practice of commendation was known as *kishin* and the rights thus acquired by the *jūnin* were known as *shiki.*[17] For the smaller landowner who could not afford to give up any part of his land, this form of commendation facilitated the securing of protection, and made it possible for him to make two or more such arrangements with his more powerful neighbors.

Commendation became more widespread and complex as the Shinto shrines and particularly the Buddhist temples entered into these arrangements. The advantage of commending land to a temple which enjoyed tax immunity on its holdings was soon realized by landlords in the provinces, including the *jūnin,* who transferred nominal ownership of their lands to a Buddhist temple. The latter registered these commended lands under its name, thus removing them from the tax rolls, then returned the lands to the donor intact as an *onchi,* or benefice. For this privilege of working

---

[17] For a brief but excellent discussion of *shiki* in English, see George Sansom, *Japan, A Short Cultural History,* 274 ff.

lands which were tax-exempt, the donor promised to the temple a *nengu,* or an annual tribute.

The practice soon spread to include the noble houses. To the large landowner in the provinces the advantage of securing the political protection of the high nobles in Kyoto was obvious. There was the possibility of partial tax immunity by transferring the lands to a noble for an annual fee. To the noble himself accepting lands commended to him was more profitable and less onerous than financing the settlement and cultivation of new lands, for he was assured an income in the form of an annual tribute without the expense and effort of subsidizing peasants to work the lands.

Such a convenient and profitable arrangement for all concerned could not be checked easily, and it is to be doubted whether the government, whose own officials were parties to these arrangements, cared seriously to check it. In fact, the nobles aided and abetted the trend toward the rapid diminution of the public domains by securing, whenever possible, complete instead of partial tax immunity for lands commended to them. They argued that lands in the provinces, whatever their present status, had been originally a part of the vast imperial ricelands which were tax-free and, as such, no taxes should be levied on them. Otherwise, the formality of obtaining tax-exemption certificates was a simple matter. These were issued by the Council of State and countersigned by an official of the Department of People's Affairs and a provincial governor. In time, certificates issued and signed only by a provincial governor became acceptable, further facilitating the process of reducing the public domain and the sources of state revenues.

How extensive and unrestrained these practices had become in the late Nara and early Heian periods can be seen from the great number of prohibitions issued against them by the government. In the fifty-year period between the 780s and 830s there were no less than fourteen official prohibitions.[18]

Meanwhile, in areas close to the capital where land allotment had been carried out in the early years of the Reform, the provision that lands be reallotted at regular six-year intervals was not being observed. In 834 the requirement was changed from six to twelve years. Even

[18] For dates and specific provisions of these prohibitions, see Zennosuke Tsuji, *Nihon bunka-shi,* III, 20–21.

so, it was not until 881, forty-seven years later, that reallotment on this basis was carried out. By the Engi Era (901–923) reallotment was given up entirely by the government.

By the late tenth century the country was dotted with private landed estates—now generally called *shōen*—nominally owned by noble families or religious orders but actually operated by local elements of society who enjoyed the political protection of the ruling class and partial or full immunity from taxes. Although the original *shōen* had developed on the estates of the Buddhist orders, their local and for the most part illegal origin made for considerable diversity in their size, organization, and degree of immunity, and in the control which their owners exercised over the people living within their boundaries. The smaller *shōen* did not exceed 10 *chō*; the larger ones covered several hundreds of *chō* and included ricelands, both wet and dry, and meadow and timber lands as well. Some were made up of scattered units of land; others were contiguous. Parcels of land within a *shōen* might be commended to different persons or institutions, such as a noble house, the provincial governor, a shrine, or a temple. Certain units in a *shōen* might enjoy full tax immunity, others only partial immunity, although the trend was definitely toward the tax-free *shōen* as commendation became widespread. Some *shōen* were managed directly by their owners, but the great size and scattered composition of others precluded direct management by a single owner, and the practice of employing managers became common.

In addition to fiscal privileges a few *shōen* enjoyed immunity from entry by public officials. This was the real, complete, private landed estate. Such a situation might come about through disputes between the owner of a *shōen* and the local representative of the central government over the question of control of the peasants who worked the lands of the *shōen*. Such workers were usually freemen who lived in villages outside the boundaries of the *shōen* and were thus subject to the authority of the local officials. However, disputes of this sort were usually settled in favor of the *shōen* whose owner appealed to the nominal owner in Kyoto over the heads of the local officials. The result might be an order from Kyoto to the local officials to refrain from entering the lands of the *shōen*. Where a *shōen* did not enjoy this privilege, called *funyū-ken,* it frequently possessed the privilege in fact through arrangements made with the local official. For example, the owner or manager of a *shōen* might effectively prevent the tax collector from setting foot on the estate by offering to collect and remit to the government the taxes owed by freemen living within the *shōen*. And thus, in one way or another, the owner of a *shōen* tended to wrest control of the people from the government.

The *shōen* of the tenth and eleventh centuries was, as a rule, a far more complex organization than it has been possible to describe here. But in the final analysis the *shōen* represented an intricate network of relationships with a great number of people owning rights to it. It involved the small cultivator, the *myōshu*, who owned the basic unit within the *shōen*, and the *ryōshu*, or *ryōke*, the individual or family in actual control of the entire *shōen*, upon whose military strength the cultivators were dependent for protection. It also included the *honjo*, or *honke*, the absentee nominal owner who might well be a Fujiwara, a member of the imperial family, or a great Buddhist temple or shrine. The manager of the *shōen* was in a position between these groups.

The rise of the *shōen* was greatly helped by the increase in peasant labor necessary for the cultivation of the land. Many peasants, who had received allotment lands in the provinces near the capital, could not as freemen pay the taxes on their land and on their persons. They defaulted on their taxes, abandoned their lands, and took to vagrancy and robbery. Some sold their lands to shrines, temples, noble houses, and even to unscrupulous local governors. Many went to the outlying regions to escape the clutches of the law, and thus, eventually, came under the control of the *myōshu* and the *jūnin*.

That the government was cognizant of the alarming growth of the *shōen* in the tenth and eleventh centuries can be seen from the great number of prohibitions which it continued to issue, although to no avail. In 902, for example, it decreed that only those *shōen* which could produce bona fide charters, or *kugen*, would be legally recognized. In 984 it issued a blanket prohibition against the establishment of any new *shōen*, a prohibition which it reissued in 987. That no one heeded these prohibitions can be clearly seen from the decree of 1040 which declared that all new *shōen* established after the prohibition of 984 were null and void. There were three more official prohibitions issued prior to 1069. The edict of that year differed from its predecessors in one important respect: it decreed the establishment of a *Kiroku-jo,* or Records Office, as a step toward curbing the growth of the *shōen.* But this measure also proved completely ineffective when its sponsor, the Emperor Go-Sanjō, died in 1073 and the Records Office was dissolved.

So long as there were many independent local lords who commended their lands to the noble families, the latter had no cause for alarm. However, the tendency in the late eleventh century was for landowners to come under the control of a few of the more powerful local lords and for lands to be commended to these powerful regional lords. This alarm of the official class is reflected in the decree of 1091 which prohibited landowners from commending their holdings to Minamoto Yoshiie (d. 1106), a local lord. This was followed in 1092 by a decree which denied official recognition to all of Yoshiie's *shōen.* This is significant, for it indicates that by the close of the eleventh century certain local lords, in particular the Minamoto family, were gaining control of the private landed estates in the provinces.

THE LOCAL LORD

It can be seen from this brief sketch of the rise of the private landed estate that it was closely connected with the rise of the local lord, the second of the basic elements which contributed to the feudalization of Japanese society between the seventh and eleventh centuries. To complete the sketch of the history of feudalism to the eve of the founding of the shogunate, it is necessary to trace the rise of the warrior class and to explain further the relationship of the warrior class to the private landed estate.

As with the development of the *shōen,* the rise of the independent local lord was closely related to the failure of the government to carry out the provisions of the Taika Reform. Among other things the Reform had established on paper an elaborate national conscript army, the details of which may be gathered from the Taihō Code of 701. All males between the ages of twenty and sixty were subject to call. Except for special troops to be stationed in the north and in

Kyushu,[19] these conscripts were to man the *gundan,* the military divisions, to be assigned to the various provinces for the preservation of law and order. But a military system which required conscripts to furnish their own weapons and sundry other equipment, as well as food for themselves and fodder for horses—a group of ten conscripts being responsible for six horses—could scarcely be expected to work in the Japan of the eighth century. Moreover, no special consideration was given the conscript with regard to the principal taxes— he was expected to continue their payment while in service. Thus among the peasantry the call to military service of one member of the family was regarded as the ruination of the family.

On the other hand, the rich and the influential found ways to escape military service, thus placing the burden of service almost entirely on the peasantry who were least prepared, economically and otherwise, to render it. The courtier could legally escape military service if he held the rank of fifth grade or higher. Nobles who held even lower ranks—from the eighth to the sixth—could also obtain exemption if they were heirs or eldest sons. If necessary, ranks could be purchased by the performance of pious acts, such as the donation of timber, other materials, or money to a temple or a shrine. If exemption could not be obtained on any of the above grounds, the courtier could always hire someone to serve in his place, or he could rear horses for the army on his estates in lieu of service. Thus, as early as 739, less than forty years after the compilation of the Taihō Code, the conscription system was abandoned. Although reactivated in 746 with changes and supposed remedies to make it work, it proved no more effective than the original system. Before the turn of the century the government dropped all pretenses at enforcing the law and formally abolished it. Although the system was later revived on a limited scale in isolated sections of the country, a national conscript army was all but abolished in 792.

The abandonment of the conscription system reflected not only the difficulty of enforcing a law essentially too advanced for the Japan of the eighth and ninth centuries, but also the general attitude

[19] Northern Japan was placed under the special jurisdiction of the *Chinju-fu,* or Pacifying-Ezo Headquarters, for defense against border incursions of the Ainu. For defense against invasions from the sea, the *Dazai-fu,* the Government Headquarters of Kyushu, was established. Its troops consisted mainly of *sakimori,* or coast guards.

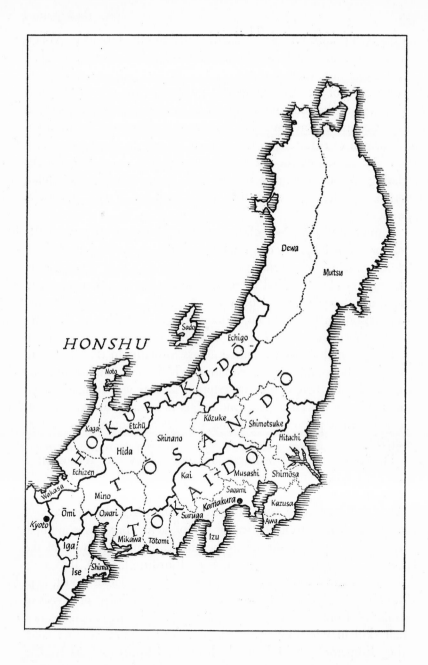

Figure 1. The circuits of Hokuriku-dō, Tōsan-dō, and Tōkai-dō, showing
the provinces and the respective positions of Kyoto and Kamakura

of the Kyoto court toward any matter affecting the provinces. When the capital was transferred from Nara to Kyoto late in the eighth century, the attention of the court was focused, understandably, on the building of the new capital to the neglect of the provinces. However, even as the court settled down in its new quarters and seemed able once more to resume the business of government, its attention was drawn to cultural pursuits, which became its chief preoccupation. As attested by the decreasing number of laws and regulations relating to the provinces which were issued during the Heian period, courtiers found no time to be concerned with provincial problems.

A more positive proof of the attitude of the court toward the provinces was its policy of strengthening the defenses of the capital while reducing troops and garrisons in the provinces. Even before the transfer of the capital from Nara to Kyoto, the government, in the thirty-two-year period between 717 and 749, had deactivated six garrisons in Ise, Echizen, Mino, Echigo, Nagato, and Kyushu. Under the circumstances, local officials were forced to rely more and more on their own resourcefulness to maintain the peace and to assert their authority, a situation which had obtained in the provinces long before the conscription system was formally abolished. Thus it was customary, and in fact necessary, for local officials to maintain a personal following, who were known generally as *shitei*.

The actual task of maintaining order, however, fell upon a smaller, more select group of *shitei*—the physically able and militarily skillful—called the *kondei*. The term was of much earlier origin and may have been used to distinguish male members of an official's family from the rest of his following; but it was applied, as the term clearly indicates, to the physically more stalwart of the personal following of an official. Soga Emishi (d. 645), for example, one of the more powerful officials of the pre-Taika Court, kept fifty *kondei* as private guards. In 642, on the occasion of a visit of a mission from Kudara, *kondei* were called upon to demonstrate their skill in wrestling before the emissaries. Twenty years later, when Emperor Tenchi despatched troops to Korea to assist Kudara in its wars, *kondei* were among the expeditionary forces.[20] Thus,

[20] See *Kokushi jiten*, ed. Fuzambō, IV, 244–45.

while the *kondei* may have on occasion served the government in some official capacity as guards at the palace or as members of the army, they came traditionally from among the private following of an influential personage, and they were, moreover, selected for their physical or military fitness.

It is important to note that the *kondei* maintained by local officials were of local origin. They were small cultivators or landowners, or sons of landowners who welcomed the political influence of the officials they served. Thus this relationship between a local official, who needed the military support of the *kondei* in order to exercise his authority, and the *kondei*, who needed the prestige of the official as protection for his private interests, represented a natural alliance. The government, in abandoning a national conscript army in the eighth century and in assigning the responsibility of preserving law and order in the provinces to its civil officials and their followers of *kondei*, had in effect transferred its police and military powers to a very select group of armed men whose interests and loyalties were intensely local and personal.

Perhaps an even more important development was the tendency among local officials to place their private interests above those of the central government. By virtue of their official position and their presence in the provinces, they were especially active in securing lands or rights to land either for themselves or for their noble patrons in Kyoto. Thus the very men upon whom devolved the responsibility of upholding the authority of the central government in the provinces tended, like the *kondei* whom they controlled, to work toward the furtherance of their own ends.

Under the circumstances it is not surprising that so many local officials settled in the provinces at the close of their terms of office. For the ex-official the advantages of remaining in the provinces far outweighed those of returning to Kyoto. He could, in the weakness of the government's authority in the provinces, continue to exercise considerable influence in local affairs long after the expiration of his tenure of office. Moreover, he could protect the private interests which he had built up during his tenure and continue to enjoy their benefits. Other officials who could not account for irregularities during their tenure found it more discreet to remain in the provinces than to return to Kyoto to face the rebuke of their superiors. Still others, even though they wished to return, were compelled to remain in the provinces until a clean bill of health, or a *geyu-jō*, was declared on their administration by their successors. The issuance of the *geyu-jō* was sometimes delayed for as long as six years with the result that many ex-officials simply settled down in the provinces.

Thus the class of ex-officials and ex-nobles in the provinces tended to grow. Moreover, beginning in the late ninth or early tenth century, this group of ex-nobles was further enlarged by a steady accretion of new arrivals from the capital. In Kyoto government was rapidly becoming a Fujiwara monopoly, a situation which had become especially marked during and after the reign of Emperor Montoku (850–858). With the assumption by Fujiwara Yoshifusa of the office of prime minister, or *dajō daijin*, in 857, and that of regent, or *sesshō*, in 858, offices which heretofore had been reserved for princes of the blood, the Fujiwara control of the Kyoto court had become well-nigh complete. In 880 the Fujiwara created a third high office, the civil dictator, or *kampaku*. Needless to say, all three offices were held traditionally in the family. Thus the Fujiwara, by assuming the regency when the emperor was a minor, or the civil dictatorship when the emperor was of age, virtually supplanted the imperial family.

The chances of a non-Fujiwara receiving office or advancing in office had become so restricted that many nobles of non-Fujiwara stock migrated to the provinces. Not a few of those who migrated to the provinces were themselves Fujiwara whose ranks had swollen beyond the capacity of the government to absorb them or the ability of the family to support them in Kyoto. In time even princely descendants sought their fortunes in the provinces, for it must be remembered that according to the provisions of the Taihō Code they were deprived of their princely ranks and privileges in the sixth generation unless they were eldest sons or heirs to the throne. In fact, the two great families of local lords, the Taira and the Minamoto, who were to emerge as the dominant families in the provinces in the eleventh and twelfth centuries, were descendants of such princely forebears. And thus, unwittingly, the government contributed toward the growth of local leadership in the provinces and of strong local forces which, eventually, were to challenge and supplant its authority in the provinces.

In one other important respect the government unconsciously weakened its own authority in the provinces. This was the practice of vesting its civil governors and nonofficial local residents with police and military powers in times of emergency. Thus a governor or a *jūnin* might be temporarily commissioned as a *tsuibushi*, or imperial gendarme, to carry out a specific mission such as the pursuit and apprehension of outlaws, as the title of the office indicates. Or, in the event of a more serious contingency, the government might commission a local lord as an *ōryōshi* to put down lawlessness and to keep order and administer justice in a certain district. These offices were intended only for the duration of the emergency; however, the tendency among the recipients was to retain them indefinitely due to the generally unstable situation in the provinces. And even when conditions warranted the cancellation of the commission, the prestige gained by the local official or the local lord in being specially designated as commissioner was not easily destroyed. In fact, descendants of such temporary officials took great pride in referring to their ancestors as the "former *tsuibushi*," or the "former *ōryōshi*." Thus measures which the government had taken to augment its faltering authority in the provinces frequently had the adverse effect of weakening its own authority and of strengthening that of local elements.

A similar development occurred with the local officials known as *kebiishi*, or police, who are not to be confused with officials of the same name in Kyoto. The latter were officials of the *Kebiishi-chō*, the Office of the Imperial Police, which had been removed from the *Konoe-fu*, or the Imperial Guards, and made into an independent police force for the protection of the capital during the reign of Emperor Saga (809–823). The local *kebiishi* were special police whom governors were authorized to commission during an emergency to assist them in preserving law and order. They were not agents of the Office of Imperial Police sent out from the capital but rather local residents deputized to assist the governor. And as these officials also tended to retain their commissions permanently and to put their private and local interests above that of the state, another element was added to the already growing force which had been steadily weakening the authority of the central government in the provinces.

From this class, composed of ex-officials, ex-nobles who had left the capital for economic reasons, and the commissioned officials of local origin, was to come the leadership which, eventually, was to challenge the government. In this connection it is interesting to note that although actual military prowess rather than the conditions of birth and rank tended to be the test of leadership in the provinces, nevertheless, it was a definite asset for any aspiring local leader to be able to point to these attributes of high birth and rank in his family background. Thus pedigree or past official connections never ceased entirely to be a factor in the social and political life of the provinces.

Similarly, although the social and political units developing in the provinces were no longer restricted to the family or related family groups but rather encompassed many unrelated families and members, the core of the social and political unit was still the family. The *uji*, the patriarchal clan of the pre-Taika era, was still the most important social unit. It was around the *uji* that warrior groups emerged. But just as the *shōen* included many unrelated families and members to meet its expanding size and needs, so the basic social units of provincial society in the tenth and eleventh centuries tended to grow in size and composition and to include more than just the immediate members of a family. Thus the term *ichizoku*, which means "one family," or "one household," actually included many members who were not related by blood to the leader of the group. Only the leadership of such a group was provided by members of a family who were called *ie-no-ko*, or "sons of the family," while the bulk of the armed retainers were not related by blood to the leader and were known variously as *kenin, rōdō,* and *rōju*. The common experience which such a group shared in providing for its own protection and in waging war to extend its control over neighboring territories served to knit these groups closely together. In time, due to the greater demands of recurring wars, the *ichizoku* coalesced into even larger groups called *tō*, which simply meant "band" or "party."

For various reasons the tendency toward closely knit groups of warriors under powerful lords was especially strong in Kanto, or Eastern Japan. Because of its later development, and because of its great distance from the nation's cultural and political center, new influences were slow to reach the east, and older local traditions and institutions tended to persist. Distance from Kyoto also accounted for the greater lack of law and order and the corresponding greater reliance by the people upon local leaders for protection. The local lord in Eastern Japan also tended to be more powerful than in Western Japan. Because of the presence of large plains and stretches of virgin land, the original cultivators in Eastern Japan had carved out large tracts of land for themselves, and thus, the *shōen* which their descendants owned or controlled were, as a rule, larger than the average *shōen* in the west. Moreover, these tracts of land had attracted a great number of the floating population of the early Heian period—the body of freemen created by the Taika Reform who for various reasons had abandoned their lands and fled east out of reach of the authorities. Thus the development of Kanto was rapid, once it was opened for cultivation and settlement, and the control of the local lord over both land and people was greater than in the West.

The people of this region early gained a reputation for their warriorlike qualities. They fought the early border wars against the Ainu, whom they pushed north. To hold the Ainu at bay in the north the government called upon these same easterners, called *azuma-bito,* to man the expeditionary forces. Even the *sakimori,* the coast guards for the defense of Kyushu, were traditionally recruited from the east. By the early Heian period a more specific cognomen, *Kanto-bushi,* or warriors of Kanto, came to displace the more general term *azuma-bito* for the fighting men of this region.

THE RISE OF THE TAIRA

Among the first families to establish a reputation as *Kanto-bushi* was the Taira, also known collectively as the Heiji or the Heike.[21] During the migration of Kyoto nobles to the provinces, one Takamochi, a grandson of Prince Katsurabara, one of the sons of Emperor Kammu (r. 781–806), received the family name of Taira

[21] See chart of Taira family, Figure 2.

and the office of vice governor of Kazusa[22] where he settled. All six
of his sons also settled in the provinces to become local leaders in
different areas in the east and the north. Kunika, the oldest, became
governor of Hitachi and shogun of the *Chinju-fu*, the Pacifying-Ezo
Headquarters, of the northern provinces. Kunika's son, Sadamori,
became governor of Mutsu, and it was from his line of the Taira
that the Hōjō of Izu, the Yamamoto, and the Heiji of Ise were to
come. Another of Kunika's sons, Shigemori, who also held the
governorship of Mutsu, was the forebear of such well-known warrior
families as the Toyoda, Iwaki, and Jō of the northern and eastern
regions.

Takamochi's youngest son, Yoshibumi, who had settled in
Musashi, was the first of a line of Taira whose descendants became
local lords in southern Kanto generally. Such familiar families of
this region as Hatakeyama, Kasai, Mikami, Kawagoe, Oyamada,
Edo, Kitami, Miura, Kajiwara, Ōba, Chiba, and many more which
we encounter in the pages of the *Azuma kagami* were of Taira
origin. As managers or actual owners of *shōen*, as governors or
constabularies, Taira descendants gradually brought Kanto under
their control. Thus Heiji lords and Heiji influence spread to all
corners of Eastern Japan. In southern Kanto, known as Bandō,
their influence was especially strong. The expression *Bandō Hachi-
Heiji*, or the Eight Heiji of Bandō, which entered the vocabulary
of the times is indicative of this influence. Other families vied with
each other to become associated with the Taira through marriage,
adoption, and vassalage. Thus local lords with large armed followings related to the Taira or aligned with them as vassals increased in
the east.

So long as these local lords confined their fighting to private wars
among themselves, or to minor infractions of the law and occasional
defiance of the local representatives of the central government, the
situation was not viewed with alarm by the government, for all lords
nominally acknowledged the distant sovereignty of the emperor.
But alliances between lords as well as increasing warfare between
them tended to eliminate the weaker and strengthen the stronger,

[22] See map of Eastern Japan, Figure 4.

and to place the government more and more in a position of dependence on the lords for the preservation of peace and order in the provinces.

The dangers inherent in such a situation were emphasized in 935 when a disturbance in the east known as the *Tenkei-no-ran* broke out. In its origins it appeared to be a strictly private—in fact, a family —affair, involving Taira Masakado, a power in Shimōsa, who at-

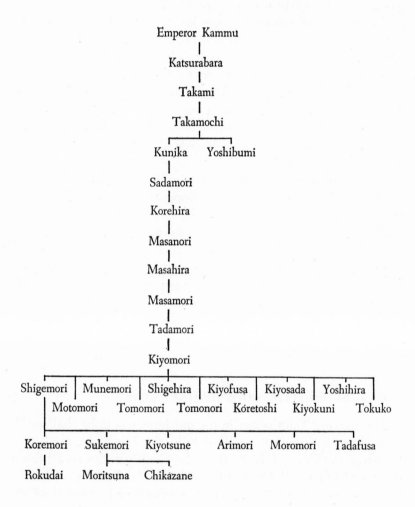

Figure 2. Genealogical chart of the Heiji (Taira)

tacked and slew his uncle Kunika, the governor of Hitachi. But before the affair was settled some four years later it had spread to several provinces and had involved many local lords and their followers as well as officials of the imperial court and their troops. In fact, it took on the character of a revolt against the imperial court when Masakado proclaimed himself the new emperor, basing his claim on his descent from Emperor Kammu, and set up his own government, complete with ministers.

The number of private warriors involved in this disturbance is significant. The total strength of Masakado's forces is believed to have been about 8,000, while Kunika's forces whom Masakado defeated numbered 3,000. Sadamori, Kunika's son and Masakado's cousin, who finally subdued Masakado in 939 in behalf of the imperial court, led an army of 4,000. These are not formidable numbers, but it must not be forgotten that they were private troops of local lords whether fighting for Masakado or for the imperial court.

This disturbance also had repercussions in Iyo Province in Western Japan, closer to the seat of the imperial court, when Fujiwara Sumitomo also revolted in 935. While the leaders of both of these revolts were subdued and killed and the threat to the court eliminated by 941, it is highly significant that local lords had become so powerful as to be able to challenge the government, and that the latter needed the cooperation and military assistance of other local lords to suppress them. In fact, the influence of the provincial warrior was being felt even at the capital where more and more the imperial guards and the imperial police were being staffed by warriors from the provinces.

THE RISE OF THE MINAMOTO

The growing Taira power in the provinces was to be challenged in time by another great warrior family, the Minamoto, familiarly known as the Genji. Like its rival, the Genji was descended from the imperial family.[23] The first to receive the family name of Minamoto was one Tsunemoto, son of a prince and a grandson of Emperor Seiwa (r. 858–876); hence the term Seiwa Genji to dis-

[23] See chart of Minamoto family, Figure 3.

tinguish this branch from other strains of the Genji. It is interesting to note that Tsunemoto served the court in various capacities in such widely separated areas as Musashi in the east, Shinano in the north, Iyo in the west, and Kyushu in the south, and that he had participated in the expeditions against both Taira Masakado and Fujiwara Sumitomo. All of his sons also served at the court, among whom the oldest, Mitsunaka, was to effect an alliance with the Fujiwara family at a time when the latter was approaching the zenith of its political power. Thus the Genji in its beginnings was more securely entrenched at the court than was the Taira.

The lands of the Genji were located mainly in the neighboring provinces. Mitsunaka settled at Tada in Settsu Province, which became the seat of the subsidiary branch of the Minamoto, called the Tada-Genji. Two other subsidiary branches were established in the neighboring provinces by Mitsunaka's sons: one in Yamato, later to be known as the Yamato-Genji; and the other at Ishikawa in Kawachi, to be known as the Kawachi-Genji.

But in Kanto the primacy of the Heiji in the tenth century was still unchallenged. Taira Sadamori, who had avenged his father's death by slaying Masakado, was rewarded by the court with high commissions, including that of *Chinju-fu* shogun, and his family and descendants continued to hold the balance of power in the north and the east until the first quarter of the eleventh century.

It was then that chance was to bring together the Taira and the Minamoto in the first test of strength between these warrior families. In 1028 Taira Tadatsune, a power in Musashi, extended his sway into Awa Province by killing the latter's governor. The imperial court sent two expeditions against him, the second under Minamoto Yorinobu, son of Mitsunaka and the founder of the Kawachi-Genji, who was successful in suppressing Tadatsune.

The above incident provided the first great impetus for the beginning of Minamoto influence in the east. On the expedition against Tadatsune, Yorinobu had taken his son Yoriyoshi who was to become the governor of Sagami a few years later and to bring most of the local lords in that province under his control. But two other wars in the north in the latter half of the eleventh century were to establish the Minamoto as a great local power. These were the so-called Nine Years' War and the Three Years' War which began in

1051 and 1083 respectively. The former involved Abe Yoritoki, a local lord of Mutsu, who had refused to remit tribute to Kyoto, and against whom Minamoto Yoriyoshi and his son Yoshiie were sent by the court. The Three Years' War of 1083 was a campaign against the Kiyowara family of Dewa. Minamoto Yoshiie, who had succeeded his father as chieftain of the clan, was sent by the court to suppress the rebellious Kiyowara. In these long years of successful campaigning in the mountains of northern Honshu against a hardy race of northerners, who themselves had earned a reputation as warriors in generations of fighting with the Ainu, the bond between Minamoto leaders and Minamoto followers was immeasurably strengthened, and the reputation of the Minamoto as warriors reached new heights. The court, having sent the Genji against the northern lords, showered them with honors in the form of appointments in appreciation of their victories. Father and son, Yoriyoshi and Yoshiie, both served as *Chinju-fu* shogun and governor of Mutsu, and between them they held the governorship of Iyo, Kawachi, Musashi, and Shimotsuke, while their warrior followers were called to Kyoto to serve as guards at the palace. The court, however, had not foreseen one of the consequences of the growing reputation of Minamoto Yoshiie, which was the commendation of lands to him in ever-increasing degree, particularly in the east and north. This movement became so pronounced that the court was compelled in 1091 to issue an official ban on the further commendation of land to him. Thus by the close of the eleventh century the Minamoto had laid the basis of its power in the provinces. Economically, it held rights to vast tracts of land. Politically, its leaders were recognized by the court. Socially, the relationship between Minamoto leaders and the warrior class in the provinces, especially in the east and the north, was firmly established.

The rise of the Minamoto in the north and the east meant that the Taira power in those areas had decreased. But the Taira, as it was giving way to the Minamoto in these areas, was quietly building the basis for a Taira resurgence in the area around Ise and points west along the Inland Sea, just beyond the Minamoto centers of Settsu and Kawachi. Korehira, a son of Sadamori, was to become governor of Ise. With Taira Masamori, Korehira's grandson, who held several governorships, Taira influence reached into Inaba on the Japan Sea and to both sides of the Inland Sea as far west as Bizen and Sanuki. Early in the eleventh century the Taira was challenged in this region by the Minamoto. Yoshichika, one of the sons of the famed Yoshiie, had defied the court and had committed excesses during his governorship of a province in Kyushu, for which he had been exiled to the island of Oki in the Japan Sea. But he had made his way to Izumo and there had seized power which he held until subdued in 1107 by Taira Masamori, who had been sent against him by the court. Thus the Taira successfully met a Minamoto challenge in the west, and continued to tighten its hold on Western Japan.

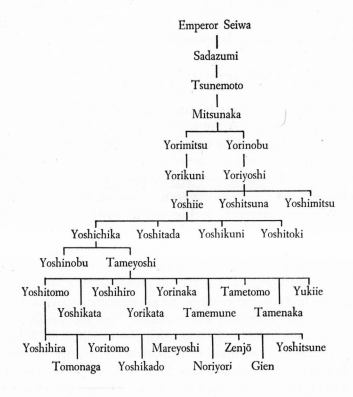

Figure 3. Genealogical chart of the Genji (Minamoto)

Masamori's son Tadamori (d. 1153) was to rise to even greater heights than his father. Because of his control over local lords in both Bizen and Sanuki, the provinces facing each other north and south across the narrowest part of the Inland Sea, he was able to subdue piracy on this ancient waterway and to gain control of shipping and commerce in the eastern end of the Inland Sea. This naval feat was to have important consequences in the subsequent history of the Taira, but for the moment it made Tadamori a power in the Inland Sea region and a favorite at the court. In fact, with Tadamori, Taira influence at the court was to increase so rapidly as to rival that of the Minamoto, who, through its alliance with the Fujiwara, had earlier entrenched itself in the capital. However, to understand the Taira infiltration into the court and the struggle for power between the Taira and the Minamoto which ensued, we must turn to a discussion of the changing political scene in Kyoto.

THE GEMPEI RIVALRY IN KYOTO

In Kyoto, as the eleventh century opened, the Fujiwara family under Michinaga was at the zenith of its power. Before his death in 1027 he had treated the capital to a spectacle of personal power, grandeur, and extravagance never before equaled by a civil official. He had ruled the court almost singlehandedly for thirty years. Three of his daughters had married emperors; four grandsons had been or were to become emperors; and he and his sons and close relatives held all the high civil posts in the government.

But actually the Fujiwara family, despite its great display of wealth and power, was dependent to a large degree upon the armed might of the Minamoto for the maintenance of its position and influence. Its vast land holdings, which were the economic basis of its power, were protected and maintained for the family by the Minamoto. One need only recall that the rebellion of Taira Tadatsune in the east occurred in 1028, only a year after Michinaga's death, and that it was quelled for the court by the Minamoto. Thus the fate of the Fujiwara, even as it attained its greatest glory under Michinaga, was dependent on the loyalty of a provincial warrior family.

Another development of the eleventh century was to threaten the position of the Fujiwara family. In the capital, where the Fujiwara had been dominant for so long, anti-Fujiwara sentiment was mounting. As early as 1034, only seven years after Michinaga's death, there was to ascend to the throne an emperor who was to devise a method of breaking, or at least of neutralizing, the Fujiwara hold on the government. This was Emperor Go-Sanjō, who abdicated in 1072, leaving an eleven-year-old son on the throne, and attempted to rule from retirement, completely removed from the influence of Fujiwara advisers and officials. Although this attempt failed, due to Go-Sanjō's unexpected demise the following year, his son Shirakawa carried out the original scheme, abdicating in 1086 and setting up the so-called *insei,* or cloistered government, with ministers and military guards of his own choosing. Thus Shirakawa, who was to rule from retirement for forty-three years, was the first emperor successfully to circumvent complete Fujiwara control.

It can be seen how this scheme of cloistered rule, though aimed at the Fujiwara, had the effect of dividing the unity of the imperial family and of weakening the imperial court against the inroads being made by the warrior class. Under such a system, differences between the emperor and the ex-emperor, to whom real authority tended to accrue, were inevitable. The relations, for example, between Ex-Emperor Toba and his successor, Emperor Sutoku, were extremely unhappy from the very beginning. There was also the possibility of more than one ex-emperor's attempting to rule from retirement. In fact, such a situation was nearly approached as early as 1141 when Emperor Sutoku abdicated while the Ex-Emperor Toba was still very much alive and in control of the cloistered government.

It was precisely at this time, the early twelfth century, when cloistered rule was becoming a cause of division within the imperial court, that Taira Tadamori was achieving fame as a warrior in Western Japan. His suppression of piracy on the Inland Sea occurred during the last years of Toba's reign and the beginning of his rule as cloistered emperor. Partly because of this coincidence, and partly because cloistered rule was aimed at weakening the Fujiwara who were aligned with the Minamoto, it is not surprising that the Ex-Emperor Toba seemed more inclined to rely on the military assistance of the Taira rather than that of the Minamoto. At any rate, both Tadamori and his son, Kiyomori, were quick to recognize the possibilities in this situation and aligned themselves with the cloistered government. Although the two courts relied on the military strength of both the Minamoto and the Taira for the preservation of peace and order in the capital, in general, the cloistered government cultivated the favor of the Taira more than it did that of the Minamoto. And it should be noted that in the first half of the twelfth century there was great need for the military assistance of warriors to put down the warfare and brawls of armed monks of rival Buddhist orders in and around the capital.[24]

Under the circumstances it was only a matter of time until warrior groups in the capital would be called upon to lend their assistance to the more strictly private quarrels of factions within the court. Just such a situation developed in 1156, when a succession dispute broke out at the court, which was settled by the force of arms of the Taira and the Minamoto. The dispute began when the Ex-Emperor Toba, who had dictated the choice of three emperors since his own abdication in 1123, died in 1156. Whereupon, Ex-Emperor Sutoku, who had been forced to abdicate in 1141 by the late Toba, sought to reascend the throne against the wishes of the incumbent, Go-Shirakawa. Factions of the Fujiwara, which was itself involved in a dispute over the headship of the family, joined the fray, and finally the Taira and the Minamoto were called upon by the dis-

[24] The subject of disturbances caused by armed monks of the various religious orders requires a more lengthy explanation than can be presented here. The causes were many. Some were feuds between two branches of a sect, particularly the so-called Sammon and Jimon branches of the Tendai Sect, over such questions as the right to conduct initiation ceremonies, and over appointments of head priests and other high ecclesiastical officials. Sometimes the monks of a monastery rose up against their own head priest and attacked and burned his residence. More often the disturbances were directed against the imperial court which made the appointments. In fact, many of these disturbances began as demonstrations by monks or priests against the court, demanding that a particular decree be rescinded or issued, or a particular official be recalled or appointed. Since the demonstrators were armed, and since the court could not disperse them except by calling on warriors, brawls in the city streets of Kyoto became frequent. Some of the more powerful monasteries were not averse to sending their armies directly against the warrior groups which earlier had assisted the court. For the nature and frequency of these disturbances during the twelfth century, see any of the detailed chronologies listed in the Bibliography, or the English chronology in the following work: R. K. Reischauer, *Early Japanese History*, Part A, pp. 367–405.

putants to give their assistance. In general, the Minamoto supported the cause of Ex-Emperor Sutoku, while the Taira threw its support to Go-Shirakawa.

Thus the *Hōgen-no-ran*, as this disturbance was known, became in effect another test of strength between these two old rivals. As a military engagement it had little significance. It was a mere skirmish of extremely short duration, and involved only a handful of troops. However, it had important political implications. The warrior, heretofore the guard and protector of the palace and the court, had been asked to settle the important political issue of who was to ascend the throne. It was obvious that after his participation in the event the warrior would no longer be content with his former duties and that he would demand a larger voice in the government of the court. In short, the provincial warrior had become, as a result of the *Hōgen-no-ran*, an integral part of the politics of the central government.

In this contest the Taira, who had supported Go-Shirakawa, emerged the victor. It promptly began to eliminate from the court all those who had supported the rival claimant. The result was that only one Minamoto of any prominence remained in the capital. This was Yoshitomo, who had chosen to support Go-Shirakawa and the Taira against the wishes of the majority of the Minamoto.

However, even this lone Minamoto in the Taira-dominated court was to meet his death within a few years and all Minamoto influence was swept out of the capital with the so-called *Heiji-no-ran* of 1159. This disturbance was engineered by elements of the Fujiwara whose places in the high councils of government were now preempted by the Taira under its leader Kiyomori. The Fujiwara, lacking troops, had alienated Yoshitomo from his former ally to assist in the revolt. The outcome was disastrous for the Minamoto. Yoshitomo met his death. His sons, among them Yoritomo who was then twelve years old, were banished from the capital and placed in the custody of Taira overlords in the provinces.

Kiyomori's rise was phenomenal after the *Heiji-no-ran*. He controlled the cloistered government, which was headed after 1158 by none other than Go-Shirakawa, whom Kiyomori had supported militarily in the *Hōgen-no-ran*. He also held firm control over the

emperor and his court, which he purged of dissident Fujiwara elements, and thus, for the first time since the introduction of
cloistered rule, there appeared to be a working harmony between the
two courts. In time Kiyomori became *dajō-daijin,* or chancellor,
with the court rank of junior first class, the first time that a member
of the military class was raised to that rank. Like the Fujiwara he
gave a daughter in marriage to an emperor, and like the Fujiwara
he became grandfather to an Emperor. Sixteen members of his
family held court ranks of the third class or higher; thirty more held
ranks of the fourth, fifth, and sixth classes. Provincial governorships
and high military offices held by Taira men numbered sixty-four.
The Taira was reputed to own more than 500 *shōen,* and thirty
of the total of sixty-six provinces which comprised the nation were
under the control of this family. While these figures may not be
wholly accurate, they nevertheless indicate the great power of the
Taira.

Although the Taira emulated the Fujiwara, the methods it employed to achieve complete dominance differed greatly from those
of its predecessor. On the whole, the Fujiwara had shunned direct
military action. Instead, it had espoused peaceful, though not necessarily honest, methods. Its chief weapons had been diplomacy,
conspiracy, and the marriage alliance, methods which were slow and
circumspect. The Taira was not averse to using these methods, but
on the whole it was impatient with them and preferred more direct
ways. Thus it refused to compromise with the Minamoto after
the *Heiji-no-ran* in 1159 and drove the family out of Kyoto. Moreover, it excluded the Minamoto and other potential rivals from the
management of the provinces. Over its 500 estates, some of which
it had seized outright, the Taira placed *jitō,* or land stewards, chosen
from among its own clan members, to assure the prompt and un-
interrupted flow of tribute to its family coffers. And, as a further
precaution against the misconduct of its *jitō* and its other appointees,
it despatched special commissioners to the provinces from time to
time to keep a watchful eye over them.

Toward the imperial family the Taira on occasion acted with
the same impatience and ruthlessness which characterized its relations with the Fujiwara and other court families. When, for exam-

ple, Kiyomori's able son Shigemori died in 1179, and the Ex-
Emperor Go-Shirakawa saw fit to have Shigemori's domain of
Echizen Province escheated to the ex-emperor's government, this act
so enraged Kiyomori that he promptly ordered the confinement of
Go-Shirakawa and the wholesale dismissal of the ex-emperor's
ministers.

And thus, as the year 1180 opened, there was little to indicate
that the Taira hold on the central government and the government
of the provinces, particularly those in the west where its economic
power lay, had weakened. True, Kiyomori tended to leave the administration of the government more and more to his sons, but no
one regarded this as anything more than the natural consequences
of advancing age. There was, according to the *Heike monogatari*,
some criticism of Taira arrogance and extravagance by the people
of Kyoto, but it is doubtful whether the Taira or anyone considered
this as a sign of declining power or influence. Thus, when a plot
to overthrow the Taira was discovered in Kyoto in the spring of
1180, it must have come as an annoying surprise to the confident
rulers.

Chapter III
The Gempei War:
Initial Phases[1]

INITIAL SETBACKS AND THE NEAR DEFEAT OF THE MINAMOTO

The events between 1180 and 1185 which brought the Taira and the Minamoto to grips again, this time in a struggle to the finish, are so familiar as to hardly warrant a lengthy repetition here. However, as these events were an integral part of the establishment of the shogunate, it is necessary to review them and to explain their relationship to the founding of the *de facto* government of the Minamoto.

The strictly military phase of the conflict was preceded by a series of important events in Kyoto. There, during the Fourth Month of 1180, a member of the imperial family had been persuaded by a Minamoto to issue a pronouncement authorizing the overthrow of Chancellor Taira Kiyomori and his supporters, and calling upon the entire nation to join in the movement.[2] The pronouncement was to be kept a secret except among the Minamoto until all preparations could be made. The member of the imperial family who authorized the pronouncement and who required little persuasion to lend his name to the plot was Prince Mochihito, the second son of Ex-

---

[1] As indicated in the Preface, all footnote citations to the *Azuma kagami* in these chapters will be given by date only. Thus the notation Jishō 4:4,9 refers to the entry in the *Azuma kagami* for the Fourth Year of Jishō, Fourth Month, Ninth Day. Some of the citations include the abbreviation "Inter." followed by a numeral such as 2. This signifies "Intercalary Second Month," an extra month added after the Second Month to make the calendar correspond more closely to the actual seasons. This process, called intercalation, was necessitated by the fact that the calendar year included only 360 days.

[2] Jishō 4:4,9.

Sovereign Go-Shirakawa. He had been bypassed for the succession twice, the second time only two months earlier when Antoku, the three-year-old grandson of Kiyomori, had been placed on the throne. The courtier who had initiated the plot was Yorimasa, a seventy-nine-year-old member of a collateral branch of the Minamoto who, for the greater part of the twenty years since the expulsion of the Genji from Kyoto, had enjoyed the dubious distinction of being a Minamoto in the service of the Taira-dominated court. But, being a Minamoto and of advanced age, he was merely tolerated and often made the butt of jokes by the Taira. Smarting under the insults of his superiors[3] but apparently not suspected by them of harboring revolutionary plans, he had taken advantage of the absence of Taira leaders from Kyoto and had secretly approached Mochihito, promising him the throne if the revolt was successful. This pronouncement, dated the ninth day of the Fourth Month, reached Yoritomo in Izu, Eastern Japan, on the twenty-seventh of the same month.[4]

However, in the following month the plot was discovered by the Taira, who moved swiftly to suppress it.[5] The prince was ordered banished to Tosa. Yorimasa, apparently not suspected at first but fearing eventual detection, burned his residence in Kyoto and fled to Onjō-ji, a monastery on the shores of Lake Biwa, to join the prince, who had evaded arrest and had preceded him there.[6] But before the month was over the plotters, realizing the inadequacy of the defenses and forces of Onjō-ji in the face of 20,000 Heike troops who had been sent against them, decided to leave for Nara and the greater protection of Tōdai-ji and Kōfuku-ji monasteries with which Onjō-ji was affiliated. En route to Nara on the twenty-sixth, they were overtaken at Uji where they perished.[7]

---

[3] The Taira scornfully referred to him as the "Junior Third Rank," a rank of no mean honor under normal circumstances; but Yorimasa had not received it until 1178 when he was seventy-seven years old. The immediate cause for his rancor, according to popular accounts, was an insult directed at his son Nakatsuna who had refused to give up to Taira Munemori a prize horse which had been imported from the east. Munemori thereupon named his own horse "Nakatsuna" to the amusement of his friends.

[4] The pronouncement is recorded in its entirety in the entry of Jishō 4:4,27.

[5] Jishō 4:5,15–27 inclusive.

[6] That Yorimasa was not suspected at first may be seen from the fact that one of his sons was assigned by the Taira to escort Mochihito to his place of exile.

[7] Jishō 4:5,26.

Meanwhile, in Izu Province in Eastern Japan, Yoritomo was attempting to rally the Genji to his banner. But this was a formidable task, as Yoritomo himself was to learn and as the delay in launching the war attests. Between the Fourth Month when Yoritomo received Prince Mochihito's pronouncement and the Eighth Month when he made his first military move against the Taira he had approximately three months in which to make preparations and to send appeals for help to the Genji in the east and the north. Even so, he was nearly compelled to postpone the opening move of the war for lack of troops. The plain fact was that the Genji, that is, Yoritomo's vassals of Minamoto stock and others traditionally associated with the Minamoto, did not respond quickly and favorably to his call.

In this connection it is important to note that those who were regarded as the Genji were not necessarily of Minamoto blood. Except for leaders of various Genji groups in the different provinces, the majority of the Genji were of non-Minamoto descent. A Genji was simply a person who paid homage to a Minamoto leader and rendered him service, usually of a military nature. A test of whether a Genji was a true, loyal retainer lay in the record of his family, that is, whether his ancestors had served Minamoto lords, and for how many generations. Those whose families held records of long and continued service were specially regarded as *ruidai no gokenin,* or "hereditary retainers."

Thus the division between the Genji and the Heiji in the provinces was a matter largely of traditional friendship rather than of blood. Had the latter prevailed as the basis of division, the Genji would have been at a distinct disadvantage, for, historically, the Taira had preceded the Minamoto as the dominant power in the north and the east and, consequently, Taira descendants comprised the majority of the lords and warrior families in those regions. Of the warrior families in the east listed in a contemporary genealogy, 161 were of Taira descent, as against 136 descended from the Minamoto.[8] This disparity may also be seen in the background of the handful of retainers who assisted Yoritomo in his initial assault on the Taira—a small but carefully executed night attack on Yamamoto

---

[8] Cited in Kingorō Ōmori, *Buke jidai no kenkyū,* I, 409–50. The genealogy in question is the *Sompi bummyaku.*

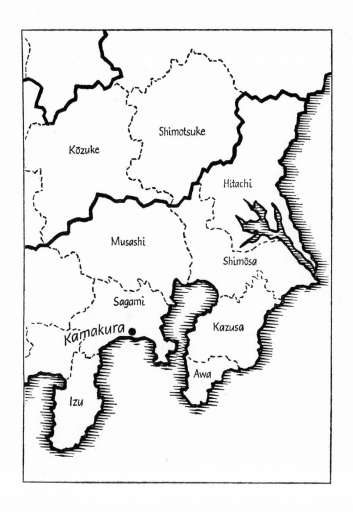

Figure 4. Kamakura and the provinces of Southern Kanto

Kanetaka, a local Taira partisan.[9] Of this group only the Sasaki and the Usumi were of Minamoto descent. The others, such as Hōjō, Kudō, Doi, and Okazaki were of Taira descent, while Amano and Katō were of Fujiwara descent. But all of them, with the lone exception of the Hōjō, had served Yoritomo's father or other Minamoto leaders.[10]

It has been noted above, as evidence of the poor response of the Genji, that Yoritomo was nearly compelled to call off the long-planned-for attack on Yamamoto Kanetaka for want of troops. This subject bears closer examination, for in attempting to overcome this difficulty Yoritomo was laying the foundation for regional control of the east and hence of a government for the east.

Among the more prominent Genji lords in the immediate vicinity of Izu on whom Yoritomo counted for assistance for the first attack on the Taira were the Shibuya, Sasaki, Hatano, Takiguchi, Chiba, and Miura. The Shibuya, despite several appeals for aid from Yoritomo, failed to respond and, in the end, joined with the Taira forces. The Hatano and Takiguchi rejected Yoritomo's plea, and even spoke harshly against it.[11] Like the Shibuya, these two lords of neighboring Sagami Province joined the enemy ranks. Only the Chiba and the Miura had sent representatives to Yoritomo to assure him of military support—although this assurance had not come until the end of the Sixth Month, causing Yoritomo much anxiety in the meantime.[12] Moreover, they were not on hand when the war was finally launched.

Of this group of six Genji lords the Sasaki were the only vassals who were on hand on the seventeenth of the Eighth Month to help Yoritomo in his first attack on the Taira. Even so, they had failed to report on the sixteenth as instructed, nearly causing Yoritomo to call off the attack. It is significant to note that the first military action of the war depended on four brothers and their small following, who

---

[9] Jishō 4:8,17.

[10] Although the *Azuma kagami* is itself one of the primary sources for genealogical data on the various warrior families, the information it contains is scattered and unorganized except for some of the more prominent families. A handy dictionary bringing together such data from the *Azuma kagami* and other sources is *Seishi kakei dai-jiten,* ed. Akira Ōta and Sanji Mikami. Another is *Dai-bukan,* ed. Hiroshi Hashimoto.

[11] Jishō 4:7,10.

[12] Jishō 4:6,27.

comprised the Sasaki. Their arrival made it possible for Yoritomo to carry out the plans in the night instead of at dawn on the seventeenth.[13] Yoritomo's desperation with regard to the smallness of his forces can be seen further in the suspicions and doubts he began to cast on some of the Genji, including the Sasaki, who held impressive records of service and loyalty to the Minamoto. Hideyoshi, the leader of the Sasaki, had fought alongside Yoritomo's father in the Heiji Disturbance. He had stood by the Genji despite reprisals against him by the Taira which included the seizure of his hereditary lands in Ōmi Province. While fleeing the Taira he had been befriended by the Shibuya of Sagami who persuaded him to settle in the east.[14] Of Hideyoshi's loyalty to the Genji Yoritomo seems to have had every confidence; yet, in the anxious moments before the arrival of his four sons, Yoritomo regretted that "he had placed complete trust in the Sasaki and that he had disclosed secret matters to them." [15] Moreover, Yoritomo remembered suddenly that the patrons of the Sasaki were the Shibuya who had not responded to his call and who were inclined to favor the Taira.[16]

There were other Genji in the immediate vicinity of Izu whose preference for the Taira was so well known that Yoritomo made no move to ask for their aid. In fact, he exercised scrupulous care in this regard, for to ask for assistance from one of this group was to expose his plans to the enemy. One such lord was Ōba Kagechika. The Ōba was a hereditary vassal of the Genji[17] and a power in Sagami Province. He and his large following had returned from Kyoto early in the Eighth Month after assisting the Taira to restore order in the capital following the Mochihito-Yorimasa incident.[18] It was he who had much to do in swaying the lesser lords of his province into supporting the Taira. The Shibuya, for example, had been influenced in their choice for the Taira by Kagechika. It was Kagechika also who had learned of Yoritomo's secret preparation and

[13] Something of Yoritomo's desperation with regard to troops can be seen from the following account in the *Azuma kagami:* "His Lordship was moved to tears at the sight of the brothers—Sadatsuna and Tsunetaka on injured horses, and Moritsuna and Takatsuna afoot" (Jishō 4:8,17).

[14] Jishō 4:8,9.

[15] Jishō 4:8,16.

[16] *Ibid.*

[17] Jishō 4:9,3.

[18] Jishō 4:8,2.

had cautioned other local lords against supporting Yoritomo should the latter rise up in revolt.[19]

To a certain extent this problem of retaining the support of the traditional Genji must have been foreseen by Yoritomo. It was, after all, twenty years since the Genji had fallen from power, and in that period many so-called hereditary Genji had, for reasons of expediency, made peace with the Taira. Most of the local lords, for example, contributed guards to Kyoto under Taira supervision. Even the Miura and the Chiba, the staunchest of Genji lords in the east, had sent warriors to Kyoto each year to provide protection for the court and the Taira.[20] Yoritomo was also aware of the predicament of some of his vassals whose lands were situated close to or between those held by Taira partisans. A vassal such as Kasai Kiyoshige, whose lands were situated between those of the Edo and Kawagoe families—lords who openly espoused the Taira—could not, for reasons of security, come forward on the side of Yoritomo.[21]

However, the fact remains that the response was poor and that Yoritomo was not prepared to launch the attack in the Eighth Month of 1180. On the other hand, he could not delay the revolt longer, for local lords of Taira persuasion like Ōba Kagechika had become extremely suspicious of Yoritomo's activities and might attack him first. And thus, with only a handful of followers, Yoritomo carried out his plans, attacking Yamamoto Kanetaka on the night of the seventeenth of the Eighth Month. Even after Miura Yoshiaki joined him a few days later with the Genji of Izu and Sagami Provinces, his total following had increased to a mere three hundred.[22]

Having announced his intentions toward the Taira by his actions of the seventeenth, Yoritomo now had no choice but to proceed with the war. Two days after the initial move Yoritomo ordered Yamamoto Tomochika, a relative of Kanetaka, to surrender control of his manor and to submit to Yoritomo's rule of Eastern Japan,[23]

[19] Jishō 4:8,9.
[20] Their delay in responding to Yoritomo's call had been due to the absence of so many of their warriors in Kyoto performing guard duty. Cf. Jishō 4:6,27.
[21] Jishō 4:9,3.
[22] The list of forty-six names of Yoritomo's principal vassals at this time, although deleted from the translation in the interest of brevity, may be found in the entry of Jishō 4:8,20.
[23] Jishō 4:8,19.

a move which had important political implications, as we shall note later. However, despite his victory over Kanetaka and his bold threat to Tomochika, Yoritomo's military position in Izu must not have been secure, for on the third day after the opening of the war, he moved out of Izu into Sagami Province toward the east. There at Ishibashi Mountain in his first field encounter, he was soundly beaten by a numerically superior Taira force composed of local lords under the leadership of Ōba Kagechika.[24]

The preponderance in numbers of the Taira over the Minamoto forces—three thousand to three hundred[25]—showed beyond any doubt how dismally Yoritomo had failed to rally the local lords to his standard. Even the forces of Itō Sukechika alone, who attacked Yoritomo's lines from the rear, were as large as the entire Genji army.[26] The final evidence of the lack of enthusiasm for Yoritomo's cause among the local lords was the presence in the enemy ranks at Ishibashi Mountain of Genji lords whom Yoritomo had earlier counted on for assistance. These were in particular the Shibuya and the Takiguchi families. And it must be remembered that the commander of the enemy forces, Ōba Kagechika, was himself a former Genji.

It was a near miracle that Yoritomo was not captured or killed at Ishibashi or in the Hakone Mountains where he hid for a few days following his abject defeat. Meanwhile, unknown to him, another Genji force under Miura Yoshiaki which had failed to join Yoritomo at Ishibashi was being defeated by the enemy at Kinugasa.[27]

The problem of rallying the Genji might not have been so serious and pressing had the leading members of Yoritomo's family and those of collateral Minamoto families come to his aid. It is true that Minamoto Yukiie, Yoritomo's uncle, had been a part of the plot since its inception in Kyoto, having delivered Prince Mochihito's pronouncement to Izu during the Fourth Month and having, moreover, left Izu on the same day for Kai and Shinano to rally the Genji in those provinces.[28] However, Yukiie's efforts can scarcely

[24] Jishō 4:8,23.
[25] *Ibid.*
[26] *Ibid.*
[27] Jishō 4:8,26–27.
[28] Jishō 4:4,27.

be regarded as effective in view of the apathy of the Genji toward Yoritomo's cause. The first Minamoto with a sizable following to declare for Yoritomo was a cousin, Kiso Yoshinaka of Shinano Province, who entered the war during the Ninth Month.[29] But Yoshinaka's action was suspiciously late, for the Genji of Kai and Shinano were the first to be notified of the plans for the revolt.[30] Moreover, Yoshinaka's declaration of loyalty had come a fortnight after the Battle of Ishibashi Mountain when it appeared that Yoritomo's cause was hopeless.

The powerful Satake family, descended from Minamoto Yoshimitsu, brother of Yoshiie who had founded Yoritomo's line of the Genji, openly defied Yoritomo. The Satake, situated in Hitachi, posed a special problem for Yoritomo, for, as Yoritomo himself acknowledged, the authority and influence of the Satake extended beyond the borders of Hitachi,[31] and there was also the possibility that the Satake might unite with Yoshinaka in Shinano, or the powerful Fujiwara of Ōshu, or other influential Minamoto in Eastern and North Central Japan, against him.

One of the latter was Shida Yoshihiro of Hitachi, another of Yoritomo's uncles. He had offered no help to Yoritomo when the war opened, and even after swearing fealty to the Genji cause,[32] he turned against Yoritomo. Together with the Ashikaga of Shimotsuke, another prominent branch of the Minamoto, he marched against Kamakura.[33]

One influential Minamoto who came out eventually for Yoritomo, but only after the latter had won important victories, was Nitta Yoshishige, the venerable great-uncle of Yoritomo. In the Ninth Month, when Genji support was sorely needed by Yoritomo, Yoshishige rallied his forces in Kōzuke, entrenched himself in Terao Castle, and refused to come forth to support Yoritomo.[34]

Thus, in the opening phase of the war, the only support which Yoritomo received from members of his own or collateral branches of the Minamoto came from Yukiie, an uncle, and Yoshinaka, a cousin. Both, however, contributed little materially to strengthen

---

[29] Jishō 4:9,7.
[30] Jishō 4:4,27.
[31] Jishō 4:11,4.
[32] Jishō 4:11,7.
[33] Jishō 5:Inter.2,23.
[34] Jishō 4:9,30.

the Genji cause. In fact, as we shall note presently, they gave Yoritomo much cause for anxiety.

It is quite apparent that Prince Mochihito and Minamoto Yorimasa, in attempting to arouse the Genji to overthrow the Heike in 1180, had rashly assumed that unity and cohesion existed among the Minamoto leaders and between them and other families traditionally associated with the Minamoto.[35] They had assumed further that the rivalry between the Minamoto and the Taira was so strong that the former would rise up as one against the Taira at the slightest excuse. Neither of these assumptions proved correct in the light of the slow and discouraging response of the Genji and the disunity among their leaders.

Yorimasa's grave error had been his failure to note that time and new developments in the provinces had greatly lessened the Gempei rivalry, however bitter and intense it had been in the past. In the twenty years since the Heiji Disturbance many Genji in the provinces had made peace with their Taira overlords. Indeed, many of them had more cause to be grateful to the Taira than to the Minamoto. For example, the head of the Ashikaga family, a branch of the Minamoto, owed the continued use and enjoyment of his manor in Shimotsuke—which was several hundred *chō* in size—to Taira Shigemori, the *honke,* or legal guardian and nominal owner of the manor. Earlier, when the head of the Ashikaga had been dispossessed of his lands, he had gone to Kyoto to plead his case with Shigemori who, consequently, restored the lands to him.[36] Thus, although a Genji by tradition, he, like other Minamoto leaders, refused to come out for Yoritomo.

Marriages between the clans, fairly common in the east and the north, also tended to erase the old rivalry between them. Yoritomo himself had taken a Taira descendant for a wife. Taira Hirotsune, the vice governor of Kazusa and one of the more influential lords of Taira descent in the east, was related by marriage to the Satake who were of Minamoto descent. The decision of Ashikaga Tadatsuna, a Minamoto, to oppose Yoritomo can be

---

[35] Note, for example, that Mochihito's pronouncement is addressed to the Genji of Tōkai, Tōsan, and Hokuriku, traditionally the regions of strongest Minamoto influence. Jishō 4:4,27.

[36] Mentioned in Juei 1:9,7.

explained in part by his marriage tie with the Fujiwara of Ōshu, who were staunch supporters of the Taira. These marriage ties, as well as many more among lesser families in the provinces, tended to obscure the old Gempei rivalry.

The immediate cause of the war—the personal insults allegedly incurred by Yorimasa from his Taira superiors whom he had chosen to serve—was hardly substantial and compelling enough to arouse the Genji to action. Yorimasa had acted hastily and impulsively. He had not consulted with Minamoto leaders in the provinces. There is no evidence in the *Azuma kagami* that he had been in communication with Yoritomo, around whom the Genji were to rally. In fact, it is extremely doubtful whether Yoritomo himself was at all enthusiastic about challenging the Taira in 1180.[37]

In 1180 the Taira were still a formidable power. Kiyomori, who had raised the Taira to dominance, was still alive. Though not as active as heretofore because of his advanced age, his word was still virtually the law at the court and his influence was considerable. Members of his family still held all the high offices in Kyoto as well as many of the governorships and vice governorships in the provinces. This latter factor was important in any consideration of war, for it was the governor who usually raised troops when they were needed. One of the Taira officials in the east, for example, was Hirotsune, the vice governor of Kazusa, who was able to raise 20,000 troops in his province alone within two months of the opening of hostilities. Moreover, the manors and lands which the Taira controlled, especially in the west, assured it of a ready source of provisions. Finally, the Taira had demonstrated in the Mochihito-Yorimasa incident that it was determined to brook no opposition to its rule and that it was capable of swift military action when provoked.

Moreover, Yoritomo seems to have been in comfortable circumstances in 1180 despite his status as a political prisoner. He ap-

---

[37] This may account in part for the existence of conflicting theories about the launching of the war. One theory ascribes Yoritomo's decision to challenge the Taira to the influence of a Buddhist priest, Mongaku. The *Azuma kagami* mentions in passing, nearly a year after the end of the wars, that "Yoritomo had raised his troops at Mongaku's persuasion" (Bunji 2:1,3).

parently enjoyed an unusual amount of freedom. He eloped with his warden's daughter on the eve of her wedding to another, and his warden not only approved the marriage but also offered to become a vassal to his son-in-law. Like so many other Genji in the provinces, Yoritomo too had made peace with his Taira overlord.

Thus it appears that circumstances beyond Yoritomo's control had compelled him to assume the initiative in the war. These circumstances were the early discovery by the Taira of the Mochihito-Yorimasa plot, and the fact that Yoritomo, as the oldest living son of Yoshitomo and hence the heir to the leadership of the Minamoto, had become the next target of the Taira. Moreover, with many known Taira partisans in Izu and Sagami, Yoritomo could not delay the war longer. Thus he struck first, hoping thereby to arouse the Genji to action.

THE TURNING OF THE TIDE AND THE UNIFICATION OF THE EAST

As already noted, within a few days of the opening of the war Yoritomo's own life, as well as Genji aspirations for a revival, was in grave peril. The tide, however, changed suddenly, once Yoritomo was able to escape from the Hakone Mountains and reestablish contact with his scattered vassals. This he was able to do from the relative security of Awa Province at the tip of the peninsula across the bay from Sagami Province. He had reached Awa by boat on the twenty-ninth of the Eighth Month.[38]

Early in the following month Yoritomo was heartened by the news that Taira Hirotsune, the powerful vice governor of Kazusa, would throw his forces on the side of the Minamoto,[39] and that Kiso Yoshinaka had risen in revolt against the Taira in Shinano.[40] He was also assured of the support of Chiba Tsunetane, perhaps the strongest of the more loyal Minamoto vassals in the East at the time.[41] By the middle of the Ninth Month the Genji of Kai Province had not only assembled in support of Yoritomo but had successfully carried out attacks on Taira supporters in Shinano.[42] Thus, on the

[38] Jishō 4:8,29 ff.   [39] Jishō 4:9,6.   [40] Jishō 4:9,7.   [41] Jishō 4:9,9.
[42] Jishō 4:9,15.

seventeenth of the month, exactly one month after the war had
begun, Yoritomo felt confident enough to quit Awa and to begin
his journey to Kamakura in Sagami Province, which had been
suggested to him by Chiba Tsunetane as being "strategically
sound" and "historically important" as a site for the military headquarters of the Genji.[43]

This journey, which Yoritomo was to complete on the sixth of
the Tenth Month, was one of the more remarkable events of the
war and constituted a turning point in the young conflict. Without
engaging in a single major battle Yoritomo increased his following
from three hundred horsemen to more than twenty-seven thousand.
In fact, the scribes of the *Azuma kagami* estimated with great
optimism that "if the Genji of Kai, Hitachi, Shimotsuke, and
Kōzuke are included, the numbers should reach fifty thousand." [44]
And it should not be overlooked that the more powerful lords who
came over to his side were former Taira supporters, such as Taira
Hirotsune, who contributed twenty thousand men, and Hatakeyama
Shigetada, who had fought Yoritomo at Ishibashi Mountain.

Yoritomo's successes in rallying local lords to his standard after
the Battle of Ishibashi Mountain can be attributed in large measure
to his willingness—in fact, his eagerness—to embrace his former
enemies. In a sense Yoritomo could take no other course, for the
Genji had not responded to his call. Although a part of the increase
in his following had been due to late arrivals of the more faithful
Genji, the greater part was composed of those who had opposed him
and had routed his forces at Ishibashi, or those who had withheld
from committing themselves to either side. In the former group
were lords such as Edo Shigenaga, Kawagoe Shigeyori, and Hatakeyama Shigetada, who had joined Yoritomo less than six weeks
after they had attacked him.[45] In this connection it is to be noted
that Yoritomo actively solicited their aid. To Edo Shigenaga, for
example, he had sent a cordial note addressing him as "the Pillar
of Musashi Province" and asking him to rally local warriors for
the Minamoto cause.[46]

[43] Jishō 4:9,9. The historical association of Kamakura with the Minamoto
stemmed from 1063, when Yoriyoshi established a branch of the Iwashimizu
Hachiman Shrine there. References to other earlier associations of Kamakura
with the Minamoto are mentioned in the account for Jishō 4:10,12.

[44] Jishō 4:9,29.   [45] Jishō 4:10,4.   [46] Jishō 4:9,28.

In the latter group was Taira Hirotsune, the vice governor of Kazusa, whose conversion to Yoritomo's cause was, perhaps, the key to the early successes. The force which he commanded was more than sixty times the size of Yoritomo's following. He had acted craftily, refusing to indicate whether he was for or against the Minamoto. But in his eventual submission to Yoritomo there were several factors which favored Yoritomo. Hirotsune was a member of the same branch of the Taira to which Chiba Tsunetane belonged. The latter's family had been faithful Genji supporters for generations, and Tsunetane's decision in this conflict to support Yoritomo must have influenced Hirotsune.[47] Another important factor was that many of Hirotsune's men recruited from Kazusa were openly for Yoritomo, and thus Hirotsune could not risk a challenge at the time. However, he harbored such a scheme even as he and his followers came up to Shimōsa to meet Yoritomo. In the words of the *Azuma kagami*, Hirotsune "would submit to Yoritomo for the time being . . . and if Yoritomo did not fare well, he would attack him and turn him over to the Heike."[48] The final factor in Hirotsune's conversion was Yoritomo's firm and aroused attitude toward his would-be betrayer. Hirotsune had been the first of the local lords whom Yoritomo had tried to reach after the Battle of Ishibashi Mountain.[49] Yoritomo had made more overtures to him than to any other lord, even offering to meet him in his home territory of Kazusa,[50] a course from which Yoritomo was finally dissuaded by his vassals.[51] After so many pleas for help, Hirotsune had come to Yoritomo expecting to be welcomed. Instead, Yoritomo showed great anger and impatience and reprimanded him for reporting late. "Completely dominated by Yoritomo, Hirotsune relinquished any thought of revolt and resolved to serve Yoritomo."[52]

This account is perhaps slightly exaggerated, especially in view of the mutual suspicion which characterized their relationship thereafter. However, there was no doubt of Hirotsune's value to Yoritomo. He played, for example, the principal role in a subsequent expedition. But the immediate effect of his conversion to the Genji

[47] Hirotsune's first reply to Yoritomo's persistent efforts to win him over was to the effect that he would first consult with Tsunetane. Jishō 4:9,6.
[48] Jishō 4:9,19.   [49] Jishō 4:9,1.   [50] Jishō 4:9,3.
[51] Jishō 4:9,4.   [52] Jishō 4:9,19.

cause was great, for by his action he had increased Yoritomo's force from three hundred to more than twenty thousand. For the first time in the war Yoritomo could back his claim to the leadership of the Genji with force. It was, therefore, no accident that the leading lords of Musashi, such as Hatakeyama, Edo, and Kawagoe, came to pay homage to Yoritomo a few days later.

In feudal terms these former and would-be enemies had been accepted as vassals. They were now as much a part of the Genji as were the Miura and Chiba whose families had been faithful for generations. In fact, the immediate importance of these new vassals to the Genji cause was even greater than that of the hereditary vassals whose followings were considerably smaller. The situation was dangerous, not only to Yoritomo's personal security[53] but also to the unity of the Genji, for the bitterness among some of the hereditary vassals toward the new Genji was very strong. The Miura in particular were thirsting for revenge on Edo and Kawagoe, who had been responsible for the death of Yoshiaki, the aged leader of the family.[54] Thus the Miura had to be reconciled and their loyalty retained. Something of Yoritomo's qualities as a leader may be seen in the manner in which he achieved the reconciliation of these bitter rivals. According to the *Azuma kagami,* Yoritomo "explained to Miura Yoshizumi that while Yoshizumi and the members of his family had served him faithfully and had distinguished themselves in battle, and while Shigenaga and the others had attacked the Minamoto, the Minamoto could not hope to achieve its objectives unless it drafted into its ranks the powerful and the influential. Yoritomo also counseled the Miura that those who would be loyal to him must forget their personal rancor. Upon the denial of any treasonable intentions on their part, Shigenaga and the others faced the Miura and took their places." [55]

And thus the momentum gained by Yoritomo as local lords joined him during the Ninth and Tenth Months of 1180 swelled his

[53] Yoritomo had been cautioned against conspirators in the region. A Taira partisan, Nagasa Tsunemoto, had made an attempt on Yoritomo's life a few days earlier. See Jishō 4:9,3.

[54] On their way to join Yoritomo in Izu the Miura had been assailed by Edo and Kawagoe at Kinugasa. The majority of the Miura managed to escape, but their aged leader had remained behind to die at the hands of the attackers. Jishō 4:8,26.

[55] Jishō 4:10,4.

following from three hundred men to twenty-seven thousand men by the time he arrived at Kamakura to establish his headquarters.

While these developments augured well for Yoritomo, he was aware of the important fact that several powerful lords, especially the hereditary Minamoto vassals such as Shida Yoshihiro, Nitta Yoshishige, and Satake Hideyoshi had not yet acknowledged his leadership, and that his new army had not yet been tested in a major battle. The test was imminent, as Yoritomo well knew, for he had been apprised of the departure from Kyoto for the east of a Heike army "several hundreds of thousands" strong under Taira Koremori on the twenty-ninth of the Ninth Month. That army had reached Suruga Province on the thirteenth,[56] and thus, on the sixteenth, after a brief stay of ten days in Kamakura, Yoritomo departed for Suruga to meet the enemy.

In this connection it is a tribute to Yoritomo's foresight that while still in Awa Province he had assigned Hōjō Tokimasa, his father-in-law and one of his most trusted lieutenants, to Kai, situated immediately to the northwest of Sagami, to rally the Genji in that area and to bring dissident local lords into line. Thus Yoritomo was able, upon a moment's notice, to move his army westward into Suruga which involved the crossing of the treacherous Ashigara Pass, with a minimum of interference from hostile local lords.

The records say that Yoritomo's army which negotiated the pass numbered two hundred thousand,[57] an increase, if true, of more than one hundred sixty thousand over the total on the sixth of the Tenth Month when the Genji army entered Kamakura. To this was added another twenty thousand from Kai and Shinano, who joined Yoritomo in Suruga.[58] These figures may not be entirely accurate, but they reflect the growing urgency on the part of local lords to acknowledge Yoritomo's leadership lest they lose control of their lands. For the vast majority of local lords the immediate issue of the war was not whether the Minamoto or the Taira cause was just and righteous; rather, the question was which of the principals would assure the continued enjoyment of one's lands. Therefore, feudal relations being what they were, the submission

[56] For the preparations, departure, and progress of Koremori's army, see Jishō 4:9,22; 9,29; 10,16.
[57] Jishō 4:10,18.
[58] *Ibid.*

of so powerful a lord as Taira Hirotsune of Kazusa meant that lesser lords in neighboring Shimōsa would have to come quickly to Yoritomo to pay homage or risk an attack and the loss of their lands. The same was true of lords in Musashi Province situated between Shimōsa and Sagami in the path of Yoritomo's growing army. Thus the figure of two hundred thousand might well represent the approximate total of Yoritomo's following from Izu, Kai, Shimōsa, Kazusa, and Awa, the provinces adjacent to and surrounding Sagami. The lords and warrior families on the outer periphery of this block of provinces could still afford, in the Eleventh Month of 1180, to ignore Yoritomo's summons so long as there remained other lords in the region sufficiently strong to challenge Yoritomo.

At any rate, a vast Genji army under Yoritomo's personal leadership arrived at Kajima on the east bank of the Fuji River in Suruga Province on the twentieth of the Tenth Month. Across the river the Taira army had established its line. Thus, for the first time in the Gempei War, a major Minamoto force faced a major Taira force.

But this confrontation at the Fuji River was to have a strange and abrupt ending with scarcely an arrow shot. On the night of the twentieth a member of the Genji, while attempting to make his way to the rear of the Taira lines, frightened flocks of birds nesting in the marshes near the river. The awesome sound of thousands of flapping wings alarmed the Taira into believing that the vast army of the Minamoto had launched a night attack. Abandoning their position without giving battle, the Taira retreated toward Kyoto, apparently in great haste, for they were reported back in the capital twelve days later.[59] The Heike reluctance to venture into Eastern Japan in the next few years may have been due in part to this experience. The following quotation, attributed to a Taira commander at the time of the retreat, is significant: "Every single warrior in the east must have answered Yoritomo's call to arms. It was reckless of us to have come here from the capital, for we stand in danger of being surrounded. We must retreat to the capital immediately, and direct our campaigns elsewhere."[60]

The strange ending of the Battle of Fuji River gave the Genji an opportunity to pursue the fleeing Taira and to press the attack

[59] Jishō 4:11,2.   [60] Jishō 4:10,20.

toward the west. Yoritomo himself prepared to make such a move, and a few eager Genji actually gave chase to the retreating Taira for a day or two. However, Yoritomo's chief vassals counseled against it. They argued that to press the war toward Kyoto was to expose the east to the ambitions and machinations of such men as Satake and Shida of Hitachi, who would not miss the opportunity to move into the heart of Kanto the moment Yoritomo vacated it. The first order of Minamoto strategy, they argued further, was the unification of the east rather than the subjugation of the Taira in the west. This counsel, which Yoritomo promptly accepted, was to prove one of the more significant decisions of the entire war. And thus, taking steps to hold his gains in Suruga by posting Takeda Nobuyoshi as *shugo*, or protector, of this province, and Yasuda Yoshisada as *shugo* of Ōmi, the province which commanded the approaches to the capital from the east and control of which would keep the Taira at bay at a safe distance, Yoritomo himself turned back toward Sagami.[61]

Meanwhile, Yoritomo's youngest brother, Yoshitsune, who figures so prominently in the subsequent phases of the war, had joined the Genji at Kisegawa. The reunion of the brothers, who had not seen each other since their exile to different parts of the country in 1160, is recounted in some detail in the *Azuma kagami*.[62]

The decision to postpone military operations against the Taira in the west in the interest of unifying the east was prompted by the need to bring lords of Minamoto descent into submission. They were the only remaining lords of any consequence in Eastern and North Central Japan who had not acknowledged Yoritomo's leadership. Moreover, because Minamoto blood flowed in their veins, they were the very lords who could dispute and might seize the leadership of the Genji. Thus the Gempei War, only two months after its inception, had assumed a peculiar turn. The rivalry among members of the Minamoto family now threatened to overshadow the real struggle between the Minamoto and the Taira.

The Minamoto who posed the greatest threat to Yoritomo's leadership was Satake Hideyoshi of Hitachi, who had shown an open preference for the Taira. Had Yoritomo's army pursued the Taira to the west after the Fuji River Battle, the Satake, it was feared, would have moved in to occupy the east. Therefore Yoritomo swung his vast army, which had assembled in Suruga to fend off the Taira, in the direction of Hitachi to subjugate the Satake.

The Satake threat was quickly disposed of in the first few days of the Eleventh Month, although Hideyoshi, the leader of the Satake, eluded capture.[63] The victory and the presence of so large a force in Hitachi had the effect of bringing other dissident Minamoto lords of the region into line, among them Shida Yoshihiro, Yoritomo's uncle, who came forward to declare his loyalty.[64]

But Shida Yoshihiro was to prove extremely troublesome to Yoritomo for several years. After Yoritomo's army had withdrawn from Hitachi, Yoshihiro turned against Yoritomo and started out from Hitachi with thirty thousand followers to attack Kamakura.[65] This was a serious threat to Yoritomo, for at the time a Taira army had been reported out of Kyoto destined for the east.[66] Moreover, another important Minamoto family, the Ashikaga of Shimotsuke, had thrown its support to Yoshihiro. In fact, Tadatsuna, the leader of the Ashikaga, had been hostile to the Minamoto from the beginning of the conflict, having supported the Taira as early as the Uji Battle in which Prince Mochihito and Minamoto Yorimasa had lost their lives.[67]

This combined force was defeated and an attack on Kamakura narrowly averted by the efforts of Koyama Tomomasa of Shimotsuke, a member of the Ashikaga who had been disputing with Tadatsuna for control of the province.[68]

While this victory by a loyal Minamoto quashed the two immediate threats to Yoritomo's leadership of the Genji, it was, in certain respects, a loss to the Minamoto cause. Yoshihiro fled toward

---

[63] Jishō 4:11,4-6; 11,8.

[64] Jishō 4:11,7.

[65] Jishō 5:1:Inter.2,20.

[66] Jishō 5:1:Inter.2,10. This army, however, returned to Kyoto approximately a month later.

[67] Jishō 5:1:Inter.2,23. Another member of the Ashikaga had earlier attacked and burned the homes of Minamoto partisans in Kōzuke. See Jishō 4:5,26.

[68] It is interesting to note that in this, as in the battle against the Satake, trickery and deceit played a large part in the Minamoto victory. Tomomasa, who was virtually without a force at the time—his father having taken the bulk of the Koyama retainers to Kyoto for guard duty—drew Yoshihiro into a narrow ravine by promising to support him, then proceeded to annihilate his forces. For details of this battle, see Jishō 5:Inter.2,23.

the west, later to join with Yoshinaka against Yoritomo. Tadatsuna, who seems to have acquired quite a reputation as a warrior,[69] also fled toward the west and remained unreconciled.

However, so far as the leadership of the Genji was concerned, the defeat of the Shida and the Ashikaga left Yoritomo in undisputed control. No other Minamoto of any power remained to challenge his supremacy. His cousin, Yoshinaka, in Shinano was allegedly for Yoritomo, and even though suspected of harboring personal ambitions against Yoritomo, he was sufficiently removed geographically not to be considered a threat. Yukiie, an uncle, had played the key role of courier of the secret pronouncement of Prince Mochihito, although his true feelings toward Yoritomo and his actions at this time are enigmas. For example, his whereabouts between the Fourth Month, when he left Kai and Shinano, and the Eleventh Month, when he suddenly appeared in Hitachi, are difficult to trace. His appearance in Hitachi in the company of Shida Yoshihiro to declare his loyalty to Yoritomo[70] is highly suspicious in the light of Yoshihiro's later actions. However, he commanded no following at the time and Yoritomo, apparently, did not look upon him as disloyal.

Yoritomo's great-uncle, Nitta Yoshishige, who held forth in Kōzuke and who had vacillated between defiance and protestations of loyalty, had also sworn fealty to Yoritomo by the end of 1180.[71] The only others who might lay claim to the leadership of the Genji were Yoritomo's brothers. But of four brothers living in 1180, Yoshitsune, the youngest, had made a difficult journey from Ōshū in Northern Japan to join Yoritomo's ranks.[72] Two others, Zenjō,

---

[69] The *Azuma kagami* says of him: "There will be no warrior in future ages like this Tadatsuna. He excelled all others in three things: namely, his physical strength, which equalled that of a hundred men; his voice, which reverberated for a distance of ten *ri*; and his teeth, which were one inch in length" (Jishō 5:Inter. 2,25).

[70] Jishō 4:11,7.

[71] Jishō 4:9,30; 12,22. Yoshishige is the lord who entrenched himself in his castle and refused to answer Yoritomo's call. Later, when Yoritomo denied him admittance to Kamakura, he explained his earlier action thus: "I had entertained no thought of demurring with Your Lordship. However, with wars waging in the provinces, it has not been easy for me to leave my castle. Thus, at the urging of my vassals, I have deferred reporting to Your Lordship."

[72] In fact, Yoshitsune could not have left the custody of the Fujiwara, his wardens, without the tacit cooperation of the latter. The Fujiwara, although reluctant to free Yoshitsune, provided him in the end with two escorts. See Jishō 4:10,21.

a priest, and Noriyori, who later was to take two armies into the field for Yoritomo, joined him at Kamakura. The fourth, Mareyoshi, was in exile in Shikoku, where he was to meet his death at the hands of the Taira in 1182.[73]

Meanwhile, other local lords and former enemies who had not voluntarily capitulated did so subsequently, or were captured or forced to flee the east. Ōba Kagechika, for example, who had led the Taira partisans at Ishibashi Mountain and who had nearly wrecked Yoritomo's cause, had surrendered.[74] Furthermore, because of the fall of the Satake, Shida, Nitta, and the Ashikaga in Hitachi, Kōzuke and Shimotsuke, lesser warrior groups affiliated with them, readily submitted to Yoritomo. Satomi Yoshinari, for example, a grandson of Nitta Yoshishige, made terms with Yoritomo.[75]

Thus by the Third Month of 1181, only eight months since the opening of hostilities, the unification of the east had been accomplished—an amazing achievement for Yoritomo who had raised his banner of revolt somewhat reluctantly and against severe handicaps.

However, the war between major Minamoto and Taira forces had all but come to a standstill. The fighting which took place did so mostly in Western Japan between small bands of Genji partisans and Taira forces. In Ōmi, for example, just east of the capital, the Genji, although defeated by Taira Tomomori,[76] continued to harass the enemy. On one occasion they effectively prevented a Taira force from crossing the Seta River by seizing and destroying boats. Elsewhere, as far away as Kyushu and Shikoku and even as close to the centers of Taira concentration of power as Kii, small bands of Genji were becoming increasingly active.

Just as the major Minamoto forces were limiting their operations to the east and their leaders were attempting to resolve their own differences, so the Taira armies were adhering to a policy of avoiding campaigns in the East and confining their activities to Kyoto and its immediate vicinity. These operations were mostly of a retaliatory nature against the monasteries which had given protection and aid to Prince Mochihito and Minamoto Yorimasa. Onjō-ji on the shores of Lake Biwa and the historic monasteries of Kōfuku-ji and

---

[73] Zenjō reported in Jishō 4:10,1. The exact date of Noriyori's arrival is not recorded. On Mareyoshi, see Juei 1:9,25.

[74] Jishō 4:10,23.   [75] Jishō 4:12,22.   [76] Jishō 4:12,1.

Tōdai-ji in Nara were attacked and burned by Taira armies,[77] thus inviting the undying hatred of the Buddhists toward the Taira and establishing the reputation that the Taira were ruthless and inconsiderate of religious institutions.

The Taira also, because of their complete domination of the Kyoto court, obtained an imperial mandate which authorized and directed the three circuits of Tōsan, Tōkai, and Hokuriku to wage war on Yoritomo.[78] The Genji and their leader were thus declared to be rebels and enemies of the imperial court, although Yoritomo was to insist throughout the war years that the Genji were fighting the Heike who were the real enemies of the emperor and his government.

An important development in this early phase of the war was, significantly, a nonmilitary measure. This was the establishment by Yoritomo, shortly after his return to Kamakura from the Hitachi campaign, of a board called the *samurai-dokoro* to assist him in the administration and control of his vassals.[79] Its establishment was clearly an indication of the vast increase of Yoritomo's following and of the expanding administrative problems of the leader of the Genji. Until this time Yoritomo had been able to meet his administrative needs with the assistance of a single *uhitsu*, or secretary.[80] In its establishment and in the growing circle of vassals and of territory under Yoritomo's control—even though largely limited to the east—may be seen the first concrete steps toward the development of the shogunate and of an organized form of feudalism.

[77] Jishō 4:12,11–12; 12,25; 12,28. For a brief report by an eye witness of the burning of Kōfuku-ji and Tōdai-ji, see Jishō 5:1,18.

[78] Jishō 4:11,7. For the location of these circuits, see map, Figure 1.

[79] Jishō 4:11,17. Wada Yoshimori was named president.

[80] This was Fujiwara Kunimichi, who wrote most of Yoritomo's letters and papers and who is one of the more frequently mentioned persons in the records.

Chapter IV
The Gempei War:
Middle Phases

THE VIRTUAL SUSPENSION
OF THE WAR, 1181–83

The Minamoto decision to unify the east before carrying the war into the west, and the Taira decision to remain out of the Mina-moto-dominated region of the east—both made as an aftermath of the brief battle at the Fuji River in the fall of 1180—were to assume great significance as the conflict entered its second and third years. During these years both sides, while making preparations to press the war, avoided frontal clashes with each other. In the entire period only one major encounter occurred between a Taira army and one of Yoritomo's forces. This was the Battle of Sunomata in Owari Province, in which Minamoto Yukiie, Yoritomo's uncle, was thoroughly routed.[1] But the victors, instead of pressing their advantage, promptly turned back toward Kyoto. Thus Owari was the easternmost point of penetration by a Taira army during this period.

Yoritomo himself made no threatening moves toward Kyoto and the west. In fact, he proposed in the fall of 1181 that the hostilities cease altogether, provided that the imperial court recognize the Minamoto as protector of the east and the Taira as protector of the west. Yoritomo also assured the court that its traditional rights to name and assign governors and other local officials would be re-

---

[1] Jishō 5:3,10. In this, Yukiie's first major assignment as commander of a Genji force, he was taken unawares by the enemy. The Genji casualty of drowned, killed, and wounded numbered 690. Later it was learned that the shameful rout was due in large part to a dispute among Genji leaders as to who should assume the vanguard position. See Juei 3:2,1. However, by that time Yukiie had deserted Yoritomo for Yoshinaka against whom he had been sent.

spected.[2] This offer of a negotiated peace, although acceptable to the ex-sovereign, was rejected by the Taira. Earlier in the year the Taira had lost their great leader, Kiyomori.[3] On his deathbed he had asked his son and successor, Munemori, to vow to destroy the Minamoto. Munemori insisted on keeping this vow and therefore would not listen to the views of the ex-sovereign, who was prepared to accept Yoritomo's proposal. Both sides, consequently, continued to husband their resources without actually engaging in combat with one another.

This does not mean that fighting between the Heike and the Genji ceased altogether in 1181. There was sporadic fighting between isolated, local groups of partisans. In Higo, for example, Harada Tanenao attacked the Genji supporters there,[4] and in Kaga Taira Tamemori attacked the pro-Genji monks of Kumano Temple.[5] The main efforts of the Taira, however, were directed toward winning the support of the hitherto uncommitted lords or coercing such lords through the instrument of imperial mandates to proceed against Yoritomo. A notable example in this connection is the imperial mandate issued to Fujiwara Hidehira, the powerful lord of Mutsu in Northern Japan, to wage war on Yoritomo.[6] Later, as an inducement to carry out the mandate, the Taira gave him an appointment as governor of Mutsu,[7] but the coy Hidehira, whose domain was situated at a safe distance from the military bases of both the Taira and the Minamoto, refused to respond.

It is conceivable that this state of suspension of hostilities between Yoritomo and the Taira might have continued indefinitely, but for developments in North Central Japan. There, since his declaration of war against the Taira in 1180, Kiso Yoshinaka, Yoritomo's cousin, had made himself an overwhelming power to the concern of both the Taira and Yoritomo. Presumably fighting on Yoritomo's side, Yoshinaka had aroused his cousin's suspicions as early as the Tenth Month of 1180, when he moved eastward from Shinano into Kōzuke instead of westward toward Taira-held territory.[8] Yoritomo

---

[2] The *Azuma kagami* is silent on this matter. It is mentioned in the *Gyokuyō*, the diary of Fujiwara Kanezane, under date of Jishō 5:8,1.

[3] The circumstances of Kiyomori's death are duly noted in the *Azuma kagami*. See Jishō 5:Inter.2,4.

[4] Jishō 5:2,29.   [5] Jishō 5:10,16.   [6] Jishō 5:4,28.   [7] Yōwa 1:8,15.

[8] Jishō 4:10,13.

had also feared the possibility of an alliance between Yoshinaka and Shida Yoshihiro of Hitachi, which could threaten his position in the east. The Taira likewise were alarmed over Yoshinaka's strength, for by the end of 1182 he had subdued the Taira governor of Shinano, defeated local lords sent against him, and extended his authority over five provinces.[9] Thus in Yoshinaka the Taira and Yoritomo found a common threat which in due time was to draw them out of the virtual armistice which they had been observing and into direct contact with each other.

But meanwhile at Kamakura Yoritomo was occupied with the task of holding his vassals together—vassals and their retainers who had been assembled for a war which seemed no longer urgent. Yoritomo's role, by the early spring of 1181, was less that of commander of an army than that of a civil ruler of a government at peace. The headquarters which he had hastily established and which was called *eichū,* or military headquarters, seemed to be a misnomer, for its functions were becoming more and more the functions of a civil government. Although Yoritomo remained alert to the possibility of a resumption of military operations, he was concerned more with the almost routine activities of a regional lord trying to maintain the unity of his vassals and the stability of the east. In short, Yoritomo's organization functioned as a regional, civil government during these years, a fact which goes a long way toward explaining the founding of the shogunate. Needless to say, the student of Kamakura history must therefore examine this phase of the Gempei War with great care if he is to understand the forces which contributed to the establishment of the shogunate.

THE CONSOLIDATION OF THE EAST AND THE BEGINNINGS OF CIVIL GOVERNMENT

Yoritomo's most urgent problem in 1181 was the consolidation of the east and the maintenance of the unity which he had achieved since the opening of the Gempei War. To do this he resorted to the classic device of the feudal lord—he offered the various local lords protection in return for their pledge of loyalty and the performance

[9] See Yōwa 1:9,6 and Juei 1:10,9.

of certain services. The offer of protection took several forms, the most common being the grant of a letter of confirmation, or the *ando-jō*. Intended to give its recipient peace of mind with regard to his holdings of lands, this form of grant answered the first and basic need of the average warrior family living in an area where feudal wars raged and where the authority of the central government was nonexistent.

The first notable grant of letters of confirmation occurred shortly after the Fuji River Battle when Yoritomo confirmed the holdings of twenty-four of his more prominent vassals, such as Hōjō, Taira Hirotsune, Miura, Chiba, and the Sasaki.[10] The holdings of Yoritomo's vassals of Musashi Province were similarly confirmed after the expedition against the Satake.[11]

This form of protection was offered not only to the warrior who rendered military service but also to land holders who performed other forms of service. Thus the temple and the shrine which constituted a large class of landowners offered prayers in behalf of the Genji, for which they sought confirmation of their holdings. For example, Yoritomo gave a blanket confirmation to shrines and temples in Musashi Province, and ordered his vassals to desist from violating their lands.[12]

Holders of offices, especially of those which commanded an economic return in the form of shares, or *shiki*, in the yield of certain lands, also requested confirmation from Yoritomo. Thus the intendant of a temple or an official of a manor frequently asked for and were granted such letters from him. The first examples of this type of confirmation appear under the date of Jishō 4:10,23, when Miura Yoshizumi's title as vice governor and Yukihira's office as manorial official of Shimokōbe were confirmed by Yoritomo.[13]

The offer of security of land and person was sometimes not enough to keep vassals in check and loyal to the lord. Thus various kinds of rewards were given to vassals for the performance of any meritorious deed. One of the more desirable forms of reward was the grant of lands seized from the enemy. For example, after the subjugation of the Satake their lands in Hitachi were promptly

[10] Jishō 4:10,23.   [11] Jishō 4:12,14.   [12] Jishō 4:11,12.   [13] Jishō 4:10,23.

claimed by Yoritomo and allocated to the more deserving of his vassals.[14]

Sometimes lands confiscated from the enemy might be assigned in trust to a deserving vassal. Thus the Koyama who had saved Kamakura from an attack by routing the Shida and the Ashikaga were given the latter's lands in trust.[15] Similarly, lands of Taira partisans who had surrendered, or who had been captured but spared capital punishment, were given in trust to a vassal, usually to the warrior to whom the prisoner was assigned for custody. It appears from these and other examples in the *Azuma kagami* that if the original holder of the land was alive or presumed to be alive, or if the original holder showed signs of becoming a loyal Genji, his lands were given in trust to or held in custody by a vassal named by Yoritomo.[16] Such grants, however, became increasingly rare after 1181, for there were few available lands in a region which was at peace and where all the lords with any sizable estates were vassals of Yoritomo.

In terms of frequency of grants, the temple and the shrine were the largest beneficiaries. When the war was but a few days old Yoritomo made a promise of a grant of two manors to the Sōtō-zan.[17] Similarly, at Awa, while Yoritomo was striving to rebuild his forces, he made the first of a number of land grants to Sunosaki Shrine.[18] After the Hitachi expedition, and especially after his return to Kamakura, Yoritomo made many grants of land, usually in small parcels, to temples and shrines.[19]

These are only a few examples of grants of land and of rights to land which Yoritomo made in the early months of the war to hold his vassals together. They represent functions and obligations quite natural to a feudal lord with regard to his vassals from whom he expected services, usually of a military nature; and thus they do not begin to indicate the number and volume of requests for confirmation and for grants which came to Yoritomo's attention during the period from 1180 to 1183.

---

[14] Jishō 4:11,8.   [15] Jishō 5:Inter.2,28.

[16] For several examples of this type of grant, see Jishō 4:10,23.

[17] Jishō 4:8,19.   [18] Jishō 4:9,12.

[19] For early examples of documents of such grants, see the grant of Hayakawa Manor to the Hakone Shrine, Jishō 4:10,16; and the grant of orchard lands to Mishima Shrine, Jishō 4:10,21.

One of the reasons for this development was the widening of the basis of vassalage which Yoritomo had made in his efforts to offset the poor response of the Genji to his call during the early weeks of the war. It has been shown that Yoritomo had admitted into vassalage virtually all the local lords of the region, irrespective of their blood or traditional connections with the Heiji or the Genji. This meant that any warrior family of any consequence remaining in the east after the disposition of the more independent Minamoto lords, such as the Satake, the Shida, and the Ashikaga, was a Genji. Thus, under Yoritomo, the term "Genji" tended to become less restrictive and more inclusive. Moreover, it is important to note that it was applied to and presumed to include not only the warrior who rendered military service but also the Kyoto aristocrat who gave administrative and even ceremonial service, as well as the temple and the shrine which offered spiritual service.

Thus a follower such as Adachi Morinaga of Fujiwara descent, who served Yoritomo mainly as a messenger and emissary rather than as a warrior was a Genji and as much a vassal, in the broadest sense of the word, as the Sasaki, Miura, and Chiba who rendered military service. Adachi's land holdings, in fact, were among the first to be confirmed by Yoritomo.[20] The temples and shrines considered to be of Genji affiliation received letters of confirmation from Yoritomo no different than those issued to warrior families.

The role played by Kyoto nobles as vassals was considerable. Among the first of this class to serve Yoritomo was Fujiwara Kunimichi, whom the *Azuma kagami* calls "a wandering visitor from the capital," and who had been recommended to Yoritomo by Adachi Morinaga, mentioned above. Kunimichi had served as Yoritomo's first spy, befriending Yamamoto Kanetaka, who was to become the victim of Yoritomo's opening attack of the wars, and making a complete sketch of Kanetaka's buildings and grounds. He served also as Yoritomo's secretary and scribe during the first several months of the war. There were others who had held office in Kyoto under the Taira and who deserted their masters for Yoritomo. Among them was Tachibana Kiminaga, secretary of the Right Horse Bureau, who was accepted as a Genji vassal as early as the Twelfth Month of 1180.[21] The most prominent Kyoto

[20] Jishō 4:10,8. [21] Jishō 4:12,19.

aristocrats to join the Genji and render invaluable service in juridical and administrative matters were Miyoshi Yasunobu[22] and Ōe Hiromoto.[23]

Thus the Genji tended to become a heterogeneous collection of people and groups—from the local lord and his following of armed men to nobles who had never wielded a sword or a bow. It was, for a clan, an unusually comprehensive group. Moreover, the domain over which it claimed control through its vassals of local lords encompassed at least eight provinces, which was an unusually large territory for a single feudal lord to oversee. In short, Yoritomo's *eichū*, or military headquarters, as it was known, tended to be not merely the typical clan or feudal administration, but a more comprehensive, regional government for the entire east.

The widening of the basis of vassalage and the general prevalence of peaceful and stable conditions in the east after the spring of 1181 strongly influenced the activities and colored the outlook of Yoritomo's government. From that date until the closing days of 1183, when Yoritomo despatched troops to Kyoto, there was scarcely a major warlike activity at Kamakura. Even after the resumption of the wars in 1184 the east was not directly affected, for all the fighting occurred near Kyoto and at points far to the west of Kyoto. Thus, as far as the east was concerned, the war had ended in 1181.

An examination of the records of Yoritomo's government for these years will impress any reader with the eminently civil character of its activities. As might be expected, there was considerable attention given at first to the building of Kamakura as a center for the Genji. In this connection it is significant to note that, although Kamakura had been selected for its strategic advantages[24] as well

[22] Miyoshi Yasunobu, son of Yoritomo's wet nurse, and the first prominent courtier to support Yoritomo. Before the wars opened he had sent couriers to Yoritomo three times a month to keep him informed of happenings in Kyoto (Jishō 4:6,19). He arrived at Kamakura in 1184 (Juei 3:4,14), was made president of the Monchū-jo, or Judicial Board (Genreki 1:10,20), and held this office for more than thirty years.

[23] Ōe Hiromoto's arrival in Kamakura is not recorded. However, he must have been in Kamakura sometime before the Tenth Month of 1184, when he was named president of the Kumon-jo (Genreki 1:10,6). Earlier Yoritomo had recommended him for the office of vice governor of Aki (Genreki 1:8,20), from which fact it may be gathered that the two were in communication with each other before the Eighth Month of 1184.

[24] Kamakura is surrounded on three sides by low-lying hills and on the fourth by the sea.

as its historical association with the Minamoto family, it was the latter on which emphasis was placed. There is, in fact, no mention in the records of the construction of military defenses of any kind at Kamakura. Instead, the greatest attention was given to the building and upkeep of the Tsurugaoka Hachiman Shrine which housed the tutelary god of the Minamoto. In fact, Yoritomo's first order of business after spending a night in Kamakura was to worship at the Tsurugaoka Hachiman Shrine.[25] Much attention was also given to the construction of residences, other buildings, and roads. Yoritomo's own residence, which also served as the headquarters, was completed in the Twelfth Month of 1180, only two months after his arrival in Kamakura, and its occupation was marked with an elaborate ceremony in which more than 300 warriors participated.[26] It is especially significant that no castle was built and that a castle was never contemplated by Yoritomo. The peaceful and civil purposes of Yoritomo's government are also reflected in the term *gosho,* or palace, by which his residence and headquarters came to be known.

In fact, Kamakura had been growing rapidly in the two months since Yoritomo and his party arrived there early in the Tenth Month of 1180. The *Azuma kagami* tells us, not without pride:

His Lordship's immediate vassals have also been constructing residences here. These houses will increase the grandeur of the entire east and will make Kamakura an important center. This had been a secluded place with but a few fixed abodes, frequented only by fishermen and aged rustics. But lanes and streets are being laid, and names are being assigned to hamlets and villages. Moreover, the tiled roofs of houses stand in a line and the doors of gates creak under the eaves.[27]

That Yoritomo personally took great pride in the rapidly developing center may be seen in the project he initiated a year later to convert three *chō* of irrigated ricelands near the Hachiman Shrine into a lake.[28] On another, earlier occasion he had noticed un-

[25] See Jishō 4:10,7. Details of its transfer to its present site and a brief history of the Shrine, recounting its association with the Minamoto family, may be found in the entry for Jishō 4:10,12.
[26] Jishō 4:12,11. Ōba Kageyoshi had been commissioned to build the residence (Jishō 4:10,9). Meanwhile Yoritomo had occupied temporary quarters (Jishō 4:10,15).
[27] Jishō 4:12,12.   [28] Yōwa 2:4,11.

sightly brambles and weeds growing in the grounds of the Hachiman Shrine and had ordered them cleared.[29]

It must be remembered that the construction of buildings, particularly of important buildings such as shrines, entailed the search for good timber and skilled carpenters. On one occasion, when two new buildings were planned for Kamakura, Yoritomo ordered local officials in Awa Province to provide carpenters.[30] For the construction of the Wakamiya, the smaller shrine within the grounds of the Hachiman Shrine, Yoritomo made special efforts to obtain the services of renowned carpenters from Asakusa, Musashi Province.[31] There was also the ceremony connected with the beginning of work on each new building, as well as the ceremony at the completion of the building, which included the giving of presents to the carpenters. Thus much time was given over to this aspect of early Kamakura history by Yoritomo.

In the area of the vassal's obligations to the lord we have the best evidence of the prevalence of peace and stability in the east between the early spring of 1181 and the late summer of 1183. The vassal, whose principal value to the lord was his armed following with whom he reported to the lord when summoned or when a battle or a military campaign was impending, was scarcely called upon to render this service during this period. His military duties were strictly peacetime duties, consisting of such services as standing watch at the headquarters,[32] attending Yoritomo on his travels and visits to shrines and temples, and providing ceremonial service for the numerous functions in which Yoritomo participated.

The vassal was also required to participate in the hunt[33] and other forms of martial exercise and competition. These forms of activity were to increase in variety and number after the subjugation

[29] Jishō 5:4,1.

[30] Jishō 5:5,23. The arrival of the carpenters is noted in Jishō 5:5,28.

[31] Jishō 5:7,3.

[32] This was called *tōban,* and there do not appear to have been any fixed rules regarding this service at this time. The vassal took up quarters in the West Room of headquarters and stood watch outside Yoritomo's bedchamber and at the gates. Depending on the occasion, the number of guards might be increased. When, for example, Yoritomo occupied his new residence, 311 guards stood watch that night (Jishō 4:12,12). On another occasion Yoritomo named eleven of his trusted vassals who were also skilled archers "to stand guard nightly for Her Ladyship." See Jishō 5:4,7.

[33] See, for example, Juei 3:3,18.

of the Heike, but it is noteworthy that there were so many occasions during the war years when such peacetime games were held. These included archery,[34] variations of archery called the *yabusame* and the *ogasagake*,[35] the ox-chase,[36] and horsemanship.[37]

An important obligation which the vassal was frequently called upon to perform and which also pointed to the peaceful atmosphere of Kamakura was the presentation of various forms of material gifts to the lord. Important events in the lord's household, such as births, coming of age ceremonies, and weddings, called for gifts as well as personal service. One is struck, for example, by the attention given to the birth of a son to Her Ladyship Masako. From the time of her announcement that she was with child, when the wife of a vassal was asked to make a gift of a girdle, to Masako's return from her lying-in quarters, all the principal vassals were concerned with little else. And then, for some days thereafter, there was the obligation of standing watch over the child.[38]

Banquets at New Year's and on other important occasions in honor of the lord were usually given by the more wealthy of his vassals. Known as the *ōban*, they were as a rule lavish affairs with several hundred guests in attendance.[39] The vassal might also be called upon to invite Yoritomo to spend a night or several days at his country residence. Miura Yoshizumi, for example, was host to Yoritomo when the latter made a trip to the country "purely for diversion and to escape the heat." [40]

Timber for buildings, silk for officiating priests, and horses—an important ceremonial gift to shrines and a practical gift to warriors—constituted some of the more common forms of presents. There are numerous examples of the presentation of horses, even to carpenters[41] and to an artist.[42]

Something of the extent of the vassal's obligations to the lord

[34] See Jishō 4:12,12, and Juei 1:6,7.

[35] The *yabusame* consisted of shooting at a target from a moving horse. See Juei 3:1,17. In the *ogasagake* the archer shot at a straw hat hung from a pole. See Genreki 1:5,19.

[36] Called *ushioumono*. See Yōwa 2:4,5, and Juei 1:6,7.

[37] Juei 1:6,7.

[38] See Yōwa 2:5,9 and the entries which follow through Juei 1:10,9. The birth occurred on Juei 1:8,12.

[39] Chiba Tsunetane was the most frequent sponsor of the *ōban*. Miura Yoshizumi also sponsored a few. See, for example, Jishō 5:1,1 and 6,13, and Genreki 1:10,6.

[40] Jishō 5:6,19.   [41] Yōwa 1:7,20.   [42] Genreki 1:8,19.

might be seen from Yoritomo's pledge toward the repair and re-construction of Tōdai-ji of Nara. The pledge, made good by vassals, included 10,000 *koku* of rice, 1,000 *ryō* of gold, and 1,000 *hiki* of high quality silk.[43]

In the matter of the lord's obligations to his vassals, one is impressed by the near absence of matters pertaining to war during this period. There were no rewards for meritorious service in battle, for there were no battles. On occasion a warrior might be honored for distinguished service which he had rendered at the beginning of the war. Kumagaya Naozane, for example, was awarded a land steward-ship in 1182 for his bravery in the Hitachi campaign of 1180.[44] Thus meritorious service in battle all but disappeared as a cause for reward. Instead, attendance to duty or past loyalty became reasons for recognition. A servant, for example, was rewarded with rights to a parcel of land for his faithful attendance on Yoritomo.[45] And, as if no other grounds for the making of an award could be found, a priest was honored for prayers which he had offered in behalf of the Genji when "Yoritomo was still in his mother's womb." [46]

Even in the more serious aspects of government Yoritomo's attention was given over mostly to the adjustment of claims on land and assistance to shrines and temples seeking relief from taxes or contributions toward the repair or construction of buildings. Thus the activities of Yoritomo and his government at Kamakura during the greater part of the war years were largely those of a government at peace. The precedents for a civil government which emerged from this period of peace and the reputation which Yoritomo built for himself as a civil administrator comprised an important factor in the later establishment of the Kamakura shogunate.

[43] Genreki 2:3,6.   [44] Juei 1:6,5.   [45] Yōwa 2:2,15.   [46] Yōwa 2:4,20.

Chapter V
The Gempei War:
Final Phases

THE RISE OF YOSHINAKA AND THE
RESUMPTION OF THE WAR[1]

The rise of Yoshinaka to a position of unchallenged preeminence
in North Central Japan between 1180 and 1183 was viewed with
grave misgivings in both Kamakura and Kyoto. However, Yoshinaka
being a Minamoto, the threat was greater to Kyoto than to Kamakura. It was the Taira, therefore, who was the first to abandon the
strategy of limited territorial operations and to launch a large-scale
military expedition outside of the provinces in the immediate
neighborhood of the capital.

Mustering an army of 100,000 men under six Taira leaders—
Koremori, Michimori, Yukimori, Tsunefusa, Kiyofusa, and Tomomori—the Heike forces departed for Shinano during the Fourth
Month. Small bands of Genji resisted the Taira in Kaga and
Echizen, but quickly gave way to the superior numbers of the
Taira. Meanwhile, Yoshinaka, in the reckless manner characteristic
of him, raced into Etchū Province to meet the Taira. There, with
the assistance of Minamoto Yukiie, he defeated Koremori's division
of the Taira army and relentlessly pursued the remnants of the Taira
toward Kyoto. Thus what had begun as a defensive war for Yoshinaka was turned into an offensive war on Kyoto itself, for by the
middle of the Seventh Month he had penetrated Ōmi Province,
directly adjacent to the capital. For the first time since the opening

[1] The *Azuma kagami* lacks accounts for the entire year of 1183, although it
makes occasional references to events of 1183 in its records of 1184 and 1185.
Thus the summary provided below has been based largely on the standard
chronologies, such as: Katsumi Kuroita, *Kōtei kokushi kenkyū nempyō;* Zennosuke
Tsuji, *Dai-Nihon nempyō;* Shōichi Heki, *Kokushi dai-nempyō,* I; and Tokyo
teikoku daigaku shiryō hensan gakari, comp., *Shiryō sōran,* III. The last-named
chronology, which gives the sources after each event noted, is by far the best.

of the war, Kyoto itself was threatened.

But there was no defense of Kyoto. The Taira, unable to re-organize its defeated contingents and to muster a new army on such short notice, and also unable to win the support of the power-ful Enryaku-ji Monastery, situated strategically on Mount Hiei between Ōmi and the capital, evacuated the city and fled westward on the twenty-fifth of the Seventh Month. In addition to the sym-bols of sovereignty—the Imperial Regalia—the Taira took with them the child Emperor Antoku and his Taira mother. The Taira had also intended to take the Ex-Sovereign Go-Shirakawa, but the latter had eluded his would-be captors on the eve of the evacuation and had fled to the Enryaku-ji Monastery. Thus, on the twenty-eighth, Yoshinaka and Yukiie and their 30,000 troops were able to enter Kyoto without opposition.

 Yoshinaka's seizure of Kyoto completely changed the political com-plexion of the war. Where formerly the Taira had received imperial mandates to chastise the rebels—who were the Minamoto—now Yoshinaka and Yukiie received, on the very day of their entry into the capital, a mandate from Go-Shirakawa to pursue and punish the rebels—who were now the Taira. This mandate was imple-mented the next day with a decree from the ex-sovereign to pro-vincial governors and local officials to pursue and destroy the Taira. Thus, overnight, the Taira had become the rebels and the Mina-moto the defenders of the imperial court and of the country.

In addition to being privileged with an edict from the ex-sovereign, Yoshinaka was designated protector of Kyoto, governor of Iyo, and director of the Left Horse Bureau; and title to one hundred and forty of the five hundred estates declared confiscated from the Taira was transferred to him. His confederate Yukiie was made governor of Bizen, and the two were given residences in the city and direct access to the ex-sovereign's palace.

But the relationship between Yoshinaka and the ex-sovereign, which had begun on this happy note, deteriorated rapidly in the next few months. One of the reasons was the disinclination of Yoshinaka to carry out the purport of the mandate he had received earlier, which was the pursuit and punishment of the Taira. The ex-sovereign was understandably concerned, for the Taira was gain-ing valuable time with each passing day. In fact, the main party of the Taira was reported to have reached Dazai-fu in Kyushu on

the twenty-eighth of the Eighth Month, approximately a month
after their abandonment of Kyoto and Yoshinaka's receipt of a
mandate to pursue them. Only after the issuance of a second mandate during the Ninth Month did Yoshinaka finally leave the city.
By this time the Taira had left their western base at Dazai-fu for
Yashima in Shikoku, a point closer to Kyoto.

However, Yoshinaka, who had penetrated Western Japan as far
as Bitchū by the twelfth of the Tenth Month, suddenly and without notice reappeared in Kyoto on the twenty-sixth of the same
month. Yoshinaka had not fared well in Bitchū, where one of his
lieutenants was defeated in a battle at Mizushima by Taira Noritsune. But his reason for returning to Kyoto was the fear that in his
absence Yoritomo might enter and seize the capital. This fear was
not entirely unfounded, for the ex-sovereign had been making
secret overtures to Yoritomo to come to the capital, the first on the
very day that Yoshinaka had occupied the city. Although Yoritomo
himself did not come to Kyoto, he took the occasion to discuss with
Go-Shirakawa, through special emissaries whom he despatched to
Kyoto, the power of Yoshinaka and other problems relating to the
wars. He also used the services of the priest Mongaku who lived near
Kyoto to persuade Yoshinaka to carry out the pursuit of the Heike
without further delay. It was this and other evidence of the growing
intimacy between Kyoto and Kamakura that brought Yoshinaka
back from the west in great haste.

Yoshinaka now pressed Go-Shirakawa for the suspension of the
mandate against the Taira and for the issuance of another authorizing him to defend Kyoto against Yoritomo. In this way the friendship between Yoshinaka and Yoritomo, which had never been
genuine from the very beginning, even though Yoshinaka had
been among the first to declare for Yoritomo, reached the breaking
point. Meanwhile, Yoshinaka's demand for a mandate to defend
Kyoto against Yoritomo was rejected by the ex-sovereign, to the
surprise of Yoshinaka, accustomed as he was to gaining his objectives quickly and by threat or force. Yoshinaka then offered to
send Shida Yoshihiro against Yoritomo. Yoshihiro, it will be recalled, was a Minamoto who had turned against Yoritomo and together with the Ashikaga had attempted to seize Kamakura. Still
the ex-sovereign refused to accede, pointing to the resurgence of
the Taira who, by the middle of the Intercalary Tenth Month, had

taken most of the western region as far east as Harima. Instead, the ex-sovereign issued the third of his mandates to Yoshinaka, ordering him to proceed without further delay against the Taira. Clearly, the relations between Yoshinaka and Go-Shirakawa had reached an impasse.

Yoshinaka's relations with his confederate Yukiie had also taken a turn for the worse. Yukiie's real reasons for supporting Yoshinaka are not known but presumably, as Yoshinaka was a Minamoto and fighting the Taira, Yukiie must have felt that serving him was not an act contrary to Yoritomo's wishes. At any rate, he took the ex-sovereign's orders more seriously than Yoshinaka, for early in the Eleventh Month he left Kyoto for the west to engage the Taira. Just before he departed he had divulged to the ex-sovereign a secret plan of Yoshinaka to seize Go-Shirakawa as hostage and to take him to the north, should the enemy enter Kyoto. About ten days later Yoshinaka, suspicious of an assembly of officials and troops at Hō-jū-ji, one of Go-Shirakawa's residences, attacked and burned the building. In the next few days Yoshinaka, while displaying for the public some one hundred heads which he had taken at Hōjū-ji, demanded and obtained from the ex-sovereign the dismissal of approximately fifty high officials. Yet on the question of a decree against Yoritomo the ex-sovereign would not yield to Yoshinaka's wishes. In fact, on the twenty-eighth of the Eleventh Month another imperial mandate was issued to Yoshinaka to proceed against the Taira. On the very next day Yukiie was routed by Taira Nori-mori in Harima Province, thus bringing the Taira closer to the capital.

Yoshinaka now resorted to communicating with Munemori, the leader of the Heike, suggesting peace between them and a joint effort against Yoritomo. When Munemori flatly rejected the offer, Yoshinaka turned his attention once again to the ex-sovereign. Finally, on the tenth of the Twelfth Month of 1183, Go-Shirakawa yielded and granted to Yoshinaka a decree authorizing him to attack Yoritomo. Also at Yoshinaka's urging a similar mandate was granted a few days later to Fujiwara Hidehira of Mutsu.

Thus Yoritomo had once again become a rebel in the eyes of the court. But this time Yoritomo took direct action. In the closing days of the year he ordered his brothers, Noriyori and Yoshitsune, to leave for Kyoto immediately at the head of 60,000 troops. This meant that the strategy of restricting his military actions to the east, which he had followed since 1180, had come to an end.

THE FALL OF YOSHINAKA AND THE EXPANSION OF THE KAMAKURA GOVERNMENT

Yoshinaka's domination of the Kyoto court during the last few months of 1183 continued into the first few days of 1184, when he was raised to the fourth rank and made Barbarian-Conquering-Great-General, or *Seii Tai-Shogun*, the nation's highest military office.[2] But his position at Kyoto with respect to his enemies was becoming more vulnerable by the day. To the west, the Taira had retaken its old headquarters at Fukuhara, and it had begun the construction of a stronghold at Ichinotani in Settsu Province. To the east Yoritomo's forces under Noriyori and Yoshitsune were reported in neighboring Ōmi Province by the sixteenth. There were troubles within his own ranks. His old confederate Yukiie—at this time in Ishikawa—deserted him, while his efforts to seek an agreement with the Heike toward a joint defense of Kyoto had been rejected.

At this point Yoshinaka made one of his typical, impetuous moves —he sent some of his much needed men to attack Yukiie, while assigning the remainder of his forces to the task of defending the approaches to Kyoto. These approaches were at Seta in Ōmi Province where the waters of Lake Biwa enter the Uji River, and at Uji in Yamashiro Province, a few miles below Seta on the same river. Yoshinaka himself remained in Kyoto, with plans to take the ex-sovereign with him to the north should the outer defenses collapse.

On the twentieth Yoshitsune's army reached Uji, where the river flows through difficult, mountainous territory. But using daring methods which were to characterize his tactics later, Yoshitsune crossed the river, broke through the defenses, and entered Kyoto on the same day.[3] Surprised by the swift advance of Yoshitsune, Yoshinaka could not carry out his plan of seizing the ex-sovereign,

[2] The *Azuma kagami* notes with surprise that Yoshinaka is only the third person in history to receive this honor, and that this conferment "is a most unusual example of imperial graciousness" (Juei 3:1,10).

and he was forced to flee the city toward Lake Biwa with a handful of followers. There his escape was blocked by Noriyori's army, which had been attempting to enter Kyoto via Seta and Ōtsu, the route of the Tōkai-dō. At Kuritsu Yoshinaka met his death. Thus his fall was swift as his rise to power had been. Ironically, the end came only two weeks after he had become shogun, and found him with only one faithful follower at his side.

The war now entered its final phase. Yoritomo's armies had established direct contact with Kyoto and the court for the first time since the beginning of the conflict. It was also the first time that an army out of Kamakura had penetrated the west. The ex-sovereign wasted no time in investing Yoritomo's lieutenants with mandates, one to proceed against the Heiji and the other against remnants of Yoshinaka's following, thus reversing Yoritomo's position from that of a rebel to that of a patriot. And the brothers, quite unlike their late cousin Yoshinaka, left on their mission on the twenty-ninth of the same month, only eight days after their entry into Kyoto.[4] Moreover, while in Kyoto their relations with Go-Shirakawa were cordial, and the conduct of the Genji troops, except for one incident involving the theft of records and papers from the residence of a court secretary, was exemplary.

By the seventh of the Second Month, only seventeen days after the entry of Minamoto troops into Kyoto, the Ichinotani stronghold of the Heike in nearby Settsu Province had fallen to the Genji. This was accomplished largely through the spectacular tactics of Yoshitsune who, with seventy of his best troops, had scaled the Hiyodori Impasse behind the fortress and had surprised the enemy. But although more than a thousand of the enemy were killed and the heads of nine Taira leaders were taken, the remainder of the Taira forces had escaped by boat to Yashima on Shikoku across the Inland Sea. The Genji, lacking boats, could not pursue the enemy, and instead returned to Kyoto to report to the ex-sovereign and to present the heads of the Taira leaders.[5]

However, the Minamoto offensive in Western Japan which had begun so auspiciously at Ichinotani was to come to a virtual stand-

[3] Juei 3:1,20.   [4] Juei 3:1,29.

[5] See the entry of Juei 3:2,5 for a roster of the leaders in Noriyori's and Yoshitsune's command. Their combined armies numbered 76,000 horsemen as against 7,000 Heike horsemen. For details of the battle, see Juei 3:2,7 and the entries following.

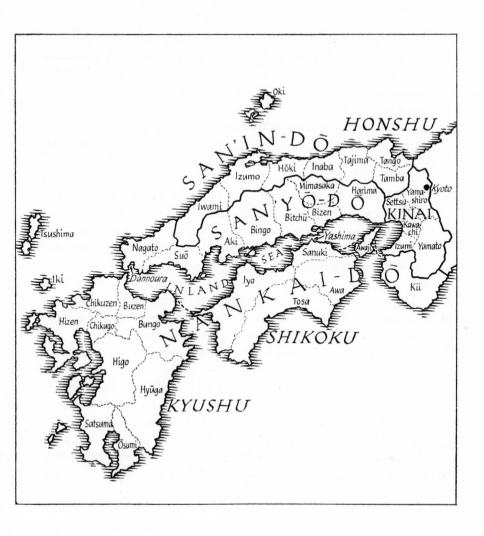

Figure 5. The circuits of Western Honshu and Nankai-dō, showing the provinces and the location of Kyoto, Yashima, and Dannoura

still in the next several months. In fact, it was six months after Ichinotani before another Genji army was to leave Kamakura for the west,[6] and an entire year before another major Minamoto victory was to be achieved.

There were several important reasons for this state of affairs. To begin with, the west was Taira territory. It was in sentiment overwhelmingly pro-Taira. It was here that some of the great heroes of the Taira Clan first emerged—men like Masamori and Tadamori. For a Genji army to make any headway in this region, it would have to lessen the hostility of as many local lords as possible and avoid, in the meantime, direct clashes with concentrations of Taira power. Accordingly Yoritomo embarked on a campaign to win over the more influential lords in the west and to enroll them as Genji vassals.

Immediately after the Ichinotani Battle Yoritomo sent Tachibana Kiminari to Sanuki Province, strategicaly situated on Shikoku commanding a narrow section of the Inland Sea, to try to win over the support of the principal lords there. Early in the Third Month of 1184 Yoritomo sent instructions to Hōjō Tokimasa, who was in Kyoto, to communicate with the local lords of Shikoku and to enroll them as Genji vassals.[7] Later in the year Tokimasa was able to report that some fourteen lords of Sanuki had abandoned the Heike and had declared their loyalty for the Genji.[8] Similarly, the lords of Kyushu were contacted by Yoritomo who sent them a directive enjoining them to support the Genji.[9] Meanwhile, during the Eighth Month, Yoritomo despatched an army from Kamakura under Noriyori and charged it with the mission of reaching Kyushu and bringing the traditionally pro-Taira lords of the region into the Genji fold. En route to Kyushu, Noriyori was instructed by Yoritomo to recognize with appropriate rewards any local warrior who might perform meritoriously for the Genji.[10]

Another reason for the delay in military operations was the lack of boats. The fact that the Inland Sea dominates the geography of Western Japan was to affect profoundly the progress of the war. Boats for transport and for naval warfare were essential. In these the Genji were woefully deficient. The only practical way to meet

[6] Genreki 1:8,8.   [7] Juei 3:3,1.   [8] Genreki 1:9,19.   [9] Juei 3:3,1.
[10] Genreki 1:10,12.

this need was to obtain the boats locally—through local lords—a factor which doubly emphasized the urgency of winning the support of western lords. Moreover, the main bulk of the Genji armies was comprised of troops from Eastern Japan with no experience in naval warfare.

If the Genji had been unaware of the importance of naval craft in the early phases of the war, they knew after the Ichinotani Battle how essential they were, for in that battle the Minamoto, despite a victory, had allowed the greater part of the defeated enemy force to escape by sea.

However, the lesson of Ichinotani had not escaped the astute Yoritomo. During the Fourth Month of 1184 he sent Nakahara Chikayori to Kyoto to instruct the Genji leaders to look into the matter of boats in order to expedite the war.[11] But so little progress had been made in this connection that Yoritomo's men were using horses whenever possible to cross from shore to island in their forays along the Inland Sea.[12]

It was precisely this problem of the lack of boats which produced one of the more disappointing failures of the Genji campaign in the west. Noriyori's army, which had left Kamakura during the Eighth Month of 1184 with instructions to operate in Kyushu, had reached Aki and Suō Provinces at the western end of Honshu by the Tenth Month, but there it languished for the next three months because of Noriyori's inability to muster boats to take the army across the narrow channel to Kyushu. Noriyori's inept handling of his mission and his slow progress not only taxed Yoritomo's patience, but also caused his own men, according to reports, to become ill-humored and restless from inactivity. Not a few deserted him to return to the east.[13] It was not until the Second Month of 1185 that Noriyori finally effected the crossing.

Lack of boats was not the only problem which plagued Yoritomo and delayed the war. There was a shortage of horses and of provisions. Early in 1185, in answer to pleas from Noriyori, Yoritomo sent thirty-two boatloads of provisions from the east.[14]

There was also the question of whether to siphon more troops out of the east to augment the expeditionary forces in the west. To draw heavily on eastern manpower was, to Yoritomo, to jeopard-

[11] Genreki 1:4,29. [12] Genreki 1:12,16. [13] Genreki 2:1,6. [14] Genreki 2:3,12.

ize the unity of the east which he had accomplished early in the war. And he had cause to be hesitant in this respect, for in Kai and Shinano there had occurred an uprising during the Fifth Month of 1184 to which he had had to despatch a special contingent of troops.[15] There were troubles also in other areas which had been won by the Genji. In Iga, for example, the laxity of the Genji had permitted Taira partisans to infiltrate the province.[16]

While these problems of a tactical and logistical nature were important, to Yoritomo the political problems created as a result of the expansion of the war into the Kyoto area and the west in general seemed to be of equally great importance. His troops were now in Kyoto in direct touch with the imperial court. He was now the defender of the court, a position which, despite several imperial decrees to the contrary, he had constantly insisted upon since the opening of the war. He strove to preserve that status.

To do so it was essential that he and his armies in the west maintain correct and friendly relations with the court at all times; hence his preoccupation with such matters as the need to discipline Genji troops—as Yoshinaka had been unable to do—and to observe established procedures in the prosecution of the war such as requesting mandates from the sovereign before launching a campaign. It will be recalled that, when Yoshinaka was dislodged from Kyoto, Yoritomo's lieutenants not only requested and obtained mandates from Go-Shirakawa but also carried them out with a minimum of delay.

In the light of Yoritomo's concern with the maintenance of proper relations with the court, it is not surprising that the first memorial which he addressed to the ex-sovereign after the Battle of Ichinotani sought to clarify the position and the aims of the Genji. An important document for an understanding of the founding of the shogunate, it contained four major items:[17]

First, it assured the court the exercise of its traditional rights with regard to local government, and expressed the hope that by the coming spring order would be restored in the country and the ex-sovereign might then resume the appointment and assignment of officials to the provinces.

[15] Genreki 1:5,1.   [16] Genreki 1:7,18.   [17] Juei 3:2,25.

Second, it requested that the ex-sovereign issue to Yoshitsune a mandate to pursue the Taira immediately and empower him to assume command of all armed warriors, irrespective of their Genji or Heiji affiliation, in the home and adjoining provinces; and also withhold the granting of any rewards to warriors until and unless recommended by Yoritomo.

Third, it declared that since "ours is the land of the gods," the lands of shrines should be confirmed as a matter of course and their right to acquire new lands recognized; and that the court should actively support the repair and upkeep of shrines damaged as a result of the wars.

And, fourth, it promised the same rights to the Buddhist temples, including the return of lands seized from them by the Heike and by Yoshinaka; but it also recommended stern measures toward the men of the church who "had aspired to military valor to the neglect of Buddhist Law," and expressed the hope that the weapons maintained by monks would be turned over to "government troops" engaged in the subjugation of the enemies of the nation.

It is significant to note that, except for the request that the court await Yoritomo's recommendations before granting awards to warriors, this memorial contained no new principles or policies. Yoritomo had consistently expressed, either in writing or in his conduct of the war, the principles enunciated in the other items. However, Item Two clearly represented a new policy. To begin with, Yoritomo would no longer seek a compromise with the Taira as he had done in 1181 when he had proposed joint rule of the country by the two clans. More important was his assumption of the role of protector of the court and its traditional rights on a country-wide basis, a role which he had maintained only on a regional basis until this time. Moreover, this was definitely a public function for the execution of which Yoritomo requested of the ex-sovereign the right to use any warrior who bore arms. At the same time Yoritomo made it clear that he did not intend to relinquish any of his customary rights as a private, feudal lord to his vassals by requesting the ex-sovereign to withhold the granting of rewards to deserving Genji vassals unless first recommended by Yoritomo. This clarification of policy is fundamental to an understanding of the later

Kamakura shogunate, for, in essence, the shogunate was a private clan government based on vassalage but also empowered with certain public functions.

This peculiar dual role of Yoritomo's government is best illustrated in the attempts made by him to enlist vassals in Western Japan. Vassalage was a private matter, but it was solicited for a public purpose—the destruction of rebels and the preservation of the imperial court. Moreover, in his directives after 1184, Yoritomo did not hesitate to refer to his own private following as *kangun*, or government troops.[18]

Meanwhile, for Yoritomo to maintain cordial relations with the imperial court while prosecuting a war in Western Japan, traditionally the home territory of the court, was a singularly difficult task. Rights to the very land over which the fighting raged were held for the most part by members of the old nobility and the imperial family. It was difficult, if not impossible, to observe the legalities of property rights in the heat of a war.

Moreover, there were many instances of deliberate violations of rights to land and property by Genji vassals whom Yoritomo, from the remoteness of Kamakura, could not effectively discipline. In fact, it was this type of outright violation by Genji warriors, or warriors claiming to be Genji, which threatened the entente between Kyoto and Kamakura.

As early as the Ninth Month of 1184, shortly after Noriyori's army had departed from Kyoto for western Honshu, the ex-sovereign addressed a decree to Yoritomo ordering him to return control of lands of the principal shrine of Tamba Province which a Genji vassal had seized arbitrarily.[19]

Such incidents increased as the campaign in the west progressed. By the Second Month of 1185 the ex-sovereign, at the insistence of holders of rights to land, addressed another decree to Yoritomo charging that "warriors have become unmindful of imperial law . . . in the various provinces of the seven circuits." [20] The list of complaints against warriors included the seizure from manors of annual tributes destined for their legal guardians or nominal owners in Kyoto, the plundering of provisions on lands of shrines and

---

[18] See, for example, his directive to the local lords of Kyushu. Juei 3:3,1.
[19] Genreki 1:9,20.   [20] Genreki 2:2,5.

temples, and the oppression of the people "on the excuse of pursuing the enemies of the imperial court." Such acts of outlawry were often inspired, as Yoritomo himself correctly surmised, "by the growing prestige of Kanto" and by the difficulty of restraining warriors at so great a distance from Kamakura.

As the volume of such complaints increased in 1184, and as they were usually brought to Yoritomo's attention through the medium of the ex-sovereign whose good will he was determined to retain, it is not surprising that Yoritomo decided, in the fall of 1184, to enlarge his administrative organization. Early in the Tenth Month he installed the *kumon-jo,* a board concerned chiefly with the writing and keeping of documents.[21] It was, in effect, a sort of foreign office, inasmuch as the scribes and officials of the board were occupied mainly with the drafting of notes and formal documents in reply to decrees and inquiries of the imperial court. In fact, its first order of business, significantly, was the disposition of "matters pertaining to shrine and temple lands" brought to Yoritomo's attention by the ex-sovereign.[22]

It is interesting to note that until 1184, when the activities of the Genji were confined mainly to the east, a single board, the *samurai-dokoro,* had comprised the headquarters. Now that the war had spread to the west, creating in its wake new problems, both military and political, the leader of the Genji found it necessary to augment his administrative organization to meet the situation.

Indeed, within a fortnight of the installation of the *kumon-jo,* Yoritomo found it necessary to add still another board to the machinery of his headquarters. This was the *monchū-jo,* a judicial board,[23] to hear and review claims pertaining to land. The cases, for the most part, were those resulting from forcible seizure by Genji warriors. Yoritomo himself sat as a member, along with Fujiwara Toshikane and Taira Moritoki. Miyoshi Yasunobu, an experienced jurist from Kyoto, wrote the decisions.

That such a board would have to be created in due time was a foregone conclusion in view of the large number of cases brought to Kamakura and awaiting adjudication. In the Tenth Month alone there were two very serious suits lodged at Kamakura, one by

---

[21] Genreki 1:10,6. Later, this board was renamed the *mandokoro* and made into the overall administrative board.

[22] Genreki 1:10,6. [23] Genreki 1:10,20.

Hirota Shrine in Awaji and the other by Iwashimizu Shrine near
Kyoto. In the former it was charged by Prince Nakasuke, the legal
guardian of Hirota Shrine, that a manor which Yoritomo himself
had given as a benefice to the shrine had been seized by followers
of Kajiwara Kagetoki, one of Yoritomo's chief vassals in the western
campaign.[24] As for the latter, the exact nature of the suit is not
recorded, but its seriousness to Yoritomo may be judged by the fact
that Iwashimizu was the parent shrine of the Tsurugaoka Hachiman
Shrine of Kamakura, where the tutelary deities of the Minamoto
were enshrined.

Thus, suddenly and in very short order, Yoritomo's headquarters
had grown from one to three boards. These boards, together with
a council of chief vassals which was to be formed later, were to
constitute the administrative machinery of the later shogunate.
That they had come into existence by 1184 through the needs of
war and that they were functioning even before the main objective of the war—the conquest of the Heike—had been achieved
is a matter of the greatest significance in the history of the Kamakura shogunate.

THE BATTLE OF DANNOURA AND THE
DEFEAT OF THE TAIRA

So far as the war was concerned, Yoritomo in 1184 was far from
satisfied with its progress. Although Genji troops had negotiated
the entire western half of Honshu by the fall of 1184, they had
shown little capacity to reach the main Taira forces on Yashima,
an island in the Inland Sea off Sanuki Province, Shikoku, or to
reach the pro-Taira local lords of Kyushu. Yoritomo was especially
dissatisfied with Noriyori in charge of the main Genji forces in the
west.

Earlier in the year, before Noriyori was named to lead a force,
Yoritomo had considered sending Yoshitsune into the field in order
to expedite the Genji campaign, for Yoshitsune had already demonstrated his abilities as a warrior and a commander. That Yoritomo
had not already done so was due to the fact that he had stationed
his brother in Kyoto as his personal deputy and representative, a

[24] Genreki 1:10,27.

position which Yoritomo regarded as being of the greatest importance. To post in the capital anyone but a warrior of the blood and of the highest reputation would be, to Yoritomo's thinking, a mark of disrespect to the imperial court.

However, by the Seventh Month of 1184, Yoritomo decided to carry out his earlier plan regarding Yoshitsune. Accordingly he petitioned the ex-sovereign to invest Yoshitsune with a mandate and to send him against the Heike.[25]

But suddenly, in the following month, Yoritomo withdrew the nomination of Yoshitsune, even though this meant a further delay in the launching of a new offensive in the west. Yoritomo's reason for this act was clear to all concerned: Yoshitsune had violated a cardinal rule of vassalage and one which Yoritomo had enunciated in his policy statement to the ex-sovereign approximately six months earlier. On or about the sixth day of the Eighth Month, the Ex-Sovereign Go-Shirakawa had conferred on Yoshitsune—and the latter had accepted—the military rank of junior lieutenant of the Outer Palace Guards, Left Division, without the prior approval of Yoritomo.[26] Concurrently, or a few days later, Yoshitsune must have accepted another office in the imperial police, for he is referred to frequently in the *Azuma kagami* as *teii*, the alternate Chinese title for the secretary, or vice president, of the imperial police.

The furor caused in Kamakura by this incident, which was to lead ultimately to the estrangement of the brothers, must be seen against the feudal background of the times. For Yoritomo to retain his position as lord over his vassals, he could not afford to have the latter accepting office and honors without his knowledge or approval. Even though Yoshitsune, in this instance, had been honored for rendering a service which Yoritomo himself had directed him to perform—namely, to protect the court and the capital from the Taira—nevertheless, it was Yoshitsune's obligation as a vassal to seek the prior approval of his lord before accepting any honors.

The reason for Yoritomo's insistence upon this rule is obvious. The court, traditionally the sole dispenser of rank and office, which all coveted, including Yoritomo, could sow disaffection among the

[25] Genreki 1:7,3. [26] Reported in the entry for Genreki 1:8,17.

Genji and could easily break their unity by bestowing on Genji vassals office and rank higher than those enjoyed by Yoritomo himself. Vassalage, by its very nature, does not admit of a situation where a vassal enjoys greater prestige and official preference than the lord himself. Moreover, in this case, Yoshitsune was no ordinary vassal. He was a vassal of the blood who had already acquired a great reputation as a warrior and who with Noriyori, Zenjō, and Yoritomo was one of the four living sons of the former chieftain of the Minamoto. Any of them, if he could command enough of a following, could claim the leadership of the Genji.

Not very long before, in the fall and winter of 1183–84, the crafty ex-sovereign had used the power of conferment to weaken the Genji. He had accorded to Yoshinaka, a vassal of Yoritomo, higher military rank and public offices, including that of a shogun, than to Yoritomo himself. Under the circumstances vassalage, so far as the two were concerned, had ceased to exist; or more correctly, it had to be remedied by the removal of the one by the other.

Yoshitsune, on the other hand, was convinced that his brother was deliberately slighting him. He had, at Yoritomo's behest, carried out every one of his missions with distinction. Yet Yoritomo had not seen fit to recommend him for a court appointment. Noriyori, his other brother, with whom he had shared joint command of the Genji armies which had driven the Taira out of Settsu Province at Ichinotani, had been recommended for and had subsequently received the governorship of Mikawa. Similarly, Ōuchi Yoshinobu had become governor of Musashi, while Ichijō Yoshiyasu, Minamoto Hirotsuna, and Taira Yasunari had become governors of Sanuki, Suruga, and Kawachi respectively—all on Yoritomo's recommendation.[27]

None of these men seemed on the record to be as deserving as Yoshitsune. Yoshiyasu and Hirotsuna were courtiers who had contributed little to the war effort, but the former was Yoritomo's brother-in-law, while the latter was the son of the late Yorimasa who had instigated the Minamoto revolt. Yasunari, who received the governorship of Kawachi, long a Minamoto stronghold, was a Taira.

---

[27] See Genreki 1:6,20, and 6,21. The latter entry adds: "Yoshitsune, who had persistently sought His Lordship's recommendation for an official appointment but who had been rejected in favor of Noriyori, was greatly displeased."

If Yoritomo had reasons of his own for omitting Yoshitsune's name from his list of recommendations, we do not know of them, unless it was jealousy of his able and popular brother, as so many historians have alleged. And Yoritomo's jealousy is readily understandable when it is remembered that no lord could afford to promote the rise to fame and power of a younger brother who might compete with him for the leadership of the clan.

Something of the determination and stubbornness of the brothers may be seen in an incident which is recounted in the *Azuma kagami*. At a ceremony honoring the carpenters who were about to begin the construction of a small shrine on the premises of the Tsurugaoka Hachiman Shrine, Yoshitsune had shown great reluctance to perform the lowly duty of leading one of the horses to be presented to the carpenters. Only after Yoritomo's second command and a reprimand did Yoshitsune finally perform this duty in which all the leading vassals had participated.[28]

But the above incident had occurred in 1181, and it is not known whether Yoritomo recalled it in 1184 when, again, his brother insisted upon an independent course of action. At any rate, the situation was not yet hopeless, although the relations between them were definitely strained. In fact, it was Yoritomo who took the first step toward a reconciliation when, in the following month, he urged Kawagoe Shigeyori, one of his vassals, to give a daughter in marriage to Yoshitsune.[29]

However, the factor which restrained Yoritomo from taking the final step of divesting Yoshitsune of his status and privileges as a Genji was the deceleration of the Genji campaign in the west. Noriyori, who had been in western Honshu since early fall, was still there at the end of the year, unable to cross the narrow channel to Kyushu. Valuable time was being lost to the enemy. In desperation Yoritomo, though still not fully reconciled to Yoshitsune, must have decided to call on his brother to take a new Genji force into the field.

Exactly when this decision was made is not clear in the records, but it must have been during the last several days of 1184; for the ex-sovereign's approval of Yoshitsune's nomination occurred on the first day of the new year. A few days after his nomination Yoshitsune

---

[28] Yōwa 1:7,20.   [29] Genreki 1:9,14.

must have left Kyoto for Settsu to prepare for his mission, for he appeared there, at a port called Watanabe, on the seventeenth of the Second Month of 1185 with a small assemblage of boats. What Yoshitsune was able to accomplish in the next few weeks—a result Noriyori had failed to achieve in months—constitutes one of the more brilliant chapters in the annals of Japanese military history.

On the seventeenth, notwithstanding a storm which broke as he prepared to leave and which destroyed many of his boats, Yoshitsune embarked with one hundred and fifty men in five boats against the counsel of other Genji leaders.[30] By the next day he was already in the vicinity of Yashima, the headquarters of the Taira and of Emperor Antoku and his court. On the nineteenth, the second day after his embarkation from Settsu, he destroyed the palace at Yashima, forcing the Taira to take to their boats and to flee westward. After approximately a month spent in Shikoku assembling naval craft and rallying allies to his cause, Yoshitsune was ready to pursue the Heike toward the west.

There are scattered references in the *Azuma kagami* to the preparations which Yoshitsune made during this brief period. One Kōno Michinobu, for example, offered him thirty boats.[31] Kajiwara Kagetoki, the Genji leader who had objected to the sailing on the seventeenth because of a storm, arrived in the meantime with one hundred and forty boats.[32] And a local commissioner in charge of boats contributed "several tens of boats." [33]

On the twenty-second of the Third Month Yoshitsune sailed with his fleet toward the Moji Strait. His point of departure is not clear, but it does not appear to have been on Shikoku. From the fact that on the day of his departure his fleet was sighted and reported to the Taira headquarters at Hikojima, situated outside and to the west of Moji Strait, it seems that by this time Yoshitsune must have been considerably west of Yashima and perhaps on the north shore of the Inland Sea off Suō. At any rate, the Heiji fleet set sail immediately and proceeded eastward through the strait to meet the Genji.

The fleets met at Dannoura, Akamagaseki, off Nagato Province, just inside of the Moji Strait, on the morning of the twenty-fourth. By 1:00 P.M., in a swift series of actions, the battle was over. The Heiji tactics had called for the encirclement of the Genji fleet by

[30] Genreki 2:2,18.   [31] Genreki 2:2,21.   [32] Genreki 2:2,22.   [33] Genreki 2:3,21.

taking advantage of the easterly flow of the current in the early morning hours. Dividing their fleet of 500 ships into three groups and riding the easterly flow of the tide, the Heiji struck at the Genji. The Heiji leaders, among them several local lords of Kyushu and Shikoku who were familiar with the tricky currents of the strait, knew that the encirclement must be completed quickly, for, in the late morning hours, the tide in the Inland Sea begins to recede and the current shifts from an easterly to a westerly course, against the direction of the Heiji attack. When this change occurred toward mid-morning and the current began to flow out toward the strait and the open sea, the Heiji could not hold the Genji boats at bay. The Minamoto boarded the enemy boats, destroyed their rudders, and rendered them prey to the swift currents of the channel. The war was over. Most of the Taira leaders either met their death or were made captives, although a few escaped. The Lady Azechi, holding tightly the eight-year-old Emperor Antoku, sank to the bottom of the sea. The Lady Azechi and Taira Tokuko, the emperor's mother, were rescued, but Antoku perished.[34]

Yoshitsune's role in the Genji victory was considerable. But not the least of his achievements was the rapidity with which he had built up a fleet. When he embarked from Settsu he had only five boats. At Dannoura, according to a record of the battle submitted to Yoritomo, Yoshitsune had a fleet of 840 boats[35]—which would make the Genji fleet considerably larger than that of the enemy. And although the total number of Yoshitsune's force at Dannoura is not given in the accounts, it is safe to assume that it included many local lords of Shikoku and western Honshu, of former Taira persuasion, who were thoroughly at home on the sea and with naval warfare, and whom Yoshitsune had won over to the Genji cause. Without them Yoshitsune would not have fared so well.

Yoshitsune's messenger bearing news of the victory reached Kamakura on the fourth of the Fourth Month.[36] Although Yoritomo must have welcomed the news, there is little doubt, from the grim tone and restraint of the passages in the *Azuma kagami*, that he had not expected so complete a victory so soon. The western campaign, especially in Kyushu, had not been progressing satisfactorily, and

[34] For details of the Battle of Dannoura, see Genreki 2:3,24, and 4,11.
[35] Genreki 2:4,11.　[36] Genreki 2:4,4.

he had sent boats and provisions to the west as late as the twelfth of the previous month. Moreover, he had been urging the ex-sovereign to issue an edict to the local lords of Bungo Province in Kyushu, promising them rewards if they would abandon their support of the Taira and render their services to the Genji. The ex-sovereign, in fact, had complied with Yoritomo's wishes and had issued such an edict on the twenty-ninth of the Third Month, not knowing then that the war had been concluded at Dannoura five days earlier.[37]

And thus the Gempei War had come to a sudden and dramatic end. With the chief members of the Taira Family killed, drowned, or captured,[38] the Minamoto under Yoritomo was now the supreme power in Japan.

THE LEGAL AND MORAL BASIS OF YORITOMO'S GOVERNMENT

Although the enemy was destroyed and the last obstacle to Genji supremacy removed at Dannoura, it is important to note that for many people, especially in Eastern Japan, the victory did nothing more than confirm what had been a fact since the war had begun in 1180, namely, that Yoritomo was their ruler and his headquarters their government. They had taken their grievances to him and to no one else, and they had received satisfaction from no one else. In the feudal system which prevailed, the vast majority of the people had little if any contact with any other government, and they did not begrudge, nor as much as question, Yoritomo's right to rule—at least in Eastern Japan.

But it is of great importance in the understanding of the founding of the shogunate that Yoritomo himself, constantly and consistently, kept before the people the image of himself and of his vassals as their legal and just protectors. By his actual conduct of government in the region he controlled, Yoritomo had accomplished more between 1180 and 1185 than simply the destruction of the enemy. He had built up precedents for rule which the people accepted and expected of him, and which, in the final analysis, con-

---

[37] Genreki 2:3,29.
[38] For a list of the principal casualties of the Taira, see Genreki 2:3,24.

tributed more to the permanence of his government than the victory at Dannoura.

What were these precedents and what was their impact on the people? One of them was the impression of the legality of his military actions against the Taira. From the beginning of the conflict Yoritomo had claimed that Prince Mochihito's pronouncement calling for the overthrow of the Taira constituted a legal authorization for his actions. To be sure, the pronouncement in question was not a public proclamation of the highest order emanating from the emperor, the ex-emperor, or the Council of State. However, it was a document from an imperial prince, and in the practices of the court, any member of the imperial family who held the rank of a prince could issue pronouncements, which were called *reishi*. Therefore, the prince's right to issue a *reishi* was never questioned. The Taira themselves, in attacking Buddhist temples which had acknowledged the prince's pronouncement, had not challenged the right of the prince to issue a *reishi*. But irrespective of its legality or illegality, its effect on the public was great. It was a document issued by a prince, and it authorized the overthrow of the Taira. Yoritomo himself, in receiving it, changed into ceremonial robes and accorded it all the respect that an imperial communication commanded.[39] Later, in his first encounter with the enemy, he attached the document to his standard to let the opposition know that his cause was just and legal.[40]

Yoritomo did much more with Mochihito's pronouncement than simply justify his military actions against the Taira. On its basis he claimed the right to rule over Eastern Japan. As early as the second day of the war Yoritomo's secretary, Kunimichi, had declared in a directive to Yamamoto Tomochika, a Taira partisan, "It is manifestly clear from the prince's pronouncement that the public and private domains in the several provinces of the east are within His Lordship's jurisdiction." [41] It matters little whether or not such a grant of power was actually made in Mochihito's *reishi*. What matters is that Yoritomo construed the pronouncement as a mandate to him not only to overthrow the Taira but also to administer the government in its place—at least in Eastern Japan where he was domiciled—and that he publicized and perpetuated this construction

[39] Jishō 4:4,27.   [40] Jishō 4:8,23.   [41] Jishō 4:8,19.

at every opportunity. Thus Kunimichi, in his communication to Tomochika, advised the latter and other neighboring lords to come before Yoritomo and seek his confirmation because he was now, by virtue of Prince Mochihito's *reishi,* the legal administrator of the east.

Another important legal precedent which Yoritomo established for the later shogunate grew out of his actions toward the local representatives of the central government. Individually, local officials were not as powerful as the feudal lords, but some of them commanded armed followings and were not entirely without power or influence. Thus Yoritomo could not ignore this group in his efforts to unify the east. Moreover, because of their official connections with the Taira-dominated court, they were more apt to support the Taira than the Minamoto, and could prove troublesome. One of the first measures Yoritomo took while attempting to rebuild his forces after the defeat at Ishibashi was to urge the vice governor of Kazusa "to rally the officials of the local government office and to report with them to him." [42] A month later he sent an emissary to the local government office of Musashi Province with instructions regarding the administration of that province.[43] By such moves he served notice on the local representatives of the central government that he was assuming rule in the east and that he desired their support. To be sure, the threat of force was behind these actions, but it is highly significant that Yoritomo did not presume to abolish the traditional system of local government. The offices held by these officials and the rights to which they were entitled by virtue of their office, such as the right to administer public lands, were recognized and left undisturbed so long as these officials acknowledged Yoritomo's leadership and did not oppose him militarily. Thus, for example, when a local official in Awa interfered with the rights of a shrine over its lands, Yoritomo ordered him to desist,[44] but at the same time he did not deny the official his right to carry on with the legitimate exercise of his office.

Yoritomo also attempted to justify the war on moral grounds. For him the war was not a rebellion but rather the removal of rebels from the high places of government. The throne had been usurped and the nation overthrown in the twenty years since the

[42] Jishō 4:9,1.   [43] Jishō 4:10,5.   [44] Jishō 5:2,10.

Taira had come to power. Therefore, the role of the Genji, as Prince Mochihito and Yoritomo saw it, was to wrest the throne and the nation from the rebel Taira. The specific charges against the Taira, enumerated in Prince Mochihito's pronouncement and repeated many times in subsequent statements and letters of Yoritomo included such crimes as the plundering of the country, confinement of the ex-emperor, infliction of banishment and death on public officials, arbitrary bestowal of rewards on the unworthy, incrimination of the innocent, apprehension and confinement of priests and student monks, and many more.[45]

Thus, the righteousness—perhaps even more than the legality—of the Genji cause was stressed by the Minamoto leader. In this Yoritomo helped his own cause immeasurably by assuming the role of a just administrator almost immediately from the opening of hostilities. In the Tomochika incident mentioned above, it was not enough for Yoritomo that legally he was authorized to demand Tomochika's submission; it was more important to him that morally there was ground for the action in Tomochika's alleged "unwarranted outrages on the peasants." [46] Similarly, his order to a local official in Awa, noted above, was prompted by the latter's interference with the lands of a shrine.

Yoritomo also showed early in the war a sense of responsibility for the conduct of his warriors which was to enhance his moral reputation. On the same day that he took the action against Yamamoto Tomochika he had also listened to complaints from the monks of Sōtō-zan, a temple in Izu, whose lands had been violated by Genji warriors answering Yoritomo's call to arms. To compensate the temple for the damages Yoritomo promised in writing that he would make, when order was restored in the east, a grant of two manors to the temple, one in Izu and another in Sagami.[47]

Sōtō-zan enjoyed a special place in Yoritomo's life. Its head priest was Yoritomo's patron priest, and it was in his care that Yoritomo had left his wife during the first few weeks of the war. However, Yoritomo showed equally considerate attention to other temples and shrines which were to bring their grievances to him throughout the course of the war.

[45] The pronouncement, dated Jishō 4:4,9, is found in its entirety in the entry for Jishō 4:4,27.
[46] Jishō 4:8,19. [47] *Ibid.*

A typical example was the grievance brought to Yoritomo by the monks of Kongō-ji, a temple in Sagami Province. A local official and his warrior-following had seized the temple lands, marked off the mountain areas as a hunting preserve, and otherwise interfered with the pursuit of the religious activities of the monks.[48] In their petition they asked: "If Your Lordship does not render a judgment, where will the wandering monks settle?" and they vowed: "If Your Lordship will accept this petition and act immediately to put a stop to the outrages, we shall, by our words, actions, and deeds, pray and strive for your everlasting success and glory."

Such petitions were filed at Kamakura not only from the religious houses close to Kamakura but also from as far away as Hitachi and, after 1184, from the western provinces. Kashima Shrine of Hitachi, for example, had complained of the seizure of its lands by the Satake. Yoritomo, as an expression of his respect and sympathy for the shrine, ordered abstinence from certain foods at Kamakura,[49] and later, after the disposal of the Satake, he remembered to make a grant of a township in Hitachi to the shrine.[50] A few years later when the shrine complained of interference by warriors in the exercise of its rights over the township, Yoritomo promptly reaffirmed the grant.[51] Still later, when the shrine sent its priests to Kamakura to lodge a charge that the land steward was interfering with its rights, Yoritomo again took measures in behalf of the shrine.[52]

That Yoritomo assumed the responsibility for injustices committed by his warriors to temples and shrines was not the only reason for his growing reputation as a just ruler. He gave ear to every manner of request for assistance which the religious houses brought to his attention. Most of these requests were for outright grants of land and confirmation of current holdings of land. However, there were requests also for fiscal exemptions and even the return of lands seized, not necessarily by the Genji, but earlier by the Heike. On occasion Yoritomo was asked to adjudicate controversies between two temples.[53]

Moreover, these appeals for redress, adjudication, and material

[48] Yōwa 2:5,25.   [49] Jishō 5:2,28.   [50] Yōwa 1:10,12.   [51] Genreki 1:8,13.
[52] Genreki 1:12,16.
[53] A notable example involved Jōju-in, a branch temple of Mount Kōya, which asked Yoritomo to effect the return of Ategawa Manor seized by Jakuraku-in. Genreki 1:7,2.

assistance came from temples and shrines throughout the east and the west as the war entered its fourth year. A partial list of the religious houses which received relief of one sort or another from Yoritomo between 1180 and the close of the war is impressive. Such shrines as Ise, Izumo, Hirota, Suwō Jōge, Mishima, Sunosaki, Hakone, Toyouke, Kibitsu, and Kamo were among the beneficiaries, as were temples such as Ikō-ji, Onjō-ji, and Tōdai-ji. The latter two temples received special consideration from Yoritomo because they had been attacked and burned by the Heike during the first year of the war.[54] Similarly, Ise Shrine, by virtue of its great historical influence and importance, received great attention from Yoritomo. When, for example, the Buddhist monks of Kumano claiming to be Genji partisans had despoiled the lands of the shrine and had attacked and burned the homes of the people living on the shrine lands, Yoritomo tried to atone for the offense with offers of help.[55]

It is apparent from these few examples that the circumstances of the war and Yoritomo's own policies had made him the sole dispenser of justice for temples and shrines, not only in the east which was under his control, but also in the west, as the above list indicates. Moreover, the majority of the cases brought to Yoritomo's attention from the west were made through the ex-sovereign's government whose members were the legal guardians of the shrines or temples in question.[56] Thus, even for the government, the only channel open to it for adjudication and redress was Yoritomo's government at Kamakura.

Yoritomo's reputation as a friend and protector of the religious institutions of the country was strengthened by his personal religious habits. The claim is made in several places in the *Azuma kagami*

[54] The petition of the high priests of Onjō-ji is regarded by many as a classic of this type of documentary writing. See Genreki 1:11,21. For the measures which Yoritomo took to assist Onjō-ji, see Genreki 1:12,1, and 12,3. For the details of the generous grant made to Tōdai-ji, see Genreki 2:3,7.

[55] Regarding Yoritomo's relations with Ise Shrine, see the following: Jishō 4:9,11; Yōwa 1:10,20; Yōwa 2:2,8; Genreki 2:3,14. Following the establishment of peace, Yoritomo continued to maintain friendly relations with Ise. On one occasion the shrine even requested from Yoritomo a pledge for expenses for the maintenance of a shrine office. See Bunji 1:10,15.

[56] The ex-sovereign lodged a complaint with Yoritomo in behalf of the historic Kamo Shrine of Kyoto. Warriors had violated some forty-one of its land holdings. Yoritomo made amends by granting control of an entire township to the shrine. See Genreki 1:4,24, and Genreki 2:1,22.

that Yoritomo performed his religious exercises every day without fail.[57] When the war began he was greatly troubled by the thought that he might have to forego these exercises, which consisted mainly of reading the sutras. He eased his conscience by asking a nun, who was his wife's religious teacher, to perform the readings for him and sent her a list of the selections.[58] Earlier he had vowed to complete the reading of one thousand passages of the *Lotus Sutra,* but the imminence of war made the fulfillment of the vow impossible. Yoritomo thereupon sought the permission of a Buddhist priest to reduce the number of passages to be recited from one thousand to eight hundred.[59]

It is also interesting to note that Yoritomo carried a rosary with him wherever he went. It is pointed out in the accounts that his rosary was a familiar sight to warriors from Sagami who had hunted with him.[60] Yoritomo also carried in his hair a small statuette of Kwannon, which he was seen to remove during the period of his hiding in the Hakone Mountains. When asked the meaning of this act, he replied that he, as the leader of the Genji, would be ridiculed by the enemy if his head were to be taken and a Buddhist statuette discovered in his hair.[61] The statuette, Yoritomo explained, had been given to him by a nun when he was three years old.

Yoritomo's devotion to religious practices and his respect for the men of the cloth may have come from his superstitious nature, about which there is much evidence in the *Azuma kagami.* However, he was probably no more superstitious than his fellow men. The important point is that he enjoyed the reputation of being a very religious man. In addition to his numerous visits to shrines and temples and the donations of land and materials which he made to them, he frequently prescribed day-long religious services for himself and his vassals, set aside days for the observance of traditional festivals of both the Buddhists and the Shintoists, and consulted with the priests on many occasions. In one notable case he pardoned a condemned man because the latter read the *Lotus Sutra* daily, saying, "I too am a devotee of the *Lotus Sutra.*" [62]

Yoritomo also enjoyed among the warrior class in the east a high reputation for fairness, a factor which accounted in large measure

---

[57] See, for example, Jishō 4:7,5, and 8,18.
[58] Jishō 4:8,18.   [59] Jishō 4:7,5.   [60] Jishō 4:8,24.   [61] *Ibid.*   [62] Jishō 5:7,5.

for the cohesion and permanence of the Genji. This reputation developed first in Yoritomo's attitude toward his former enemies, especially toward those who had opposed him and had nearly destroyed him at Ishibashi. To these men Yoritomo showed a generosity and trust unusual in the warrior society of the time. Edo Shigenaga, for example, was assigned to an important mission the day after he had renounced his former allegiance to the Heike.[63] Hatakeyama Shigetada, who had come to swear fealty to Yoritomo on the same day as Shigenaga, was given the honor of leading Yoritomo's army of 27,000 men into Kamakura the next day.[64]

But these men had come voluntarily to serve Yoritomo. There were many others who had served the Heike cause at Ishibashi and who had resisted Yoritomo until they were captured. Even some of these were given reprieves and enrolled in the ranks of the Genji. In fact, the *Azumi kagami* says that after the Fuji River Battle Yoritomo punished only one out of ten captives.[65]

There were some like Shibuya Shigekuni who were received back into the Genji without a question or reprimand from Yoritomo, although in Shigekuni's case, it was reported that he was "full of remorse and shame" for his earlier action.[66] There were others whom Yoritomo was determined to behead for their treachery but who were pardoned in the end. Takiguchi Tsunetoshi is a case in point. Yoritomo had expected him in his lines; instead he had joined the enemy lines at Ishibashi Mountain and had even shot an arrow at Yoritomo which had pierced his armor. Determined to confront Tsunetoshi with the evidence Yoritomo had saved the armor and the arrow—on which was inscribed Tsunetoshi's name —still buried in the armor where it had struck. Yet Yoritomo pardoned him on the plea of the condemned man's mother, who pointed to the long record of service of her family to the Minamoto.[67]

Another example of Yoritomo's fairness and willingess to forgive involved one of his old enemies who had attacked him at Ishibashi. This was Itō Sukechika who, until his capture just before the Fuji River Battle, had hopes of reaching the Taira lines. Sukechika, a lay priest, expected no less than immediate execution. But Yori-

[63] Jishō 4:10,5.　[64] Jishō 4:10,6.　[65] Jishō 4:10,23.　[66] Jishō 4:8,26.
[67] Jishō 4:11,26.

tomo, realizing that Sukechika was father-in-law to Miura Yoshi-zumi, one of his most trusted vassals, postponed passing sentence on the prisoner and instead remanded him to the custody of his son-in-law. A year and a half later Yoritomo, in an outburst of generosity, granted Sukechika a pardon. But Sukechika, "conscience-stricken over his earlier position," took his own life upon receipt of the news of his pardon.[68] Although Yoritomo's forgiveness saved Sukechika's life for only a limited time, this incident was regarded at Kamakura as an "inspiring episode" in warrior relations.[69]

It must be said for Yoritomo that his judgment of his former foes was excellent, for they served him loyally throughout the remainder of the war. Their names appear on the rosters of the Genji armies which fought at Ichinotani, Yashima, Dannoura, and in western Honshu and Kyushu.

But while his handling of his former enemies was on the whole praiseworthy and established for him the respect of the warrior class in the east, his relationship with one of his more influential vassals was far from ideal. This was Taira Hirotsune. He served Yoritomo loyally and, in fact, conspicuously in the early months of the war. In the Hitachi expedition he was given the principal role because of his knowledge of the country. But it appears that Hirotsune could not forget that his decision to join with Yoritomo in the early weeks of the war had been a turning point in the fortunes of the Genji and that at the time he commanded a larger following than any of the other vassals. In the summer of 1181, when Yoritomo was visiting with the Miura, Hirotsune and some fifty of his followers had gone to meet Yoritomo. To the dismay of Yoritomo's hosts, Hirotsune refused to dismount at the meeting. Later that evening, at a banquet given by the Miura, Hirotsune had objected to the presentation by Yoritomo of his ceremonial robe to Okazaki Shirō Yoshizane who had requested it, saying: "This beautiful robe should be proffered to someone who is worthy of it, such as I. I had not thought that it would go to someone as old as Yoshizane." [70]

Although Yoritomo did not venture to intervene in the quarrel over his robe, he was visibly disturbed by Hirotsune's self-assertion

[68] Yōwa 2:2,14.   [69] Yōwa 2:2,15.   [70] Jishō 5:6,19.

and sense of self-importance. During the ensuing months Hirotsune was definitely not in Yoritomo's good graces.[71] However, the two appeared to wish to restore friendly relations. Hirotsune sent Taira Tokiie, his Kyoto-born son-in-law, to placate Yoritomo.[72] Yoritomo honored Hirotsune a few months later by naming him to stand watch over his newborn son on the fifth night after the birth.[73] But their mutual overtures seem to have been in vain, for in the following year Hirotsune was assassinated by Kajiwara Kagetoki at Yoritomo's instigation.

Had this incident ended there, Yoritomo's reputation as a just leader of the Genji and of the east might have been damaged. However, Yoritomo was to learn later that his suspicions of Hirotsune were unfounded. He quickly acknowledged his error, released members of Hirotsune's family whom he had been holding, and restored them to his good graces.[74]

If Yoritomo was vindictive and at times impatient and unfair, it was usually in cases involving close members of his own family and household. For example, in an infamous incident Yoritomo ordered Shimizu Yoshitaka, his own son-in-law, killed. It does not appear that Yoritomo had any sound reasons for the slaying except that he suspected Yoshitaka of disloyal motives. The suspicion, moreover, was based not on Yoshitaka's conduct but on the record of the victim's father. This episode had other ramifications. The wife of the victim of Yoritomo's suspicions—his own daughter—languished in grief. Masako, Yoritomo's wife and the mother of the grief-stricken widow, blamed Yoritomo for this state of affairs and compelled him to order the execution of the man who had slain Yoshitaka on Yoritomo's orders.[75]

One other family controversy which might have had serious consequences for Genji unity began over Yoritomo's interest in a

[71] Yōwa 2:1,28.   [72] *Ibid.*   [73] Juei 1:8,16.

[74] A written vow which Hirotsune had made and deposited with his armor at a shrine in his native province of Kazusa, swearing allegiance to Yoritomo and expressing his wishes for Yoritomo's success, had been discovered. See Juei 3:1,17. Another acknowledgment by Yoritomo that he had erred with respect to Hirotsune, "who had given his life for an offense of which he was entirely innocent," appears in Juei 3:3,13.

[75] See Genreki 1:4,21; 4,26; 5,1; and 5,2. The unfortunate vassal who was decapitated for having carried out Yoritomo's order was a follower of Hori Chikaie. Regarding his death, see Genreki 1:6,27.

mistress. To keep the matter from his wife Yoritomo housed her in
a vassal's home situated at a distance from his own residence.[76] It
appears that Yoritomo changed her quarters from time to time so
as not to arouse his wife's suspicions. But eventually the secret
reached Masako's ears. In great anger she ordered Maki Munechika
to destroy the mistress's quarters, which happened to belong to
Yoritomo's secretary and close friend, Fujiwara Hirotsuna.[77] Yoritomo retaliated by cutting off Munechika's topknot. Expecting his
wife's reprimand, Yoritomo spent the night away from Kamakura,
but he had not foreseen the effect of this incident on Hōjō Tokimasa,
his father-in-law and faithful vassal. The man who had been
humiliated was a member of the Hōjō household, and thus Tokimasa, as chief of the Hōjō, was displeased. In sullen anger he left
Kamakura for his native Izu.[78] Although this incident seems to
have been quickly forgotten and amicably settled, it placed many
vassals who were followers of the Hōjō under severe strain, for
they had to choose between staying at Kamakura with Yoritomo or
leaving for Izu to join their immediate lord.

Although Yoritomo was not entirely consistent in his policies
and measures toward the warrior class in general, it is apparent that
certain principles of conduct for vassals in their relationship to each
other and to the lord were evolving at Kamakura. These principles
were still vague and not formalized into anything like a code, but
the basic ideas and ideals to which Yoritomo subscribed and which
he wished to instill among his followers were quite clear before
the war was a few months old. Basically, and quite naturally for
a feudal lord, Yoritomo emphasized the principle of loyalty. He
made it clear early in the war that he would not tolerate treachery
or acts of betrayal among his own followers. Thus he summarily
beheaded Ogino Toshishige who had deserted to the enemy at
the Battle of Ishibashi.[79] He refused to acknowledge a service
rendered to him by Kiryū Rokurō in killing Fujiwara Toshitsuna
whose head Yoritomo was seeking, for Rokurō was a follower of
Toshitsuna and hence his act represented for Yoritomo the basest
kind of disloyalty. Rokurō had offered Toshitsuna's head to Yoritomo
on condition that he be made a vassal. Yoritomo answered that "anyone who is so unprincipled as to harbor treacherous intentions

[76] Juei 1:6,1.   [77] Juei 1:11,10.   [78] Juei 1:11,14.   [79] Jishō 4:11,12.

against his own hereditary lord and to kill him is not deserving of an award" and ordered that Rokurō be decapitated.[80]

By the same token, Yoritomo honored acts of loyalty even among the enemy. The most notable example involved a youth captured in Hitachi during the battle against the Satake. Before Yoritomo the boy spoke his mind fearlessly, condemning Taira Hirotsune who had ambushed and killed one of the Satake leaders by luring him to the middle of a bridge to talk terms. He was also critical of Yoritomo for setting aside the chastisement of the Heike for the killing of a fellow Genji, for the Satake were of Minamoto stock. Yoritomo admired the youth's fearless loyalty to his own lord, and against the wishes of Taira Hirotsune and other vassals, who would have killed the boy at once, Yoritomo gave the youth the name of Iwase Yoichi Tarō and admitted him into the ranks of his immediate vassals.[81]

Again, Yoritomo honored a member of Taira Hirotsune's family for his loyalty to Hirotsune during the period when the latter was out of favor at Kamakura.[82] In many similar cases Yoritomo made allowances for the loyalty of warriors to enemy lords. Minamoto Mitsuyuki, for instance, had served a Taira lord faithfully for many years in Buzen. To Yoritomo, this alone was not cause enough for punishment and he quickly granted Mitsuyuki's request for pardon.[83]

It is clear that Yoritomo was attempting to instill loyalty among his vassals in a manner morally acceptable to the warrior class. He was not entirely consistent in the handling of his men, sometimes sacrificing principle for expediency. Thus a follower of Hori Chikaie in the Shimizu incident described above was sacrificed for the sake of peace in the Minamoto-Hōjō family. Asaba Munemori, a manorial official in Ōmi Province, had refused to provide labor for the construction of defenses and had, moreover, insulted Yoritomo's chief vassal in the region. On the plea of the latter to Yoritomo to authorize punishment and the seizure of Asaba's lands, Yoritomo ruled in favor of Asaba against his own vassal on the ground that the Genji needed the services of Asaba's sons and numerous following in an area such as Ōmi, where the Genji following was

---

[80] Yōwa 1:9,7; 9,13; 9,16; and 9,18.　　[81] Jishō 4:11,4; 11,8.
[82] This was Hara Takaharu of Owari, son-in-law of Hirotsune. See Juei 3:3,13.
[83] Juei 3:4,14 and **Genreki** 1:4,22.

small.[84] But on the whole Yoritomo was remarkably successful in inculcating high ideals of loyalty among his vassals.

One other aspect of loyalty which contributed toward the establishment of the shogunate later was Yoritomo's own loyalty to the throne and that of his vassals to the throne. Normally this was not a matter of serious concern to the warrior class generally; for their service was given to their lord, and it was the lord who determined the nature of that service. If, as was the custom, the lord prescribed guard duty at the Kyoto court for the vassal, the latter, in carrying out the order, would still be performing a service to his lord. However, in this case, he would be performing a private service to his lord and a public service to the court at one and the same time. Feudal service, in other words, could be and frequently was a public service.

This confusion of public and private service had begun in Japan much earlier. When the Fujiwara family controlled the Kyoto court, it was frequently difficult to make a distinction between an order issued by them as private individuals and an order issued by them as officials of the government. The fact was that an order emanating from the *mandokoro*, the private family administration of the Fujiwara, carried with it virtually the same authority as an order from a department of the government, and there was an equal vagueness as to whether a service given in compliance with such an order was private or public. Similarly, in the provinces it was hardly expected of the people to distinguish between public and private authority. To many in the east Yoritomo represented authority of both a private and public nature.

Certain developments in the provinces clearly reflected this amalgamation and confusion of authority. Terms such as *kan* and *tsukasa* (or the Sinico-Japanese reading of *shi* and *ji*), meaning "office" and "official" and used initially only in a public sense, had come, by the twelfth century, to be applied to private officials as well, as in *shōkan* and *shōji*, the terms for "manorial officials."

In fact, even the term *hōkō* meaning "service" or "to render service," used in the Nara period for services given to the emperor and the government, had acquired a private, feudal connotation. Yoritomo used it for services rendered to him by his vassals. But it is

[84] See Jishō 5:3,13; 3,14; and 4,30.

important to note that he used it frequently with the connotation that loyal service given to him was at the same time service given to the throne. Thus, in his letter to the local lords of Sanuki praising them for their offer of *hōkō,* or service, to him, Yoritomo prescribed that service to be their immediate submission to his deputy in the region and participation in the war against the enemies of the imperial court.[85] It must also be remembered that Yoritomo had consistently maintained that his purpose in waging war was to destroy the enemies of the imperial court, and hence any service rendered to him was, indirectly, a service rendered to the throne. The only condition of *hōkō* was that it must be offered directly to him, a necessary means for the control of his vassals.

At any rate, the impression which Yoritomo created among his vassals and the people generally was that his war against the Heike was just and that any military service contributed toward his victory was a service contributed toward the preservation of the throne. And this impression was strengthened by his policy of leaving the traditional system of local government intact as far as possible, by his assurances in writing to the court that it might resume local rule throughout the country in due time, and, in general, by the deference he showed toward the ex-sovereign. This record of insistence upon loyalty to the throne gave to Yoritomo's government a strong legal and moral claim to continue to operate as the protector of the court and the country. It explains in part the wide acceptance and the permanence of the Kamakura shogunate.

[85] Genreki 1:9,19.

Chapter VI
The Establishment
of the Shogunate

THE IMMEDIATE RESULTS OF DANNOURA

The thoroughness of the defeat of the Taira at Dannoura is apt to leave one with the impression that the authority of the victor, the Minamoto, now extended over the entire country. This is, of course, erroneous. The Minamoto, it must be remembered, did not wage war over the question of who should rule the country. The war, in its origins, was a feudal conflict in which the principals, particularly the Minamoto, were concerned primarily with the preservation of their customary feudal rights and interests in the areas where such rights and interests were concentrated. True, the victors were also interested in the spoils of war, but the latter was limited to the private property and private rights of the defeated foe and included none of the vast public powers once exercised and enjoyed by the conquered Taira. In fact, the Minamoto disclaimed any interest in succeeding the Taira as the dominant family or group in Kyoto.

But Minamoto influence prevailed in Eastern and North Central Japan, and it expected official recognition of this fact after the Battle of Dannoura. The area in question included Kanto, or the eight provinces of Sagami, Izu, Kai, Musashi, Shimōsa, Kazusa, Hitachi, and Awa, as well as the central provinces of Shinano, Kōzuke, and Shimotsuke. It included also the remote northern province of Dewa and the provinces of Echizen, Kaga, and Etchū facing the Japan Sea. The provinces stretching along the eastern shore between Sagami and the Kyoto region and including Suruga, Tōtomi, Mikawa, Owari, Mino, and Iga comprised another area where Minamoto interests were dominant. Beyond these areas the only other province in which the Minamoto enjoyed priority was Bungo in northeastern Kyushu. In other words, Minamoto influence extended over twenty-two provinces, or only one third of the total number of sixty-six provinces which comprised Japan. Moreover, the degree of Yoritomo's control over the region recognized as being within his sphere of influence differed from province to province.

It is important to note that the areas mentioned were brought under Yoritomo's control before the Battle of Dannoura—the eastern provinces as early as 1181, and the central provinces early in 1184 following the death of Yoshinaka. After Noriyori's army reached Bungo in Kyushu in the Second Month of 1185, two months before the victory at Dannoura, that area was also brought under Minamoto control. Thus, territorially, the final victory at Dannoura gave to the Minamoto little that it had not already gained earlier in the war.

Even in the matter of the so-called Heike *mokkan-ryō,* or "lands confiscated from the Heike," the Minamoto did not gain much. Actually Heike lands were extensive, numbering some five hundred separate manors. However, since the Heike had arbitrarily seized most of these lands at the height of their power and influence, their former owners, including many temples and shrines, promptly claimed them as their lawful property upon the fall of the Taira. Since Yoritomo was pledged to return such lands to their lawful owners, he personally and the Minamoto as a group profited little in this respect by defeating the Taira. However, his claim to such lands and his right to dispose of them as he saw fit was recognized not only by feudal custom but also by the imperial court.[1]

In theory the victory gave Yoritomo complete military rights over his vassals and complete civil authority to appoint and dismiss officials for his private government at Kamakura, to make grants of land and other forms of awards to his vassals, to confirm the holdings of his vassals or to dispossess them, and, in general, to expect and if necessary to compel various kinds of services from his vassals. But, again, these were the customary rights of a feudal lord which Yoritomo had exercised and enjoyed before Dannoura. The

[1] For examples of Yoritomo's disposition of former Heike lands, see Genreki 1:6,23 and 12,1.

difference in his power and authority after the victory was, therefore, one of degree.

From another point of view, however, the results of Dannoura
were of extreme significance. Yoritomo's defeat of the Taira forces
meant that he was the undisputed military power in the entire
nation. He had successfully challenged his most formidable foe.
He was now free to carry on in Eastern Japan as the leader of the
Genji. However, any success in governing the region presupposed
his control over his vassals. And this was a problem as great as, if
not greater than, prosecuting a war.

THE CONTROL OF VASSALS

The victory at Dannoura had, in fact, only aggravated the difficulties of controlling the Genji. Great distances now separated
Yoritomo from his vassals. With the prestige of a Minamoto victory
behind them the Genji warriors in the west tended to become more
assertive and independent of his control.

The gravity of the situation was emphasized by the fact that the
misbehavior of Genji warriors centered for the most part in Kyoto
and its immediate environs, the center of most of the private and
public interests of the imperial court. This seriously complicated his
attempts to retain the goodwill of the court which he had so studi-
ously cultivated during the war. Even before Dannoura, Yoritomo
had to order a vassal in Kyoto to desist from interfering with lands
belonging to the imperial storehouse and to remind him that its
control was vested in the minister of the treasury.[2]

There were many forewarnings of this problem on the eve of
Dannoura. Frequently Yoritomo was compelled to send special
groups of warriors from Kamakura to arrest members of the Genji
accused of perpetrating all manner of crimes and fraud. There was,
for example, the instance of warriors claiming to be members of
the Genji who had commended lands to a sister of Kiso Yoshinaka,
using old, canceled documents for the purpose, "then, claiming to
be her agents, they intruded on private and public land." [3] There
were also complaints from the court that the Genji, on the pretext
of prosecuting the war against the Heike, were seizing provisions

[2] Genreki 2:3,2.   [3] Genreki 2:3,3.

in the home provinces.[4] The court, in fact, implored Yoritomo to stop sending more Kanto troops to Kyoto. In reply Yoritomo assumed responsibility for the conduct of his men, but at the same time reminded the court that it was imperative to press the war against the Heike, and that the present deplorable situation with regard to Kanto warriors in Kyoto would be corrected at the conclusion of the war.[5]

Meanwhile, as an expression of his good faith, Yoritomo had despatched a mission to Kyoto and charged it with the responsibility of checking the lawless activities of isolated groups of warriors. The mission, headed by Nakahara Hisatsune, a courtier and a scribe by training, and Kondō Kunihira, a warrior, was ordered to begin its policing in the provinces of western Honshu and to proceed to Kyushu and Shikoku later.[6]

Shortly after this mission arrived in the west to begin its work the Gempei War came to an end, and incidents of open disregard for law and order involving Genji warriors increased in the western provinces. Only a month after Dannoura even deputies of Yoritomo's chief vassals in the home provinces, who had been assigned to the various districts to maintain order, were being accused of ignoring the rights of land owners and the orders of local officials, and of seizing provisions and lands, including parcels belonging to the imperial family.[7]

In Kyoto itself an outbreak of robbery was reported, although Yoritomo was informed that the perpetrators in this instance were former Heike warriors. However, as Yoritomo assumed the responsibility of maintaining law and order, and as the danger existed of Genji warriors being among the bands of thieves or of becoming involved with them, he issued strict orders to his principal vassals in the Kyoto area to put down robbery and lawlessness immediately.[8] He rewarded Genji followers who performed meritoriously in suppressing outlawry in the capital. Thus a Genji warrior was specially honored by Yoritomo for having apprehended a thief who had attempted to rob the imperial palace of one of its sacred swords.[9]

Yoritomo was also to learn that the lawless elements of the Genji frequently made no distinction as to those whom they victimized.

[4] Genreki 2:2,5.　[5] Genreki 2:3,4.　[6] Genreki 2:2,5.　[7] Genreki 2:4,26.
[8] Genreki 2:5,19.　[9] Genreki 2:5,27.

Even respected Genji were among the victims. Thus Minamoto Shigetō, the eighty-year-old governor of Dewa and a descendant of a collateral branch of the Minamoto, made the long journey from Ōmi where he had been living to declare before Yoritomo that "since the assumption of authority by Your Lordship, when I had expected my anxieties to diminish, instead my troubles and cares have increased, due to the conduct of Your Lordship's warriors residing in the capital. I have been subjected to their oppressive demands for military levies and guard duty. . . . I have not been subjected to such indignities even under the Heiji. . . ." [10]

Shigetō appears to have been a resident of Ōmi Province at the time, but in neighboring Tōtomi Province the situation seems to have been worse. There Genji vassals, high in Yoritomo's regard, were reported to have intimidated provincial officials and lords of manors into handing over their titles to land and to have seized forcibly the agricultural produce of smaller cultivators. Among those believed to have acquired large parcels of private and public lands in this way was Minamoto Aritsuna, son of Nakatsuna, the governor of Izu. [11]

To Yoritomo personally perhaps the most shocking news of this sort to reach him from Kyoto was that regarding his old and revered friend, the priest Mongaku. The priest, it was reported, was using questionable means to increase the land holdings of his temple. Using an earlier recommendation which Yoritomo had given him, Mongaku had gained access to the ex-sovereign and had obtained the imperial seal on a history of his temple, the Shingo-ji. As the history, verified by an imperial seal, contained false claims to land which were held by others, Mongaku confronted the latter with this certified evidence and forced such persons to make "donations" of land to his temple. [12]

Fortunately for Yoritomo, these acts of Genji outlawry were committed for the most part by small, isolated bands of warriors. His principal vassals in the west, such as Noriyori and Wada Yoshimori in Kyushu, and Doi Sanehira and Kajiwara Kagetoki in the home provinces, remained loyal to him and attempted to carry out his orders conscientiously. They had stayed at their posts at Yoritomo's specific command to hold the gains made in the war and

[10] Genreki 2:4,28.   [11] Genreki 2:5,19.   [12] Genreki 2:7,15.

to stabilize the situation in the west.[13] And thus, through their efforts and the cooperation they gave to the special Nakahara-Kondō mission, outlawry was greatly reduced and the relationships among land owners, the court, the people in the west, and the victorious Genji improved noticeably.

There were other problems of vassalage which were, in certain respects, unique to Yoritomo. During the last phase of the war when the need for men, provisions, and boats was great, Yoritomo had dispensed with some of the customary procedures connected with vassalage and had enrolled many warriors of Shikoku and Kyushu as vassals. Most of these men he had never met, but he had taken the word of his deputies in the region and had enrolled them without a question. Their obligation to Yoritomo was to oppose the Heike and to contribute men and materials to the war effort. This they seem to have done. On the other hand, Yoritomo had promised to confirm their holdings and to protect them. However, as many of them had been Taira partisans until the last few weeks of the war, their lands, in many instances, were seized by Genji warriors after the war. To straighten out the confusion with regard to lands which might or might not be seized was one of the reasons for the extension of the Nakahara-Kondō mission from Honshu to Kyushu and Shikoku.

YORITOMO AND THE COURT

The conduct of his men in the west was important to Yoritomo not only as an indication of his control over them but also because of the need to retain the friendship and the good will of the ex-sovereign, the court, and the people of the west for his government at Kamakura. Since 1180 Yoritomo had twice suffered the degradation of being officially named as a rebel of the state by the ex-sovereign, and he was determined not to suffer a third degradation, especially in the wake of a great victory.

On the whole, Yoritomo's relations with the ex-sovereign had been cordial since the disposal of Yoshinaka early in 1184. Yoritomo's troops in Kyoto were ordered to seek the approval of the ex-sovereign for any action they might take. As a mark of respect to

[13] Genreki 2:4,12.

the ex-sovereign, members of his court who were apprehended by Yoritomo's troops as partisans of Yoshinaka were turned over to the imperial police for prosecution.[14] Just before Dannoura the ex-sovereign had complied with Yoritomo's request for a special proclamation directed to local lords of Kyushu to join in the war against the Heike.[15] Following the victory the ex-sovereign congratulated Yoritomo with a proclamation, crediting his success "entirely to Yoritomo's skillful military strategy," and expressing his pleasure at the victory.[16] In the same month the ex-sovereign raised Yoritomo's rank to junior second rank.[17]

Meanwhile, Yoritomo sought to console the ex-sovereign for one of the casualties of the war—the loss of the Sacred Mirror—and ordered Noriyori in Kyushu to make every effort to retrieve and return it to the court.[18]

The establishment of good will toward Yoritomo and his government was immeasurably promoted by the work of Nakahara Hisatsune and Kondō Kunihira. Yoritomo himself attached great importance to their mission. He had originally instructed them to suppress lawlessness among the warriors but, at the same time, to act only in accordance with the decrees of the ex-sovereign. Later, as evidence of the importance with which he regarded it, he assigned six special servants to serve the mission which was occupied at the time with the adjudication of claims to land. It is interesting to note that Yoritomo took the occasion to caution Hisatsune against accepting "material support from others" and Kunihira from showing any bias in the execution of his duties.[19]

That this mission assisted the court in other ways may be seen in the request made to it by the ex-sovereign regarding a local lord in Owari who had disobeyed orders of the imperial court. When this matter was reported to Kamakura by the mission Yoritomo took prompt measures to remedy the situation. The same entry notes that Yoritomo was greatly pleased with the work of the mission.[20]

Shortly thereafter Yoritomo ordered the mission to Kyushu to

---

[14] Juei 3:2,23.
[15] The decree is dated Genreki 2:2,2. It appears in the entry for Genreki 2:3,29.
[16] Genreki 2:4,14.
[17] The rank was conferred on the twenty-seventh of the Fourth Month; the announcement reached Kamakura on Genreki 2:5,9.
[18] Genreki 2:3,14.   [19] Genreki 2:5,25.   [20] Genreki 2:6,16.

look into the matter of unrestrained outlawry by warriors and the confused situation with regard to the ownership of manors. Its immediate purpose, which was pleasing to court members who were the nominal owners of many lands there, was "to restore lands to their original owners, whether provincial officials or lords of manors, so that the payment of annual tributes might be resumed." [21]

Another aspect of both the control and discipline of his vassals and of his relationship with the imperial court was the problem of the acceptance of court ranks and offices by Genji warriors without his prior approval. Actually the records do not indicate that many Genji received appointments without Yoritomo's recommendation. But this was a matter of such importance to Yoritomo that he took some of his sternest measures against his men who violated this rule. Thus, even as scattered reports of the victory at Dannoura were coming in to Kamakura, Yoritomo issued a directive charging twenty-four Genji warriors with having accepted posts, mostly military positions in the imperial guard, without merit and without his recommendation. They were forbidden to return to Kanto "east of Sunomata" except at the risk of their lives and dispossession of their lands.[22]

It may be added that, with the exception of Koyama Tomomasa, none of these men was prominent at Kamakura. Yet Yoritomo used the most vindictive and in some instances the vilest of language in accusing them of perfidy and disloyalty. He wrote of one of them, "He has the eyes of a rat," and of another, who had received the post of lieutenant, "There is a softness about his face which makes his appointment unusual." Of still another he wrote: "It cannot be forgotten that he has declared the Lord of Kamakura to be an evil man. . . . Rarely might one find a more villainous lieutenant." [23] Although these men were permitted to serve the court on condition that they remain out of Kanto, Yoritomo demanded cancellation of the appointment of some of them.[24] But in all of these cases Yoritomo placed greater responsibility on his vassals for having disobeyed his orders than on the ex-sovereign.

The one serious development of the postwar period which marred the good will for the Genji at the court and in the west generally

[21] Genreki 2:7,12.   [22] Genreki 2:4,15.   [23] *Ibid.*
[24] See the case of Shibuya Shigesuke, Genreki 2:5,9.

was the deterioration of Yoritomo's relationship with his brother, Yoshitsune, and the eventual involvement of the ex-sovereign in their quarrel.

Since Yoshitsune's acceptance of court favors in 1184 without having obtained his brother's prior approval, Yoritomo had become suspicious and jealous of his younger brother. Furthermore, the latter had emerged from the war a greater hero than ever. It was duly noted at Kamakura that the ex-sovereign had first sent a special emissary to congratulate Yoshitsune for his achievement at Dannoura,[25] and only subsequently despatched another emissary to Kamakura to congratulate Yoritomo, even though the latter was the chief of the Genji.[26]

Yoritomo's suspicions of his brother were heightened by a lengthy letter from Kajiwara Kagetoki who had served with Yoshitsune at the battles of Yashima and Dannoura. Kagetoki, a member of the *samurai-dokoro,* had been assigned to Yoshitsune's command to look after the affairs of the troops as Wada Yoshimori, the president of the *samurai-dokoro,* had been assigned to Noriyori's command in western Honshu and in Kyushu. His message accused Yoshitsune of highhandedness and excessive pride, and of harboring ambitions of his own. Kagetoki also charged that Yoshitsune was suffering under the delusion that the victory was the result mainly of his own efforts, and that he refused to countenance the suggestion that the victory was due "to the cooperative efforts of a large force." Kagetoki declared that his own life was in danger for having made the suggestion that Yoritomo might not be pleased with Yoshitsune's attitude. He asked Yoritomo for permission to terminate his attendance on Yoshitsune and that he be recalled to Kamakura.[27]

Following Kagetoki's charges, events moved rapidly toward a complete break between the brothers. Yoritomo ordered his vassals in the west not to serve under Yoshitsune.[28] In particular he instructed Noriyori to ignore any orders issued by Yoshitsune.[29]

Meanwhile, rumors to the effect that Yoshitsune was planning to seize control of Kyushu reached Kamakura.[30] In fact, Noriyori, in complaining to Yoritomo through a succession of messengers that his freedom to discharge his duties in Kyushu had been curtailed,

[25] Genreki 2:4,14.   [26] Genreki 2:4,21.   [27] *Ibid.*   [28] Genreki 2:4,29.
[29] Genreki 2:5,5.   [30] *Ibid.*

implied that interference by Yoshitsune was the cause.[31] And thus, although Yoshitsune himself took the trouble to send a messenger to Kamakura to deny the allegations against him and to declare his loyalty,[32] Yoritomo seems to have made up his mind as to how he would treat his brother. Yoritomo had already sided with Kagetoki in his quarrel with Yoshitsune, and had relieved him from any further obligation to serve Yoshitsune.[33] Moreover, Yoritomo was irked that, whereas Noriyori had maintained a steady communication with him, Yoshitsune had not. The latter had taken the trouble to explain his point of view only after he had learned of Yoritomo's displeasure.[34] This was conduct unbecoming of a loyal vassal.

The fact is that Yoritomo's men watched Yoshitsune's every move and act and interpreted them in the worst light. When, for example, Yoshitsune had stopped in Kyoto between the twenty-fourth of the Fourth Month and the seventh of the following month, he had participated in a ceremony in observance of the return of the Sacred Mirror to the palace. On that occasion the penetrating eyes of Yoritomo's men had not failed to detect that Yoshitsune wore the uniform of an imperial police under his armor.[35] The implication was that Yoshitsune showed preference for the ex-sovereign who had conferred the office of imperial police on him against Yoritomo's wishes.

But meanwhile Yoritomo continued to act as Yoshitsune's lord and ordered him to escort the high prisoners of war captured at Dannoura to Kamakura. Yoshitsune complied with the order and he and his party left Kyoto on the seventh of the Fifth Month. On the fifteenth, the day before he was expected on the outskirts of Kamakura, Yoritomo assigned a delegation of vassals headed by Hōjō Tokimasa to meet Yoshitsune, receive the prisoners from him, and to instruct him not to enter Kamakura.[36] Yoritomo had decided to cut off his brother from the ranks of the Genji.

The meeting took place as planned. The site was Koshigoe, the entrance to Kamakura, and, ironically, the execution grounds for the Kamakura government. Yoshitsune waited at Koshigoe for nearly ten days, hoping that his brother would change his mind or that he himself might be given the opportunity to explain his position.

---

[31] Genreki 2:5,7.　[32] *Ibid.*　[33] Genreki 2:5,4.　[34] Genreki 2:5,7.
[35] Genreki 2:4,24.　[36] Genreki 2:5,15.

When it appeared highly improbable that Yoritomo would reverse
or modify his earlier decision, Yoshitsune wrote a letter, the now
classic "Letter from Koshigoe," addressing it to Ōe Hiromoto and
imploring him to speak to Yoritomo in his behalf.[37] In the letter
Yoshitsune made it clear that he had expected to be honored for his
"prodigious deeds" on the field of battle and that he was profoundly
hurt by the vicious slander against him. He declared that his slander-
ers not only were keeping him out of Kamakura but also made it
impossible for him to prove the falseness of their slander, for, he
wrote, "good medicine is bitter to the taste and true words are
harsh to the ear. . . ." Yoshitsune even defended his acceptance of
the military title of lieutenant of the fifth rank, arguing that such
an appointment was an honor to the house of Minamoto.

But despite his eloquence there was no reply from his brother.
Instead, he was given the assignment, his very last as a Genji, of
taking Taira Munemori, one of the prisoners he had brought from
Dannoura, back to Kyoto.[38] Thus, on the ninth of the Sixth Month,
Yoshitsune left Koshigoe for the west, "his resentment more profound than ever." A few days later Yoshitsune was dropped from
the ranks of the Genji when his brother dispossessed him of the
twenty-four estates of confiscated Heike lands which had been given
to him earlier.[39]

But the Yoshitsune problem was far from solved. His ability,
personal charm, and popularity were a constant threat to Yoritomo's
leadership. Rumors reached Kamakura of an alliance developing
between Yoshitsune and Yukiie, Yoritomo's uncle. Therefore a
secret mission was sent from Kamakura to Kyoto to probe into
Yoshitsune's intentions and to determine the whereabouts of Yukiie.[40] The report of the mission convinced Yoritomo that the alliance between Yoshitsune and Yukiie might materialize and that
it threatened his leadership of the Genji. The only solution to this
threat appeared to be to destroy Yoshitsune.

Although this decision was arrived at by Yoritomo in council
with his chief vassals, it could not have been a very popular one;
for a virtually unknown warrior-monk, Tosabō Shōshun, volun-

---

[37] The letter in its entirety may be found in the entry for Genreki 2:5,24.
[38] Genreki 2:6,9.   [39] Genreki 2:6,13.   [40] Bunji 1:9,2: 10,6.

teered for the mission "when many others had excused themselves." [41] At any rate, Shōshun was able to muster eighty-three men
and to depart for Kyoto. The Shōshun mission was to end disas-
trously. His surprise attack on Yoshitsune at the latters' residence in
Kyoto failed and Shōshun himself was hunted down by Yoshitsune's
retainers and killed.[42]

The political consequences of the failure of the mission were far
more disastrous to Yoritomo than the military defeat. It brought
Yoshitsune and Yukiie, whom Yoritomo was trying to separate,
closer together. It also brought the two allies closer to the ex-
sovereign whose good will Yoritomo had been trying to cultivate.
The incident convinced the ex-sovereign that the private feud
within the Minamoto family was a matter directly affecting the
safety of the court and that the only persons in or near the capital
capable of protecting the court were Yoshitsune and Yukiie. Therefore, he acceded to the persistent demands of Yoshitsune to declare
Yoritomo's action as being contrary to imperial law and to authorize
Yoshitsune and Yukiie to take up arms against Yoritomo.[43]

Yoritomo's indignation at this latest development was great, being
directed especially toward the ex-sovereign, to whom he had been
showing every courtesy. Only a few days earlier, at the request of
the ex-sovereign, he had taken steps to punish a vassal in Owari
who had seized lands belonging to Ise Shrine.[44] He had even ac-
ceeded to the ex-sovereign's request to remit expenses for the office
of the high priestess of the Ise Shrine.[45] Taking advantage of a gathering of his vassals at Kamakura for the dedication of the *Shōchōju-in,*
the Buddhist temple to honor the memory of Yoshitomo, Yoritomo
made plans to lead an expedition personally to Kyoto.[46]

It is interesting to observe, as an indication of the extent of Yoritomo's anger, that throughout the war he had not ventured farther
west than the Fuji River in neighboring Suruga Province nor anywhere farther than Hitachi. It is also interesting to note, as an indication of the limited strength of the Genji, that, though there were
2,916 principal vassals who assembled at Kamakura for the dedica-

[41] Bunji 1:10,9.   [42] Bunji 1:10,17; 10,26.
[43] The decree is dated Bunji 1:10,18. For earlier developments on the relationship between Yoshitsune and the ex-sovereign, see Bunji 1:10,13; and 10,17.
[44] Bunji 1:10,14.   [45] Bunji 1:10,15.   [46] Bunji 1:10,24.

tion ceremony, only sixty-eight of them signified their willingness
to join in the expedition.[47]

Although Yoritomo did not reach Kyoto on this occasion, having
turned back to Kamakura upon learning of Yoshitsune's flight from
the capital, he had sent a smaller force to Kyoto in advance of his
own party to convey to the ex-sovereign his indignation at the court's
authorization of punitive measures against him.[48] Meanwhile the
ex-sovereign, in anticipation of Yoritomo's protests to him, had
issued orders to provincial officials in the west to make a search for
Yukiie and Yoshitsune.[49] After Yoritomo's protests were formally
conveyed to him, the ex-sovereign issued an official decree directing
provincial governors in the west to apprehend Yoshitsune and
Yukiie.[50]

In these moves of the ex-sovereign his crafty diplomacy must not
be overlooked. On the one hand, he had acceded to Yoritomo's demands by reversing his position with regard to Yoshitsune and
Yukiie but, on the other, he had not authorized Yoritomo himself
to press the search for them. There is little doubt that the ex-
sovereign was anxious to keep Genji troops out of the home
provinces where Yoshitsune and Yukiie were believed to be hiding
at the time, and also out of Shikoku and Kyushu, their ultimate
destination. This region, with the exception of Bungo in Kyushu,
was outside Yoritomo's realm of authority and the ex-sovereign knew
that the governors in these areas would probably not make any
effort to capture Yoshitsune and Yukiie.

But Yoritomo did not fall prey to the ex-sovereign's wiles. He
continued to express dissatisfaction with the official attitude, and
ordered an intensive search for his brother and uncle in the home
provinces. When it was explained to Yoritomo by one of the ex-
sovereign's ministers that it was never His Majesty's will to grant
authorization to Yoshitsune, and that the whole incident was "the
work of the devil," Yoritomo replied that the person authorizing
rebels to strike at him who had rescued the throne from the enemies
of the state was "the greatest devil of Japan." [51] These were the

---

[47] *Ibid.* These figures, however, are not indicative of the local strength of the
Genji, for each of the vassals commanded armed followings of his own.
[48] Yoshitsune and Yukiie left Kyoto on the third of the Eleventh Month. Yoritomo turned back from Kisegawa, Suruga Province, on the eighth.
[49] Bunji 1:11,6.   [50] Bunji 1:11,11.   [51] Bunji 1:11,15.

harshest words that Yoritomo was to apply to the ex-sovereign and an indication of his anger toward anyone who would impugn the wisdom of his actions against Yoshitsune. Yoritomo, in fact, backed his harsh words against the throne with action, sending another force to Kyoto, this time under Hōjō Tokimasa, perhaps the best known of his vassals. The ex-sovereign reacted quickly to this "strong representation." On the day of Tokimasa's arrival he issued a decree authorizing Yoritomo to search for and apprehend Yoshitsune and Yukiie.[52]

In this incident the ex-sovereign had failed to appreciate the intensity of Yoritomo's feelings against Yoshitsune and his determination to rid the Genji of any challenge to his leadership. At the time that the ex-sovereign complied with Yoshitsune's request for a mandate, his ministers with whom he had consulted had remarked casually that if the reasons for the court's action were subsequently explained to Yoritomo, he "would not be seriously provoked."[53] These courtiers and the ex-sovereign had completely misjudged Yoritomo. Little did they realize that Yoritomo would be so aroused as to alert his vassals west of Suruga to be in readiness for a major military campaign,[54] or that he would press his demands with a show of force. Nor did they guess in the Tenth Month that within a few weeks Yoritomo would be making other demands.

For, the granting of an imperial mandate to Yoritomo to proceed against Yoshitsune did not bring the issue to a close. Yoritomo next demanded punishment of the officials who had played a part in encouraging the ex-sovereign's friendly attitude toward Yoshitsune. Takashina Yasutsune, the minister of the Treasury, who had transmitted to the ex-sovereign Yoshitsune's request that he be allowed to attack Yoritomo, was the first high official to suffer the consequences of Yoritomo's ire. Hōjō Tokimasa, on the day after his arrival in Kyoto, persuaded the ex-sovereign to sentence Yasutsune to house confinement.[55] Yoritomo then sent to the court a list of twelve high officials whose immediate dismissal he demanded for their alleged endorsement of Yoshitsune and Yukiie.[56] Others, unnamed, who had encouraged or joined in the revolt, including the retainers of Yoshitsune and Yukiie and even monks and diviners, were or-

[52] Bunji 1:11,25. [53] Bunji 1:10,18. [54] Bunji 1:11,12. [55] Bunji 1:11,26.
[56] Bunji 1:12,6.

dered to be apprehended and to have their degree of complicity determined and appropriate penalties meted out to them.[57]

Yoritomo did not stop with a demand for the dismissal and punishment of all, high and low, implicated with Yoshitsune. He named the officials to be appointed by the ex-sovereign to replace those dismissed or to fill other vacancies. He maintained that "both the provincial officials and the more influential of the local lords have been sympathetic to the Yoshitsune rebellion," and hence the new appointments required his personal attention. Consequently he included himself among the persons recommended as governors and requested that he be appointed to Bungo.

In fact, Yoritomo's memorial to the ex-sovereign of the sixth of the Twelfth Month in which these recommendations were made constituted the most sweeping demands that he had ever made or was to make to the court. He named ten high officials of the court to be appointed by the ex-sovereign as advisory councilors. He requested that they be empowered to deliberate and advise the ex-sovereign on all matters of state, "including matters pertaining to shrines and temples." Perhaps his most drastic request to the ex-sovereign concerned Fujiwara Kanezane, the minister of the right. Yoritomo recommended Kanezane as an imperial adviser and also demanded that he be named *nairan,* or imperial examiner, whose duties were to read and approve prior to their promulgation all decrees to be issued by the ex-sovereign and to inform Yoritomo of all that occurred at the court.[58]

Compliance of the court with these measures was more or less assured by the presence of Hōjō Tokimasa and his troops in the capital. However, it was evident that Yoritomo was relying also on the support of high officials within the court, in particular, Minister of the Right Fujiwara Kanezane. Yoritomo's designation of Kanezane as the spokesman for Kamakura in the councils of the court was not made at random. Yoritomo had already taken Kanezane into his confidence. He had written Kanezane a long letter explaining his reasons for the stern measures he was taking and had urged him to speak for the carrying out of his aims.[59] It had been noted earlier at Kamakura that "the great minister of the right had consistently supported Kanto" when the question of whether to issue

[57] *Ibid.*   [58] *Ibid.*   [59] *Ibid.*

a mandate to Yoshitsune was being deliberated at the court.[60] It was also maintained at Kamakura that Kanezane's position on the Yoshitsune issue was based on sound, "coherent" reasoning and not on selfish partisanship for Kamakura.[61]

One other influential courtier whom Yoritomo expected to serve as a spokesman for Kamakura was Yoshida Tsunefusa, who held the office of provisional governor-general of Dazai-fu and middle councilor and who was also one of those recommended for imperial adviser. In Tsunefusa's case, however, it appears that he had taken the initiative in cultivating Yoritomo's friendship. As early as the Ninth Month of 1185 it was noted that Tsunefusa had been communicating with Yoritomo, that they thought alike on many issues, and that "they share[d] each other's good and bad fortunes."[62] Tsunefusa, in fact, was not without ulterior motives in befriending Yoritomo, for he sought the latter's recommendation for a promotion at the court.[63] Thus it is not surprising that he was the more vociferous of the two principal supporters of Yoritomo at the court, or that Yoritomo's communications to the court were usually transmitted through him.

It is also important to note that Yoritomo was able to make inroads into the court's authority without changing the traditional forms of court administration. Neither the office of imperial adviser nor that of imperial examiner was an innovation, but Yoritomo, by insisting on men of his choice to fill them, assured himself of a voice and a measure of control in the government without upsetting the system of government to which the court was accustomed.

The Yoshitsune incident had thus resulted in drawing Yoritomo out of the east into the very heart of the central government. Ironically, the latter had been desirous of keeping Yoritomo out of the west and preventing him from meddling in its affairs, while Yoritomo, until the eruption of the Yoshitsune incident, had shown no signs of wanting to interfere with the powers and functions of the court. Now the court lost full control of its own operations and Yoritomo, through his spokesmen at the court, was very much a part of the central government.

Needless to say, Go-Shirakawa, the ex-sovereign, had overplayed his hand. In the past he had maintained a favorable position for

[60] Bunji 1:11,7. [61] Bunji 1:11,11. [62] Bunji 1:9,18. [63] *Ibid.*

the court by playing one powerful warrior against another. He had succeeded in causing Yoshinaka to break with Yoritomo. He had kept the Taira from regaining entry into the capital by supporting the Minamoto. He had, in fact, succeeded in driving a wedge between Yoritomo and Yoshitsune by showering the latter with honors without consulting the former. That Yoritomo placed the greater share of the blame on Yoshitsune rather than on Go-Shirakawa was another evidence of the ex-emperor's masterful diplomacy. But Go-Shirakawa, needlessly and without considerate judgment, sided with Yoshitsune in the quarrel between the brothers. He had thereby transformed a private quarrel between a lord and his vassal into a public matter by ordering Yoshitsune, through the instrument of an imperial mandate, to wage war on Yoritomo. Under the circumstances, it is not surprising that Yoritomo took such determined measures against the court. By thus acquiring control of the vital operations of the central government Yoritomo had taken another step toward the establishment of the shogunate.

THE POSTING OF CONSTABLES AND STEWARDS

The excuse for the involvement of Kamakura in the affairs of the central government had been Yoshitsune. So long as he and his confederate Yukiie remained at large, the security of the Kamakura government was in jeopardy, and the court, having committed the indiscretion of endorsing Yoshitsune, had no recourse but to cooperate with Kamakura, even to the extent of sacrificing some of its traditional prerogatives. However, if the excuse for this state of affairs was Yoshitsune, his capture and disposal would in turn provide the court with an excuse to demand the withdrawal of Genji troops from Kyoto and the surrender of their newly won privileges at the court. This no doubt was Go-Shirakawa's plan. But meanwhile Yoritomo made the best of the situation and continued to press the court for more political powers.

When Hōjō Tokimasa was despatched to Kyoto with an army to coerce the court into granting an imperial mandate to Yoritomo to pursue and chastise Yoshitsune and Yukiie, he had been instructed to make a "strong representation" for another request. This was a request for the grant of authority to Yoritomo to post *shugo*, or constables, and *jitō*, or stewards, in all the provinces, and for the right to levy *hyōrōmai*, or commissariat rice tax, of 5 *shō* per *tan* on all lands, whether public or private.[64] Presumably, the first would expedite the capture of the rebels and facilitate the maintenance of peace and order in the provinces, and the second would help defray the cost of instituting such a system. Tokimasa presented the request to the ex-sovereign on the twenty-eighth of the Eleventh Month through the Middle Councilor Yoshida Tsunefusa,[65] and on the very next day the request was approved.[66] It is interesting to note, again as an example of the artful ways of the ex-sovereign, that he did not make the grant in writing. He merely ordered the middle councilor to transmit the approval orally to Hōjō Tokimasa.

The idea of posting Kamakura appointees throughout the land with the express approval of the court was the brainchild of Ōe Hiromoto, the president of the *kumon-jo* and one of Yoritomo's distinguished courtier-vassals. It had occurred to him that rebellions and disturbances outside of Eastern Japan, such as the present Yoshitsune-Yukiie incident, which required an outlay of men and material from Kamakura, could be reduced or prevented entirely if such a plan could be put into operation. He pointed out that Eastern Japan was remarkably free of troubles because of Yoritomo's presence in the region. If, therefore, his influence could be made to be felt elsewhere in the country through constables and stewards named by him, there would be peace in the land.[67]

It was a simple yet an eminently practical suggestion. To Hiromoto the east seemed to be at peace, and that peace was secure because of Yoritomo's control of the region. Yet incidents occurring elsewhere in the country where Yoritomo lacked political authority could threaten that security. Thus Yoritomo could not afford to ignore the dangers implicit in the current situation. Hiromoto reasoned further that to deal with similar incidents or disturbances in the future would require the manpower and resources of the Genji in the east. Hence the best way for Yoritomo and his vassals to enjoy the peace which they had won and to reduce to a minimum the burden of maintaining that peace and of preserving their supremacy was to seek the approval of the court for the present plan.

---

[64] A *shō* was 0.05 of a bushel. For *tan,* see Part One, Chapter II, Note 5. [65] Bunji 1:11,28. [66] Bunji 1:11,29. [67] Bunji 1:11,12.

As with so many of the measures of the Kamakura government, the merits of this proposal lay in the fact that it did not deviate radically from past practices and older institutions. Neither the *shugo* nor the *jitō* was a new kind of official. The *jitō* in particular was a well-known official whose history is closely linked with that of the manor. Known in the past by different names, he had served as an agent or manager of the owner of a manor and had performed such functions as apportioning and delivering the yield of the manor among the various shareholders. He had also collected and transmitted the taxes which the manor might owe to the government. In this latter respect he was performing a public service although he was essentially a private official. The Taira themselves had assigned *jitō* to some of their manors, so that *jitō* were, by the latter part of the twelfth century, a familiar official in the provinces. It explains in large part the court's ready acceptance of Yoritomo's proposal.

The *shugo*, whose function was to protect and to guard, as the term indicates, was no more an innovation than the *jitō*. He was heir to the *ōryōshi* and *tsuibushi* of the Heian period, the officers commissioned by the emperor in times of emergency, usually from among the ranks of local lords. During the late war Yoritomo had posted *shugo* in certain strategic provinces such as Suruga, just west of Kamakura, and Ōmi, just east of Kyoto. He had also assigned one to Iga Province, where in 1184 the Taira had threatened Genji positions. In certain respects Yoshitsune's role in Kyoto during the war had been that of a *shugo*, for in addition to looking after Genji interests there, he had been responsible for the protection of the court and the capital. Yoritomo's proposal, therefore, to assign his vassals as *shugo* to the various provinces in the emergency created by Yukiie and Yoshitsune must not have seemed unreasonable to the court.

Furthermore, the ex-sovereign could not counter Yoritomo's proposal with the argument that no emergency existed to warrant such measures, for he had as much as admitted the existence of one when he gave Yoshitsune a mandate to attack Yoritomo. Then, in rescinding the mandate and issuing another in its place, this time authorizing Yoritomo to pursue and chastise Yoshitsune, he had merely compounded the gravity of the emergency. Indeed, in the light of the ex-sovereign's own acts, it would have been difficult for him to prove that the emergency was not of his own making.

But whether or not an emergency existed, Yoritomo now had the authority to post his *jitō* and *shugo* throughout the country. It meant that his vassals, as constables and stewards, were to restore order and preserve the peace as well as collect the taxes necessary for the maintenance of peace and order throughout the land. It marked the formal recognition of Yoritomo's government as the police and military arm of the imperial court.

Important as this event was to the establishment of the Kamakura shogunate, it cannot be overemphasized that in many respects this development was the culmination of a trend which had begun in the early Heian period. The court was, after all, a government without an army. For centuries it had been dependent on private warriors for protection and for the preservation of law and order. But where formerly the court could call on a number of local lords independent of one another and each a power in his own locality to put down a rebellion or a disturbance, now, after the Gempei War, few such lords remained. Local lords were either vassals of Yoritomo or of so little power and influence that they had no value to the throne as protectors of the interests of the court, even on a local basis.

As for Yoshitsune, whose disagreement with Yoritomo had touched off the series of events which led to the establishment of Kamakura authority at the court, he managed to elude his stalkers and to escape to the comparative safety of northern Honshu and the protection of the Fujiwara. His uncle and confederate Yukiie was not so fortunate. The hapless Yukiie, who had figured in the entire history of the Gempei War in a prominent but aimless manner— offering his services first to Yoritomo, then to Yoshinaka, tiring of the latter and returning to the former, only to desert him again for Yoshitsune—was tracked down and killed in Izumi Province in 1186. It could not be said of him that he was denied the opportunity to compile a more honorable record. He had led armies on at least three occasions. In two of them he had performed miserably; in the third, as a partner of Yoshinaka in the campaigns against the Taira, he had been completely overshadowed by Yoshinaka.

Although Yoshitsune was effectively isolated from the court,

Yoritomo did not enjoy full peace of mind so long as his brother lived. The fact that the Fujiwara family, the former warden of Yoshitsune, now protected and honored its former ward with the grant of Koromogawa, a fortress reputed to be impregnable, served only to emphasize to Yoritomo the necessity of a military expedition to the north to destroy both Yoshitsune and the Fujiwara. The latter, it must be remembered, had carefully avoided embroilment in the late war. They had been strongly pro-Taira in sentiment, and now they dared to offer refuge to Yoshitsune. Moreover, it was known to Yoritomo that the imperial court was looking to the Fujiwara as a potential ally and a counterweight against Minamoto influence.

These threats were finally removed in 1189 when Yoritomo organized and personally led a military expedition to northern Japan. The Fujiwara were easily subjugated, proving that the vaunted reputation of this northern clan had been grossly exaggerated. Yoshitsune, betrayed at the last moment by the Fujiwara, preferred to take his own life, thus bringing to a close the celebrated feud of the brothers. So much sentiment—overwhelmingly in favor of Yoshitsune—has been injected into this episode by later generations of dramatists and novelists that it has been difficult for the Japanese to regard it with any degree of impartiality and fairness. Jealousy, a cold and calculating attitude, and a willingness to sacrifice even a brother for the sake of personal power are often the traits attributed to Yoritomo in popular Japanese literature. But Yoshitsune's stubborn refusal to acknowledge an indiscretion —his acceptance of honors from Go-Shirakawa without his brother's approval—and his sense of self-importance so irritating to his lord and to his peers must not be overlooked in any fair appraisal of the popular hero. Moreover, it must not be forgotten that to the leader of the Genji, anyone of stature, and in particular a Minamoto and one with a proven reputation for bravery and leadership, was a constant threat to his own leadership. Yoshitsune, by his fame and by his command of the sympathy of the ex-sovereign and the court, could easily become the rallying point for a movement to displace Yoritomo. By the very nature of vassalage, the lord can not for long tolerate a vassal who is more popular, famous, and influential than the lord himself.

Fundamentally, it was just such problems of lord and vassal relationship, complicated by the Gempei War and the victory of the Minamoto, which lay at the bottom of the increased power of Yoritomo. The system of constables and stewards was essentially an attempt of a feudal lord to keep control of his vassals, now greatly increased in number and scattered throughout the country. That the system, intended to reduce the incidence of rebellions and disturbances in the country, was sanctioned by the court meant that the maintenance of the public peace was now, formally and officially, the responsibility of Yoritomo and his vassals. Yoritomo's headquarters was no longer a strictly private administration. And thus, except in name, the Kamakura shogunate was established by the close of 1185.

Chapter VII
Conclusion

THE SCOPE AND SIGNIFICANCE OF THE WAR

Although there were long periods of inactivity in the Gempei War, it had lasted for five years. It had spread from Eastern Japan to the western tip of Honshu. There had been fighting in Kyushu and Shikoku, as well as in Central Japan. Although no battles were fought in northern Honshu, its local lords, especially the Fujiwara, were constantly a factor in the strategy of the warring armies. Even Tsushima, off western Honshu, was affected, its governor fleeing for safety to Korea.[1] And thus, for a feudal conflict, the Gempei War was unusually extensive.

The war also embroiled all classes of society. The imperial family could not escape it, losing in the course of the conflict its seat of government, one of its three symbols of sovereignty, and two of its members on opposing sides. Temples and shrines were drawn into the conflict, some by virtue of their long association with the families of the warring principals, and others because their lands were seized or violated by warriors. Thus the Gempei War was not a typical feudal war between two warrior families and their vassals and followers. It was a war of national scope and significance.

In one important respect the Gempei War was destined to assume a wider significance than a typical feudal war, for one of its principals, the Taira, was virtually the government. Its hold on the

[1] Fujiwara Chikamitsu, governor of Tsushima and a Genji supporter, while traveling to the capital in 1183, was compelled to return to Tsushima when the Taira evacuated Kyoto and began their flight to the west. After three attacks on Tsushima by Heike supporters of Northern Kyushu, Chikamitsu fled to Korea in Juei 3:3,4, where, it was reported, he was received by the king of the kingdom of Kōrai and honored with a grant of three provinces. Yoritomo's instructions to Noriyori in Kyushu to receive Chikamitsu and to provide safe passage for him appear in the *Azuma kagami* under date of Genreki 2:3,13. For other references to Chikamitsu's experiences in Korea, see Genreki 2:5,23; and especially 6,14.

imperial court was so complete that it was impossible at times to distinguish its private from its public role. To oppose the Taira was to oppose the government. And thus, from the opening of the war, the Genji had to bear the onus of being rebels to the state while the Taira enjoyed the advantage of being the *kangun,* or government troops.

To surmount this disadvantage of being called the rebels to the government, the Genji themselves attempted to present their cause to the public as a just and righteous effort to overthrow "the enemies of the imperial court." They called the Taira usurpers of the throne, offenders of the native gods, persecutors of government servants, and despoilers of private and public lands. The Taira, it was pointed out, had ignored the best traditions of the country. Consequently it was not the Genji alone who had suffered during the twenty years of Taira rule: the entire nation had been the victims of Taira despotism. Accordingly the Genji called on all elements of society —the Fujiwara, the bureaucracy both in Kyoto and in the provinces, the Buddhist Church and the Shinto Shrine, and bands of armed men anywhere in the country and of whatever family affiliation— to join in the war against the Taira. Thus the Genji denied any private motives in the war and made of it, from the very beginning, a war of national concern.

Obviously such a war, with the broadest of aims, presuming national support for their attainment, could not be prosecuted adequately by the methods, based on local needs and local conditions, of the feudal lord. The first requirement of the war, a large armed following and the control of this following, called for an administrative organization larger than the single *uhitsu,* or secretary, with whom Yoritomo had launched the war. There were messages and orders to be written and sent and even judicial cases to be heard as the warriors began to assemble. Thus, within two months after the opening of the war, Yoritomo had established a permanent headquarters at Kamakura, and within another month, he had added a board, the *samurai-dokoro,* to assist him with the management and control of his vassals and their followers. It will be recalled that paralleling the development of his headquarters, his following had increased from 300 mounted men to 200,000 men.

Thus one of the first effects of the war was the creation by the

Genji of an administrative organization, more elaborate than one customary for a feudal lord, and capable of governing and controlling a large area. By the autumn of 1184, when the Genji troops were in Kyoto and in western Honshu, and the requirements on Yoritomo's headquarters had increased proportionately, two more boards—the *kumon-jo* and the *monchū-jo*—were established. In addition to these permanent boards there was an increasing tendency at Kamakura to use the services of *bugyō*, or commissioners, to carry out specific assignments. Frequently these assignments amounted to no more than the presentation of gifts in Yoritomo's behalf to a carpenter, a priest, or a warrior for services rendered, and the writing of a congratulatory document appropriate for the occasion.

In the actual prosecution of the war itself, especially in the last phase of the struggle, there was a degree of organization unusual for a feudal army. Yoritomo created two armies, each under a separate commander. To each field commander he assigned an official of the *samurai-dokoro* to assist him with the administration and control of the warriors and with the problem of obtaining provisions and supplies. He kept in constant touch with each army, sending instructions to the commanders and receiving reports from them regularly. By such measures Yoritomo tried to keep his large following in widely separated regions under his control.

The need for greater organization meant that the highly personal character of the lord and vassal relationship could not be maintained at all times. Although Yoritomo attempted to give his personal attention to all matters, even down to the smallest detail, the demands of a large-scale war and of a large following compelled him frequently to assign others to represent him. Therefore he interposed two deputies, the field commander and a representative of the *samurai-dokoro,* between himself and even his closest vassals fighting in the west. In fact, the establishment of the *samurai-dokoro* in 1180 meant that, in theory at least, he had placed the president of the *samurai-dokoro* between himself and all of his vassals. It has also been shown that Yoritomo, as a war expediency, even enrolled many lords of Shikoku and Kyushu as vassals without meeting them and without a knowledge of their character or background. Thus the older, more simple and direct relationship between lord and vassal was affected by the scale and geographical extent of the war.

It may be noted that, because of the circumstances of a war which had wide, national implications and which were beyond the normal means of a feudal lord to cope with, "organized feudalism" had come into being. In this development adjustments in practices and customs had been necessary, not only between vassal and lord, and vassal and vassal, but also between the Genji as a group and the Kyoto court. The victor of such a war, in order to hold and enjoy the gains of the struggle, could hardly be expected to relinquish the control, the organization, and the adjustments he had achieved.

Thus Yoritomo's government at Kamakura represented the adjustments which had evolved during the struggle between the warrior class and the civilian aristocracy, and between feudal customs and imperial law. Yoritomo's administration, therefore, had to have both a feudal, local significance and a broader, national significance. In its role as headquarters of the Genji it retained its essentially feudal character. In its new role as defender of the public peace through its constables and stewards it assumed a national role. Thus after 1185 Yoritomo's government at Kamakura was no longer a purely feudal nor yet a completely national institution. However, because of this duality, it was able to meet the needs of both the warrior and court societies and to stabilize the nation.

THE CONSERVATISM OF THE
KAMAKURA SHOGUNATE

Of equally great significance was the fact that this adjustment had been achieved without a drastic, violent overturning of the established political, social, and economic institutions of either the Kyoto court or the provincial warrior society. There was surprisingly little change after the war in the life of the Kyoto noble and that of the provincial warrior. This is to say that Yoritomo's government was, essentially, a conservative institution. On the whole, it preserved traditions and strengthened precedents. The war was not intended, like the palace revolution of 645 which had ushered in the Taika Reform, to destroy an old set of values and substitute new ones. On the other hand, the purpose of the Gempei War was to solidify institutions which had been created by the war. Politically the administration and the powers of the imperial court remained virtually intact. While the court gave away some of its powers concerned with maintaining the public peace, this grant of powers merely formalized a practice which it had tacitly recognized for a long time. In many respects the court gained in power and prestige by being freed from the direct domination of the Taira. It could now, for example, appoint and assign governors to more provinces than it had been able to do under the Taira. It could exercise its customary rights in such matters as conferring rank and office with less interference than it had experienced under the Taira who had reserved every high office for members of its own family. Indeed, in this matter of conferring rank and office which it guarded jealously, it could be more assertive than ever, even toward its benefactor Yoritomo, from whom it withheld the title of shogun until 1192.

Economically the court's prospects were brighter than they had been for years. With peace restored, with measures taken by Yoritomo to return lands seized earlier by the Taira to their original owners, most of whom were members of the court, and with other measures taken by Yoritomo to reduce the incidence of violations of property rights, the prospects of an increase in public revenues and in the private incomes of the nobility were vastly improved.

For the warrior class, as for the nobility, the establishment of the Kamakura government meant the continued enjoyment of its traditional rights. There was now, in fact, a greater security for the warrior class under a strong government of its own making. True, it had made minor concessions to organization and unity, but essentially it rendered to the lord the same obligations after the war as it did before. If anything, the probability of being called upon to render the more onerous of the obligations—military service—was greatly reduced. In return for the traditional services he gave to his lord, the vassal received the protection of the lord and the guarantee, in the form of an *ando-jō,* or letter of confirmation, of his rights to land and to his following of armed men. Thus, although in theory he was less independent in 1185 under a strong leader, in practice he enjoyed greater freedom and security in the exercise of his customary rights.

Yoritomo's policies toward the temple and the shrine also showed a deep understanding of the religious traditions of the country.

The Taira, on the other hand, showed a shocking callousness towards religious traditions when it attacked and burned the Onjō-ji, Tōdai-ji, and Kōfuku-ji monasteries, and seized their lands.

The strength of Yoritomo's government lay in its adherence to custom and tradition and in the promise it held for all classes of Japanese society for the continued enjoyment of their customary way of life.

THE DUAL BACKGROUND OF MINAMOTO YORITOMO

The creation of an institution which answered the immediate needs of societies as distinct and opposed as that of the Kyoto noble and that of the provincial warrior, which was accomplished with a minimum of sacrifice to the established institutions of both, could not have been possible under a leader who was a product solely of either society. It demanded a leader who knew both societies and who understood and appreciated the values of both. In Yoritomo the country had just such a leader.

Yoritomo was a product of Kyoto rather than of the provinces. He was born in or near Kyoto. His mother was a Kyoto woman, a daughter of Fujiwara Sukenori. His wet nurses were all Kyoto women, the best known among them being the mother of Miyoshi Yasunobu. Until he was twelve years old, when he and his younger brothers were exiled from Kyoto following the Heiji Disturbance, Yoritomo was acquainted only with the life of the warrior in service at the court and knew nothing of the life of the warrior in the provinces. Although he was a mere youth of twelve years at the time of his exile, he was of an impressionable age, old enough to remember many details of his early life in Kyoto.

Thus Yoritomo was a Kyoto-bred warrior and not a typical provincial warrior as were his father-in-law Tokimasa and his cousin Yoshinaka. And hence it is not surprising that he showed a pronounced predilection for the cultural values of the courtier. He seems to have preferred the company of the courtier over that of the provincial warrior. Among the small number of retainers who visited or served him during his exile were men with court backgrounds, such as Kochūta Mitsuie, who was a Nakahara, and

Adachi Morinaga, who was a Fujiwara. Both were in his original band which launched the war in 1180, as was another courtier, Fujiwara Kunimichi, who joined the group just before the initial military action and who became Yoritomo's scribe, or secretary.

Yoritomo's favoritism for the Kyoto-trained man was well known among his vassals. Taira Hirotsune, for example, when he was out of favor at Kamakura, sent his Kyoto-bred son-in-law, Taira Tokiie, to Yoritomo to help restore friendly relations. The *Azuma kagami* notes that Tokiie was received warmly by Yoritomo, "for [His Lordship] likes guests from the capital." [2]

Even among the provincial warriors Yoritomo showed a definite preference for those who were lettered. When, for example, he accepted the services of Kajiwara Kagetoki, one of the local warriors who had opposed him at Ishibashi Mountain, Yoritomo noted that although Kagetoki did not like to meddle in literary matters, he was, nevertheless, "most adept with words." [3] Years later Yoritomo showed appreciation for Kagetoki's written reports from the west over the oral reports of Noriyori's messengers.

That Yoritomo's tastes were more aristocratic than provincial may be seen also in the activities in which he indulged, such as outings to view the cherry blossoms or the maples, [4] and in the fact that on these occasions he always invited his courtier friends or visitors from Kyoto to accompany him. It may be seen also in his efforts to bring Kai Shōshirō Akiie to Kamakura "because of his reputation as a singer of ballads," [5] and in his invitation to Fujiwara Tamehisa, a talented artist, to paint a portrait of Kwannon for him. [6] In fact, Yoritomo was probably as well versed in art as any courtier. On one occasion he criticized a mural depicting auspicious symbols of paradise and the figures of twenty-five bodhisattvas as not conforming to the original text and ordered the artist to correct the defects. [7]

Yoritomo was also interested in and well informed on the political aspects of court life. No ordinary provincial warrior could have had the knowledge of court procedure or the appreciation of the political

---

[2] Yōwa 2:1,23.

[3] Jishō 5:1,11. It may be noted that a few years later Kagetoki inadvertently put his talent with words to Yoritomo's use by writing him in a convincing manner that Yoshitsune harbored treasonable intentions toward his brother.

[4] Juei 3:4,4; Genreki 1:10,15.

[5] Genreki 1:6,18.   [6] Genreki 1:4,18.   [7] Bunji 1:10,11.

traditions of the court which Yoritomo possessed. In this regard he was far more respectful of the customary prerogatives of the throne than were the Taira. Even when he made his demands on the ex-sovereign, he was careful, first, to observe the proper procedures, sending his requests up to the throne through the middle councilor, and second, to keep his demands as far as possible within the bounds of accepted practices. The very form which his administration at Kamakura took was patterned after that of private governments of noble houses. The *samurai-dokoro,* for example, was named and patterned after an office maintained by the Fujiwara to administer the numerous guards and attendants under its control.

But while Yoritomo was an aristocrat by background and inclination, he was at the same time very much a part of the warrior society of eastern Japan of which he had been compelled to become a part and in which he had spent more than two thirds of his life. He knew the customs and traditions of the provinces as well as any provincial warrior. His interest in and promotion of the hunt, archery, horsemanship, and other martial games came from his intimate knowledge and observation of warrior life in the provinces. Even if he himself does not seem to have excelled in any of these activities nor to have participated in them, he knew the value to a warrior society of competitive games and the skills necessary for them.[8] Thus he promoted these games and personally attended them.

Again, by virtue of his understanding of the needs of a warrior society, he discouraged practices among his vassals which in his opinion were unnecessary and detrimental to that society, even if the practices in question were derived from the Kyoto court that he admired so much. Foremost among such practices were luxury and ostentation, so characteristic of court life and so unnecessary, debilitating, and demoralizing to the life of a warrior. On one occasion, when Fujiwara Toshikane appeared before his lord "dressed in a most fashionable manner, wearing ten wadded silk

---

[8] In the *Azuma kagami* there are very few references to Yoritomo's skills as a warrior, and even these are obviously exaggerated and written for their literary effect. For example, it is said of his abilities as an archer that "his arrows find their mark with unerring accuracy" and that "without fail, His Lordship's arrows —shaft and feathers—buried themselves in their mark and killed many an enemy" (Jishō 4:8,24).

garments and a skirt of many colors," Yoritomo asked for Toshikane's
sword and cut off the skirt. As if the lesson to Toshikane was too
sudden and direct for comprehension, Yoritomo spelled out a reprimand to his startled vassal. Pointing to the example of some of his
vassals who used their wealth for the support and general welfare
of their retainers, Yoritomo ordered Toshikane to cease wasting his
wealth on ostentation and luxury.[9] In such ways Yoritomo, who
was intimate with the culture of both the court and the provinces,
and who could, therefore, assess the values of the one in the light of
the other, contributed greatly to the formulation of the creed of
the warrior class.

Fundamentally, Yoritomo represented the balance necessary to
stabilize a society characterized by a distinct duality. In twelfth-century Japan there was, on the one hand, a hereditary class of aristocrats, proud of its cultural heritage, jealous of its prerogatives, pacifist
to a point of effeminacy in its attitude toward life, and disdainful of
its uncultured brethren in the provinces. It was opposed, on the
other hand, by a vigorous class of warriors, unlettered and uncultured but equally proud of its heritage which was martial rather
than pacifist, quick to assert itself, and practical and realistic almost to a fault in its attitude toward life. The fortuitous emergence
of a leader such as Yoritomo, whose life was rooted in these two
societies, not only influenced the kind of government which evolved
at Kamakura but, more important, made its establishment and its
acceptance by both societies possible.

[9] Genreki 1:11,21.

Part Two

Selected Translations from the
AZUMA KAGAMI

Translator's Note

To avoid excessive footnoting and the frequent use of various devices within the body of the text, such as brackets and parentheses, and to give the accounts a degree of readability, the translator has taken certain liberties with the original text.

The first is in the matter of names. Since the *Azuma kagami* was written and put together by a number of scribes over a period of years, there is a bewildering inconsistency in the use of names. A person may be referred to in a dozen different ways. Adachi Morinaga, for example, appears in these pages as simply Morinaga, or Fujiwara Morinaga, or Tō Kurō, or Tō Kurō Morinaga, or Adachi Tō Kurō Morinaga. It may be explained that Adachi, a place name where his lands were situated, was probably his surname, but he was of Fujiwara descent and perhaps wished this fact to be known. Tō is the Sinico-Japanese reading for *Fuji* of Fujiwara, while Kurō was his adolescent name. This example, however, does not begin to convey the difficulties involved in another exasperating practice of the writers of the *Azuma kagami*. This was the use of alternate Chinese titles, often combined with abbreviated names. Thus Minamoto Yoshitsune who held a position in the office of *kebiishi*, or imperial police, was frequently referred to as *teii*, the alternate Chinese title for *kebiishi*. He was also *Yoshū*, the abbreviation for Iyo Province, of which he was governor. Finally, the name Minamoto was often given its Sinico-Japanese reading of *Gen*, especially with reference to Yoshitsune. Hence Gen Kurō was none other than Minamoto Yoshitsune, Kurō being his adolescent name. Yoritomo, the principal personage in these pages, was addressed more often as *buei*, the Chinese title for *hyōe*, or military guards, in which he once held office. After his elevation to the second court rank, his vassals presumed to refer to him as *nihon,,* a special title reserved for members of the imperial family who held the second rank. In all these cases the translator has taken the liberty of identifying the person in question with one or more names, without burdening the translations with bracketed explanations and footnotes. Needless to say, this liberty was taken only where the identification was reasonably certain.

Another liberty has been exercised by the translator in the reading of personal and place names. Anyone familiar with the Japanese language knows how frustrating it is to establish the correct reading of names. A surname such as Tako may well be read as Ōko, and Amawa as Amō. A strong case for either reading can be made in each instance. Again, the translator has made no attempt to crowd these pages with footnote citations to the authorities who might favor one reading over the other. However, biographical and geographical dictionaries have been carefully checked. In this connection, the most useful dictionary for the identification of archaic and medieval place names, as well as surnames, is Yoshida Tōgo's *Dai-Nihon chimei jisho* in seven volumes.

In the translation of titles, offices, and ranks, the translator has followed for the most part the suggestion of Jean and Robert Karl Reischauer in their book, *Early Japanese History*. However, many of the translations have been shortened in these pages. For example, the title, lieutenant of the Outer Palace Guards, Right Division, has been shortened in some places to lieutenant of the Right Outer Palace Guards. Other references which are extremely useful in this regard are: Coates and Ishizuka, *Honen the Buddhist Saint*, pp. 109–19; and G. B. Sansom, "Early Japanese Law and Administration," *TASJ* (2nd Series), IX, 67–109; XI, 117–49.

For each entry the translator has provided at the beginning an italicized summary of the main points covered in the entry. Where the entry is extremely brief only the summary appears. Some of the longer entries, especially if they contain details already touched upon in an earlier entry, have also been reduced to summaries. Finally, repetitious matter has sometimes been deleted in these translations. Where such deletions occur they have been indicated with the usual marks.

Chapter I

FOURTH MONTH

9th day. *Minamoto Yorimasa in Kyoto plots the overthrow of the Taira.*

The lay priest[1] and courtier, third rank, Minamoto Yorimasa had been planning for a long time to overthrow the lay priest and chancellor Taira Kiyomori. But realizing the difficulty of accomplishing this long-cherished ambition by his stratagem alone, he, together with his son Nakatsuna, the governor of Izu, secretly called this evening on Prince Mochihito, the second son of the ex-sovereign, at the Sanjō-Takakura Palace and urged him to join in the destruction of the Taira and to assume the rule of the country himself. He would be aided in the effort by Minamoto Yoritomo, the former assistant captain of the Military Guards, Right Division, and his followers of the Minamoto clan. The Prince instructed Munenobu, Scattered Rank,[2] to issue a pronouncement[3] rallying the country against the Taira. As Minamoto Jūrō Yoshimori, the youngest son of the imperial police Minamoto Tameyoshi, happened to be in the capital, he was ordered to take the pronouncement to Yoritomo and to the other members of the Minamoto clan in the eastern provinces. Yoshimori, ap-

[1] *Nyūdō,* literally, "one who has entered the way," a title given to those who had taken the Buddhist tonsure but who had not actually joined or entered a monastery. It was fashionable among members of the titled nobility to become lay priests, usually after retirement from civil office.

[2] *San'i.* It was customary for one's court rank to correspond with his office—the higher the office, the higher the court rank. However, when one's office and rank did not correspond, the latter was termed "scattered."

[3] This was technically a *reishi,* i.e., a pronouncement by any member of the imperial family, and not a formal, public edict or decree by the emperor. Examples of the latter, of which there was a bewildering variety, appear later in these pages.

pointed a private secretary to Hachijō-in,[4] has changed his name to Yukiie.

27th day. *Yoritomo receives Prince Mochihito's pronouncement.*

Prince Mochihito's pronouncement borne by Yukiie reached Yoritomo today at the Hōjō residence in Izu Province. Wearing ceremonial robes and bowing respectfully toward distant Otoko-yama,[5] Yoritomo gave instructions to have the pronouncement opened and read. Meanwhile, Yukiie departed for Kai and Shinano to notify the Minamoto of the purport of the prince's directive.

It is twenty sad years since the 11th day of the Third Month of Eireki 1 [1160] when Yoritomo, involved in the disturbance created by the former captain of the Right Outer Palace Guards Nobuyori[6], was exiled to this province. During this period the lay priest and chancellor Kiyomori ruled the country despotically, meting out sentences on his ministers as he pleased, and even daring to confine the ex-sovereign in the Toba Detached Palace. He has aroused the indignation of the reigning emperor and has caused him extreme anxiety. The prince's pronouncement, reaching Yoritomo at such a time, has caused him to resolve to raise an army of justice. This is the will of Heaven, and the destruction of the Taira will come to pass.

Now, Hōjō Shirō Tokimasa, descendant in the fifth generation of the *ason*[7] and vice governor of Kōzuke Taira Naotsune is a powerful lord of this region. He is father-in-law to Yoritomo, to whom he has shown indisputable loyalty. Thus, on this occasion,

---

[4] Hachijō-in, the title of Akiko, daughter of Ex-Sovereign Toba [d. 1156]. The suffix *-in*, affixed to names or titles, indicated retired members of the imperial family.

[5] Otoko-yama, a low mountain along the south bank of the Kizu River in Yamashiro near Kyoto on which is situated the Iwashimizu Hachiman Shrine. Hachiman is the tutelary deity of the Minamoto.

[6] Fujiwara Nobuyori (1133–1159) and Minamoto Yoshitomo, Yoritomo's father, had opposed the Taira and the Ex-Sovereign Go-Shirakawa in the so-called Heiji Disturbance. The Taira victory in that incident led to the expulsion of the Minamoto from Kyoto.

[7] *Ason,* one of eight honorary titles given originally to clan chieftains by their clansmen. As these titles were hereditary, and as certain families became more powerful and influential than others, a kind of order of nobility developed by the late seventh century. Traditionally, *ason* ranked second.

it was he above all others who was invited by Yoritomo to open the pronouncement. It reads:

ORDERED: That the Genji and bands of troops in the various provinces of the three circuits[8] of Tōkai, Tōsan, and Hokuriku proceed forthwith against the master of Buddhist Law[9] Taira Kiyomori, his partisans and rebels

The foregoing is decreed by the *ason* and former governor of Izu Minamoto Nakatsuna. The pronouncement of His Excellency the prince declares that Kiyomori, Munemori, and others, using the prestige of their office and their influence, have incited rebellion and have overthrown the nation. They have caused the officials and the people to suffer, seizing and plundering the five inner provinces and the seven circuits. They have confined the ex-sovereign, exiled public officials, and inflicted death and banishment, drowning and imprisonment. They have robbed property and seized lands, usurped and bestowed offices. They have rewarded the unworthy and incriminated the innocent. They have apprehended and confined the prelates of the various temples and imprisoned student monks. They have requisitioned the silks and rice of Mount Hiei to be stored as provisions for a rebellion. They have despoiled the graves of princes and cut off the head of one, defied the emperor and destroyed Buddhist Law in a manner unprecedented in history. Now the country is saddened and the ministers and people alike grieve. In consequence thereof, I, the second son of the ex-sovereign, in search of the ancient principles of Emperor Temmu,[10] and following in the footsteps of Prince Shōtoku,[11] proclaim war against those who would usurp the throne and who would destroy Buddhist Law. We rely not on man's efforts alone but on the assistance of providence as well. If the temporal rulers, the Three Treasures,[12] and the native gods assist us in our efforts, all the people everywhere must likewise wish to assist us immediately. This being so, let those of the Minamoto, the Fujiwara, and the brave now living in the provinces of the three circuits

[8] Japan was divided into circuits for administrative purposes, the system known collectively as *go-ki shichi-dō*, or five inner provinces and the seven circuits. The circuits mentioned here were generally in the east and north.

[9] *Hōshi*, a title given usually to famous Buddhist priests, is used here in place of lay priest.

[10] Emperor Temmu [d. 686] ascended the throne in 668 and continued the reforms known as the Taika Reforms begun by his brother and predecessor Tenchi. Temmu was also a devout Buddhist.

[11] Prince Shōtoku [d. 621], one of the great figures of Japanese history, is frequently referred to as the patron saint of Japanese Buddhism. As regent to his aunt, the Empress Suiko, he promoted Buddhism and made possible its firm establishment in Japan.

[12] The Three Treasures—the Buddha, the Law, and the Priesthood—stood for Buddhism.

add their efforts to the cause. If there be those who are not of like mind, they shall be regarded as partisans of Kiyomori and they shall suffer pain of death, exile, or imprisonment. If there be those who perform meritoriously, despatch missions to me and inform me of their names and deeds, and I shall, without fail, following my enthronement, bestow rewards upon them according to their wishes. Proclaim this message in all the provinces and carry out the terms of this pronouncement.[13]

Jishō 4:4,9

> Minamoto Nakatsuna, *Ason*
> Former Governor of Izu
> Senior Fifth Rank, Lower Grade

FIFTH MONTH

10th day. *Shimokōbe Yukihira despatches a messenger to Yoritomo to inform him of Yorimasa's preparations.*

15th day. *The Heike discover the plot and move to check it.*

Cloudy. An imperial decree was issued banishing Prince Mochihito to Tosa. The presiding officer of the meeting taking this action was the major councilor Sanjō Sanefusa, and the secretary was the private official and Minor Controller of the Right Yukitaka. This action was the result of the disclosure of the granting of an imperial pronouncement by the prince exhorting the country to rise up in arms against the Heike. Thus today, at 7 P.M., the imperial police Kanetsuna, Mitsunaga, and others, leading a guard of soldiers, went to the Sanjō-Takakura Palace. However, the prince, forewarned by Yorimasa, had fled the palace, and thus the imperial police could find no trace of him despite a thorough search of the premises. Meanwhile, Hasebe Nobutsura, captain of the Military Guards, taking up a long sword, attempted to fight off the police and succeeded in wounding five or six of Mitsunaga's men. But subsequently Nobutsura was overcome by Mitsunaga who bound him, one or two household officials, and three ladies in waiting and departed.

---

[13] The form and other peculiarities of this document lead one to believe that it is a reconstruction of the original pronouncement which was probably lost by the time of the compilation of the *Azuma kagami*. Nakatsuna, who despatched it, appears to be quoting the prince; however, all prior and subsequent references to the pronouncement indicate that it had reached Yoritomo in Nakatsuna's communication of this date.

16th day. *The Heike make a search for Mochihito.*

Clear. This morning the imperial police surrounded the prince's palace and made a further search for the prince, tearing open the ceilings and removing the floors, but to no avail. However, the Middle Councilor Taira Yorimori, on orders from the lay priest and chancellor, proceeded to the Hachijō Palace with picked troops and apprehended the prince's young son, whose mother is a lady in waiting to Princess Hachijō and a daughter of Nariaki, and removed him to Rokuhara.[14] It is impossible to say how great the confusion was within and without the capital.

19th day. *Prince Mochihito flees to Onjō-ji.*

Rain. On the 15th Prince Mochihito secretly entered Mii[15] Temple where quarters have been provided for him by the monks. Meanwhile, Minamoto Yorimasa set fire to his residence at Konoe-Kawara and with his children, nephews, and retainers left to join the prince.

23rd day. *The monks of Onjō-ji strengthen the defenses of the temple.*

24th day. *Yorimasa's villa is destroyed by fire.*

26th day. *The principals of the Minamoto plot die at Uji.*

Clear. Because of the inadequacy of forces at Mii Temple, the prince departed at 5 A.M. for Nara, to seek the protection of the monks there. He was escorted by Yorimasa's family and the monks of the temple. The sons of the lay priest and chancellor—the *ason* and captain of the Left Outer Palace Guards Tomomori, and the *ason* and provisional vice governor and minor captain Koremori— leading a force of 20,000 government troops, pursued the prince to Uji, where a battle ensued. Yorimasa, his sons Nakatsuna, Kanetsuna, and Nakamune, and the secretary Ashikaga Yoshifusa were killed by the Heike and their heads pilloried. It is being said that the head purported to be that of Yorimasa is actually that

[14] Rokuhara, name of a district in Kyoto on the east bank of the Kamo River where the main Taira residence was located.

[15] Mii-dera, a popular name for Onjō-ji, located at Mii in Ōmi Province and overlooking Lake Biwa.

of someone else. The prince took his own life before the sacred gate of Kōmyō-zan. He was thirty years old.

27th day. *The Heike burn Mimurodo; they plan an attack on the Nara temples.*

Because the monks of Mii Temple had constructed defenses around Mimurodo at Uji, this building was burned and razed by the government troops. On the same day action was taken at the ex-sovereign's palace to proceed punitively against the Genji in the provinces and the monks of the two temples of Kōfuku-ji and Onjō-ji who had acknowledged the pronouncement of the late prince.

SIXTH MONTH

19th day. *The courtier Miyoshi urges Yoritomo to flee to Ōshu.*

A messenger of Miyoshi Yasunobu arrived at Hōjō, and, meeting with Yoritomo in the seclusion of his residence, reported thus: "In the wake of the death of Prince Mochihito on the 26th of the past month, there has been a court action to proceed punitively against the Genji and all others who had endorsed the prince's pronouncement. This is of special concern to Your Lordship, the legitimate heir to the chieftainship of the Minamoto clan. It is suggested that Your Lordship flee immediately to Ōshu." Yasunobu's mother is a younger sister of the woman who had been Yoritomo's wet nurse. Because of this close relationship between their families Yasunobu has always leaned toward the Minamoto. Through messengers who endure the dangers of the mountains and the rivers Yasunobu has been reporting on the details of the happenings in the capital three times a month. On this occasion he had sent his younger brother Yasukiyo because of the seriousness of the news of punitive action against the Genji. In order to bring the message to Yoritomo Yasukiyo had taken leave of his court duties by pleading illness.

22nd day. *Yoritomo thanks Miyoshi for his services.*

Yasukiyo has departed for the capital. Yoritomo has entrusted him with a detailed letter to Miyoshi Yasunobu expressing his appreciation for his services. The scribe was Kunimichi, the secretary of Yamato.[16] Included in the packet were His Lordship's brush and seal.

24th day. *Yoritomo attempts to mobilize his vassals.*

Since His Lordship does not regard as mere rumor the information contained in Yasunobu's letter that the Heiji, following Minamoto Yorimasa's rout, were planning to attack the Genji in the provinces, he has summoned the hereditary vassals to his side that they might devise ways to check the Heiji. Yoritomo's messengers for this purpose were Adachi Morinaga and Kochūta Mitsuie.

27th day. *Miura Yoshiaki and Chiba Taneyori swear fealty to Yoritomo.*

Miura Jirō Yoshizumi, second son of Miura Yoshiaki, and the fifth rank[17] Taneyori, sixth son of Chiba Tsunetane, have come to visit at Hōjō. Normally, they are on duty in Kyoto. In the middle of the past month, when they had hoped to return to the provinces, they were detained at the capital by government troops because of the occurrence of the Uji Battle. The purpose of today's visit was to dispel any doubts His Lordship might have had regarding them who, because of guard duty in Kyoto, had failed to report earlier to their lord. His Lordship met with the two in the seclusion of his residence. Others were barred from the meeting.

SEVENTH MONTH

5th day. *Yoritomo is excused from reading one thousand passages of a sutra.*

The sky is clear and the winds are gentle. Monyō-bō Kakuen, the resident monk of Sōtō-zan whom His Lordship had summoned by letter yesterday, has arrived today at the Hōjō residence. Yoritomo addressed the priest thus: "It has been my long-cherished ambition to recite a thousand passages of the *Lotus Sutra*. To demonstrate

[16] This is Fujiwara Kunimichi, Yoritomo's secretary. One of Kunimichi's ancestors had been an official of Yamato Province: hence the expression "secretary of Yamato."

[17] *Taifu*, or *tayū*, was originally an honorary title for holders of the first to fifth ranks inclusively. But in this period the tendency was to use this title for holders of the fifth rank only. When it is clear that the older usage is meant, the title may be translated as "grandee."

my sincerity I had undertaken the recitations several days ago, but now an emergency has arisen making it impossible for me in the coming days to carry out this vow. I wish instead to address eight hundred passages to the Buddha. What is your opinion?" Kakuen replied: "To address to the Buddha less than a thousand recitations meets with my humble approval." Then, making an offering of incense and flowers before an idol of Buddha, the priest explained thus: "Your Lordship is a member of the clan of the Bodhisattva Hachiman.[18] Your Lordship upholds the eight chapters of the *Lotus Sutra*. Your Lordship, as the recipient of the heritage of Hachiman Tarō Yoshiie, has been the leader of the brave warriors of the eight provinces of the east, and it is within your power to subjugate the eight major crimes and the family of the lay priest and chancellor Hachijō. This Your Lordship can do by reciting eight hundred passages of this sutra." Yoritomo was moved to great admiration for this priest, and upon the conclusion of the meeting presented him with a gift, which Kunimichi, the secretary, received for the priest. At nightfall the priest, having taken leave of Yoritomo, had reached the area just beyond the gate when the latter recalled him and said: "Donations which I should have made to you this day I shall attend to at Hirugashima when there is peace and order in the world." Kakuen, in great joy, took his departure.

10th day. *The Hatano and Takiguchi oppose Yoritomo.*

Adachi Morinaga has reported to His Lordship that while many in Sagami Province have indicated their acceptance of the prince's pronouncement, several, such as Hatano Yoshitsune, and Takiguchi Saburō Tsunetoshi of Yamanouchi, have not only refused to respond to the gracious call but have also spoken harshly against it.

23rd day. *A Shinto priest offers his services to Yoritomo.*

Saeki Masasuke, the priest of Sumiyoshi Shrine of Chikuzen

---

[18] It will be noted that the priest's explanation is a form of numerology and a play on the word "eight," or *hachi*. Hachiman is the native god of war and the tutelary deity of the Minamoto. Yoshiie, Yoritomo's great great grandfather, was popularly known as Hachiman Tarō, while "the east" consisted of eight provinces. Similarly, the major crimes enumerated in the laws of the period consisted of eight offenses. Finally, one of the residences of the Taira in Kyoto was situated at Hachijō.

Province, had been banished by the Heike to Izu Province on the
3rd day of the Fifth Month of the past year. Previously, on Jishō
2:1,3 [1178], a priest of the same shrine had been exiled to this
province. Now the younger brother of this Masasuke has come to
pay homage to Yoritomo for the first time. A descendant of the
priest of the Ise Shrine and in recent years a retainer of Hatano
Yoshitsune, he has of late turned against his lord and has come to
do homage to Yoritomo. As these two have secretly indicated their
desire to serve the Minamoto cause, and as they are greatly experienced in matters of Shinto ritual, His Lordship has accepted
their offer of service that they might conduct prayers in his behalf.

EIGHTH MONTH

2nd day. *Ōba Kagechika returns to Sagami from Kyoto.*

The principal resident of Sagami, Ōba Saburō Kagechika, and
a great number of his followers from Eastern Japan who had been
in the capital for the military engagements of the Fifth Month have
returned to the east.

4th day. *Yoritomo plans his initial attack.*

The former imperial police Taira Kanetaka, now called the
secretary Yamamoto, had been exiled to Izu on charges brought
against him by his father Nobukane, the governor of Izumi. But
due to his relationship with the Heike, his prestige in the local
districts and villages increased gradually as the influence of Taira
Kiyomori increased. Besides being an enemy of the nation, Kanetaka
harbors ambitions of his own. Thus Yoritomo decided to test the
strength of the Minamoto clan by attacking Kanetaka first. However, Kanetaka's residence is strategically located and its approaches,
both from the front and the rear, are well guarded. To offset these
difficulties Yoritomo a few days ago ordered Kunimichi, a wandering
visitor from the capital who, by an act of fate, had been recommended to him by Morinaga, to make his entry into Kanetaka's
domains and to make a sketch of the terrain and of the residence.
Kunimichi joined Kanetaka at the latter's residence, where he was
entertained with song and drink, and in the course of several days
he had made a complete sketch of the terrain. Yoritomo summoned

Lord Hōjō to his residence and with the sketch between them
instructed him thoroughly as to the route the troops should take.
It appears from the plans that Kanetaka's territory can be taken.

6th day. *Yoritomo sets the day and the hour for the launching of
his attack.*

His Lordship, wishing to determine a propitious day and hour
for the launching of his attack on Kanetaka, summoned Kunimichi
and Sumiyoshi Masanaga to conduct a divination ritual. This has
been set for the coming 17th between 3 and 5 A.M.

Then His Lordship singled out from among the warriors presently visiting him those whom he trusts implicitly and who would
not hesitate giving their lives for the cause, and summoned them
individually to his residence to discuss the forthcoming military
action. These men were Kudō Shigemitsu, Doi Jirō Sanehira,
Okazaki Shirō Yoshizane, Usami Saburō Sukeshige, Amano Tōnai
Tōkage, Sasaki Saburō Moritsuna, and Katō Kagekado. Although
His Lordship did not say expressly that he depended entirely on
them for the success of the attack, each man came away from his
meeting with His Lordship convinced that his efforts were absolutely necessary for the success of the initial attack. Thus each
man, moved by the sincerity of His Lordship's words and rejoicing
in the conviction that he had been singled out by His Lordship,
is determined to exert his utmost for the cause. Although these
men have been forbidden to take any independent course, it is
His Lordship's intention to honor their wishes when the Minamoto
is established. However, no one, with the exception of Lord Hōjō,
knows the true details of His Lordship's plans.

9th day. *Ōba Kagechika hears a rumor about Yoritomo's plans.*

Sasaki Gensan Hideyoshi, a principal resident of Ōmi, had distinguished himself in battle in the service of Minamoto Yoshitomo
during the Heiji Disturbance. After Yoritomo's banishment he continued to hold in esteem the friendship of the Minamoto and refused
to bow to the growing power of the Heike. As a result he was deprived of Sasaki Manor, a hereditary estate. Subsequently, while
passing through Sagami Province with his sons and followers en-
route to Ōshu to seek the protection of Fujiwara Hidehira, a close

relative by marriage, he was prevailed upon to live in Sagami by the manorial official Shibuya Shigekuni, who admired Hideyoshi's bravery and daring. It is now twenty years since Hideyoshi settled in Sagami. During this period his sons Sadatsuna and Moritsuna have been serving Yoritomo.

Today Ōba Kagechika invited Hideyoshi to his residence and said to him: "While sojourning in the capital I met the vice governor of Kazusa Taira Tadakiyo. On that occasion he read me a letter addressed to him from the lay priest Osada who averred that Hōjō Yoshitoki and Hiki Yoshikazu, secretary of the housekeeping office, were planning to bolt the Taira and join in the revolt under Minamoto Yoritomo's leadership. Then Tadakiyo said to me: 'This is no ordinary matter. This letter, coming after the Prince Mochihito incident and in the very midst of Taira preparations to attack the Genji in the various provinces, portends serious consequences. It should be shown immediately to the lay priest and chancellor Kiyomori.' I replied, 'I cannot say how Hōjō feels about this matter, as he is now related to Yoritomo.[19] As for Hiki Yoshikazu, he is presumed to be dead.'" Kagechika, who left the capital after this meeting, was greatly disturbed, but he revealed the matter to Sasaki Hideyoshi, his guest and old friend, and cautioned him to be on guard, as the latter's oldest son was in Yoritomo's service. Alarmed by the disclosure and unable to discuss the matter further, Hideyoshi took his leave of Kagechika.

10th day. *The Sasaki alert Yoritomo.*

Hideyoshi, through his son and heir Sadatsuna, notified Yoritomo of the gist of yesterday's conversations with Kagechika. A few days ago Sadatsuna had come to Shibuya from Utsunomiya where he had been residing of late.

11th day. *Yoritomo commends the Sasaki on their loyalty.*

Sadatsuna arrived at Hōjō on his father's mission and reported the details of Kagechika's assertions to His Lordship. Whereupon His Lordship remarked, "The fact is I have been contemplating

---

[19] It should be remembered that the Hōjō were of Taira descent and that the exiled Yoritomo was a ward of the Hōjō. But Yoritomo had won over his warden's friendship and had even become attached to the Hōjō family by marrying his warden's daughter.

the matter earnestly since the Fourth Month, and I hope to reveal my plans shortly. You are to be commended highly for reporting to me when I was about to summon you for your services. Hide-yoshi's action in conveying information to me without delay is also most praiseworthy."

12th day. *Yoritomo summons Okazaki Yoshizane and Doi Sanehira.*

The date for the attack on Kanetaka had been fixed for the 17th. However, as His Lordship is counting on the services of Okazaki Shirō Yoshizane and his son Yoichi Yoshitaka, he despatched instructions today to Yoshizane to report with his son and Doi Jirō Sanehira before the 17th.

13th day. *Yoritomo instructs the Sasaki to report by the 16th.*

When Sasaki Sadatsuna informed His Lordship that he plans to leave for home on the morrow, the latter tried to detain him. However, His Lordship consented when Sadatsuna explained that he wished to collect his arms and armor. His Lordship's instructions to him as he took his leave were: "Report back to me on the 16th without fail, for I am determined to initiate this war of justice by attacking Kanetaka on the 17th as planned." Yoritomo also entrusted Sadatsuna with a letter to Shibuya Shigekuni, expressing confidence in his services.

16th day. *Yoritomo is forced to postpone the hour of launching the war.*

The rain which had begun yesterday continued to fall unceasingly throughout the day. Prayers were offered for the success of the engagement tomorrow. Sumiyoshi Masanaga conducted the ritual to exorcise the spirits of disaster and calamity in which His Lordship, handing over the mirror to Masanaga, participated. The secretary Nagae Yorikane performed one thousand purification prayers.

Although the Sasaki brothers had been instructed to report today, they had failed to appear by nightfall. Thus, lacking the personnel to attack Kanetaka at dawn tomorrow, His Lordship was compelled to postpone the attack. On the other hand, it would not do to postpone the attack until the 18th, the day for the Buddhist ceremony of the liberation of all living things from confinement, which His Lordship had observed before an image of the Goddess of Mercy for many years since his boyhood. Nor would it do to postpone the attack to the 19th, for the probability of exposure of the plans was great. The failure of his men to report today has caused His Lordship great anxiety and regret that he had placed complete trust in the Sasaki and had disclosed secret matters to them. The Sasaki, moreover, are friendly with Shibuya Shigekuni, who at present appears to be sympathetic to the Heike cause.

17th day. *The Sasaki arrive; Yoritomo launches the war.*

Clear. This being a festival day of Mishima Shrine, His Lordship sent Adachi Morinaga as an emissary to worship and make an offering at the shrine. Morinaga completed his mission before the festivities began. At 1 P.M. the four Sasaki brothers—Tarō Sadatsuna, Jirō Tsunetaka, Saburō Moritsuna, and Shirō Takatsuna—arrived at Hōjō. His Lordship was moved to tears at the sight of the brothers—Sadatsuna and Tsunetaka on injured horses, and Moritsuna and Takatsuna afoot. However, when His Lordship expressed great chagrin at having had to call off the attack which had been planned for dawn this day because of their late arrival, Sadatsuna explained that unexpectedly high flood waters had caused the delay.

At 7 P.M. a servant of Kanetaka was captured in His Lordship's kitchen, according to prearranged plans, by a servant of Morinaga. The captured servant is husband to a maidservant in Yoritomo's household and comes here nightly, and his suspicions might be aroused at the gathering of many warriors. Thus the initial attack, in His Lordship's opinion, could not wait another day and must be launched immediately. Accordingly Yoritomo ordered his men to proceed immediately to Yamamoto, after reminding them that this is an act which will affect their entire lives. Yoritomo also ordered the men to set fire to the Yamamoto residence during the engagement so that he might see the smoke rising to the sky. Although the troops were eager to commence activity, Lord Hōjō cautioned them, saying, "This is a festival day of Mishima Shrine, and the streets are full of worshippers. If we proceed along the main thoroughfare of Ushikuwa, the passers-by will object. Should we not proceed along Hirugashima Street?" Yoritomo replied: "That is true, but a war should be launched on a great thoroughfare and not on a quiet back street. Moreover, Hirugashima Street would restrict our horsemen." Sumiyoshi Masanaga, girding himself with a belt, was assigned to conduct prayers for the troops, while Moritsuna and Kagekado were assigned to stand night watch. The troops, proceeding north from Ibaragi, reached Hidahara. There Lord Hōjō stopped his mount and said to Sadatsuna: "Kanetaka's guardian, the vice governor Tsutsumi Nobutō, whose domains lie north of Yamamoto, is a superior warrior. If we do not kill him as well as Kanetaka, he will prove troublesome later. You and your brother will attack Nobutō, and I shall assign a guide for you." Sadatsuna accepted the assignment, and at 11 P.M. he and his party proceeded east on Ushikuwa. Stopping for a moment at the head of the rice field in front of Nobutō's residence, the brothers, accompanied by the guide whose name was Minamoto Tōta, a servant of Lord Hōjō, encircled Nobutō's residence to the rear. Then Takatsuna moved up to the edge of the courtyard and released an arrow. This was the moment of the beginning of the Minamoto war against the Taira. A bright moon above made the night as bright as midday. Nobutō's followers, seeing Takatsuna's challenge, shot their arrows at him, while Nobutō, his long sword in hand, went forth toward the southwest to confront Takatsuna. The latter discarded his bow, grasped his long sword, and, facing his adversary to the northeast, engaged him in combat. Both excelled in bravery, but Takatsuna was struck by an arrow. At that moment Sadatsuna came up from the rear and slew Nobutō. Meanwhile, Lord Hōjō and his followers had advanced to the vicinity of Temman Hill in front of Kanetaka's residence and had begun to release arrows and to hurl rocks. Many of Kanetaka's men, having gone to worship at Mishima Shrine and having stopped subsequently to tarry at Kisegawa Inn, were not at the scene. However, the stalwart warriors who had remained behind were contemptuous of death and gave battle. During the struggle Sadatsuna and his brother, having disposed of Nobutō, arrived to offer assistance.

Meanwhile, Yoritomo, anxious about the battle, looked for signs of smoke from the porch of his residence. Failing to detect any smoke, he ordered Eda Shimpeiji, an attendant of the sovereign's dining room, to climb a tree and to look for signs of smoke. When he too failed to detect smoke after a few moments, His Lordship summoned Katō Kagetaka, Sasaki Saburō Moritsuna, and Hori Tōji Chikaie, who had been detained for guard duty, and ordered them to go to Yamamoto immediately and join in the battle. Then, presenting a long sword to Kagekado, His Lordship commanded him to return with Kanetaka's head. The three, without benefit of horses, dashed out on the embankment of Hirugashima toward Yamamoto. Moritsuna and Kagekado entered Kanetaka's residence, slew him and his followers according to Yoritomo's command, and set fire to the building, which was completely destroyed. Soon it was dawn. The warriors returned and assembled in the courtyard as Yoritomo stepped out on the porch to inspect the decapitated heads of Kanetaka and his followers.

18th day. *Yoritomo asks a nun to perform penances for him.*

Over the years Yoritomo has been accustomed to performing his religious penances every day without fail, whether or not there was immediate cause for purification. Troubled by the thought that he would have to forego these daily exercises because of the wars, he has instructed Her Ladyship Masako to order Hōon of Izu-yama, a nun pure and chaste, who is Her Ladyship's teacher of the sutras, to perform the penances in his behalf. A list of exercises has been sent to her. The nun has indicated her acceptance. . . .

19th day. *Yoritomo proclaims his rule over Kanto; Sōtō-zan complains of violation of its lands.*

The clerk fifth rank[20] Tomochika, a relative of Kanetaka, has been inclined to commit unwarranted outrages on the people at Uraya *mikuri*[21] where he resides. Yoritomo commanded him through Kunimichi to cease such acts. This is the beginning of His Lordship's administration of Kanto.[22] His Lordship's directive reads:

[20] See note 17 above.

[21] A *mikuri* was one of several types of domains owned by shrines. A *mikuri*, which means "kitchen," was land whereon grains and other crops were raised for the shrine which owned it or had rights to it.

[22] Kanto, literally "east of the barrier," referred generally to Eastern Japan. The barrier was the Ashigara Pass in the Hakone Mountain Range.

ORDERED TO: The local gentry of Uraya *mikuri*

That the commission of the clerk fifth rank Tomochika cease forthwith. It is manifestly clear in the language of Prince Mochihito's pronouncement that the public and private domains in the provinces in the east are within His Lordship's jurisdiction. The attention of residents of this region is directed to this order and they are advised to take steps to have their holdings confirmed. Thus ordered, in accordance with His Lordship's instructions.

Jishō 4:8,19

Of late the lands belonging to Sōtō-zan have become a thoroughfare for warriors traveling between Doi and Hōjō, and the monks of Sōtō-zan have complained to His Lordship that the warriors have been committing outrages on their lands. In a letter sent to the monks to console them His Lordship declared that, when peace and order are restored, he would donate manors to the temple, one in Izu and another in Sagami, in the interest of promoting the prestige of the Izu Incarnate[23] in Kanto. In this way, His Lordship has soothed the anger of the monks.

At night Her Ladyship, accompanied by Kunimichi and Masanaga, went to Sōtō-zan and called on Monyō-bō Kakuen. Her Ladyship will lodge here in quiet and peace during this unsettled period.

20th day. *Yoritomo leaves Izu for Sagami.*

The vice governor Miura Yoshiaki and his band of followers reported to His Lordship only this day. Yoshiaki explained that although there had been men who had come forward and offered their services to Yoritomo in the past few days, they were delayed in reporting for various reasons: some had to take a sea route across treacherous waters; others had chosen a direct but difficult route. But now that his immediate vassals of Izu and Sagami were assembled, Yoritomo has decided to take them out of Izu. Leading his party, he made his way toward Doi District in Sagami. . . .

22nd day. *The Miura and Wada families and their followers prepare to join Yoritomo.*

[23] *Gongen,* a Buddhist term meaning "incarnation." It was used frequently in this period for a Shinto deity who was regarded as a Buddha Incarnate and worshiped at both shrines and temples. The amalgamation of native and foreign cults was a characteristic feature of the religion of this period.

23rd day. Yoritomo is defeated at Ishibashi.

Cloudy. A heavy rain fell last night. Today, at 3 A.M., Yoritomo led his three hundred horsemen, including Hōjō and his sons, Morinaga, Mochimitsu, and Sanehira, to Ishibashi Mountain in Sagami, where he established a position. Carrying the standard to the top of which was attached Prince Mochihito's pronouncement was Naka Shirō Koreshige. Yoritaka, holding a pole to which were tied sacred emblems,[24] attended His Lordship.

The Taira line was established beyond a ravine by the local lords of Sagami, such as Ōba Saburō Kagechika, Matano Gorō Kagehisa, Kawamura Saburō Yoshihide, Shibuya Shigekuni, the provisional governor Kasuya Morihisa, Ebina Gensan Sukesada, Soga Tarō Sukenobu, Takiguchi Saburō Tsunetoshi, Mōri Tarō Kageyuki, Nagao Shingo Tamemune, Nagao Shinroku Sadakage, Haramune Saburō Kagefusa, Haramune Shirō Yoshiyuki, Kumagaya Jirō Naozane, and their three thousand horsemen. Among Kagechika's troops is one Iida Gorō Ieyoshi, who wishes to serve Yoshitomo and who intends to flee Kagechika's camp, but who remains reluctantly in the enemy camp because enemy troops are stationed between him and Yoritomo's lines. On the mountain to the rear of Yoritomo's lines the master of Buddhist Law Itō Jirō Sukechika, commanding more than three hundred mounted men and with intentions of pressing Yoritomo, has established a position.

Meanwhile, under cover of night, Miura and his men encamped near the Maruko River and set fire to the homes of some of Kagechika's men. As the smoke rose to the sky Kagechika, who had seen it from afar, summoned a council and said: "Although it is not quite dusk, we must initiate the battle now. We cannot wait until tomorrow, for Miura's men will arrive by then to reenforce the enemy, which would make it extremely difficult for us to defeat them." As soon as the deliberations ended, Kagechika's men—several thousands strong—assailed Yoritomo's lines. Although in number the Minamoto could not compare with Ōba's great army, Yoritomo's men cherished their friendship for their leader and all fought with a determination to die, if necessary, for Yoritomo. In

---

[24] *Hakuhei,* strips of white paper cut into small angular bunches, representing offerings of cloth. The origin of the shape of the emblems is obscure, but the Japanese continue to observe this custom during festivals. The paper is usually tied to branches of the *cleyera* tree, considered sacred.

this way Sanada Yoichi Yoshitaka, Butō Saburō, and the follower Bunzō Ieyasu lost their lives. Finally, Kagechika attained victory as dawn was breaking, and Yoritomo fled toward Sugiyama. At the time there were gale winds and torrential rains to plague him. Kagechika's men, loosening arrows and hurling rocks, gave chase. Just then Iida Ieyoshi, who was in Kagechika's ranks, led six of his own horsemen against Kagechika, thus giving Yoritomo a chance to escape to Sugiyama.

24th day. *Yoritomo flees; he narrowly averts capture.*

Yoritomo took up a position at Horiguchi in Sugiyama but, pressed by the pursuing forces of Kagechika and his three thousand horsemen, he fled to a ridge above Horiguchi, while Katō Kagekado and Ōmi Sanemasa remained at Horiguchi to cover his flight. Kagekado's father, Kagekazu, and Sanemasa's older brother, Masamitsu, concerned over the safety of their son and brother respectively, refused to retreat. They stopped their mounts to shoot their arrows, while Sasaki Takatsuna, Amano Tōkage, Mitsuie, Hori Chikaie, and Sukemasa likewise turned their horses and charged into the enemy. Many of Kagekazu's horsemen were felled in the fray by enemy arrows. Time and again Yoritomo himself, whose arrows found their mark with unerring accuracy, ordered his own conveyance turned toward the enemy so that he might join in the fray. Without fail His Lordship's arrows—shaft and feathers—buried themselves in their mark and killed many an enemy.

Meanwhile, His Lordship had exhausted his supply of arrows. Thereupon Kagekado, taking the reins of His Lordship's mount, guided it farther into the mountains, as four or five columns of Kagechika's men advanced closer upon them. Seeing this, Takatsuna, Tōkage, and Kagekado countered repeatedly with their bows and arrows.

Lord Hōjō, who with his two sons had been battling with Kagechika, was so exhausted that he could not escort Yoritomo to the ridge of the mountain. Saying, "I cannot possibly accompany His Lordship; you must do so," Lord Hōjō ordered Kagekazu, Mitsukazu, Kagekado, Sukemochi, Chikaie, and Sanemasa to go and search for Yoritomo immediately. The party scaled a treacherous precipice several *chō*[25] high and found Yoritomo, with Sanehira in attendance, standing on a fallen log. Yoritomo was overjoyed, but Sanehira remarked: "That you have been able to come to His Lordship without incident is a matter for rejoicing, but it is unquestionably more difficult to keep His Lordship concealed in this mountain if so many of us remain with him. I shall remain here and find a way to keep him concealed, if need be, for ten months." The others protested and insisted upon attending His Lordship at his side, but Sanehira persisted, saying: "Our parting now will be our great fortune later. Each of us, high or low, by going his separate way and striving for the realization of our aims, can help to avenge this disgrace." Influenced by his words, the men took their leave and scattered. Tears filled their eyes and they could scarcely see their way.

Later Ieyoshi sought out Yoritomo, bringing with him a rosary which His Lordship had lost earlier in the day during the course of the battle. It was a rosary familiar to many of his men from Sagami, who had hunted with His Lordship in the past. Yoritomo had missed it earlier and had been greatly upset. Thus he was overjoyed to retrieve it and thanked Ieyoshi repeatedly. However, when Ieyoshi offered to stay in attendance on His Lordship and was counselled against it by Sanehira, he departed tearfully.

Lord Hōjō and his son Shirō intend to cross the Hakone Mountains into Kai Province. His other son, Saburō, had descended from Doi to Kuwabara and, while passing through Hirai District, he was surrounded by Itō Sukechika's men in the vicinity of Hayakawa and was wounded and taken captive by the landlord Kiroku Hisashige. Kudō Mochimitsu, a follower of Saburō, unable to proceed further, had retreated and killed himself. His Lordship lamented the fact that he as commander could not console his wounded men, separated as he was from the battlefield by mountains and ravines.

Ōba Kagechika had discovered the steep mountain peak where Yoritomo was hiding. But one of his men, Kajiwara Kagetoki, who knew exactly where Yoritomo was hiding and who bears good will toward Yoritomo, took Kagechika's hand and directed him to the

[25] *Chō*, the distance of a city block.

adjoining peak, saying, "There are no traces of anyone in this mountain."

Meanwhile, Yoritomo had removed from his topknot a statuette of the Goddess of Mercy and had installed it in a cavern. When asked the meaning of this by Sanehira, Yoritomo replied, "If by chance my head is taken by Kagechika, I as the commander in chief of the Genji would be ridiculed if an image is found in my hair." His Lordship explained that when he was an infant of three his wet nurse had shut herself in Kiyomizu Temple to offer prayers in his behalf, and on the 27th day of prayer she was blessed with a divine revelation. Thereupon, she had obtained this two-inch image of the Goddess of Mercy to present to him.

Lord Hōjō has arrived at Sugiyama. Accompanying him was the monk Eijitsu on a mission for his older brother, Gyōjitsu, the intendant of Hakone-yama. He had come to present His Lordship with provisions of food. Earlier, when the monk had met Lord Hōjō and had inquired about Yoritomo, Lord Hōjō had replied: "The commander was surrounded by Kagechika's men and was unable to break out." To this Eijitsu had remarked, "I do not know whether Your Honor is testing my patience, but I daresay that if the commander had perished, Your Honor would have also." Lord Hōjō had burst out in laughter and had consented to Eijitsu's accompanying him in his search for Yoritomo. The food which Eijitsu brought was greatly appreciated by His Lordship who, with his attendant, might have perished from starvation. Sanehira offered the suggestion that when peace is restored His Lordship should grant Eijitsu the post of intendant of Hakone-yama, to which he agreed. Then, with Eijitsu serving as guide, Yoritomo made his way secretly to Hakone-yama. There it was decided that His Lordship should stay at Eijitsu's residence rather than at Gyōjitsu's abode, where the secret of Yoritomo's presence would be difficult to maintain because of the many monks going there to worship. Earlier, during the time of his father Ryōjin, Gyōjitsu had gone to Kyoto to seek the post of intendant of Hakone-yama which he was able to obtain because of his father's acquaintance with Minamoto Tameyoshi and Minamoto Yoshitomo. Before Gyōjitsu returned to the east Tameyoshi had said to him, "If the men in the eastern provinces seek you out, comply with their wishes," and he had presented him with a letter of investiture which directs the Minamoto retainers in Suruga and Izu Provinces to comply with Gyōjitsu's wishes if he should seek them out. Thus, since the time of Yoritomo's arrival at Hōjō, Gyōjitsu has been most faithful in offering prayers in His Lordship's behalf. Grief-stricken at the news of the defeat at Ishibashi Mountain, he had despatched his brother Eijitsu, who is skilled in the military arts, rather than any of several apprentices under him, to search for Yoritomo.

The news of the defeat reached the men of Miura in the region near the Maruko River. They had come there the previous night and were awaiting the dawn to join Yoritomo, but the news caused them to turn back. As they withdrew toward Miura they were challenged to battle at Yuinoura by Hatakeyama Shigetada. In this engagement Tatara Saburō Shigeharu and his follower Ishii Gorō lost their lives. However, Shigetada retreated when more than fifty of his followers were killed. Thus Yoshizumi and his men reached Miura safely. Meanwhile, Taira Hirotsune, the provisional governor of Kazusa, and his younger brother Kanada Yoritsugu and seventy horsemen have joined Yoshizumi's band.

25th day. *The Genji in Kai resist Ōba Kagechika; a priest assists Yoritomo.*

To prevent Yoritomo's escape, Ōba Kagechika had dispersed his troops and had set up barriers on roads everywhere. Meanwhile, his following increased by the forces of Matano Kagehisa and the deputy governor of Suruga Tachibana Tōmochi, Kagechika had set out for Kai to attack the Takeda, Ichijō, and other Genji bands in that province. At dusk yesterday, while Kagehisa's army was bivouacked at the northern foothills of Mount Fuji, rats had gnawed at and cut one hundred bowstrings belonging to his men. While thus inconvenienced, Kagehisa and his men were attacked by Yasuda Saburō Yoshisada, Kudō Kagemitsu, his son Yukimitsu, and the commissioner Ichikawa Yukifusa, who were leaving Kai Province for Ishibashi Mountain to assist Yoritomo. When they encountered Kagehisa at Hashida Mountain, they turned their horses and attacked him. Caught without bowstrings and forced to resort to their long swords, Kagehisa and his men could not defend themselves adequately against the arrows and stones, and many of them were struck. Although Yasuda's men could not escape the enemy swords entirely, nevertheless, Kagehisa pocketed his pride and quietly took flight.

At Hakone Mountain where Yoritomo was situated, a younger brother of Gyōjitsu, called Chizō-bō Ryōsen, who had been a prayer official for the late Kanetaka, turned against his brothers and, collecting other ignoble men around him, plotted to kill Yoritomo. When Eijitsu informed Yoritomo and Gyōjitsu of the plot, the latter said, "There is nothing to fear so far as Ryōsen's military abilities are concerned, but there is the danger that Kagechika will hear of the plot and come here to join forces with Ryōsen. Therefore Your Lordship must leave this place immediately." Accepting his counsel, Yoritomo, escorted by Sanehisa, Eijitsu, and a guide for the mountains, turned toward Doi District by way of the Hakone Road. At the same time Lord Hōjō, accompanied by Nankō-bō, who had been assigned to him by Gyōjitsu, and taking a trail used by itinerant priests, departed for Kai to apprise the Genji there of the present situation. However, Lord Hōjō, realizing the difficulty of rallying the Genji of Kai Province without definite knowledge of Yoritomo's future location, and believing that it would be better to depart for this mission later after Yoritomo's headquarters is established, turned away from Kai toward Doi in search of His Lordship. Nankō turned toward Hakone Temple.

26th day. *The Miura are besieged at Kinugasu; Shibuya Shigekuni repents.*

Hatakeyama Jirō Shigetada of Musashi, desirous of returning his debt of gratitude to the Heiji, on the one hand, and of avenging the humiliation he suffered at Yuinoura, on the other, planned to attack Miura and his men. He sent word to Kawagoe Tarō Shigeyori to rally the various bands of warriors in Musashi and to report to him. . . . Today, when word reached Miura of this activity, the group withdrew into Kinugasa Castle at 5 A.M. to prepare its defenses. The east gate, which is the main outer gate, was assigned to Yoshizumi and Yoshitsura; the west gate to Wada Yoshimori and Kanada Yoritsugu; the center position to Nagae Yoshikage and Ōto Yoshihisa. At 7 A.M. several thousands of horsemen under Kawagoe Shigeyori, Nakayama Shizane, Edo Shigenaga, Kaneko,

and Murayama advanced upon the castle. Miura Yoshizumi gave
battle, but he lacked both strength and arrows, this being the
second successive day of fighting which had begun at Yui yesterday, and he decided to abandon the castle. He had planned to take
his father Yoshiaki with him, but Yoshiaki refused to go, saying,
"As a hereditary vassal of the Minamoto I rejoice at the revival of
that venerable clan. I am now more than eighty years old, and
I have not much longer to live. It is my wish that I may die for
Yoritomo and that my descendants should perform meritoriously
for him. I command you to withdraw from the castle immediately
and to help Yoritomo achieve his destiny. I alone will remain in
the castle and, putting up the appearance of a large force, I will
face Shigeyori." Yoshizumi and his followers, weeping without
restraint, yielded to Yoshiaki's command and dispersed.

Ōba Kagechika had sought out Shibuya Shigekuni and had
said to him: "The four Sasaki brothers have turned against the
Heike and have gone over to serve Yoritomo. This is inexcusable.
To draw them out we should make hostages of their wives and
children." Shigekuni replied: "These men are serving Yoritomo
because they have always borne good will toward him. If they
still esteem their old friendship for the Minamoto, how can we
restrain them? Have you forgotten that at your command I have
reported to you at Ishibashi, bringing with me Yoshikiyo, a Sasaki
and the son of my own daughter? Now you order me to make
hostages of the wives and children of the Sasaki. This I cannot do."
Kagechika, convinced by Shigekuni's logic, did not press his demand
further and departed.

When night fell Sasaki Sadatsuna, Moritsuna, and Takatsuna
arrived at Shigekuni's residence in Shibuya with the priest Zenjō[26]
of Daigo, whom they had met as they were quitting the Hakone
Mountains. Shigekuni, happy to see them but fearing disclosure of
their arrival, invited them into his warehouse, where he entertained
them with food and drink. When Shigekuni inquired whether
Tsunetaka, the second son, had been captured and killed, Sadatsuna replied: "We urged him to come with us, but he refused."
Shigekuni said, "I understand his position. It is many years since
I resolved to serve Yoritomo, but I have not made good this resolu-

---

[26] Zenjō, also known as Imawaka, is a younger brother of Yoritomo.

tion. I am full of remorse and shame, especially now at Yoritomo's defeat." Then Shigekuni vowed that he would send his men to search for Yoritomo. His hearers were deeply touched by his expressions of remorse.

27th day. *Miura Yoshiaki dies; the Katō flee.*

A slight drizzle fell during the morning. At 3 P.M. the wind and the rain increased in intensity.

For lack of help Miura Yoshiaki, aged eighty-nine, was taken captive and killed at 7 A.M. by Kawagoe Shigeyori and Edo Shigenaga. His son Yoshizumi had left for Awa Province, while Lord Hōjō, his son Shirō, Okazaki Yoshizane, and Kondō Kunihira had embarked from Iwaura for Bōshū. On the sea they met with the men of Miura, with whom they exchanged accounts of their sad experience. Meanwhile Kagechika, who with several thousands of horsemen had advanced into Miura, withdrew from that area, for their adversary, Yoshizumi, had embarked for Awa.

For three days, since the 24th, Katō Kagekazu and his sons, Mitsukazu and Kagekado, had remained in the Hakone Mountains, their provisions exhausted, their spirits depressed, and their minds vacant. In particular, Kagekazu, who was old and decrepit, could walk no longer. Turning to his sons he said, "I am an old man. Even supposing that I had no cause for anxiety, I have no desire to prolong my life. You are in the prime of your life; do not throw your lives away wantonly. Leave me in this mountain and go out and search for Yoritomo." Although the sons were determined to disembowel themselves rather than abandon their father, in the end they assisted him and brought him to Sōtō-zan Temple. There the aged father took the tonsure, while the sons turned toward Kai Province. At 9 P.M. this evening the brothers arrived at Haraedo in Kokufu, Izu Province, where the local inhabitants, suspicious of them, fled. This led them to decide to proceed on their way separately. Thus at present they do not know each other's whereabouts.

28th day. *Yoritomo flees by boat to Awa Province.*

The brothers Mitsukazu and Kagekado came upon each other once again on the grasslands of Ōoka in Suruga and wept with joy.

They are now hiding somewhere in the foothills of Mount Fuji.

Yoritomo has embarked for Awa Province from Manazuru in Doi. On Sanehira's instructions, Sadatsune, a principal resident of Doi, is escorting Yoritomo in a smaller craft. From Manazuru before his embarkation Yoritomo despatched Doi Yatarō Tōhira to Her Ladyship with news of his sad experiences since their parting.

29th day. *Yoritomo reaches Awa.*

The small craft bearing Yoritomo and Sanehira reached Ryūgashima in Hirakita District, Awa Province. There they were met by Lord Hōjō and his men, and in the brief moment of reunion the anxiety and anguish of several days were dispelled.

NINTH MONTH

1st day. *Yoritomo orders Taira Hirotsune to report to him.*

Yoritomo has announced that he will meet with Taira Hirotsune, the vice governor of Kazusa, and he expects Lord Hōjō and his followers to accompany him to Kazusa. His Lordship's letter to Hirotsune was despatched in the care of Anzai Kagemasu, a principal resident of Awa and an intimate friend of Yoritomo since his youth. The letter directs Hirotsune to rally the officials of the local government office and to report with them to him. It adds that those in Kazusa who are sympathetic to the Taira should be apprehended and presented to him.

2nd day. *Yoritomo's messenger apprises Masako of latest developments.*

3rd day. *Ōba Kagechika rallies local lords of Musashi and Sagami; Yoritomo plans to meet Taira Hirotsune.*

Although a hereditary vassal of the Genji, Ōba Kagechika had, on this occasion, taken up arms against the Genji. Not only does he obey implicitly the commands of the Heiji but he also appears to have ambitions of his own. But so far only the local lords of Musashi and Sagami have joined his traitorous band. Among the local gentry who have refused to serve Kagechika and who are assisting Yoritomo are the Miura and the Nakamura. His Lordship, in an effort to determine the extent of Kagechika's conspiracy, despatched letters to Koyama Tomomasa, Shimokōbe Yukihira, the provisional governor Toyoshima Kiyomoto, and Kasai Kiyoshige, urging them to rally the pro-Genji forces in their localities and to report to him. Of this group Kasai Kiyoshige has been conspicuously loyal to the Minamoto, but his indecision to report might have been due to the fact that his lands are situated in the Edo and Kawagoe regions whose lords are for the Taira. His Lordship suggested in his letter that they report to him via a sea route. His Lordship has also sent word to the wife of Toyoshima Tomotsune, secretary of the Right Horse Bureau, who is presently away at the capital, that he is sending her a silk garment.

Today His Lordship left Hirakita District for Hirotsune's domain. As darkness approached he stopped for the night at a peasant's hut along the way. There Miura Yoshizumi, who is serving His Lordship as his guide in this region, heard of a conspiracy engineered by Nagasa Rokurō Tsunetomo, a Taira partisan and a principal resident of this area, to attack Yoritomo this evening at his lodging. Yoshizumi intercepted the attack and after a spell of fighting repulsed Tsunetomo.

4th day. *Yoritomo is warned against conspirators.*

In connection with the mission of delivering His Lordship's letter, Anzai Saburō Kagemasu reported to Yoritomo with his band of followers and two or three officials from the local government office. Addressing Yoritomo, Kagemasu said: "Your Lordship must not attempt to go to Hirotsune's territory without more aides. The road is full of conspirators like Nagasa Tsunetomo. Instead, Your Lordship should first send an emissary to Hirotsune and instruct him to come to meet you." Accordingly Wada Tarō Yoshimori was despatched to Hirotsune and Adachi Tō Kurō Morinaga was sent to vice governor Chiba Tsunetane with instructions for them to report to Yoritomo immediately. Meanwhile, His Lordship was taken to Kagemasu's residence.

5th day. *Yoritomo worships at Sunosaki Shrine.*

His Lordship, praying with sincere devotion, worshipped at the Sunosaki Myōjin[27] Shrine. He vowed in writing that if his prayers

[27] Myōjin, a Shinto deity. The word, like *gongen*, is actually of Buddhist significance, showing the influence of Buddhism on Shinto.

for the arrival of all the warriors whom he had summoned are answered, he would present to the shrine a benefice of merit rice-lands to promote the glory of its deity.

6th day. *Taira Hirotsune replies to Yoritomo's summons.*

At night Wada Yoshimori returned from his mission and reported to His Lordship as follows: "Taira Hirotsune declares that he will report to Your Lordship after he has conferred with vice governor Chiba Tsunetane."

7th day. *Kiso Yoshinaka in Shinano joins in the war against the Heike.*

The Lord of Kiso, Minamoto Yoshinaka, is the second son of Minamoto Yoshikata, chief of the bodyguard of the crown prince. When Yoshikata was killed by Aku Genta Yoshihira in the Eighth Month of 1155, Yoshinaka, who was a mere infant of three, was taken to Shinano Province and reared there by Nakahara Kanetō, the provisional governor and husband of his wet nurse. Now in his manhood, Yoshinaka is endowed with great military skill and a will to overthrow the Heike and to establish his family. When word reached him in distant Shinano of the launching of the war at Ishibashi Mountain by Yoritomo, he sought to assist in the war and to make known his long-cherished ambition of reestablishing the Minamoto. Now there was in Shinano a partisan of the Heike called Kasahara Heigo Yorinao who today rallied his troops together in an attempt to attack Yoshinaka. But when Murayama Yoshinao and the intendant of Kurita Temple, the master of Buddhist Law Hankaku, who are allies of Yoshinaka, heard of this, they assembled their forces at Ichihara and challenged Yorinao. However, Yoshinao, who had hoped to check Yorinao and thus to protect Kiso Yoshinaka, was forced, much against his pride, to send a messenger to Yoshinaka and to ask for help when at nightfall, and still in the midst of fighting, his supply of arrows was depleted. Yoshinaka responded with a vast army. As he approached the scene of battle, Yorinao, fearful of Yoshinaka's vaunted forces, fled toward Echigo Province to seek the protection of Jō Shirō Nagamochi.

9th day. *Chiba Tsunetane suggests Kamakura as Yoritomo's headquarters.*

Adachi Morinaga, returning from his mission to Chiba, reported to His Lordship thus: "Shortly after I announced myself at the gate of Chiba Tsunetane's residence, I was invited in. Tsunetane, flanked by his sons Tanemasa and Taneyori, received me in his guest room. Although he listened patiently to what I had to say, he remained silent and appeared to be asleep. But his sons spoke up, almost in unison, saying, 'Yoritomo seeks to arouse the brave to action so that the cruel and the avaricious might be overthrown. He has summoned us at the very outset of his venture. Is there any reason to defer our acceptance? We shall forward our letter of acceptance immediately. Tsunetane contemplates no action except to concur. Tears fill his eyes and he is speechless, for he is grateful for the chance to restore the House of Minamoto which has been held in abeyance.' Later, as I was being entertained with drink, Tsunetane suggested, 'The location of His Lordship's present headquarters is neither strategically sound nor historically important. His Lordship should move his headquarters forthwith to Kamakura in Izu Province.' Tsunetane also declared that he will join Your Lordship with his band of followers."

11th day. *Yoritomo tours Maro* mikuri *and vows to assist shrines.*

Guided and attended by Nobutoshi, Yoritomo toured the Maro *mikuri* in Awa. This land had been the first grant made by an emperor to Yoritomo's ancestor Yoriyoshi at the time of the latter's conquest of the barbarians of eastern Japan. Other Minamoto ancestors, such as Tameyoshi and Yoritomo's own father Yoshitomo, had received imperial confirmations of this grant. However, in Heiji 1:6,1 [1159] Yoritomo had granted this land to the Great Shrine of Ise in return for prayers by the shrine toward Yoritomo's advancement at the court. Then on the 28th of the same month the shrine placed this land in charge of a secretary. Now, after more than twenty years, as Yoritomo revisited this place which holds many memories for him, he was moved to tears. His Lordship, declaring that a *mikuri* cannot but enhance the glory of the gods, and believing that the glorification of the gods would remove obstacles in the path of his cherished ambitions, vowed to establish new *mikuri* throughout the province and to offer them to the gods. So saying, His Lordship committed his vow to writing.

12th day. *Yoritomo grants a rice field to Sunosaki Shrine.*

13th day. *Yoritomo plans to quit Awa; the Chiba attack Heike partisans.*

His Lordship, who plans to quit Awa Province for Kazusa, has more than three hundred picked troops who will accompany him. However, his departure has been delayed because of the failure of Taira Hirotsune and his troops to assemble here.

Today, as Chiba Tsunetane, his sons, and his relatives were readying themselves to report to Yoritomo, Taneyori spoke to his father, saying: "The provisional governor of Chiba, a Taira partisan, harbors sinister designs which he will undoubtedly execute the moment our clan crosses the provincial border to join with the Minamoto. We should therefore dispose of him first." Tsunetane agreed and sent his nephew Shōtarō Maritane and his followers to attack the residence of the provisional governor who, strong as ever, stood off the attack with several tens of men. However, as there was a brisk wind blowing at the time, Naritane sent a servant to the rear of the house to set fire to the place. As the building was consumed, and as the governor frantically sought safety from the fire, Yoritane slew and beheaded him.

14th day. *A Taira partisan attacks the Chiba.*

The secretary Chikamasa, lord of the Chida manor in Shimōsa Province, is a son-in-law of Taira Tadamori, the minister of justice. As he is a supporter of the lay priest and chancellor Kiyomori, he attacked Chiba Tsunetane when he heard of the slaying of the provisional governor. But Tsunetane's great grandson Naritane gave battle and took Chikamasa a prisoner.

15th day. *The Takeda and Ichijō return to Kai from Shinano, after subduing Heike partisans there.*

Takeda Nobuyoshi and Ichijō Tadayori and their men, having successfully subdued the insurgents in Shinano, returned last night to Kai and encamped for the night at Hayami-yama. Today Lord Hōjō arrived at the same place and conveyed His Lordship's instructions to Nobuyoshi and Tadayori.

17th day. *Yoritomo quits Awa for Shimōsa, where he is joined by Chiba Tsunetane.*

Yoritomo has departed for Shimōsa without awaiting the arrival of Taira Hirotsune. Meeting him at Kokufu in Shimōsa were Chiba Tsunetane, his sons Tanemasa, Morotsune, Tanemori, Tanenobu, Tanemichi, and Taneyori, and his grandson Naritane, the eldest son of Tanemasa. Yoritomo's following now numbers three hundred mounted men.

At the meeting of Chiba and Yoritomo, Tsunetane first presented for His Lordship's inspection the prisoner Chikamasa. Then he presented Yoritomo with a supply of food provisions. Inviting Tsunetane to sit at his right, Yoritomo said: "It is most proper that I address you as my father." Tsunetane, coming forward with a young man and directing the lad to take a position before Yoritomo, said, "This is my gift to Your Lordship today. Permit him to attend you." This youth, who is called the young lord Yoritaka, is the sixth son of Minamoto Yoshitaka of Mutsu. Clothed in a blue-spotted coat of mail, the youth knelt beside Tsunetane. From the youth's appearance Yoritomo saw immediately that he was a scion of the Minamoto and invited him to take his place with Tsunetane. The youth's father, Yoshitaka, had given his life for Yoshitomo in the 12th month of Heiji 1 [1159] at Ryūgegoe on Mount Hiei. At the time Yoritaka was an infant of fifty days, but because of his father's involvement with Yoshitomo, he was placed in Tsunetane's care in Shimōsa during the 12th month of Eireki 1 [1160].

19th day. *Taira Hirotsune reports to Yoritomo with twenty thousand men.*

The vice governor of Kazusa, Taira Hirotsune, leading a force of twenty thousand horsemen drawn from Sutō, Susai, Inan, Ihoku, Chōnan, and Chōhoku in Kazusa, reported to Yoritomo near the Sumida River. Yoritomo, angered at Hirotsune's delay in responding to his call, was in no mood to condone the delay. Hirotsune, on the other hand, secretly reasoned that since not all of his own men were supporters of the Taira as he was, he would submit for the time being to Yoritomo, leading the latter to believe that it was a simple matter for him, an exile, to raise troops for a cause. If, on the other hand, Yoritomo did not fare well, Hirotsune would attack him and turn him over to the Heike. Thus Hirotsune had come to Yoritomo, outwardly professing submission but inwardly prepared to betray him. But Hirotsune, who had expected Yoritomo to welcome him and his large force, was stunned at being reprimanded instead by Yoritomo for reporting late. Completely dominated by Yoritomo, Hirotsune relinquished any thought of revolt and resolved instead to serve Yoritomo. Many years ago when Taira Masakado, the son of Yoshimasa, junior fifth rank, lower grade, and the former general of the Pacifying-Ezo Headquarters, had planned to subjugate Eastern Japan and to raise a revolt, Fujiwara Hidesato, under guise of serving Masakado, had gained entrance into Masakado's lines. In his joy, Masakado had come forward to receive him without so much as binding his hair or putting on his ceremonial cap. Hidesato took his leave, convinced by the careless demeanor of his host that the time had come to attack Masakado. Subsequently, he was able to carry out his plan and to take Masakado's head. . . .[28]

20th day. *Yoritomo prepares to set up a line of defense in Suruga.*

Tsuchiya Saburō Munetō has left for Kai Province on a mission for His Lordship. Since the warriors of the three provinces of Awa, Kōzuke, and Shimōsa have been reporting to His Lordship, it is planned to despatch these troops, as well as those of Musashi, to Suruga Province to prepare to face the Heiji which may be sent against the Genji. Munetō's mission is to instruct Lord Hōjō to establish contact with the Genji followers of Takeda Nobuyoshi and to proceed with them to Kisegawa, Suruga Province, to await His Lordship's arrival.

22nd day. *The Taira in Kyoto prepare to invade Eastern Japan.*

The *ason* and minor captain of the Left Inner Palace Guards Taira Koremori, who is planning to depart for the east to subjugate the Minamoto, was presented with a horse by the regent Fujiwara Motomichi. The presentation was made for the regent by Kiyokata,

---

[28] This is an episode from the so-called Tenkei-no-ran, the civil war brought about by Taira Masakado during the Tenkei era [938–947].

clerk of the military guards and official of the sovereign's dining room, and the gift was accepted for the minor captain by an emissary. The precedent for this custom began in Kashō 2:12,19 [1107] when Taira Masamori, the governor of Inaba, upon receipt of an imperial mandate to chastise Minamoto Yoshichika, the governor of Tsushima, called upon the regent Tadazane to beg his leave. Following the visit the regent had made a gift of a horse to Masamori's family through Tamesada, the clerk of the military guards and official of the sovereign's dining room.

24th day. *Yoritomo orders the Genji of Kai to proceed to Suruga.*

Today, at 11 P.M., Yoritomo's emissary, Munetō, reached Lord Hōjō and the Genji of Kai at Isawa *mikuri* where the latter had arrived from Hayami Mountain. In accordance with Yoritomo's instructions Takeda Nobuyoshi and Ichijō Tadayori resolved to assemble their men and to proceed to Suruga Province.

28th day. *Yoritomo invites Edo Shigenaga to join him.*

Yoritomo has sent an emissary to summon Edo Tarō Shigenaga. Although Shigenaga had opposed Yoritomo at Ishibashi Mountain at the urging of Kagechika, he was told to comply with the directive of Prince Mochihito. Yoritomo's message to Shigenaga reads: "In the absence of Hatakeyama Shigeyoshi and Oyamada Arishige at the capital, you are the chief pillar of Musashi Province. It will be my pleasure to have your support. Rally what warriors you can and be in readiness."

29th day. *Yoritomo's following increases to twenty-seven thousand men; a Taira army departs for the east.*

Yoritomo's following now numbers twenty-seven thousand horsemen. If the Genji of Kai, Hitachi, Shimotsuke, and Kōzuke are included, the number should reach fifty thousand mounted.

The failure of Edo Shigenaga, still favorably disposed toward Ōba Kagechika, to respond to Yoritomo's letter of yesterday has led His Lordship to take measures against him. He has despatched Naka Shirō Koreshige to Kasai Saburō Kiyoshige with instructions to inspect the defenses of Ōi and to draw out Shigeyori by deceit so that he might be killed. Although the Edo and Kasai are members of the same clan, Kiyoshige is loyal to His Lordship and is not known to practice duplicity.

Owing to a special regard for Sanada Yoichi Yoshitada, who had given his life for Yoritomo at Ishibashi Mountain, His Lordship sent an emissary to the mother of the late Yoshitada. To assure her the safety of the young sons of Yoshitada from Kagechika and his rebel followers of Sagami and Izu, who had been posing as members of the Minamoto in order to do harm, Yoritomo wisely urged her to send the youths immediately to his present location in Shimōsa.

Today the minor captain Taira Koremori has departed from the capital for the east. With him are the governor of Satsuma Taira Tadanori and the governor of Mikawa Taira Tomonori. The decision to embark on this campaign had been reached after Kagechika's messengers, despatched on the 28th of the Eighth Month with news of the Battle of Ishibashi Mountain, reached the capital on the 2nd of the Ninth Month.

30th day. *Nitta Yoshishige and Ashikaga Toshitsuna are reported hostile to Yoritomo.*

Because he is the grandson and heir of the late Minamoto Yoshiie, governor of Mutsu, Nitta Yoshishige, the lay priest and assistant director of the palace kitchen, who is known by the priestly name of Jōsai, has tended to act independently of Yoritomo long before the outbreak of hostilities in Eastern Japan. Yoritomo, nevertheless, has written to him soliciting his aid. Yoshishige, refusing to respond, has withdrawn to Terao Castle in Kōzuke and is reported to be rallying troops. Also, Ashikaga Tarō Toshitsuna, a Taira partisan, has burned and destroyed the homes of the people at the local government center in Mutsu, claiming that the people there had given shelter to Minamoto men.

TENTH MONTH

1st day. *Tachibana Tōmochi moves to intercept the Genji; Yoritomo reaches Shimōsa; Zenjō reports to Yoritomo.*

The acting governor of Suruga, Tachibana Tōmochi, having had word that the Genji of Kai were approaching Suruga, has rallied troops in Tōtomi and Suruga and has ordered them to Yosu.

Many of the Minamoto who had dispersed at Ishibashi Mountain have reported today to Yoritomo at his quarters in Washinuma. Among those reporting to His Lordship was Zenjō[29] of Daigo. Zenjō, upon learning of the prince's pronouncement, had secretly left his temple in Kyoto, and under guise of going on a pilgrimage had made his way to the east. Yoritomo was moved to tears by Zenjō's zeal for his cause.

2nd day. *Yoritomo crosses the Ōi and Sumida Rivers.*

Directing his course toward Musashi Province, Yoritomo and his following of more than thirty thousand picked troops crossed the Ōi[30] and Sumida rivers on boats provided by Chiba Tsunetane and Hirotsune. Among the first to report to Yoritomo were the provisional governor Toyoshima Kiyomitsu and Kasai Saburō Kiyoshige. Also awaiting His Lordship's arrival, in compliance with orders from Yoritomo a few days ago, was Adachi Tō Kurō, the secretary of the Right Horse Bureau.

The late Hatta Munetsune's daughter, wife of the senior secretary Koyama Masamitsu, and now known as the nun Kanka, had been His Lordship's wet nurse. Today she has come to call on Yoritomo. With her is her youngest son, to whom she is greatly devoted. Summoning her before him, Yoritomo graciously listened to her reminiscences of the past. When she indicated her desire to have her son serve him, Yoritomo summoned him and, placing his own ceremonial cap on the youth's head, personally conducted the coming-of-age ceremony.[31] He was given the name of Koyama Shichirō Munetomo, which was later changed to Tomomitsu. He is fourteen years old.

3rd day. *Chiba Tsunetane, on orders from Yoritomo, attacks and kills Tsunenaka of Kazusa, a brother-in-law of Nagasa Rokurō.*

4th day. *Hatakeyama Shigetada, Kawagoe Shigeyori, and Edo Shigenaga pay homage to Yoritomo.*

Hatakeyama Shigetada has come to report to His Lordship at the

---

[29] See note 26, above.

[30] The Ōi River is the present Tone River.

[31] *Gembuku*, or *shufuku*, a ceremony indicating that a young man has come of age. It consisted of wearing the hat and clothes of an adult, and changing the personal name. The ceremony could take place at any time between the fifth and twentieth years of a boy's life.

Nagai Crossing. Kawagoe Shigeyori and Edo Shigenaga have also come to pay homage. These two men had been responsible for the death of Miura Yoshiaki. Yoritomo explained to Miura Yoshizumi that while he and the members of his family had served him faithfully and had distinguished themselves in battle, and while Shigenaga and the others had attacked the Genji, the Genji could not hope to achieve its objectives unless it chose and drafted into its ranks the powerful and the influential. Yoritomo also counseled the Miura that those who would be loyal to him must forget their rancor. Upon the denial of any treasonable intentions on their part, Shigenaga and the others were permitted to face the Miura and to take their places in the ranks.

5th day. *Edo Shigenaga is assigned a mission.*

Edo Shigenaga has been assigned to see that the officials of the provincial capital of Musashi, as well as those of the districts, carry out various matters pertaining to the provinces.

6th day. *Yoritomo arrives at Kamakura.*

With Hatakeyama Shigetada at the vanguard and Chiba Tsunetane at the rear, Yoritomo and his party arrived in Sagami Province. It is not known by how many thousands His Lordship's following of warriors has increased. Since the party arrived here directly, no measures had been taken previously to build quarters for His Lordship. Therefore a peasant's house has been selected as his quarters.

7th day. *Yoritomo worships at Tsurugaoka Hachiman Shrine and inspects the remains of Yoshitomo's residence.*

Yoritomo journeyed to Tsurugaoka Hachiman Shrine to worship, following which he inspected the remains of Yoshitomo's residence at Kamegayatsu. Earlier Yoritomo had planned on building his own residence at Kamegayatsu, but he abandoned the plan because of the geographic restrictions of the location and because Okazaki Yoshizane had built a temple there in memory of Yoshitomo.

8th day. *Adachi Morinaga's holdings are confirmed.*

For his constant support of the Minamoto, Adachi Morinaga has been summoned by His Lordship and given assurance of title to his present holdings of certain districts and villages.

9th day. *Yoritomo commissions Ōba Kageyoshi to build his residence.*

The work of constructing His Lordship's residence, assigned to Ōba Kageyoshi, has begun. However, because of the time required to complete it, His Lordship will occupy for the time being the mountain residence of the private official [32] Kanemichi, which has been requisitioned for this purpose. Kanemichi's dwelling, which will be moved and rebuilt, was originally constructed in the Shōreki era [990–994], and it has never been in a fire. . . .

11th day. *Masako arrives at Kamakura.*

At 5 A.M. Her Ladyship arrived at Kamakura, where she was met by Yoritomo's emissary for the occasion, Ōba Kageyoshi. . . . Also arriving at Kamakura in fulfillment of an agreement made with His Lordship several days ago was the priest Senkō-bō of Sōtō-zan. He had been Yoritomo's religious teacher in the past.

12th day. *The Tsurugaoka Shrine is transferred to a new site.*

Weather clear. That his ancestors might be venerated, His Lordship went to Kitayama in Kobayashi District at 3 A.M. to designate a place for the construction of an ancestral mausoleum and the Tsurugaoka Shrine, which will be transferred from its present site. Senkō-bō has been named intendant for the time being, while Kageyoshi has been assigned to administer the affairs of the shrine. Meanwhile, in order to purify himself, Yoritomo has been observing strict abstinence from animal food. So that there will be no question as to the wisdom of abandoning the old for the new site, the matter of selecting the exact location for the shrine was left to divine discretion, His Lordship drawing a lot before the Altar. Although the embellishment of the building remains to be done, the roof has been thatched.

The shrine was secretly established in the Eighth Month of Kōhei 6 [1063] by Minamoto Yoriyoshi, the governor of Iyo, who invited the spirits of Iwashimizu Shrine to come and dwell here. At the time Yoriyoshi wished to offer prayers to the ancestral gods in connection with the subjugation of Abe Sadatō to which he had

[32] *Chikeji,* or *chikaji,* an official serving in the *mandokoro,* or administrative board, of a private family, such as the Fujiwara. His duties consisted mainly of drafting documents. Here, the term is freely rendered as private official.

been assigned by imperial decree during the reign of the Ex-Sovereign Goreizei. Located originally in Yui District, the shrine, now designated as the lower sub-shrine,[33] had been repaired during the Second Month of Eihō 1 [1081] by Minamoto Yoshiie, governor of Mutsu. Now it has been transferred to Kobayashi District, and elaborate rites to commemorate the occasion were held.

13th day. *Kiso Yoshinaka invades Kōzuke Province; the Genji arrive in Suruga Province.*

Kiso Yoshinaka, emulating the deeds of his late father, Yoshikata, has invaded Kōzuke. In his efforts to pacify the local gentry he has warned Ashikaga Toshitsuna to desist from harassing the people and from causing further alarm and apprehension.

At nightfall the Genji of Kai and the Hōjō, father and son, stopped at Ōishi Station on their way to Suruga. There a report reached them that the acting governor of Suruga and the lay priest Osada were planning to attack them at 7 P.M. by way of the Fuji plains. The Genji in council decided to intercept them. Takeda Nobuyoshi, Ichijō Tadayori, and Kaneyori, the lieutenant of the military guards Takeda Ariyoshi, Yasuda Yoshisada, Hayami Mitsunaga, Kawachi Yoshinaga, and Izawa Nobumitsu crossed Washikoji at the northern foothills of Mount Fuji into Suruga Province. There they were joined by Katō Mitsukazu and Katō Kagekado who had fled toward Kai after the Battle of Ishibashi Mountain.

14th day. *The Genji slay Osada and take the acting governor of Suruga prisoner.*

At 11 A.M., in the vicinity of Hachita, the acting governor of Suruga Tachibana Tōmochi and his force, while proceeding toward Kai, were surprised by Takeda, Yasuda, and their men, who had come upon them by way of Kamino and Harutaji. The enemy, confined by a range of mountains and by towering boulders along the road, could neither advance nor retreat. However, Izawa Nobumitsu and Katō Kagekado, making their way to the head of the Genji columns and mustering every military might they could, attacked the enemy. Although Tōmochi was able to put up a de-

---

[33] *Wakamiya*, a sub-shrine or a small shrine, usually built within the precincts of a principal shrine. The term, also meaning "young prince," was sometimes applied to shrines built especially for imperial princes.

fense for a while, he was finally taken prisoner, while the lay priest Osada and his two sons were slain and beheaded. It is not known how many of Osada's followers were killed and wounded. The remainder of his men, unable to shoot their arrows from their position at the rear of their column, turned and fled. At 5 P.M. their heads were pilloried in the vicinity of Ide at the edge of the Fuji plains.

15th day. *Yoritomo occupies his new quarters.*

16th day. *Yoritomo proceeds to Suruga; en route he makes a grant of a manor to Hakone Shrine.*

At Yoritomo's request religious exercises lasting throughout the day were held at the Tsurugaoka Sub-shrine. . . . His Lordship has designated Kuwabara Township in Sagami Province as support-lands[34] for the shrine.

However, upon receipt of a report that the commander Taira Koremori, leading a force of several tens of thousands of mounted men, had arrived at Tegoshi Station in Suruga on the 13th, His Lordship departed immediately for Suruga. Tonight he arrived at Rokusho Shrine at the provincial capital of Sagami. Here he made a grant of the Hayakawa Manor in Sagami to the Hakone Incarnate[35] Shrine. With the directive making this grant His Lordship enclosed a personal letter to Gyōjitsu, the intendant of the shrine, which he despatched in the care of the servant Tsurutarō. His Lordship declared that, notwithstanding his failure to write to Gyōjitsu, he had never doubted his loyalty, and exhorted him to devote himself to prayer. His Lordship's directive is as follows:

Granted to the Hakone Incarnate Shrine
Hayakawa Manor in Sagami Province
  To be given forthwith to the control of the intendant of Hakone Shrine
This grant of the aforementioned manor has been made at the instruction of Minamoto Yoritomo, former assistant captain of the military guards. There shall be no interference in the exercise of the grantee's rights thereto. This grant is thus documented for future reference.
Jishō 4: 10,16

---

[34] *Kuryō-jo,* literally, "places for provisions to be used as offerings."
[35] See note 23, above.

17th day. *Hatano Yoshitsune takes his own life.*

When Hatano Yoshitsune, the secretary of the Right Horse Bureau, learned that Yoritomo had despatched troops with orders to slay him, he took his own life in Matsuda Township before Shimokōbe Yukihira and the others could reach him. Absent from the scene and thus escaping death was Aritsune, Yoshitsune's son, who is presently serving Ōba Kagechika. . . . Yoshitsune's father, Yoshimichi, had served Yoshitomo in the past, but in the spring of Hōgen 3 [1158], a breach had occurred in their relationship, and Yoshitsune, quitting the capital without notice, had taken up residence in Hatano.

18th day. *Yoritomo leads two hundred thousand troops across Ashigara Pass and arrives at Kisegawa in Suruga Province.*

Yoritomo, at the head of two hundred thousand of his mounted troops, has crossed the Ashigara Mountains, thus checking the further advance of Ōba Kagechika and his one thousand mounted men who had started out to reach the Taira lines. Kagechika has fled to the Kawamura Mountains.

During the day His Lordship was overtaken on the road by a manorial official of Izu Temple who presented him with a letter from the monks of the said temple. The letter appealed to him to put a stop to the outrages of warriors on the temple's lands which, owing to the war, had become a highway for troops. Yoritomo, in an effort to pacify the monks, has issued an order to the effect that such outrages must cease forthwith.

. . . His Lordship has arrived at Kisegawa at nightfall and has designated the coming 24th as the opening day of battle. The Genji of Kai and Shinano, as well as Lord Hōjō and twenty thousand mounted men have arrived here in accordance with the arrangements made with His Lordship a few days ago. . . . The eighteen prisoners captured from the ranks of the acting governor in the recent battle were presented for His Lordship's inspection. At the same time His Lordship was apprised of the deeds of his men. Katō Mitsukazu had slain the acting governor and had taken a prisoner; Katō Kagekado had killed two and taken one prisoner; Kudō Kagemitsu and Kagehisa had charged into the enemy at Hashita Mountain. His Lordship has declared that these men would be rewarded. He has also announced that he holds no rancor for those who had served Ōba Kagechika against the Minamoto. Whereupon, persons such as Ogino Toshishige and Soga Sukenobu came forward with their hands clasped to pay homage to Yoritomo.

At night Doi Sanehira and Tsuchiya Munetō entertained with wine while Lord Hōjō, his son, and followers from Izu and Sagami, were each presented with a horse and a ceremonial robe. Following this His Lordship despatched Doi Sanehira and Munehira, the manorial official of Nakamura Manor, to Matsuda to repair the old residence of the late Minamoto Tomonaga.

19th day. *Itō Sukechika is captured; Kagami Nagakiyo joins Yoritomo's forces.*

While launching a boat at Kohina, Izu province, in the hope of reaching Taira Koremori's lines, Itō Sukechika, master of Buddhist Law, was discovered and captured by Amano Tōnai Tōkage who presented him to His Lordship today at his Kisegawa quarters. But as Miura Jirō Yoshizumi is a son-in-law of Sukechika, His Lordship remanded the former to the custody of the latter until formal sentence is pronounced. In the past year Sukechika had plotted against Yoritomo, who escaped dire consequences when Sukeyasu, Sukechika's second son, secretly informed Yoritomo of the plot. Thus, today, Yoritomo sought to reward Sukeyasu for his services, but the latter declared: "Does the son of a hated enemy and captive deserve a reward? I ask only that Your Lordship grant us leave to go to the capital to join the Heike." It is an inspiring episode.

Kagami Jirō Nagakiyo has presented himself to His Lordship. He had left the capital early in the Eighth Month but, en route, he had been stricken with illness. After resting at Kōzuchi in Mino for approximately two months, he had, with assistance, made his way to Kai, where he learned that his band had joined the Genji. Thus he too has come to join the cause. His older brother, Akiyama Tarō Mitsutomo, still remains in the capital. . . .

20th day. *The Genji confront the Heiji at the Fuji River.*

Yoritomo arrived at Kajima in Suruga. On the west bank of the

Fuji River, Left Minor Captain Taira Koremori, the governor of
Satsuma Taira Tadanori, and the governor of Mikawa Taira
Tomonori have established their lines. At night, as Takeda Nobuyoshi was making his way stealthily to the rear of the Taira
lines, he frightened flocks of water birds nesting in the marshes.
Their flapping wings sounded like a huge army on the march.
There was consternation in the Heiji ranks. The second in command, Taira Tadakiyo, vice governor of Kazusa, suggested to
Koremori: "Every single warrior in the east has answered Yoritomo's
call to arms. It was reckless of us to have come here from the capital,
for we stand the danger of being surrounded. We must retreat to
the capital immediately, and direct our campaign elsewhere." Persuaded by his counsel, Koremori and his subordinates withdrew
their lines without awaiting the dawn and retreated toward the
capital. Iida Ieyoshi and his son Tarō crossed the river to pursue the
Taira. Tarō was killed by Butō Jirō, a local lord of Ise, who had
paused in his flight to give battle, but Butō in turn was killed by
Ieyoshi. Intō Jirō Tsuneyoshi was killed at Sameshima.

21st day. *Yoritomo abandons pursuit of the Taira; Minamoto
Yoshitsune joins his brother.*

When His Lordship ordered his men to prepare to pursue Taira
Koremori to the capital, Chiba Tsunetane, Miura Yoshizumi, and
Taira Hirotsune counseled him, saying: "In Eastern Japan there
are still men like Satake Yoshimasa and Fujiwara Hideyoshi of
Hitachi and several hundreds of troops under them who refuse to
acknowledge Your Lordship's leadership. Takayoshi, Hideyoshi's
father, especially, is a strong supporter of the Heike and is presently
residing in the capital. Besides these men there are many more in
the east who remain stubborn and obstinate. Under the circumstances, would it not be wiser to subjugate these eastern barbarians
first before going to Western Japan?" Accepting their counsel,
Yoritomo withdrew to Kisegawa, after taking measures to post
Yasuda Saburō Yoshisada in Tōtomi and Takeda Nobuyoshi in
Suruga as constables.[36]

Today a lad posting himself on the stone pavement before His
Lordship's quarters requested an audience with the Lord of Kama-

---

[36] *Shugo*, literally, "protector."

kura. Suspicious of the boy, Sanehira, Munetō, and Yoshizane refused to honor his request. In time, however, Yoritomo heard of the boy, and, surmising from the age of the youth that he might be Kurō from Ōshu, ordered that he be brought before him immediately. When Sanehira carried out the order, Yoritomo discovered that as he had surmised this was Yoshitsune. The two, recalling the past, wept with joy. Yoritomo recalled in particular the incident of the Ninth Month of Eihō 3 [1083] during the reign of the Ex-Sovereign Shirakawa, when their great grandfather Yoshiie, the governor of Mutsu, waged war in Ōshu against the shogun Saburō Takehira and his son Iehira. When Minamoto Yoshimitsu, lieutenant of the Left Military Guards, who was then serving in Kyoto, heard of the war, he resigned his post and, leaving his bowstrings at the palace, rushed to Ōshu to join his older brother. Together they routed the enemy. Yoritomo was touched by the similarity of this fine example to Yoshitsune's action in coming to assist him on this occasion. In Heiji 2:1 [1160], when his father passed away while Yoshitsune was still in swaddling clothes, he was taken by his stepfather, Ichijō Naganari, minister of the treasury, and placed in a temple in Kurama Mountain. There, as he grew to manhood, the urge to avenge the humiliation to his family became so strong that Yoshitsune administered the coming-of-age ceremony to himself and made his way to Ōshu to be with the powerful Fujiwara Hidehira. When, however, Yoshitsune stole out of Hidehira's manor house, the latter, forgetting his selfishness, sent the warrior brothers Tsugunobu and Tadanobu to escort Yoshitsune.

As the time to light the candles approached, His Lordship bathed, then went to Mishima Shrine to pray. Convinced that the divine assistance of Myōjin[37] had made possible the realization of his prayers, His Lordship, in gratitude, made a grant of land in this province to the shrine. The document reads:

Kawaraya and Nagasaki, orchard lands in Izu Province
> The said lands shall be yielded forthwith to the *Dai-Myōjin* of Mishima

The aforementioned orchard lands are hereby granted to the said shrine that it may conduct its prayers with peace of mind and equanimity. Granted thus.

Jishō 4:10,21   The *Ason Minamoto*

[37] See note 27, above.

22nd day. *Iida Ieyoshi reports to Yoritomo.*

Iida Gorō Ieyoshi, presenting himself before Yoritomo with the decapitated head of the Heike vassal Butō Jirō, reported on the details of his battle and of the death of his son Tarō. He was not able to report yesterday because of His Lordship's pilgrimage to the shrine. Yoritomo, impressed by Ieyoshi's bravery, said: "In our land there is no one braver. Although you fought alongside Ōba Kagechika at Ishibashi, you have come to serve me. Moreover, on this occasion you have distinguished yourself. There will be no one braver to match you in later generations." All present agreed with His Lordship.

23rd day. *Yoritomo rewards his vassals for their service; Ōba Kagechika surrenders.*

His Lordship has arrived at the provincial capital of Sagami and, for the first time, he has made awards to his men for meritorious services rendered in his behalf. The men whose present holdings were confirmed or to whom new grants were made were: Lord Hōjō, Takeda Nobuyoshi, Yasuda Yoshisada, Chiba Tsunetane, Miura Yoshizumi, Taira Hirotsune, Wada Yoshimori, Doi Sanehira, Adachi Morinaga, Tsuchiya Munetō Okazaki Yoshizane, Kudō Chikamitsu, Sasaki Sadatsuna, Sasaki Tsunetaka, Sasaki Moritsuna, Kudō Kagemitsu, Amano Tōkage, Ōba Kageyoshi, Usami Sukemochi, Ichikawa Yukifusa, lay priest Katō Kagekazu, Usami Sanemasa, Ōmi Iehide, and Iida Ieyoshi. In addition Yoshizumi was confirmed as vice governor of Miura and Yukihira as manorial official of Shimokōbe.

Ōba Saburō Kagechika has come here to surrender himself to Yoritomo. He has been placed in the custody of the provisional vice governor of Kazusa Taira Hirotsune. Owari Tamemune has been remanded to the custody of Okazaki Shirō Yoshizane, while Owari Sadakage has been remanded to Miura Yoshizumi. The township of Kawamura, claimed by Kawamura Saburō Yoshihide, has been confiscated and given to the custody of Ōba Kageyoshi. Takiguchi Saburō Tsunetoshi has been divested of his Yamanouchi manor, which has been given to the custody of Sanehira. Although there are others who had opposed the Genji at Ishibashi, only one out of ten received punishment.

25th day. *Yoritomo occupies the Matsuda residence.*

26th day. *Yoritomo orders the execution of Kawamura Yoshihide.*

27th day. *Yoritomo departs for Hitachi Province.*

His Lordship has departed for Hitachi to subdue the young lord Satake Hideyoshi. Although some of the men questioned the advisability of embarking on a campaign on His Lordship's day of abstinence, Yoritomo pointed out that the departure must take place on this day, the 27th, without delay, for Prince Mochihito's pronouncement authorizing his subjugation of Eastern Japan had reached him on the 27th of the Fourth Month.

ELEVENTH MONTH

2nd day. *Taira Koremori and his army reach the capital.*

4th day. *Yoritomo arrives in Hitachi; the Satake resist the Genji at Kanasa.*

His Lordship arrived at the provincial capital of Hitachi and ordered his elder retainers—Tsunetane, Hirotsune, Yoshizumi, and Sanehira—to hold a council and to plan a strategy of attack with utmost care and without error and oversight, for the authority and influence of the Satake extend beyond the boundaries of Hitachi, while within the province the Satake has numerous supporters. That such a strategy might be devised, the elders asked Taira Hirotsune, who is related to the Satake, to probe the feelings of the enemy. Returning from his mission he reported that Yoshimasa was in favor of capitulating to Yoritomo, but his son, the young lord Hideyoshi, and his followers had overruled Yoshimasa and had refused to surrender. It was also reported that Yoshimasa's father, Takayoshi, had always been a supporter of the Taira and that he and Hideyoshi had agreed earlier not to capitulate to the Genji. Thus Hideyoshi has withdrawn into Kanasa Castle.

Yoshimasa was persuaded by Hirotsune to appear at Ōya Bridge. There, at the suggestion of Yoritomo, Yoshimasa ordered his men to withdraw as he came forward to the middle of the bridge to meet Yoritomo. Thereupon Hirotsune slew him and with such great dispatch that Yoshimasa's followers either capitulated immediately

or turned and fled. Then Yoritomo sent Doi Jirō Sanehira, Wada
Yoshimori, Tsuchiya Munetō, Sasaki Sadatsuna, Sasaki Moritsuna,
Kumagaya Jirō Naozane, the guardsman Hirayama Sueshige, and
several thousands of his best warriors against Satake Hideyoshi.

Hideyoshi, ensconced behind the strong walls and defenses of
Kanasa Castle, remained obstinate and, in fact, commenced the
battle by hurling arrows and stones. The positions of the opposing
forces—the castle atop a mountain, the concentration of His Lordship's men in the ravine below—were as heaven is to earth. Thus
many of the flying arrows and the hurtling rocks from above struck
Yoritomo's men below, while the arrows of Yoritomo's men could
scarcely reach their objective atop the mountain. Moreover, huge
boulders blocked the way to the castle, and the men and horses lost
their footing. However, Yoritomo's men, despite their wasted efforts
and their bewilderment as to strategy, could not withdraw. In the
midst of this foolhardy attempt at battle the sun sank in the west
and the moon rose in the east.

5th day. *Yoritomo's men rout Satake Hideyoshi.*

At 3 A.M. Sanehira and Munetō sent a message to Yoritomo,
saying: "The fortress which the Satake has built cannot be broken
by human strength, and the troops ensconced within, except for
one in a thousand, cannot be hit by our arrows. We seek your wise
counsel." At a meeting summoned by Yoritomo, Hirotsune suggested: "Among Hideyoshi's uncles is one who is known as the
private official Satake. He excels in strategy and is above selfish
motives. If Your Lordship would agree to reward him for services
rendered, he would suggest a strategy to overthrow Hideyoshi."
Accepting the counsel, Yoritomo despatched Hirotsune to seek out
the private official. The latter, elated over Hirotsune's visit, . . .
was told: "There is not a single relative of yours who has not
acknowledged Yoritomo's leadership except Hideyoshi, who remains hostile. And thus, although Hideyoshi is of your own flesh
and blood, is there any reason why you should not assist us in
attacking him? Go quickly and pay homage to Yoritomo; then go
and slay Hideyoshi and receive his domains." The private official
promptly accepted the offer and, knowing the region well, led him
to the rear of the castle. There the men emitted a war cry which

reverberated through the castle. Surprised out of their wits, Hideyoshi and his followers fled from the castle in great confusion as
Hirotsune pressed the attack. Hideyoshi has disappeared, leaving
no traces of his whereabouts.

6th day. *The Genji burn Kanasa Castle and pursue remnants of the
Satake; Hideyoshi flees to Hanazono Castle in Ōshu.*

7th day. *Shida Yoshihiro and Minamoto Yukiie join Yoritomo.*
    Taira Hirotsune and his men reported to Yoritomo at his quarters
to recount the details of the battle, the flight of Hideyoshi, and the
burning of the castle. His Lordship announced that among the
men Kumagaya Jirō Naozane and the guardsman Hirayama Sueshige had distinguished themselves by rushing forward from time
to time without regard for their own safety and by killing many
of the rebels.
    The private official Satake also appeared before His Lordship
and expressed his wish to serve him. Because of the services he had
rendered, His Lordship granted the request.
    Today, the official of the office of the bodyguard of the crown
prince Shida Saburō Yoshihiro and the private official Minamoto
Yukiie arrived at the provincial capital and had an audience with
His Lordship.

8th day. *Yoritomo seizes the lands of Satake Hideyoshi and redis-
tributes them among his vassals; he makes Iwase Tarō a vassal.*
    Seven districts in eastern Hitachi, as well as Ōta, Kasuda, and
Sakaide, which had been Hideyoshi's domains have been confiscated and allocated as awards to those who had rendered distinguished service. Also, Yoritomo ordered Taira Hirotsune and
Miura Yoshizumi to apprehend and assemble in the courtyard the
ten or so Satake retainers who had been rumored to wish to acknowledge Yoritomo's leadership. As Yoritomo scanned their faces
to determine whether any of them harbored treasonable intentions,
he noticed among them a youth attired in ceremonial robe, and
weeping, with bowed head. When asked to identify himself and
to give his lineage, the youth declared that he could find no reason
for the killing of Satake Yoshimasa. His Lordship declared: "If that

is your opinion, why did you not give your life for him at the time
of his death?" The youth replied: "At the time Yoshimasa's retainers were not permitted on the bridge; My Lord alone was summoned to come forward. When he was killed I fled, fearful of the
consequences. Although my appearance here now is not becoming
to a true warrior, nevertheless, I have requested this audience with
Your Lordship, for I have something I wish to say." Encouraged to
continue, the youth added: "To set aside the chastisement of the
Heike and to destroy, instead, a member of your own clan is a
grievous error.[38] Against an enemy of the state the combined
force of all the warriors of the land should be brought to bear.
If you slay those of your own clan who have committed no wrong,
to whom would you turn to carry out the subjugation of your foes?
Moreover, who will be the protectors of your own heirs? This is a
matter of deepest concern for Your Lordship." All who heard the
boy were distrustful of his motives, and they were certain that the
youth's protestation of submission to Yoritomo was not sincere. But
Yoritomo remained silent. Whereupon Hirotsune declared: "There
is no doubt that the boy has treasonable motives. He should be
killed at once." However, His Lordship not only rejected Hirotsune's
suggestion and comforted the boy, but also admitted him into the
ranks of his immediate vassals. This is he whom we know as Iwase
Yoichi Tarō.

   Today Yoritomo departed for Kamakura, stopping for the night
along the way at the Hatta Manor House in Oguri *mikuri,* which
is held by Oguri Jūrō Shigenari.

10th day. *Yoritomo makes a grant of a manor to Kasai Kiyoshige.*

   His Lordship has made a grant of the Mariko Manor in Musashi
Province to Kasai Saburō Kiyoshige, at whose residence he is lodging
tonight. The table was laid out for His Lordship by Kasai's wife,
a fact which was withheld from the guest out of deference for his
pleasure. His Lordship was told that she was a young woman invited by the host for the occasion.

12th day. *Ogino Gorō Toshishige is beheaded.*

   When His Lordship arrived in Musashi, he ordered the decapita-

   [38] The Satake were descended from Minamoto Yoshimitsu, brother of Yoshiie,
who had founded Yoritomo's line of the Genji.

tion of Ogino Gorō Toshishige. Although Ogino had served His Lordship for some time and appeared to be loyal, he had espoused the cause of Ōba Kagechika at the time of the Ishibashi Battle. Yoritomo took this action, because, if such villainy is not rectified now, it would be difficult to discipline his men later.

14th day. *Yoritomo orders warriors in Musashi to desist from violating temple and shrine lands.*

15th day. *Ikōji Temple of Masashi is given fiscal exemption.*
    Since the tradition of Ikōji Temple of Musashi, which has offered prayers in behalf of the house of Minamoto for generations, is being carried on by Zōen, the head priest, the privilege of fiscal exemption for the priest's residence and the temple's lands will be continued to be recognized by His Lordship.

17th day. *Wada Yoshimori is made President of the* Samurai-dokoro.[39]
    His Lordship has returned to Kamakura. He has granted clemency to Soga Tarō Sukenobu.
    Wada Tarō Yoshimori has been appointed president of the *samurai-dokoro.* Yoshimori had requested the office in the Eighth Month during the flight from Ishibashi Mountain when His Lordship's safety was uncertain. Now His Lordship has given his consent and has issued instructions today to reserve this office for Yoshimori.

19th day. *Yoritomo installs his younger brother Zenjō as priest of Nagao Temple in Musashi.*

20th day. *Ōba Kageyoshi seeks pardon for Matsuda Yoshitsune, his brother-in-law.*

26th day. *Yoritomo exonerates Takiguchi Tsunetoshi.*
    A decision had been arrived at in secret to behead Takiguchi Saburō Tsunetoshi of Yamanouchi. But word of this decision

---

[39] *Samurai-dokoro,* formerly a chamber in the civil dictator's mansion for the reception of members of the military class. At Kamakura it was intended for the management of the affairs of the warriors.

reached Tsunetoshi's aged mother, who had been Yoritomo's wet nurse. Appearing before His Lordship, and pleading tearfully for her son's life, she said: "For generations, ever since the lay priest Sukemichi entered the services of Lord Hachiman Minamoto Yoshiie, and since I became a wet nurse to Minamoto Tameyoshi, we have rendered loyal service on innumerable occasions to the house of Minamoto. In particular, Toshimichi gave his life for the Minamoto at Rokujō-Kawara in the Heiji Battle. As for Tsune-toshi, it is true that he supported Ōba Kagechika, which is a grievous offense. However, he did so only out of fear of Heike reprisals later. At the very time he established his line at Ishibashi, he was thinking of asking for Your Lordship's pardon. Moreover, is not the fact of Tsunetoshi's past deeds cause for mitigation?" Without replying to her directly, Yoritomo ordered Doi Sanehira to bring forward a long, four-legged chest. Opening the lid, he took out a coat of mail, which he placed before the woman. The armor which Yoritomo had worn in the Ishibashi Battle was pierced at the sleeve by an arrow shot from Tsunetoshi's bow. On the arrow, just above the surface of the armor where it had struck, were inscribed the words "Takiguchi Saburō Fujiwara Tsunetoshi." It is indeed re-markable that His Lordship had kept the arrow to this day— buried in the armor where it had struck and with the portion of the shaft above the inscription broken off. When the name on the arrow was read aloud, Tsunetoshi's mother was rendered speechless, and, wiping her tears, retired from Yoritomo's presence. Yoritomo had kept the arrow for this purpose. However, although Tsune-toshi's offense is hardly excusable, His Lordship, moved by the grief of the aged mother and out of consideration for the exploits of Tsunetoshi's predecessors, granted him an immediate pardon.

TWELFTH MONTH

1st day. *Taira Tomomori attacks the Genji in Ōmi Province.*

Taira Tomomori, captain of the Middle Palace Guards, Left Division, leading a force of several thousand government troops, has descended on Ōmi to attack Yamamoto Yoshitsune, the former lieutenant of the palace guards and his younger brother, the young lord Saeki Yoshikane. Although Yoshitsune and his men challenged Tomomori with utter disregard for their lives, Tomomori and his vast forces set fire to the Yamamoto manor house and the houses of the Yamamoto followers, thus causing consternation in the Genji ranks and forcing them to flee. By choosing to remain in Ōmi ever since the Genji in the east had raised their standard of revolt during the Eighth Month, Yoshitsune and Yoshikane had exposed themselves to Taira attacks. By constantly flouting the authority of the lay priest and chancellor Taira, they are serving Kanto's cause loyally.

2nd day. *Taira Shigehira, Taira Kiyofusa, and Yamamoto Sadayoshi depart for the east against the Minamoto but return to the capital.*

4th day. *The* ajari[40] *Sadayoshi, exiled to Kazusa by the Taira, is summoned to Kamakura and installed as altar priest at Tsurugaoka.*
    The *ajari* Sadayoshi has come to Kamakura from Kazusa Province on the summons of His Lordship. Sadayoshi had been banished to Kazusa on Angen 1:4,26 [1175]. But his fame as an authority on Buddhism and the absence in Kamakura of anyone so virtuous led His Lordship to order Taira Hirotsune to instruct Sadayoshi to report to Kamakura. Today he was installed as altar priest at Tsurugaoka.

10th day. *Yamamoto Yoshitsune arrives at Kamakura.*
    Yamamoto Yoshitsune has arrived at Kamakura. Doi Jirō Sanehira, speaking in his behalf, reported thus to His Lordship: "Yoshitsune has always espoused Kanto's cause. Throughout the period of Heike rule he demonstrated his partisanship for Kanto whenever the occasion demanded. On the first of the month his castle was attacked and destroyed by the enemy. Now, in accordance with his fixed resolve, he has come to pay homage to Your Lordship. He declares that, when the time comes to strike at the rebels, he will be, without fail, at the vanguard of one of Your Lordship's armies. It is praiseworthy of him to have reported promptly to Your Lordship. For the present he requests permission to serve Your Lordship in Kanto." Yoshitsune is a descendant in the fifth generation of Minamoto Yoshimitsu, secretary of the Ministry of

───────────────

[40] *Ajari*, from the Sanskrit word *ācārya*, meaning "holy teacher." It was an honorary title for priests of high rank who were skilled in ritual prayers and mystic practices and who presided over initiation of novices.

Justice. In the two arts of archery and horsemanship he yields to no one. In Angen 2:12,30 [1176], due to vilification by the Heike, he was banished to Sado, and it was only last year that he received an imperial pardon. Now, again, because of the attack on him by the Taira, he has been rendered homeless. His Lordship consented to give Yoshitsune the opportunity to realize his cherished ambition.

11th day. *Taira Kiyomori despatches Taira Shigehira to Ōmi to destroy Onjō-ji.*

Taira Kiyomori has despatched Shigehira against the monks of Onjō-ji because of the latter's compliance during the Fifth Month with Prince Mochihito's pronouncement. It is also the intention of the Taira to destroy the southern capital. The Taira claims that it had never contemplated these moves until compelled to do so by Yoritomo's orders which had aroused the monks to warlike acts.

12th day. *Yoritomo moves into his new residence; Onjō-ji is burned by the Heike.*

Sky clear. Winds gentle. At 9 P.M. Yoritomo[41] observed the ceremony of removal to a new house.[42] The work on the building, which is situated in Ōkura Township, had begun in the Tenth Month under the supervision of Ōba Kageyoshi. At the scheduled hour His Lordship left the residence of the provisional vice governor of Kazusa Hirotsune and entered the new residence. His Lordship was dressed in ceremonial robe. His mount was chestnut-colored and mottled. Attending His Lordship at his front was Wada Yoshimori. Kagami Jirō Nagakiyo was in attendance to the left of His Lordship's mount, and the young lord Moro Hidemitsu at the right. . . . After His Lordship entered his bedchamber, the men gathered in the *samurai-dokoro,* which has eighteen rooms, and, with Wada Yoshimori seated in the center, took their places in two rows facing one another. There were three hundred and eleven men in attendance.

His Lordship's immediate vassals have also been constructing residences here. These houses will increase the grandeur of the entire east and will make Kamakura an important center. This had

[41] In the text the term "shogun" is used here. Obviously, it was inserted at a later date.

[42] *Owatamashi-no-gi,* after a custom observed among the nobles.

been a secluded place with but a few fixed abodes, frequented only
by fishermen and aged rustics. But lanes and streets are being
laid, and names are being assigned to hamlets and villages. Moreover, the tiled roofs of houses stand in a line and the doors of gates
creak under the eaves.

Today, Onjō-ji was razed by the Heike. The main hall, the large
and small halls, and the stupa, as well as the *Mahayana* and
Hinayama Sutras and the sacred writings of exoteric and esoteric
Buddhism, have been virtually reduced to ashes.

14th day. *Yoritomo grants confirmation of present holdings to principal residents of Musashi.*

16th day. *Yoritomo attends an exposition of the* Saishōō Sutra[43] *at
Tsurugaoka.*

19th day. *Tachibana Kiminaga and his two sons desert the Taira
and are accepted as vassals by Yoritomo.*

20th day. *Yoritomo indulges in a banquet, an archery contest, and a
visitation.*

Miura Yoshizumi gave a banquet[44] in His Lordship's honor at
the latter's new residence. Following the banquet an archery contest[45] was held. Although unscheduled, the contest was ordered by
His Lordship when he was told of the special skill of Tachibana
and his sons. . . .

For his first visitation[46] since his removal to his new residence
His Lordship chose the Amanawa residence of Adachi Morinaga.
His Lordship presented him with a horse. The horse was led by
Sasaki Moritsuna.

22nd day. *Nitta Yoshishige comes to Kamakura; Satomi Yoshinari
comes from Kyoto to pay homage.*

Nitta Jōsai, the lay priest and assistant director of the bureau of
the palace kitchen, has been summoned by His Lordship. At the
express order of Yoritomo not to enter Kamakura at his own dis-

---

[43] The abbreviated title for the *Konkōmyō saishōō Sutra.*
[44] *Ōban.*   [45] *Yumi-hajime.*   [46] *Gokō-hajime.*

cretion, it being rumored that he had gathered troops and with-drawn himself in his Terao manor house in Kōzuke, Jōsai had been staying at Yamanouchi. Adachi Morinaga was despatched to Yama-nouchi to escort Jōsai to Kamakura. Jōsai gave the following ex-planation to His Lordship: "I entertained no thought of demurring with Your Lordship. However, with wars waging in the provinces, it has not been easy for me to leave my castle. Thus, at the urging of my vassals, I have deferred reporting to Your Lordship. I am therefore astonished to be served with this order." At Morinaga's avowal that he was convinced of Jōsai's sincerity, His Lordship accepted the explanation.

Satomi Tarō Yoshinari, a grandson of Jōsai, has also reported to His Lordship. Although he had been a supporter of the Heike in the past, he has come to pay homage to Yoritomo, having heard of the increasing successes of the Minamoto. His intentions differ from those of his grandfather. Yoshinari, pleading to be permitted to serve at Yoritomo's side, explained: "Since the Battle of Ishibashi the Heike have not ceased discussing and making preparations for the destruction of every member of the Genji. I therefore deceived the Heike with the proposition that I would go to Kanto to attack Yoritomo. To this they were agreeable and gave me leave. At Sembon Matsubara in Suruga I met Nagai Saitō Sanemori, the intendant, and Seshimo Shirō Hirochika, who told me that the warriors in the east are all supporters of Yoritomo, who consequently had assembled tens of thousands of mounted troops in Kamakura. As for the two, they were on their way to the capital, having promised to serve the Heike a few days ago. Hearing this, I hastened on my way."

24th day. *Kiso Yoshinaka returns to Shinano Province.*

The young lord Kiso Yoshinaka is vacating Kōzuke and is pro-ceeding toward Shinano. Although he has declared that the purpose of this action is to lay claim to Tago Manor in Shinano which had belonged to his late father, his intention is to establish his autonomy in Shinano. The fact is that Yoritomo's growing prestige in the east has prompted him to return to Shinano.

25th day. *Yoritomo retrieves the statuette of Kwannon; Taira Shigehira departs from Kyoto to subdue the monks of Nara.*

26th day. *Sasaki Gorō Yoshikiyo is remanded to the custody of his brother.*

28th day. *Taira Shigehira burns the Tōdai-ji and Kōfuku-ji in Nara.*

Izumo Tokizawa has been named by His Lordship to be the superintendent of servants. Although there are many servants who render service to His Lordship morning and night, Tokizawa had distinguished himself during the recent campaigns.

Today Taira Shigehira burned the southern capital of Nara. The compounds of Tōdai-ji and Kōfuki-ji, including the halls and stupas, did not escape the fires. Likewise, the Buddhist statues and sutras have been consumed by the fire.

Chapter II

FIRST MONTH

1st day. *Yoritomo worships at Tsurugaoka, then attends a banquet.*

At 5 A.M. Yoritomo worshiped at the sub-shrine of Tsurugaoka. He has suspended all activities for the day and has fixed the morning of the first day of each lunar month as a day of worship at Tsurugaoka.² Last night, shortly after midnight, Miura Yoshizumi, Hatakeyama Shigetada, and Ōba Kageyoshi and their followers posted themselves as guards at every intersection. His Lordship arrived at the worship hall on horseback. Waiting here to attend His Lordship was Senkō-bō Ryōzen. First, a sacred horse drawn by Usami Sukemochi and Nitta Tadatsune was led to the altar; then His Lordship listened to a reading of the *Lotus Sutra,* as offerings of food were made to the spirit of the dead. At his residence, after the services, Chiba Tsunetane gave a banquet in His Lordship's honor. The table was laid with a three-foot carp and an abundance of fruits and wine.

5th day. *Hatano Tadatsuna and Hatano Yoshisada capture Gō Shirō and his sons.*

On the basis of a rumor that the warriors of Kanto were planning to enter the capital via a sea route around the Nankai circuit,³ the Heike had posted their retainers at various points along the coast. One of these men, Gō Shirō of Izu, who had been assigned to guard Shima Province, was attacked today on Nakiri Island by the monks

¹ The era designation of Jishō was changed to Yōwa on the fourteenth day of the Seventh Month.
² Literally, "as the day for the offering of *nusa* at the shrine." The *nusa,* originally cloth offerings, were symbols of sanctity or divinity made of cloth or paper and hung on a pole. See also note 24, Part Two, Chapter I.
³ *Nankai-dō,* the administrative circuit comprising the provinces of Shikoku, the island of Awaji, and Kii on the main island.

of Kumano,[4] who inflicted many casualties on Gō's followers and caused them to flee. While fleeing toward Izuoka by way of the sacred mountains of the Great Shrine of Ise, Gō and his followers came across Hatano Tadatsuna, the second son of Hatano Yoshimichi, and Hatano Yoshisada, Yoshimichi's grandson, and their followers. There ensued a battle, the Hatano being loyal followers of the Minamoto, and the two sons of Gō were killed. Tadatsuna and Yoshisada, succeeding to their father's estate, had been living in Ise; but their father Yoshitsune, the secretary of the Right Horse Bureau, had been condemned to death by His Lordship for his unprincipled behavior.[5] However, his descendants—Tadatsuna and Yoshisada—have not forgotten their friendship for the Minamoto and they continue to render loyal service to the Genji.

6th day. Kudō Kagemitsu captures Hirai Kiroku who had attacked Hōjō Munetoki; he is placed in the custody of Wada Yoshimori.

18th day. A report is made on the burning of the Tōdai-ji and Kōfuku-ji.

Today, the details of the burning by the Heike of the halls, stupas, and living quarters of the Tōdai-ji and Kōfuku-ji in the southern capital on the 28th of the Twelfth Month have reached Kanto. Only the special warehouses with the imperial and temple seals escaped the fire. When the fire reached the Hall of the Great Buddha, three persons, unable to bear the sight, threw themselves into the fire and were burned to death. More than 100 persons of the two temples sustained burns from this unexpected fire. The report was brought here by the monk Inkei, a local lord of Mōri Manor of Sagami Province. For the past two or three years he had been living in the southern capital to pursue his studies. Now, with the destruction of these temples, he has returned to his native province.

21st day. The monks of Kumano attack the Heike in Ise and Shima Provinces.

Battles have been raging in various places in Ise and Shima

---

[4] A historic shrine in southeast Kii.

[5] On Hatano Yoshitsune's differences with Yoritomo, see Jishō 4:10,17.

Provinces since the 5th of the month, when the armed monks[6] of Kumano first burst into these provinces. By the 19th they had seized the homes of the people in seven places along the coast and, inflicting death and injury, they had forced the retainers of the Heike to abandon their fortified areas and to flee. Impelled by the momentum of these victories, the monks today burned the homes of the people at Futami-ura. As they carried their onslaught to Kosegawa, the governor of Dewa Nobukane and his nephew Itōji, who are members of the Heiji, organized their followers to resist the monks. They met the monks in the vicinity of Funae, where a battle ensued. When Kaikō, . . . the leader of the monks, was struck down by one of Nobukane's arrows, the monks withdrew to Futami-ura, where they took to their boats for Kumano-ura, forcing more than thirty people, including maidservants between the ages of thirty and forty and children about fourteen or fifteen years old, to go along with them.

The cause of this disturbance was the desire of the Kumano monks, who have been praying for the success of Kanto, to attack and overthrow Heiji partisans in the Nankai circuit, which had been seized by the lay priest and chancellor. The lay priest and chancellor had insulted the imperial government by his excessive pride and pomp; he had been heedless of the glory of the gods; he had been destructive of Buddhist Law; and he had tormented and demoralized the people. Of late he had sent messengers into the three districts of Ise, where the Great Shrine is located, to levy a commissariat rice tax[7] on the people and to seize their homes. This is unprecedented in the one-thousand-year history of this shrine dedicated to the Heaven-Shining-Great-Deity. In the last two or three years the people in high and low places and in the cities and the rural areas alike have had but one hope—the destruction of the said lay priest, his sons, his grandsons, and his great grandsons. And thus the people, though essentially different one from another, think alike on the subject of the aforementioned family.

---

[6] *Akusō*, literally, "evil monks." The term was usually applied to those members of a monastery or a temple not concerned primarily with religious studies and exercises. Thus it was an inclusive term for the guards, servants, and other general-duty monks maintained by the monasteries.

[7] *Hyōrōmai*.

23rd day. *Yoritomo names the priest Chōei to administer Nagao and Kumyō Temples in Musashi.*

SECOND MONTH

1st day. *At Yoritomo's urging, Ashikaga Yoshikane marries Lord Hōjō's daughter, and Kagami Nagakiyo marries Taira Hirotsune's daughter.*

9th day. *Minamoto Yoshimoto, captured by the Heike last winter, is beheaded; his head is claimed by Ishikawa Yoshisuke and Kōbe Yoshihiro who are prisoners of the Heike in Kyoto.*

10th day. *Yoritomo receives a complaint from Sunosaki Shrine.*
    There has been a complaint from the Sunosaki Shrine in Awa Province to the effect that it has been harassed by officials of the provincial capital. Today His Lordship issued an order directing the officials to desist.

ORDERED: To the Priests of Sunosaki Shrine
    That, forthwith, the Sunosaki Shrine of Awa Province is exempted from all public obligations[8]
Lately the aforementioned shrine has been exempted from all public obligations; but regarding the exercise thereof, its shrine officials have complained repeatedly. If this is true, it is indeed audacious of those who ignore the order. It is ordered that the exemption be honored forthwith. The attention of the provincial office is directed hereto and it is decreed that it comply with this order without fail.
Jishō 5:2

12th day. *Taira Tomomori returns to Kyoto with the heads of the Genji of Mino.*

18th day. *A son-in-law of Miura Yoshiaki is pardoned by Yoritomo.*

27th day. *Taira Michimori, Taira Koremori, and Taira Tadanori lead troops to Owari.*

28th day. *Yoritomo orders Wada, Okabe, Kanō, Usami, and Tsuchiya to Ōmi to intercept the Heike; he orders abstinence from cer-*

    [8] *Manzō-kuji,* an inclusive term for the three public obligations or taxes; *so,* or rice tax; *chō,* or tax in kind; and *yō,* or corvee.

tain foods out of respect for Kashima Shrine of Hitachi, whose lands have been seized by Shida Yoshihiro.

29th day. *Kikuchi Takanao of Higo and Ogata Koreyoshi of Bungo oppose Harada Tanenao in Kyushu.*

INTERCALARY SECOND MONTH

4th day. *Taira Kiyomori dies.*

The lay priest and chancellor passed away at 7 P.M. at the home of Kujō Kawaraguchi Morikuni. He had been ill since the 25th of the past month. His verbal will specified that the funeral services be held three days later; that his remains be interred in the Lotus Hall at Yamada, Harima Province; that memorial services be held every 7th day and not daily; that no mass be held in Kyoto; and that his sons and grandsons continue to work for the subjugation of eastern Japan.

7th day. *Yoritomo observes his birthday.*

On the occasion of his birthday, His Lordship summoned his wet nurse, the nun Mama, who resides at Hayakawa Manor in Sagami. Out of deep regard for her and to assure her the continued enjoyment of her house and lands, including ricelands and dry fields, His Lordship has made her land steward [9] of the entire domain of Hayakawa.

10th day. *Taira Munemori and more than a thousand troops depart from Kyoto for the east.*

12th day. *Kōno Shirō and Ochi Michikiyo of Iyo seize the province and defy the Heike.*

15th day. *Taira Shigehira departs for the east with a mandate from the ex-sovereign.*

Bearing a decree from the ex-sovereign's government addressed to the provinces in the Tōkai circuit and enjoining all to chastise Yoritomo, the director of the sovereign's private office Taira Shigehira

[9] *Jitō.*

has departed from the capital for the east at the head of a thousand picked troops.

17th day. *Yasuda Yoshisada entrenches himself at Hamamatsu Manor near Hashimoto, Tōtomi Province, and awaits the Taira armies.*

19th day. *Miyoshi Yasunobu's letter arrives at Kamakura.*

20th day. *Shida Yoshihiro turns against the Genji; Yoritomo strengthens defenses west of Suruga; Seki Masahira deserts Yoritomo for Yoshihiro.*

It has come to light that Yoritomo's own flesh and blood, his uncle Shida Yoshihiro, leading a force of several tens of thousands of rebels, has left Hitachi for Shimotsuke with intentions of attacking Kamakura.

Meanwhile, as word of the approaching Heike armies has reached Kamakura, Yoritomo has despatched many of his warriors from Kamakura with orders to strengthen the defenses west of Suruga. In his efforts to devise a strategy to meet the enemy moves, Yoritomo has been pleased by the gallantry of Shimokōbe Yukihira and Koyama Tomomasa who, without awaiting orders from His Lordship, have gone to Shimōsa and Shimotsuke respectively to assist in the cause of the Genji. In this connection, Tomomasa's younger brother Munemasa, his followers, and Seki Masahira, who is Tomomasa's uncle, have departed today for Shimotsuke to reinforce Tomomasa's forces. When these men were summoned before Yoritomo prior to their departure, Masahira begged to be excused. Yoritomo suspected duplicity on his part, and this has come to pass; for Masahira, without joining Munemasa on the road, has taken a secret road to join Yoshihiro's lines.

21st day. *Yoritomo worships at Tsurugaoka Shrine.*

Because of the outbreak of insurrections in the east and the west, Yoritomo has vowed that beginning today and for the next seven days he will worship at the sub-shrine of Tsurugaoka for the return of peace and tranquility. This morning His Lordship visited the shrine before dawn. The sacred dance was performed.

23rd day. *Ashikaga Tadatsuna joins with Shida Yoshihiro to oppose Yoritomo; Koyama Tomomasa gives battle to Yoshihiro.*

Shida Yoshihiro, proceeding toward Kamakura with thirty thousand mounted men, stopped to confer with Ashikaga Matatarō Tadatsuna. The latter, having been hostile to the Minamoto from the beginning of the conflict, agreed to support Yoshihiro. The Ashikaga and the Koyama, although of the same clan, had been rivals for power in the same province. Last summer, when Prince Mochihito's pronouncement authorizing the overthrow of the chancellor Taira and his family reached the provinces, Koyama had acknowledged it, while Tadatsuna had taken exception. Tadatsuna, in fact, greatly provoked by the directive, had joined the Heiji in the Uji Battle and had broken the lines of the lay priest and courtier third rank Yorimasa and that of Prince Mochihito. He is still hostile to the Minamoto; thus he has agreed to support Yoshihiro, hoping at the same time to break the power of the Koyama.

When word of Tadatsuna's decision to support Yoshihiro reached Koyama Tomomasa, he, ever loyal to Yoritomo, called a council of his elders to devise a stratagem for killing Yoshihiro. At the time Tomomasa was virtually without an army, for his father Masamitsu had taken most of the Koyama following to Kyoto to do guard duty at the imperial palace. His elders suggested: "Let us first deceive Yoshihiro by telling him that we support him." When this message was relayed to Yoshihiro, he, happy at the thought of having made an ally, came forward toward Tomomasa's manor house. Tomomasa, in the meantime, had withdrawn into the Nogi Shrine, and as Yoshihiro reached the shrine, Tomomasa's men, who had climbed the trees at Todorokizawa and at Jigokutani, emitted battle cries according to a prearranged plan. The cries reverberated through the ravine, giving the impression of a huge force. In his astonishment and confusion Yoshihiro was attacked by Tomomasa's followers, such as Ōta Kango, Mizushiro Rokuji, Wada Ikejirō, Kagesawa Jirō, and Shichirō, and Tomomitsu's follower Hoshi Chinsaburō. Tomomasa, wearing an armor with plates threaded in red, and astride a chestnut-colored horse, dashed about in all directions with the full vigor of his twenty-five years and killed many a rebel. But one of Yoshihiro's arrows struck him and threw him off his horse. Although Tomomasa was not killed, his horse ran away toward Todorokizawa, where it was discovered neighing by Naganuma Gorō Munemasa, age twenty, who was returning from Kamakura. Recognizing the horse and believing Tomomasa to be dead, Munemasa hurried toward Yoshihiro's lines. As he did so, he saw to his left Tawayama Shichita, the son of Yoshihiro's wet nurse, fleeing from the scene, and captured him. Munemasa's page took Shichita's head. Meanwhile, Yoshihiro had withdrawn slightly to the southwest of Nogi Shrine and had established his line. Tomomasa and Munemasa attacked from the east. At the time, strong winds blowing from the southeast raised a cloud of dust from the burning fields and obscured the vision of the men and horses, causing many to break ranks and to lose their footing and to die in Jigokutani and Todorokizawa. However, remnants of the fleeing enemy were checked at Koga and Takano by Shimokōbe Yukihira and his brother Masayoshi, who had posted themselves at these passes.

Also, Ashikaga Aritsuna, his heir Mototsuna, his fourth son Asonuma Hirotsuna, his fifth son Kimura Nobutsuna, and Ōta Yukitomo, the junior provisional governor,[10] had set up their lines at Kodesashihara and at Kotsuzumi. However, others, such as the guardsman Hatta Tomoie, Shimotsuma Shirō Kiyouji, Onodera Tarō Michitsura, Oguri Jūrō Shigenari, Utsunomiya Tokoro Nobufusa, Kamada Shichirō Tamenari, and the manorial official of Minatogawa Kagesumi, have joined with Tomomasa. Likewise, the young lord Ura Noriyori has come to join Tomomasa's ranks. The said Tomomasa's ancestor, the *ason* Hidesato, had subdued the enemy of the court, Taira Masakado, during the Tenkei era [938–946]. He had been given the governorship of two provinces and the grade of junior fourth rank, lower grade, and he had left a record of distinguished service. He had protected the provinces for a long period and had been the leader of the clan. Now Tomomasa, hearing of Yoshihiro's defection, has met him on the battlefield in a spirit of loyalty and with disdain for his own life, and has defeated him.

25th day. *Ashikaga Tadatsuna hides in Kōzuke, then flees to Saikai.*[11]

[10] *Shō gon-no-kami.* The son of an officeholder was frequently addressed by his father's title with the word *shō*, here rendered as "junior," prefaced to the title.

[11] *Saikai-dō*, one of the seven administrative circuits. It included the nine provinces of Kyushu and the islands of Iki and Tsushima.

Although Ashikaga Tadatsuna had espoused the cause of Shida Yoshihiro, after the defeat at Nogi Shrine he regretted his error and, desirous of avoiding future opprobrium, secluded himself at Tatsuoku, Yamakami Township, Kōzuke Province, with a follower, Kiryū Rokurō. After several days of hiding Tadatsuna, at Kiryū's suggestion, departed for Saikai via the San'in circuit.[12]

There will be no warrior in future ages like this Tadatsuna. He excelled all others in three things: namely, his physical strength, which equalled that of a hundred men; his voice, which reverberated for a distance of ten *ri*; and his teeth, which were one inch in length.

27th day. *Yoritomo concludes his seventh day of prayer; Koyama Tomomasa sends word of his victory.*

Yoritomo worshiped at the sub-shrine for the seventh day, thus fulfilling his vow. While kneeling at the altar he had expressed his anxiety about the outcome of Yoshihiro's insurrection. Holding His Lordship's sword and attending him at the time was Koyama Shichirō Tomomitsu, who ventured an answer, saying: "I wonder if Yoshihiro has not been defeated by Tomomasa by now." Yoritomo studied Tomomitsu's face, then said: "Your words have not come entirely from your own heart; they have been inspired by the gods. And if what you say does come to pass, you will be rewarded." Tomomitsu is fifteen years old this year.

On his way from the shrine His Lordship was met by Tomomasa's messenger and by Shimokōbe Yukihira, who reported the news of Yoshihiro's defeat. At night the messenger reported to His Lordship that the heads of Yoshihiro's men had been brought to Kamakura. Yoritomo instructed Miura Yoshizumi and Hiki Shirō Yoshikazu to take the heads to Koshigoe[13] and to display them to the public there.

28th day. *The conquerors of Shida Yoshihiro are honored by Yoritomo.*

Naganuma Munemasa, representing Tomomasa, who could not appear because of his injuries, and the group of men who had given assistance on this occasion have reported to Kamakura. Yoritomo met them and expressed his appreciation for their conspicuous deeds.

[12] *San'in-dō,* the provinces west of Kyoto facing the Japan Sea.
[13] Koshigoe, located west of Shichirigahama, the entrance to Kamakura.

Munemasa, Yukihira, and their groups of followers took their position on His Lordship's left; Hatta Tomoie, Shigenari, and their followers took their position on His Lordship's right. Of the twenty-nine prisoners, some were ordered to be beheaded and others were remanded to the custody of Yukihira and Aritsuna. Then the lands in Hitachi, Shimotsuke, and Kōzuke of those who had supported Yoshihiro were declared confiscated and were given in trust to Tomomasa and Tomomitsu as their reward.

THIRD MONTH

1st day. *Yoritomo observes the anniversary of his mother's death.*

As the anniversary of the death of his mother falls in this month, Yoritomo today attended a mass at Kamegayatsu in a hall built by Tsuchiya Jirō Yoshikiyo. The officiating priest was Gyōjitsu, the intendant of Hakone Shrine. Five other priests . . . were invited for the occasion. His Lordship presented a horse and two *hiki*[14] of *chōken*[15] to the officiating priest, and two *tan* of cloth to each of the invited priests.

6th day. *The despoilment of Ise Shrine by monks of Kumano is reported to Kamakura.*

A communication from Ōnakatomi Yoshichika of Ise to Yuri Nakahachi Korehira reports that men claiming to be followers of Tanzō of Kumano had burst into the precincts of Ise Shrine on the 19th of the First Month and had wrecked the inner hall and despoiled its sacred objects. When Narinaga, the assistant head of the shrine, requested restoration of the objects to the inner shrine, the men reappeared on the 26th of the same month, burning and destroying homes of the people in the two townships of Yamada and Uji, and taking by force whatever they could. Never in the one thousand and one hundred years since the august reign of the Heaven-Shining-Great-Deity, nor during the six hundred years of the descent of the emperors has there been anything comparable to this. At this time of the revival of the house of Minamoto, the greatest respect must

---

[14] *Hiki*, a measure of cloth equal to two *tan*. A *tan* was a piece of cloth from twenty-five to twenty-eight feet long.

[15] *Chōken*, silk used for making various kinds of robes including *suikan*, or a ceremonial robe; *shitatare*, a long silk robe worn by court nobles; and *kariginu*, a silk garment worn during the hunt and for hawking.

be shown to the gods. His Lordship, reading Korehira's letter and alarmed that the incident had been perpetrated in Tanzō's name, has ordered that special prayers be offered to the gods.[16]

7th day. *Takeda Nobuyoshi is rumored to oppose Yoritomo.*

A letter from Miyoshi Yasunobu to His Lordship states: "On the 7th of the past month, at a council held at the ex-sovereign's palace, a decision was reached to issue to Takeda Nobuyoshi a mandate from the ex-sovereign's office to chastise Yoritomo. However, the rumor that the order directs punitive action against all the Genji in the provinces is without foundation. Only Yoritomo's name is specified. This is the substance of the rumor."

As a consequence, Nobuyoshi is no longer entirely above suspicion in Yoritomo's eyes. Pressed by Yoritomo for details, Nobuyoshi, who had been in Suruga, arrived at Kamakura today. In a written pledge he disavowed receipt of any order to strike at His Lordship and declared that, if ever such an order should come to him, he would not carry it out. He reminded His Lordship of his frequent services to him during the past year and that he had always espoused his cause. Writing thus in a spirit of deep apology and adding that his sons and grandsons would never draw their bows against His Lordship's descendants, Nobuyoshi moved Yoritomo to grant him an audience. Even so, His Lordship was cautious, summoning Yoshizumi, Yukihira, Sadatsuna, Noritsuna, and Kagetoki to attend him at his side. Nobuyoshi, on his own initiative, handed his sword to Yukihira, retrieving it after His Lordship retired to his inner quarters.

10th day. *Minamoto Yukiie is defeated at Sunomata, Mino Province.*

His Lordship's uncle, the secretary Minamoto Jūrō Yukiie, and Yukiie's sons—the secretary Tarō Mitsuie, Jirō, the priest Gien— and Izumi Tarō Shigemitsu and the warriors from Owari and Mikawa Provinces had established a position near the Sunomata River.[17] The Heiji, under their commander Taira Shigehira, who is the director of the sovereign's private office and assistant master of the empress's household, and such leaders as the minor captain

---

[16] Yoritomo was especially alarmed at this incident because Tanzō was one of his uncles. He had been adopted by the intendant of Kumano.

[17] Also known as the Nagara River.

of the Left Inner Palace Guards Taira Koremori, the governor of
Echizen Taira Michimori, the governor of Satsuma Taira Tadanori,
the governor of Mikawa Taira Tomonori, the governor of Sanuki
and lieutenant of the Left Outer Palace Guards Taira Moritsuna,
who is also known as Takahashi, and the lieutenant of the Left
Military Guards Taira Morihisa had established their position on
the west bank of the same river.

Yukiie's preparations to surprise the Heike with a night attack
were discovered by Kaneishi-maro, Shigehira's page, who had gone
down to the river to wash his master's horse. Therefore the Heike
under Shigehira launched an attack immediately, catching Yukiie
and the Genji unaware. Although the Genji fought back, they were
ineffective. The priest Gien was taken prisoner by Moritsuna; the
secretary Jirō was captured by Tadanori; and Izumi Tarō Shigemitsu
and his younger brother Jirō were taken by Morihisa. In addition,
many men drowned in the river or were wounded and killed. More
than six hundred and ninety men were lost.

12th day. *Yoritomo makes a grant of land to Kashima Shrine.*

Yoritomo, concerned about the unsettled situation in the provinces, has vowed to assist the various shrines. Today he has
granted Shiohama, Ōkubu, and Seya in Hitachi Province to the
Kashima Shrine. Moreover, out of reverence for the gods, he has
assigned Kashima Saburō Masamiki to the shrine as constable[18] to
prevent violence and disorderliness on the lands of the shrine.

13th day. *Yasuda Yoshisada asks Yoritomo to punish Asaba Munenobu and Sagara Nagayori.*

Butō-go, Yasuda Yoshisada's messenger, has arrived at Kamakura
from Tōtomi Province. Reporting to His Lordship, he said, "Protecting Tōtomi as Your Lordship's deputy, Yoshisada has been
making preparations to meet the Heiji attack. When he sought, in
pursuance of Your Lordship's orders, to secure workers to strengthen
the defenses around Hashimoto, the manorial official Asaba Munenobu and Sagara Saburō Nagayori acted contemptuously and refused to give assistance. In fact, on one occasion, while Yoshisada
was dismounted, the said persons rode by him without dismounting.

[18] *Sōtsuibushi.*

These men are ambitious and treacherous, and many of their followers are presently supporters of the Heike. Your Lordship should
punish them swiftly."

14th day. *Yoritomo replies to Yasuda Yoshisada.*

When His Lordship explained to Butō-go that it is difficult to
punish Asaba and Sagara for their disagreeable behavior, Butō-go
replied: "It is known throughout Tōtomi that I have been sent here
to protest the impudence of these men. If I should return without
a judgment against them, Yoshisada's influence will come to naught.
If, subsequently, Your Lordship should determine that these charges
are false, then I should be punished." Whereupon Yoritomo wrote
a reply to Yoshisada declaring that the lands of the defendants
should be held by Yoshisada, but if, subsequently, Asaba Munenobu
should vindicate himself, then the plaintiff would be punished.

19th day. *Ōya Yasusuke of Owari prepares to meet the Heike at
Atsuta Shrine.*

Ōya Yasusuke has arrived in great haste at Kamakura. He reported to His Lordship thus: "On the 10th Yukiie's army was completely destroyed by the Heiji at Sunomata. In the face of the
Heike victory I withdrew from Sunomata to Atsuta Shrine. Taira
Shigehira, having broken one line, must now be advancing toward
the east." Yoritomo commended Yasusuke's loyalty, noting that
such loyalty was rare at this time when so many of the provincial
officials of Tōtomi Province were turning toward the Heike.

27th day. *Kataoka Tsuneharu defies Yoritomo.*

Upon receipt of a report that Kataoka Tsuneharu was hostile to
the Genji, His Lordship had sent a servant to his residence in
Shimōsa to summon him to Kamakura. Tsuneharu, claiming that
the messenger had broken into his lands, wounded and bound him.
Therefore today Yoritomo sent word to Tsuneharu, who has now
committed two offenses, that he was being dispossessed of his holdings and that he should release the servant in question.

FOURTH MONTH

1st day. *The grounds of the Tsurugaoka Shrine are cleared of
brambles and weeds.*

Yoritomo worshiped at Tsurugaoka. Seeing that the mausoleum was overgrown with brambles and the fence around the shrine hidden by weeds, he ordered the shrine grounds weeded and set in order. At the end of the day Ōba Kageyoshi reported to His Lordship that the matter had been attended to.

7th day. *Trusted vassals are assigned to stand guard at night before Masako's chambers.*

The best archers among the vassals who are at the same time above suspicion have been designated by His Lordship to stand guard nightly for Her Ladyship. They are: Ema Shirō, Hangaya Shirō Shigetomo, Shimokōbe Yukihira, Kasai Saburō Kiyoshige, Wada Jirō Yoshimochi, Miura Jūrō Yoshitsura, Kajiwara Genta Kagesue, Chiba Tarō Tanemasa, Usami Heiji Sanemasa, Hatta Tarō Tomoshige.

19th day. *Hirai Kiroku, who had attempted to kill Hōjō Munetoki, is beheaded at Koshigoe.*

20th day. *Oyamada Shigenari is accused of claiming lands not belonging to him.*

Oyamada Saburō Shigenari, having offended His Lordship and fearing the consequences, has secluded himself. Last year, when His Lordship confirmed the holdings of his immediate vassals of the eastern provinces, Shigenari, who had laid claim to Yoshitomi, Ichinomiya, and Renkōji in Tama District, Musashi Province, had been among those who had received confirmation. However, Heita Hirosada has since claimed these lands. An investigation followed, which confirmed Hirosada's claim. Thus these lands have been assigned to Hirosada.

30th day. *Asaba Munenobu's holdings are restored.*

Although His Lordship, at Yasuda Yoshisada's instigation, had confiscated the holdings of Asaba Munenobu, the latter has tendered his apologies through the good offices of Yasuda himself. His Lordship has restored Asaba's rights to Shibamura Village and to the rice fields within his original manor. His Lordship has taken this action because he needs the services of Asaba's numerous sons and followers.

FIFTH MONTH

8th day. *The priest Nichie of Onjō-ji arrives at Kamakura.*

The priest Nichie, . . . a novice of Ritsujō-bō Nichiin of Onjō-ji, has arrived at Kamakura. The said Nichiin is a son of Chiba Tsunetane, and he is Yoritomo's patron priest. In the Fifth Month of the past year Yoritomo had sent him a written prayer from Izu. Nichiin then betook himself to Iwashimizu Shrine, where he planned to remain for one thousand days to read in silence the *Mahā-prajñāpāramitā Sutra*. On the evening of the 600th day, Nichiin saw a vision of himself receiving golden armor from the direction of the altar. Believing that His Lordship's prayers had been answered, and learning on the following morning of Prince Mochi-hito's flight to Miidera, he ordered Nichie to attend to the matter of completing Yoritomo's prayer, and hastened to be at the prince's side. On the 26th of the same month he was killed by the Heike at the gate to Kōmyō-zan. However, Nichie continued with his late master's vow, completing his mission of one thousand days of prayer, but his arrival at Kamakura had been delayed to this day because of the disturbances in the capital and in the provinces.

13th day. *Plans are made for the renovation of the sub-shrine of Tsurugaoka.*

The matter of timber for the building of the sub-shrine of Tsuru-gaoka has been attended to. The commissioners for this project are Doi Sanehira and Ōba Kageyoshi. This shrine, built last year, was intended to be a temporary structure. Thus it is extremely simple, consisting of pine pillars and a miscanthus roof. The shrine will be decorated to enhance the glory of the gods.

16th day. *Yoritomo confirms the holdings of Murayama Yorinao.*

His Lordship has ordered that there shall be no change with respect to the estates now held by Murayama Shichirō Yorinao. The document states that Murayama and Yonemochi are to be held as before by Lord Murayama. Yorinao had been especially solicitous of Yoritomo when the latter was still in great danger, and

he had fought against Jō Shirō Nagamochi in His Lordship's behalf. And thus, in acknowledgment, Yoritomo has taken this action.

23rd day. *Two new buildings are planned for Kamakura.*

It has been decided to construct alongside His Lordship's residence a separate residence for His Lordship's daughter and a storehouse for offerings to the gods. In order that construction might begin before the period of the greatest heat in summer, His Lordship
has ordered that the question of the ownership of the land involved,
whether public or private, be set aside for the moment, and that
the provincial government office in Awa provide carpenters within
the next two days. Shōkan is in charge.

24th day. *Work begins on the new buildings.*

The land for the building of a residence for His Lordship's
daughter and a storehouse has been cleared. Kageyoshi, Kagetoki,
and Shōkan are in charge. The immediate vassals have contributed
workmen.

28th day. *Carpenters arrive from Awa.*

The carpenters requisitioned from Awa have arrived last night.
Thus the raising of the pillars and the beams for the buildings will
take place today.

SIXTH MONTH

13th day. *The new residence for Yoritomo's daughter is completed
and appropriate ceremonies are held; a banquet for the occasion is
given by Chiba Tsunetane.*

19th day. *Yoritomo visits in Sagami; Okazaki Yoshizane and Taira
Hirotsune have words.*

Purely for diversion and to escape the heat, Yoritomo, at the
invitation a few days ago of Miura Yoshizumi and his family, has
gone to Miura. His Lordship was accompanied by the young lord
of Mutsu Yoritaka and his followers. Also, in compliance with Yoritomo's orders of a few days ago, Taira Hirotsune and some fifty
of his followers came to meet His Lordship at Sagaokahama. On

this occasion Hirotsune's men dismounted and made obeisance on the sand to Yoritomo. However, Hirotsune remained on his mount and, loosening his hold on the reins, bowed toward Yoritomo. Whereupon, Miura Jūrō Yoshitsura, stepping before His Lordship's mount, indicated to Hirotsune that he should dismount to pay his respects. Hirotsune replied, "For three generations we have not observed such etiquette, in public or in private."

When the party arrived at the old home of the late Miura Yoshiaki, Yoshizumi gave a most elaborate banquet. During the drinking, when all, high and low, had been soothed by the wine, Okazaki Shirō Yoshizane made a request for His Lordship's ceremonial robe. When Yoritomo obliged and Yoshizane attempted to put on the robe at once, Hirotsune, green with envy, remarked: "This beautiful robe should be proffered to someone who is worthy of it, such as I. I had not thought that it would go to someone as old as Yoshizane." Yoshizane replied angrily: "Hirotsune may believe that he is worthy of this robe, but no one can match me in length of service to Yoritomo. I have been with His Lordship since the beginning of the conflict, and I have never entertained a single thought against His Lordship." There followed insulting words between Hirotsune and Yoshizane and a challenge to fight. Although His Lordship remained silent, Miura Yoshitsura, perhaps sensing that the quarrel was getting out of hand, rushed in and, upbraiding Yoshizane, said: "Yoshizumi has seen fit to present this banquet on the occasion of His Lordship's visit. At such a time how could anyone think of engaging in a brawl? Is this the behavior of a crazed old man? Surely Hirotsune is not capable of such conduct, but if you insist on fighting, agree to do so on a later day. There is absolutely no reason to interfere with this party in His Lordship's presence." His repeated efforts to stop the quarrel brought an end to the angry words and the altercation was resolved. Yoritomo's special esteem for Yoshitsura comes from this incident.

21st day. *Yoritomo returns to Kamakura with a gift of armor and a horse from Miura Yoshizumi.*

25th day. *A strange star appears in the northeastern heavens.*
   At 7 P.M. a strange star appeared in the northeastern heavens.

It was reddish green, the color of Saturn, and it had a beard. This is the first appearance of such a star since Kankō 3 [1006].

27th day. *Timber for Tsurugaoka arrives at Yui Bay.*

Timber for the sub-shrine of Tsurugaoka, including thirteen pillars and two beams, has arrived at Yui Bay this morning.

SEVENTH MONTH

3rd day. *Shōkan is commissioned to bring the carpenter Kyōshi of Asakusa, Musashi Province, to Kamakura.*

5th day. *Nagao Sadakage is pardoned for his devotion to the Lotus Sutra.*

Nagao Shinroku Sadakage has received His Lordship's pardon. Yoritomo had strongly resented the audacity of this man, who had killed Sanada Yoichi Yoshitada during the Ishibashi Battle. But Yoritomo had placed Sadakage in the custody of the father of the man whom he had killed. This is Okazaki Shirō Yoshizane, who is by nature forgiving and merciful, and thus he refused to demand execution of the man who had killed his son. Instead, he held him as a prisoner and gave him a copy of the *Lotus Sutra*, which he has been reading every day. Last night Yoshizane received a message in a dream and going before His Lordship, he said: "As Sadakage is my son's enemy, I should not rest until we dispose of him. However, as I am a believer in the teachings of the *Lotus Sutra*, my resentment toward the prisoner has gradually subsided as I hear him intoning the sutra. If we kill him, would it not affect the happiness of my dead son?" His Lordship replied: "For your peace of mind I shall pardon the prisoner. I too am a devotee of the *Lotus Sutra*. Your request will be fulfilled immediately." Thus Sadakage was pardoned.

9th day. *Work is begun on the Tsurugaoka Sub-shrine.*

The carpenters from Asakusa have arrived and work on the sub-shrine has begun. First, the sacred objects were removed to a temporary hall in a ceremony conducted by a necromancer summoned by His Lordship from the shrine ricelands of Ōba Mikuri in Sagami. In charge of the removal were Sukemichi and Kageyoshi.

The construction of the shrine should be completed by the 15th of the coming month, when it is planned to return the sacred objects to their proper place.

YŌWA 1 [1181]

14th day. *The era name is changed.*
  The era name has been changed from Jishō 5 to Yōwa 1.

20th day. *Yoritomo reprimands Yoshitsune; Shimokōbe Yukihira is rewarded for capturing a would-be assassin.*
  The ceremony for the raising of the beams of the sub-shrine of Tsurugaoka was held in a temporary hut built for the occasion to the east of the main shrine building. As Yoritomo arrived and took his seat, his immediate vassals took their places, flanking him to the north and south. When Yoritomo, in the presentation of horses to the carpenters, ordered Yoshitsune to lead the horses in, the latter replied that he had no servants at the moment to carry out the order. His Lordship repeated the instruction, saying, "When Hatakeyama Jirō and Sanuki Shirō are serving in this capacity, how can you say such a thing? It is a lowly function which must be repugnant to them, but they are performing it in accordance with my orders." Yoshitsune stood up apprehensively and took the reins of two horses. The first to lead the horses in was Hatakeyama, followed by Sanuki. Others who participated were Doi Sanehira, Kudō Kagemitsu, Nitta Tadatsune, Sano Tadaie, and Usami Sanemasa.
  The ceremony ended at 3 P.M. and, as Yoritomo was about to take his leave, a man who had never been seen before was noticed among His Lordship's escorts. A man of more than seven feet in height and of extremely suspicious features, he was seen hurrying toward His Lordship but, before His Lordship could say a word, Shimokōbe Yukihira apprehended him. Upon Yoritomo's return from the ceremonies, His Lordship summoned the man before him. Under his robe the man wore a bellyband, and in his topknot he had placed a card. On the card were the words "Sachūta Tsunezumi, follower of the late Nagasa Rokurō Tsunetomo of Awa." Because of the suspicious circumstances, the man was interrogated. However, he would not speak, except to insist on death. Yukihira said to the

man, "We shall of course behead you, but unless you tell us your reasons, we have no cause for such action. Tell us your reasons immediately." In time Tsunezumi answered, saying, "Last winter when my master was sentenced to death in Awa, his followers went into hiding. Since then, whether awake or asleep, we have had no peace of mind. I had placed this card in my hair to let all know who I am, in the event I am killed." His Lordship then issued an order, saying: "Execute this man without further ado. However, as this is the day for the raising of the beams of the shrine, postpone the execution until tomorrow." The prisoner was placed in the custody of Kajiwara Kagetoki. Then Yoritomo summoned Yukihira before him and said: "You have conducted yourself meritoriously today. Is there anything you wish as a reward?" Yukihira replied, "I do not have any particular wish, but my people have found it extremely difficult to meet the annual tribute of horses." Yoritomo then said: "In the granting of awards for meritorious services, it is quite proper for those seeking office and salary to state their wishes. Although your request is a difficult one to fulfill, it shall be carried out immediately." Then Yoritomo wrote out an order, assigning Jōjin as commissioner.

ORDERED TO: The intendant of shrine lands for Shimōsa Province
   Regarding the immediate suspension of payment of tribute horses
   Tribute horses required of Yukihira
The obligation for the payment of tribute horses devolving on the afore-mentioned Yukihira is hereby canceled. Be it thus understood by the intendant of shrine lands, and let there be no negligence in carrying out the terms of this order. Thus ordered.

21st day. *Sachūta is executed.*

EIGHTH MONTH

13th day. *The ex-sovereign issues mandates against Yoritomo and Yoshinaka.*

At the urging of the Heiji, imperial mandates, directing Fujiwara Hidehira to proceed against Yoritomo, and Jō Sukenaga to proceed against Kiso Yoshinaka, have been issued.

15th day. *The sacred objects are restored to the sub-shrine; the governor of Kashima Tsunemasa departs for the north to attack Yoshinaka.*

16th day. *Taira Michimori departs for the north to attack Yoshinaka;
the governor of Ise Kiyotsuna, the vice governor of Kazusa Tadakiyo, and Date Sadayasu depart for the east to attack Yoritomo.*

26th day. *Miyoshi Yasunobu sends word of the departure of government troops for the east and counsels readiness to Yoritomo.*

27th day. *Shibuya Shigekuni receives fiscal exemption.*
The manorial official Shibuya Shigekuni has received exemption
from annual taxes for the lands he holds in Shitasato.

29th day. *Yoritomo orders temples and shrines to conduct prayers
in behalf of a Genji victory over the Heiji.*

NINTH MONTH

3rd day. *Jō Sukenaga dies.*
Jō Shirō Sukenaga, governor of Echigo, died suddenly this morning while rallying troops in his province to attack Kiso Yoshinaka in
compliance with an imperial decree. He has incurred the curse of
Heaven. . . .

4th day. *Yoshinaka launches a campaign against the Heike.*
Kiso Yoshinaka has embarked on a campaign against the Heike,
departing for the capital by way of the Hokuriku region.[19] His vanguard under Nenoi Tarō Yukichika has already engaged in battle
with the forces of Taira Michimori at Suitsu in Echizen Province.

7th day. *Fujiwara Toshitsuna and Ashikaga Tadatsuna are defiant
of Yoritomo.*
Fujiwara Toshitsuna . . . is a descendant of the governor of
Musashi Hidesato. . . . He holds several thousand *chō*[20] in the
district and is a power in the province. During the Nin'an era
[1166–68] he was dispossessed of his rights to Ashikaga Manor in
Shimotsuke Province. The legal guardian of the manor, Taira
Shigemori, then granted the manor to the young lord Nitta Yoshishige. Whereupon Toshitsuna went to the capital to plead his case.

---

[19] I.e., the region along the Japan Sea containing the provinces of Wakasa,
Echizen, Kaga, Noto, Etchū, Echigo, and the island of Sado.
[20] A *chō* is 2.45 acres.

Consequently, the manor was returned to him. Because of this debt to the Heike, he has been of late a supporter of the Heike. His oldest son Ashikaga Tadatsuna had supported Shida Yoshihiro, for which reason he has not come to pay homage to Yoritomo. Yoritomo himself thinks ill of him and has issued an order to Wada Jirō Yoshimochi to proceed against Toshitsuna. Today Yoshimochi has left Kamakura with Miura Yoshitsura, Kasai Kiyoshige, and Usami Sanemasa.

13th day. *Kiryū Rokurō slays his lord, Fujiwara Toshitsuna.*

A messenger of Wada Yoshimochi has arrived from Shimotsuke and has reported to His Lordship as follows: "Before Yoshimochi arrived in Shimotsuke, Kiryū Rokurō, one of Toshitsuna's principal warriors, slew his master to show his secret loyalty for Yoritomo. After the slaying he had been hiding in the mountains. When he heard of Yoshimochi's mission, he came forward to Yoshimochi's line. However, he would not produce Toshitsuna's head. What shall we do about Kiryū?" Yoritomo replied: "Tell him to produce the head immediately." The messenger hastened back to Shimotsuke with Yoritomo's order.

16th day. *Kiryū Rokurō produces Toshitsuna's head.*

Kiryū Rokurō has presented Toshitsuna's head to Yoshimochi. . . . Without being brought to Kamakura, it was taken directly to Koshigoe via Fukazawa in accordance with Yoritomo's orders. When Yoritomo sought to find someone among his followers who might identify the head, Sano Shichirō spoke up, saying, "Shimokōbe Masayoshi has seen him many times. Shouldn't he be summoned?" Thus Masayoshi was sent out to inspect the head. Returning, he reported that, although the face had changed considerably, it being several days since the killing, it was without doubt Toshitsuna's head.

18th day. *Kiryū Rokurō is decapitated on Yoritomo's orders.*

Kiryū Rokurō has requested through Kajiwara Heizō that he be invested as His Lordship's vassal. But Yoritomo, saying that anyone who is so unprincipled as to harbor treacherous intentions against his own hereditary lord and to kill him is not deserving of an award, ordered him killed. Kagetoki beheaded Kiryū and exposed his head alongside that of Toshitsuna's. His Lordship then took steps to confiscate Toshitsuna's lands. However, Yoritomo assured Toshitsuna's wife and children of their rights to their residence and personal property. The directive which he has drafted and despatched in care of Wada Jirō is as follows:

ORDERED TO: Wada Jirō Yoshimochi
  Desist from punishing Toshitsuna's sons and followers who would pay homage to His Lordship
Spare the lives of the sons, brothers, and followers of the aforesaid Toshitsuna, including members of the Kiryū family, who would submit to His Lordship. Moreover, desist from seizure of, or inflicting harm on, the wives and children, or the private dwellings, of members of Toshitsuna's followers. Thus ordered.
Yōwa 1:9,18

27th day. *Taguchi Nariyoshi invades Ise Province for the Heike; Kōno Michinobu surrenders to Nariyoshi.*

28th day. *Wada Yoshimochi returns to Kamakura.*

TENTH MONTH

3rd day. *Taira Koremori leaves his castle for the east.*

6th day. *Zen'ei of Sōtō-zan is appointed as altar priest for Tsurugaoka Shrine; Genshin is also named as altar priest.*

12th day. *Yoritomo grants the Tachibana Township in Hitachi Province to Kashima Shrine.*

20th day. *The provisional assistant head Shinto priest of Ise Shrine arrives at Kamakura.*

Yesterday the provisional assistant head Shinto priest of the Great Shrine of Ise Watari Mitsutomo . . . arrived at Kamakura. Here to conduct prayers for His Lordship, he was received in audience today. Mitsutomo said to His Lordship: "On the 19th of the past month, upon orders from the Heike that I pray for the submission of the eastern provinces, I made an offering of metal armor at the shrine, following a precedent set in the Tenkei era [938–946]. Prior

to the presentation of the armor, Sadataka, the junior assistant head
of the department of Shinto, and the eldest son of Chikataka, the
high priest of the Great Shrine of Ise, died suddenly at Ichishi Station in Ise. Again, on the 16th of the same month, when the decision was made in Kyoto to make the offering of the said armor,
it was noticed that on the rafters of the main building of the Ise
Shrine hornets had built a nest, swallows had hatched their chicks,
and snakes had brought forth their young. These ominous signs
caused me to reflect upon the past, and I came to the firm conclusion
that now is the time to eliminate treasonable ministers who make
light of imperial rule and who endanger our land." His Lordship
replied: "When I took leave of the capital in Eireki 1 [1160], I saw
a vision. Ever since, I have had a special regard for all matters
pertaining to the Ise Shrine. If the prayer is answered, I shall, without fail, make a benefice of new lands to the shrine."

ELEVENTH MONTH

5th day. *Yoritomo learns that Taira Koremori is still in Ōmi Province; therefore, he postpones his departure for the west.*

11th day. *Hanyū Morikane, attendant of the late Minamoto Yorimasa, takes his own life to avoid capture by the Taira.*

21st day. *Taira Michimori and Taira Yukimori return to Kyoto.*

29th day. *Yoritomo grants exemption of annual dues to Hayakawa
Manor.*

TWELFTH MONTH

7th day. *Masako is taken ill.*

11th day. *The priest Nichie dies.*
    Nichie has passed away from a stomach ailment. This evening
he was interred at Yamanouchi. Out of deep compassion for the
deceased, Yoritomo attended the cremation. Pure and learned in
both esoteric and exoteric Buddhism, and a disciple of Nichiin of
Onjō-ji, he had come to Kamakura during the Fifth Month because

of his teacher's regard for Yoritomo. Thus His Lordship has had complete faith in him.

YŌWA 2[21]

FIRST MONTH

1st day. *Yoritomo worships at Tsurugaoka Shrine.*

3rd day. *Yoritomo makes his first visitation of the year.*

For his first visitation of the year Yoritomo has gone to the Amanawa residence of Adachi Morinaga. . . .

8th day. *Yoritomo decrees daylong services at Tsurugaoka Shrine.*

23rd day. *Taira Tokiie comes to pay homage to Yoritomo.*

The governor of Hōki Taira Tokiie has come to pay homage to His Lordship. This is the first meeting of the two. He is the son of the courtier Tokitada. Through a scheme of his stepmother he had been exiled to Kazusa. Taira Hirotsune, admiring him, had made him his son-in-law. Because Hirotsune had not been in His Lordship's good graces the past year, Tokiie had been sent to placate Yoritomo. Yoritomo received him warmly, for he likes guests from the capital.

28th day. *Yoritomo makes a donation to Ise Shrine.*

Measures having been taken earlier for the presentation of sacred horses and gold dust to Ise Shrine, the purification ceremony for the men who are making the offerings was held at headquarters today. The gifts received included 100 *ryō*[22] from Chiba Tsunetane and Koyama Tomomasa. Ten sacred horses were led into the courtyard. The reins of these horses were held by Toshikane, who was in attendance on a bamboo matting.

1 horse, cream-colored, given by Edo Shigenaga
1 horse, gray-colored, given by Shimokōbe Shirō
1 horse, chestnut-colored, given by Takeda Nobuyoshi

[21] The era name was changed from Yōwa 2 to Juei 1 on the 27th of the Fifth Month.
[22] A *ryō* is 1.32 ounces avoirdupois.

1 horse, dappled chestnut, given by Azuma Hachirō
1 horse, blackish green, given by Takaba Jirō
1 horse, cream-colored, given by Toyota Tarō
1 horse, fawn-colored, given by Oguri Jūrō Shigenari
1 horse, grayish white, given by Kasai Saburō Kiyoshige
1 horse, light chestnut, given by Kawagoe Tarō Shigeyori
1 horse, dark gray, given by the manorial official Nakamura Munehira

After their presentation the horses were left in the custody of the shrine priest Naritomo. For each a groom was assigned.

SECOND MONTH

2nd day. *Narusawa Gorō incurs Yoritomo's displeasure but is pardoned.*

Narusawa Gorō, a follower of Takaba Jirō, having incurred His Lordship's displeasure, had been placed in the custody of Koyama Shōshirō Tomomasa. He had been negligent about feeding the horses before their presentation, despite instructions to be especially diligent about the matter. However, at the intercession of the priest Naritomo, who pointed out that such punishment would not accord with the divine will, Narusawa was pardoned.

8th day. *Yoritomo addresses a prayer to Ise Shrine.*

His Lordship has sent a prayer to the Great Shrine of Ise. Drafted by the master clerk and lay priest Miyoshi Yasunobu, its purpose is to ask for peace and tranquility in the country and for the wealth and prosperity of the people. Naritomo, attired in his robe and cap, appeared at headquarters to receive the prayer, and then departed. Naka Shirō Koreshige was assigned to accompany him. Also taking leave was Nagae Tarō Kageyoshi as commissioner of sacred objects. Gon Gorō Kagemasa, Kageyoshi's ancestor, had faithfully revered the gods. On Eikyū 5:10,23 [1117] he had given his lands in Ōba, Sagami Province, to the Ise Shrine, to be held by the shrine in virtual perpetuity. His Lordship has appointed Kageyoshi for this post, confident that a descendant of Kagemasa in the third generation would not displease the gods. His Lordship's prayer reads:

As a token of my respect and reverence for the emperors descended from the Heaven-Shining-Great-Deity, I, Minamoto Yoritomo, former Assistant Captain of the Middle Palace Guards, Right Division, and *Ason*, Junior Fifth Rank, Lower Grade, make this presentation of gold dust and sacred horses. My lineage begins with Emperor Jimmu, at the very beginning of Japan at Toyoashihara Mizuho, and descends to Emperor Seiwa, the 56th emperor after Jimmu, and thence to Seiwa's third grandson, who was skilled in the martial arts, and who protected the state and enhanced the glory of the imperial court through his services in the palace guards. For the next 300 years my ancestors, blessed with imperial favor and famed for their military prowess, rendered meritorious service in subjugating the traitors and in eliminating the murderers, and in making Yamato a safe and peaceful country. But beginning in the Hōgen era [1156–58] there were military disturbances in the capital. The people gave no thought to the teachings of the founder, nor were they desirous of protecting the country. Awards and punishments were pronounced without regard to justice. Thus, in the Heiji era [1159], though I had committed no offense, I was punished. And while I was thus spending many years in bitter resentment, the former chancellor Taira ordered his strong men two years ago to slay me. But by a stroke of fortune I have escaped the traitor's arrow. Having done no wrong, I received on this occasion the assistance of the gods. But the chancellor Taira has alarmed the emperor with the contrary notion that I was the rebel. My reports to the imperial court have been to no avail. Without the opportunity to explain my case to the court, I have had no recourse but to gaze at the blue sky, while throughout the country, in the capital and in the provinces, insurrections have piled on insurrections, and there is no peace. Meanwhile, there has been the burning of the seats of Buddhism, unprecedented in the more than four hundred years since the establishment of these temples by Emperor Shōmu. Who among the people has not grieved over this? The Taira has conducted government despotically, destroying districts and townships. Is this not an insurrection? It is clear that the gods are displeased at the sudden rise to power of the chancellor Taira.

I am especially concerned about the rumor that monks claiming to be from Kumano had broken into Izawa Shrine, a branch shrine of Ise, during the First Month of the past year, and had despoiled the main hall and had taken the sacred objects therein. These objects were later irreverently abandoned on the stone pavement of the shrine at Isuzu. Again, in the same month, the said ruffians broke into the homes of the people at two places in the vicinity of the Ise Shrine, seizing property and burning the houses, and causing the shrine priests to gather in the interior of the shrine in fear and in great commotion. Revering the gods, I completely disavow any part in these two incidents. Now I shall make a visit to the capital, restrain the enemies of the court, restore administration of the country to the ex-sovereign, seek the love and compassion of the founder, conduct the worship of the gods before our very eyes, and carry on the traditions of the True Law.

Injustice will be punished and loyal service will be rewarded, irrespective of whether the candidate is a Taira or a Minamoto. Moreover, I vow to establish, according to precedent, new holdings for the two shrines and to restore the Izawa Shrine and retrieve its sacred objects. As for the present holdings of these two shrines in the east, there shall be no change, and I shall grant, in writing, fiscal exemptions in accordance with precedent and the wishes of the shrines. I shall not be remiss in presenting this prayer to the inner shrine so that there shall be benevolent protection, peace, and tranquility for the government and ruler above and the officials and people below. Yoritomo declares with humble reverence that he and his men—through the nights and the days—will provide protection to the utmost of their ability and strive for the prosperity of the shrine.

Yōwa 2:2,8

Minamoto Yoritomo, Former Assistant Captain of the Middle Palace Guards, Right Division, and *Ason,* Junior Fifth Rank, Lower Grade

14th day. *Itō Sukechika commits suicide.*

Since the year before last the master of Buddhist Law Itō Jirō Sukechika had been in the custody of Miura Yoshizumi. When Yoshizumi, hearing of Her Ladyship's pregnancy, inquired of her health, he was told, unexpectedly, that Sukechika was being pardoned. Yoshizumi immediately sent word to Sukechika, who indicated to a messenger that he would come presently to pay homage to Yoritomo. As Yoshizumi waited for him at headquarters, a retainer rushed in to say that the lay priest, upon receiving word of the pardon, had indicated his intention of despatching himself, declaring that he was conscience-stricken over his earlier position. Although this had occurred but a moment ago, and Yoshizumi hurried to his side, Sukechika had already expired.

15th day. *Itō Sukeyasu is praised for his loyalty.*

Yoshizumi appeared at the gates of the headquarters and through Hori Tōji Chikaie reported the details of Sukechika's suicide to His Lordship. Yoritomo lamented his death and was also moved to admiration for Sukechika. Summoning Itō Kurō Sukeyasu, Sukechika's son, His Lordship said to him: "Although your father's crime was a serious one, I was about to pardon him when he took his own life. However, it is of no use to repent now. Indeed, to you who have reasons to feel great compassion for the deceased, I shall make a special award." Sukeyasu replied: "My father is now dead. There is no profit in honor after death. He has begged your leave and has killed himself." It is an inspiring story for all. . . .

THIRD MONTH

5th day. *An attendant is made a land steward.*

In consequence of his constant and considerate attendance on His Lordship, Yamada Tarō Shigezumi has been awarded today with the stewardship of a village.

9th day. *Masako is with child.*

Her Ladyship being with child, Yoritomo has made a special request to the wife of Chiba Tsunetane to present Masako with a girdle. The presentation was made through her grandson Shōtaro Tanemasa. At Yoritomo's urging, Her Ladyship put on the girdle. The Lady Tango attended her at her meal.

15th day. *A new road is built to Tsurugaoka Shrine.*

For the convenience of worshipers the winding road between Tsurugaoka Shrine and Yui Bay has been straightened. Yoritomo had long planned to do this, but had done nothing so far. However, his concern that Her Ladyship, now with child, might make pilgrimages to the shrine has prompted him to initiate the project. Lord Hōjō and his retainers assisted in the carting of soil and stones.

20th day. *Yoritomo's special emissary to Ise Shrine returns.*

Yoritomo's emissary to Ise Shrine has returned with the report that the offerings had been presented to the assistant head Shinto priests of the two shrines. Each has accepted the offerings and promised to offer prayers in earnest. However, they have refused to present Yoritomo's written prayer to the shrine for fear that the Heike might hear of it later and take reprisals.

FOURTH MONTH

5th day. *Yoritomo visits Enoshima; he watches an ox-chase.*

Out of a deep sense of gratitude to Mongaku *shōnin*[23] of Takao, who had installed a statuary of the Goddess of Riches at Enoshima,

[23] Priests of superior virtue were addressed as *shōnin*, or "superior man."

near Koshigoe, to pray for the success of Yoritomo's undertaking,
. . . His Lordship made a visit there. Inspecting the statuary, Yoritomo prayed for the subjugation of Fujiwara Hidehira, the general
of the Pacifying-Ezo headquarters,[24] and before departing for
Kamakura he ordered that a Shinto gate be erected at the spot.

On the way home, in the vicinity of Kanearai, an ox-chase[25] was
held. The manorial official Shimokōbe, Wada Shōtarō, Oyamada
Saburō, and Aikyō Saburō, having made the most hits, each received
dyed hides and dark-blue silk from His Lordship.

11th day. *The Heike press the people of Kyushu for provisions.*

Taira Sadyoshi has been in Kyushu on a mission for the Heike.
Posing as an emissary of the government, and deceiving the people
with the pretense that the government had levied a commissariat
rice levy, he and several of his personal representatives have been
collecting provisions from the people of the various districts and
subjecting the people to an ordeal of fire and water. As a result the
population of these districts has greatly decreased. Kikuchi Jirō
Takanao, a local lord of Higo, has submitted to the Heike in order
to avoid the ordeal.

24th day. *A lake is planned at Kamakura.*

Three *chō* of irrigated ricelands near the Tsurugaoka Shrine are
to be converted into a lake. The work is in charge of Senkō-bō and
Ōba Kageyoshi.

FIFTH MONTH

12th day. *Yoritomo names Fujiwara Hirotsuna as his secretary.*

The young lord of Fushimi, Fujiwara Hirotsuna, has come to pay
homage to Yoritomo for the first time and to become his secretary.
He had been recommended by Yasuda Yoshisada upon an inquiry
by Yoritomo for someone who is acquainted with Kyoto. Normally,
Hirotsuna resides in the vicinity of the Kake River in Tōtomi.

16th day. *Toyouke Shrine complains against Yasuda Yoshisada.*

During the day an old man . . . appeared at headquarters
and assumed a place on the west corridor, attended by two servants,

---

[24] *Chinjufu Shogun.*   [25] *Ushioumono.*

. . . each carrying a branch of *sakaki*.[26] They made a strange figure. However, to inquiries as to the purpose of their visit put to them by the men who gathered on the stone pavement, they would make no reply. Not until Taira Tokiie, the former Minor Captain, questioned them did they utter a sound. . . . Yoritomo, who had seen them through a curtain, was impressed by the holy appearance of the old man and offered the party an audience. The old man addressed Yoritomo thus: "I am Tameyasu, the assistant head Shinto priest of Toyouke Shrine. Since the Enchō era [923–30], the Kamada *mikuri* in Tōtomi has been held by the shrine as a hereditary possession. But it has been forcibly seized by Yasuda Saburō Yoshisada, who refuses to answer my entreaties for an explanation. I request Your Lordship's intercession and a considerate judgment on this matter." Then, producing old records, the priest explained the extraordinary importance of the shrine. His Lordship, thoroughly convinced of the truth of the case, but unable to question Yasuda, granted the priest an order and named Shintō Toshinaga as his emissary to assure Tameyasu's representative the resumption of control of the said land.

19th day. *Minamoto Yukiie is ordered to Kyoto.*

It has been decided in council to order Minamoto Yukiie, who is now in Mikawa Province, to proceed to the capital to attack the Heike. Preparatory to the move, the acting governor of Mikawa Ōnakatomi Mochimichi has been prevailed upon secretly to issue a manifesto to the two shrines of Ise to solicit their prayers. . . .

25th day. *The monks of Kongō-ji, Sagami Province, file a complaint with Yoritomo.*

A party of resident monks of Kongō-ji, Sagami, has come to headquarters to present a bill of complaint against the unlawful acts of Kondō Yoshinari of Furushō Township. The bill of complaint was read before His Lordship by Aiga, the captain of the guards of the crown prince's household.

The monks of Kongō-ji petition the Lord of Kamakura for a judgment:
A letter requesting special consideration regarding the seizure of

---

[26] *Sakaki*, the *Eurya ochnacea*, traditionally regarded as a sacred tree.

Furushō by the local official Kondō who has committed unparalleled outrages and has obstructed the conduct of our religious affairs
ATTACHED AND SUBMITTED: A bill of particulars

The resident monks of the aforementioned temple respectfully submit this memorial after a most careful consideration of the present situation. The temple lands are the sacred grounds of Acala,[27] avatar of Maha-Vairochana.[28] The monks who live thereon in Acala's beneficence have sought to destroy evil spirits, to abominate enemies, and to attain the highest virtues. The monks and priests of this temple have cleared the heavily forested mountains and have installed an image of Acala thereon. They have assembled kindred monks who, in the performance of their religious austerities day and night, sound the bells and gongs in the morning to offer prayers to their great master and at night, in their coarse garments, pray for the peace and the safety of the country. However, the official of the township, absorbed in his covetousness, has for long ignored the divine assistance of the Three Treasures. Because of his oppressive ways, the resident monks have bolted their doors and abandoned their religious implements. The rice fields and farms of the temple remain uncultivated, and the monks eke out a bare existence on the fruits of the forest. In particular, the mountains have been made into a hunting preserve and the monks are prohibited from entry. This is unprecedented. Under such oppressive conditions the monks have had to flee and disperse. Moreover, the priests have repaired the buildings, but who is there to assure their safety? If Your Lordship does not render a judgment, where will the wandering monks settle? If Your Lordship will accept this petition and act immediately to put a stop to the outrages, we shall, by our words, actions, and deeds, pray and strive for your everlasting success and glory. Thus petitioned.

Yōwa 2:5   Monks of Kongō-ji

26th day. *Yoritomo renders a judgment on the plea of Kongō-ji.*

Night had fallen as attempts were being made yesterday to dispose of the charges brought by the monks of Kongō-ji. Today, before the arrival of Shōkan,[29] who had been delayed, a decision was reached and the judgment duly noted on the petition as follows:

The levying of taxes, the use of the mountain areas for hunting and the cultivation of silk worms, and other deplorable acts on the lands of the said temple shall cease forthwith. Thus ordered.

[27] Fudō, literally, "immovable," one of the so-called power gods, as distinguished from the benign gods, of Buddhist tradition.
[28] *Dai-Nichi.*
[29] I.e., Shōkan was the commissioner for this particular case. As commissioner, he entered the decision in the margin of the petition and delivered it to the plaintiff.

27th day. *The era name is changed.*

The era name has been changed from Yōwa 2 to Juei 1.

JUEI 1 [1182]

SIXTH MONTH

1st day. *Yoritomo provides quarters for a concubine.*

Yoritomo's favorite concubine, who is styled Kizen, has been provided with quarters at the Kokubo residence of Kochūta Mitsuie. The selection of a place at a distance from His Lordship's own residence was made so that he might visit her without arousing public attention. Moreover, this place is conveniently located for trips to the bay. Kizen is the daughter of the lay priest Yoshihashi Tarō. The acquaintanceship began during Yoritomo's visit to Izu. Her facial features, like her constancy for His Lordship, are warm and affectionate. The intimacy began last spring, and His Lordship is greatly enamored of her.

5th day. *Kumagaya Jirō Naozane is rewarded for his bravery.*

For his constant loyalty to Yoritomo and particularly for his bravery during the campaign against the young lord Satake in Jishō 4, Kumagaya Jirō Naozane's rights to lands in Musashi, which had been seized by Naomitsu, had been restored to him earlier by Yoritomo. However, the order of investiture had not been delivered to Naozane until today, when he arrived here from the provinces.

TO: Kumagaya Jirō Naozane of Ōsato District, Musashi Province
   Regarding holdings assigned to him
Naozane is hereby granted the office of land steward of the aforementioned place which had been transmitted in his family for generations and which had been interfered with by Naomitsu. . . . Having distinguished himself in the campaign against Satake Shirō, this award, to wit, the land stewardship of Kumagaya Township, is hereby granted. These rights, which may be transmitted to his sons and descendants in perpetuity, shall not be interfered with. The attention of cultivators is directed to this order, and their compliance with its terms is thus decreed.
Juei 1:5,30

7th day. *Yoritomo indulges in martial games and in fellowship with his men.*

Yoritomo went out to Yui beach, where his men participated in games of archery and horsemanship, beginning with the ox-chase. . . . Following the games the time was passed in drinking. After nightfall Katō Kagekado suddenly lost his senses and fell prostrate at his seat. As everyone gathered around him in great commotion, Sasaki Moritsuna brought a large tent and, wrapping Kagekado in it, carried him out to his quarters, where medical attention was given. As a result of this incident, His Lordship called a halt to the drinking and ordered everyone home.

8th day. *Yoritomo inquires after Kagekado's condition, then visits at Kochūta's home.*

20th day. *A shining object is noticed at Kamakura.*

At 5 A.M. a shining object moving in the direction of Maehama was seen near Tsurugaoka. The object, several *jō*[30] in size, remained lighted for some time.

SEVENTH MONTH

12th day. *Her Ladyship is removed to her lying-in quarters.*

To await the birth of her child, Her Ladyship has gone to Hikigayatsu. . . . Kajiwara Kagetoki has been assigned to be in charge of all matters connected with the forthcoming birth.

14th day. *Nitta Yoshishige incurs Yoritomo's displeasure.*

The young lord Nitta Yoshishige has incurred His Lordship's displeasure. Yoritomo had induced the young lord of Fushimi Hirotsuna to write a love letter on his behalf to Yoshishige's daughter, who is the widow of Aku Genta, Yoritomo's older brother. She failed to respond favorably and, moreover, turned to her father, Yoshishige, for advice. Yoshishige, having given the matter some thought earlier, and wishing to avoid arousing Her Ladyship Masako's anger, gave his widowed daughter away to Sochi Rokurō. This is the cause of Yoritomo's displeasure.

EIGHTH MONTH

5th day. *The priest Zen'ei receives fiscal exemption.*

Zen'ei, an altar priest of Tsurugaoka, has filed a bill of complaint

[30] A *jō* is a linear measurement equal to 3.31 yards.

with His Lordship, declaring that, although he had not been
negligent in the matter of conducting prayers, his benefice of ricelands and dry fields has been subjected to public obligations in the
same way as those of the common people. . . . His Lordship summoned Zen'ei and granted him a decree absolving him from all
public obligations.

ORDERED: The prompt cessation of taxes on the residence and on the
one *chō* of cultivated barley field belonging to Zen'ei, the altar priest
of the sub-shrine
It is not in the interest of amicable relations to subject, in the same
manner as the people, the aforementioned person, an altar priest of the
sub-shrine, who has conducted prayers faithfully, to all forms of public
taxes on his residence, situated in his native township. It is ordered that,
hereafter, all public obligations, including taxes on his enclosed dry
fields, shall cease. Thus ordered.
Juei 1:8,5

11th day. *Masako indicates that the birth of her child is imminent.*
Yoritomo has gone to visit Her Ladyship, who has indicated this
evening that the birth is imminent. Many people are gathering to
await the event. In the past few days many immediate vassals from
the provinces have been coming to Kamakura for the occasion. Also,
to pray for Her Ladyship, special emissaries bearing offerings have
been sent to the Izu and Hakone shrines as well as to other shrines
in the nearby provinces.

12th day. *Her Ladyship gives birth to a son.*
Clear. At 5 P.M. Her Ladyship gave birth to a boy. The priests in
attendance were Senkō-bō Ryōzen and the great master of Buddhist
Law Kanshū. The twanging of bow strings to keep away the evil
spirits was performed by Morooka Shigetsune, Ōba Kageyoshi, and
the provisional governor Tatara Sadayoshi. The conjuration to
destroy evil spirits by shooting an arrow was performed by Taira
Hirotsune. At 7 P.M. the wife of Kawagoe Shigeyori, who is a
daughter of the nun Hiki, was admitted into the chamber to serve
as wet nurse.

13th day. *Yoritomo invites vassals to make presents to his son.*
In accordance with the best practices on the occasion of the birth

of a prince, His Lordship has invited his immediate vassals to make presents of swords. Therefore, swords were presented by the lieutenant of the Left Outer Palace Guards Utsunomiya Tomotsuna, Hatakeyama Shigetada, lieutenant of the military guards Tsuchiya Yoshikiyo, Wada Yoshimori, Kajiwara Kagetoki, Kajiwara Kagesue, and Yokoyama Tokikane. The immediate vassals have also made presents of horses, which now number two hundred. Then His Lordship selected the physically best of his warriors who had not lost either of their parents to present these fine horses as offerings to Tsurugaoka Shrine, the Provincial Shrine of Suruga, the shrine ricelands of Ōba, the Miura Jūniten Shrine, and the Kurihama Daimyōjin Shrine.

14th day. *Attendance upon the young prince on the third night since his birth is assigned to Koyama Shirō Tomomasa.*

15th day. *Lectures on the six monthly fast days*[31] *are begun at Tsurugaoka Shrine.*

16th day. *Attendance upon the young prince on the fifth night is performed by the vice governor of Kazusa Taira Hirotsune.*

18th day. *A special ceremony for the young prince is observed.*
Attendance for the seventh night was performed by Chiba Tsunetane and his six sons. The father, Tsunetane, dressed in a white ceremonial robe, and Tanemasa's mother, who is the daughter of the fifth rank Chichibu Shigehiro, personally attended the young prince. There was also the presentation of gifts in which the oldest son, Tanemasa, and the second son, Morotsune, bore the armor; Tanemori and Tanenobu, the third and fourth sons, led the sacred horse, which was saddled; Tanemichi, the fifth son, carried the bow and arrow; and Taneyori, the sixth son, carried the sword. Yoritomo was greatly impressed by the splendid and stalwart deportment of the brothers. It was a grand sight for the others, as well, who witnessed the ceremony.

[31] *Roku-sai,* the six monthly *posadha,* or fast days, fall on the eighth, fourteenth, fifteenth, twenty-third, twenty-ninth, and thirtieth.

20th day. *Attendance on the young prince for the ninth night is assigned to the prince's maternal grandfather, Hōjō Tokimasa.*

NINTH MONTH

15th day. *The Heike return from Hokuriku to Kyoto.*

The Heiji troops who had embarked for Hokuriku on a campaign against Kiso Yoshinaka have all returned to Kyoto. Although the Heike have announced that the cold weather had forced them back, the truth of the matter is that they fear the military prowess of Yoshinaka.

20th day. *The hōgen[32] Engyō visits at Kamakura.*

The Middle Counselor and *hōgen* Engyō has arrived here from Kyoto. He is a grandson of the *ason* and governor of Mutsu Minamoto Yoshiie, who was a grandson of Prince Sukehito, a descendant of the Ex-Sovereign So-Sanjō. Yoritomo, learning of the visitor's relationship to the family, has invited him to headquarters. Engyō, wishing to offer prayers in connection with the birth of a child to Her Ladyship, had stopped at the Great Shrine of Ise on his way from the capital; thus his delay in arriving at Kamakura. Escorts for Engyō for the greater part of the journey were provided by the high priest of Ise Shrine Chikataka.

23rd day. *Engyō is made intendant of Tsurugaoka.*

Yoritomo and Engyō have gone to the Tsurugaoka Shrine. The visit was made to invest Engyō with the office of intendant of Tsurugaoka. The arrangement was consummated before the altar.

25th day. *Mareyoshi, Yoritomo's brother, is killed in battle.*

During the Eireki era [1160] Yoritomo's younger brother, the young lord of Tosa Mareyoshi, whose mother is a daughter of Fujiwara Suenori, was exiled to Tosa because of his relationship to the late Minamoto Yoshitomo. When Yoritomo rose up in arms in the east, the Heike, expecting Mareyoshi to join with Yoritomo, ordered him to be killed. Eager to distinguish themselves in service, the provisional governor Hasuike Ietsuna and Hirata Tarō Toshitō,

[32] *Hōgen,* abbreviation for *hōgen-washō-i,* the second highest of priestly ranks.

local lords of Tosa who are vassals of Taira Shigemori, launched an attack on Mareyoshi. The latter quit his castle at Kera to join Yasu Shichirō Yukimune, a local lord of Tosa, with whom he had been on friendly terms. But en route to the Yasu Manor, Ietsuna and Toshitō overtook him in the Toshikoe Mountains in Agawa District and killed him. . . .

26th day. *Work is begun on the residence of the intendant of Tsurugaoka.*

The western foothills of Tsurugaoka have been marked off as the site for the residence of the intendant of the Tsurugaoka Shrine. Today the ceremony of the raising of the pillars and the beams was begun under the supervision of Ōba Kageyoshi. Yoritomo attended the ceremony.

28th day. *Jō Nagamochi of Echigo defies the Genji.*

Word has been received to the effect that Jō Shirō Nagamochi of Echigo has constructed a castle at Akatani, Kogawa Manor, in Echigo, and that, moreover, he has installed an image of the Beautiful Sight Bodhisattva before which he will invoke maledictions on the Minamoto.

TENTH MONTH

9th day. *Kiso Yoshinaka attacks the governor of Hitachi.*

Sukemoto, the governor of Hitachi and older brother of Jō Nagamochi of Echigo, has taken up his brother's cause and has opposed the Minamoto. Thus Kiso Yoshinaka, at the head of troops drawn from the Hokuriku circuit, launched a battle against Sukemoto near the Chikuma River in Shinano. By nightfall Sukemoto had been defeated and routed.

17th day. *Masako returns to her residence.*

Her Ladyship and the young prince have returned to headquarters from the lying-in quarters. Carrying the young prince's sedan chair were Sadatsuna, Tsunetaka, Moritsuna, and Takatsuna of the Sasaki family. Carrying the prince's bow and arrows was Koyama Munemasa. The sword was carried by Koyama Tomomitsu. The offerings to ward off the evil spirits were borne by Hiki Yoshi-

kazu, he being the husband of the prince's wet nurse. For her devotion to Yoritomo, he had granted the Hiki District in Musashi
Province to her custody in Eireki 1 [1160] during his exile. She,
together with her husband, the secretary of the housekeeping office,
had come to Hiki from Kyoto, and until the fall of Jishō 4 [1180],
a period of twenty years, she had never ceased inquiring after Yoritomo's welfare.

ELEVENTH MONTH

10th day. *Masako learns of Yoritomo's concubine.*

Of late His Lordship's favorite, Kizen, has been residing at the
Iijima residence of the young lord of Fushimi Hirotsuna. However,
the secret reached the ear of Her Ladyship, who was greatly angered.
The matter had been divulged to her by Lord Hōjō's wife, the Lady
Maki. Today Her Ladyship ordered Maki Munechika to destroy
Hirotsuna's residence, thus subjecting Hirotsuna to great humilia-
tion. Hirotsuna, however, had luckily escaped from his home with
Kizen and had gone to Ōtawa Gorō Yoshihisa's residence in Abumi-
zuri.

12th day. *Yoritomo punishes Maki Munechika.*

Yoritomo, announcing that he was going on an outing and summoning Maki Munechika to accompany him, has gone to Ōtawa
Yoshihisa's residence in Abumizuri. Upon his arrival there he summoned Hirotsuna to explain the extraordinary happenings of the
10th. Then His Lordship summoned Munechika, who, stunned beyond words, prostrated himself in abject apology with his face on
the ground. The irate Yoritomo, unable to contain his anger, cut off
Munechika's topknot, while rebuking him in these words: "It was
most praiseworthy of you to have carried out Her Ladyship's orders,
but why did you not inform me first of the nature of her orders?
It was extremely impudent of you to scheme to humiliate others."
Munechika, weeping, fled from the scene. This evening Yoritomo
lodged at Yoshihisa's residence.

14th day. *Hōjō Tokimasa is displeased at Yoritomo's punishment of
Munechika.*

Yoritomo returned to Kamakura as the evening shadows began to

appear. Then, tonight, Lord Hōjō, dejected over Yoritomo's rebuke
of Munechika, suddenly departed for Izu. When this information
was conveyed to Yoritomo, he was greatly disturbed. Summoning
Kajiwara Kagesue, he said, "Although Yoshitoki, Tokimasa's son,
is on friendly terms with me, we must determine whether he has
followed his father, who in unjustified resentment has gone home
to the provinces without my leave." When Kagesue reported a few
moments later that Yoshitoki had not left for home, Yoritomo ordered Kagesue to bring Yoshitoki before him. Through the secretary
Kunimichi His Lordship told Yoshitoki: "Lord Hōjō, dejected over
the rebuke which His Lordship administered to Munechika for the
impudence he displayed, has gone back to his native province. This
was against His Lordship's will. But you, on your own judgment,
did not accompany your father. It was for this praiseworthy act
that you have been summoned." Yoshitoki, in no position to com-
ment on the propriety of the matter, expressed his regrets over the
incident and retired.

20th day. *Yoritomo despatches Minamoto Aritsuna to Tosa to
avenge the death of Mareyoshi.*

His Lordship has despatched the lieutenant of the Right Outer
Palace Guards Minamoto Aritsuna of Izu against Ietsuna and
Toshitō, the principal residents of Tosa. With Yasu Shichirō Yukimune as guide Aritsuna took his leave at dawn this morning. This
action was taken against Ietsuna for the crime of killing the young
lord of Tosa.

TWELFTH MONTH

1st day. *The Heike place the Ise Shrine under surveillance.*

According to a letter from the priest Naritomo, the Heike have
indignantly memorialized the throne over the accession to the cause
of Kanto of the assistant head Shinto priest of the two shrines of Ise.
Placed under the surveillance of the nobles last month, the priests
are in great anxiety.

2nd day. *Yoritomo assures the Ise Shrine of support.*

In connection with Naritomo's letter, His Lordship has sent the
following note to the Great Shrine:

I am alarmed at the charge brought by the Heike against the assistant head Shinto priest for espousing my cause. However, the gods accept reason, as will, I am certain, the ruler. The two shrines, so long as they continue to offer prayers in earnest, are hereby assured of continued control of their holdings in the east. Respectfully forwarded.

Twelfth Month, 2nd day

TO: The Lord Fifth Rank Naritomo

7th day. *Yoritomo rewards a priest for devotion to duty.*

In the deep of the night after the people had retired Yoritomo went to Tsurugaoka to worship, escorted only by Sasaki Moritsuna and Wada Yoshimochi. As Yoritomo intoned prayers in the worship hall, a ritualist of the shrine, Eikō, appeared and reproved him thus: "Who is it that has the audacity to occupy His Lordship's place? Take your leave immediately!" Yoritomo, moved by this act, called Eikō before him and made him a grant of 1 *chō* of riceland in the vicinity of Amanawa.

10th day. *Yoritomo removes his concubine to Kochūta's residence.*

His Lordship's favorite, Kizen, has been moved to Kochūta Mitsuie's residence in Kotsubo. Although she is in great fear of incurring Her Ladyship's displeasure, she has acceded to His Lordship's every wish, as the latter's love for her continues to grow from day to day.

16th day. *Fujiwara Hirotsuna is banished to Tōtomi Province at the instance of Masako.*

30th day. *Yoritomo confirms the holdings of Susai Suketada and his followers.*

A judgment confirming the control of their present residences has been granted to Susai Jirō Suketada, an immediate vassal residing in Kazusa, and his followers.

Chapter III

JUEI 3 [1184]

FIRST MONTH

1st day. *Yoritomo foregoes worship at Tsurugaoka Shrine.*

Clear. Although the religious dance was held at the Tsurugaoka Hachiman Shrine, Yoritomo, because of the defilement of the headquarters as a result of the Taira Hirotsune incident of the past winter,[1] did not attend. Instead, His Lordship made his offerings to the shrine through his secretary, Fujiwara Kunimichi. Kunimichi sat in the corridor of the shrine as the intendant Engyō intoned and explained the eight volumes of the *Lotus Sutra*.

3rd day. *Yoritomo makes a grant of land to Toyouke Shrine.*

8th day. *Yoritomo attempts to retrieve Hirotsune's armor.*

According to a letter from the priest of the Principal Shrine of Kazusa, the shrine is in possession of armor given to it as an offering by the late vice governor Taira Hirotsune. Wishing to examine it, His Lordship despatched Fujiwara Kunimichi and Ippon-bō to the shrine with two sets of armor to be exchanged for the one presented by Hirotsune. As the latter set of armor is now a sacred shrine property, it is believed that such an exchange of two sets for one would not offend the gods.

10th day. *Kiso Yoshinaka is made shogun.*

It has been reported that the governor of Iyo Kiso Yoshinaka has been given the additional office of Barbarian-Conquering-Great-General.[2] Although there have been seventy imperial appointments

---

[1] The headquarters had been the scene of Hirotsune's assassination. The act had been committed by Kajiwara Kagetoki at Yoritomo's instigation.

[2] *Seii-tai-shogun,* usually abbreviated to *shogun.*

of Ezo-Pacifying generals[3] from the reinstatement of Sakanoue to
the appointment of Fujiwara Norisue in Angen 2:3 [1176], there
have been only two appointments of Barbarian-Conquering generals.
These were that of the imperial investigator and governor of Mutsu
Sakanoue Tamuramaro in Enreki 16:11,5 [797] during the reign
of Emperor Kammu; and that of the councilor and captain of the
Right Outer Palace Guards Fujiwara Tadabumi in Tenkei 3:1,18
[940] during the reign of the Ex-Emperor Suzaku. Since then, during a period of twenty-two imperial reigns and two hundred forty-
five years, there has been no appointment to this office except for
Yoshinaka's, which is only the third in history. It is a most unusual
example of imperial graciousness.

17th day. *Yoritomo regrets the slaying of Taira Hirotsune.*
   Bearing Hirotsune's armor, the secretary Fujiwara Kunimichi,
Ippon-bō, and the Shinto priest Kaneshige have returned to Kamakura from the Principal Shrine of Kazusa. Upon examining it, Yoritomo noticed a written document tied to the armor strings. Reading
it, His Lordship discovered that it was a vow made by Hirotsune
to pray and work for the success of Yoritomo and his cause. Thus
His Lordship, realizing that Hirotsune had not harbored treasonable intentions toward him, regrets the slaying of Hirotsune, and
is making plans to pray for the vice governor's afterlife. Moreover,
His Lordship has ordered that Hirotsune's younger brothers—the
manorial official Amawa Naotane and Sōma Kurō Tsunekiyo, who
are now held as prisoners because of their relationship to the deceased—be pardoned. Hirotsune's vow follows:

Respectfully submitted to the August Principal Shrine of Kazusa
   Regarding the vow which I have made
Item: I shall make a benefice of ricelands amounting to twenty *chō*
   within the next three years.
Item: I shall reconstruct the shrine within three years.
Item: I shall shoot ten thousand arrows from a moving horse within
   three years.
The foregoing resolutions have been made in behalf of the former
assistant captain of the Middle Palace Guards Yoritomo and for his
prayers to establish peace in the east. If each of the foregoing vows is

---

[3] *Chinjufu-shogun.*

fulfilled, it will enhance the glory of the gods of your shrine. Thus
vowed.
Juei 2:6,7   Taira Hirotsune,
                                              Provisional Vice Governor of Kazusa

20th day. *Yoshitsune and Noriyori enter the capital.*

Representing Yoritomo, his brothers Noriyori and Yoshitsune have
made their way into the capital at the head of several tens of
thousands of troops. This move was made to pursue and punish
Kiso Yoshinaka. Noriyori entered the capital today via Seta, while
Yoshitsune entered via the Uji Road. Although attempts to check
these advances were made by Yoshinaka, Shida Yoshihiro, Imai
Kanehira, and their men, they were routed. Noriyori and Yoshitsune
. . . rushed over to the palace at Rokujō to offer protection to the
ex-sovereign, while Ichijō Tadayori and his followers of gallant men
went out in various directions in pursuit of Yoshinaka and his men.
Finally, in the vicinity of Kuritsu in Ōmi Province, Yoshinaka was
overcome and killed by the local lord of Sagami, Ishida Jirō. . . .

21st day. *Higuchi Kanemitsu, a retainer of Yoshinaka, is captured.*

Gen Kurō Yoshitsune has notified the throne by letter that he
would present the head of Yoshinaka. Today, at nightfall, Yoshitsune captured and bound Higuchi Jirō Kanemitsu, one of Yoshinaka's principal vassals. Kanemitsu, on a mission for Yoshinaka,
had sought to kill the secretary Ishikawa Yoshisuke, who resides
in Kawachi. Ishikawa, however, had escaped. While returning
empty handed to the capital, Kanemitsu learned of his master's
death in the vicinity of Yawata Ōwatari; but nevertheless he attempted to enter the capital. There he was challenged by Gen Kurō
and his retainers who fought with him and took him prisoner.

22nd day. *A painter is invited to Kamakura.*

Summoned by His Lordship, the provisional governor of Shimōsa
Fujiwara Tamehisa has come to Kamakura from Kyoto. He is the
third son of the governor of Buzen Fujiwara Tametō. He is a
talented painter and is without a peer.

23rd day. *A strange omen is reported to Yoritomo.*

The assistant head Shinto priest of Kashima Shrine of Hitachi
has sent a messenger to Kamakura, who reported as follows: "On

the 19th the priest of the shrine was told in a dream that the gods of the shrine had gone to Kyoto to pursue and chastise the Heike and Kiso Yoshinaka. Then, on the 20th, at 7 P.M., a dark cloud descended on the worship hall, and there was darkness everywhere. The hall rumbled and vibrated. The deer and the chickens all gathered in groups. After a while the dark cloud spread to all directions. One of the chickens was enveloped by the cloud, and it looked like a human eye. It was the strangest of omens." Upon hearing this, Yoritomo stepped down from the bathhouse to the courtyard and prayed in the direction of Kashima Shrine.

26th day. *The Genji in Kyoto turn over the heads of Yoshinaka and his lieutenants to the imperial police.*
    Clear. This morning at Shichijō-Kawara the imperial police formally received the decapitated heads of Yoshinaka, Takanashi Tadanao, Imai Kanehira, and Nei Yukichika, which were exposed to public view on the trees before the prison. Also, the captive Kanemitsu was turned over to the police. The director was the Middle Councilor Fujiwara, who was assisted by Mitsumasa, the director of the sovereign's private office and controller.

27th day. *Yoritomo receives reports on the battle against Yoshinaka.*
    At 1 P.M. messengers . . . arrived at Kamakura to report on the battle of the 20th and on the disposal of Yoshinaka and his followers. As Yoritomo listened to the details, . . . Kajiwara Kagetoki's messenger arrived with a roster of those who had been killed and captured. His Lordship was especially pleased at Kagetoki's thoughtfulness in submitting a written record for, although many messengers have been streaming into Kamakura, none had brought written reports.

28th day. *More messengers arrive to report that Yoritomo's armies had suffered no serious casualties in the recent battle.*

29th day. *Noriyori and Yoshitsune leave Kyoto for the Heike lines.*

SECOND MONTH

1st day. *Noriyori incurs the displeasure of Yoritomo.*
    Noriyori has incurred His Lordship's displeasure. Only today

Yoritomo received the details of the battle at the river crossing of Sunomata in Owari in which Noriyori, on his way to the capital to attack Kiso Yoshinaka, had fought with fellow vassals as to who should assume the vanguard position of the army.[4] His Lordship has declared that surely there must be a more conciliatory way of settling a dispute than to indulge in a private war, especially just prior to launching an attack on the enemies of the imperial court.

2nd day. *Higuchi Kanemitsu is beheaded.*

Higuchi Kanemitsu has been beheaded. The execution had been assigned to Shibuya Shigekuni, who in turn had ordered a follower, Heita, to carry it out. However, Heita faltered in carrying out the order. Whereupon Takashige, son of Shigekuni, assumed the role of executioner and performed the decapitation with one arm. Takashige had injured an arm in the battle on the 20th.

There had been efforts in some quarters to spare Kanemitsu's life, he being a close associate of the men of Kodama in Musashi, who are deserving of honors for their meritorious services. Accordingly Yoshitsune had brought the matter to the attention of the throne, but, Kanemitsu's crime being of serious proportions, a pardon was denied.

4th day. *The Heike fortify Ichinotani.*

The Heike, having assembled several tens of thousands of mounted troops from the Saikai and San'in circuits, have fortified and manned a castle at Ichinotani on the border of Settsu and Harima. Today the Heike conducted a Buddhist memorial service on the occasion of the third anniversary of Kiyomori's death.

5th day. *The Genji armies reach Settsu Province.*

The two Genji commanders reached Settsu at 5 P.M. and they have fixed the coming 7th at 5 A.M. as the time for the launching of the attack. The frontal attack will be commanded by Noriyori.[5] . . . In his command there are 56,000 mounted troops. The attack on the rear of the enemy position will be commanded by Minamoto

---

[4] For an earlier report on the Sunomata Battle, see Yōwa 1:3,10.
[5] The names of thirty-two Genji vassals are listed in the text.

Yoshitsune.[6] . . . In his command there are 20,000 mounted troops.

The 7,000 Heike troops are under the command of the Middle Captain Sukemori who was recently raised to the third rank, the Minor Captain Komatsu Arimori, the governor of Bitchū Moromori, the lieutenant of the Middle Palace Guards Hirauchi Kiyoie, and Emi Jirō Morikata. Having been apprised of the arrival of the Genji in Settsu, the Heike established their position to the west of Mikusa Mountain. The Genji formed their line to the east of the Mikusa Mountain. Thus, the Taira and the Minamoto face each other with three *ri*[7] separating them. Then Yoshitsune, Nobutsuna, and Sanehira decided in council to attack Taira Shigehira at night without awaiting the dawn. Thus they created consternation in the Heike ranks and forced them to disperse.

7th day. The Genji and the Heiji battle at Ichinotani.

Snow fell. At 3 A.M. Minamoto Yoshitsune, leading seventy of his best troops, arrived at the far end of Ichinotani, which is called the Hiyodori Impasse. At 5 A.M. Kumagaya Jirō Naozane of Musashi and Hirayama Sueshige made their way stealthily to the front approaches to Ichinotani and, seizing control of the area from the shore to the edge of the buildings, they announced in a loud voice that they represented the vanguard of the Genji. The Heike opened the castle gates and the lieutenant of the Left Outer Palace Guards Hida Saburō Kagetsuna, the military guard Koshi Chūjirō Moritsugu, the lieutenant of the military guard Kazusa Gorō Tadamitsu, and the military guard Akushichi Kagekiyo and twenty-three mounted men came out to battle the Genji. Kumagaya Jirō Naoie was injured, and a follower of Sueshige was killed. After that Minamoto Noriyori, Ashikaga, Chichibu, and Miura with their men from Kamakura mixed in battle with the Taira, as did the red and white colors of their standards. The fierce combat caused the mountains to reverberate and the ground to tremble. And despite the efforts of the men from Kamakura, an easy victory was not in sight, for the castle walls towered high on the boulders which could

[6] The names of seventeen Genji vassals assigned to Yoshitsune's command are listed.

[7] A *ri* is equal to 2.44 miles.

not be negotiated by the horses, and the deepness of the ravine cut off penetration.

But Yoshitsune, leading the gallant followers of Miura Jūrō Yoshitsura, attacked the castle from the Hiyodori Impasse, which is a precipice frequented only by wild boar, deer, rabbits, and foxes. The Heike were thrown into panic, some whipping their horses and dashing out of the castle, others taking to boats to flee toward Shikoku. Taira Shigehira, the Minor Captain, third rank, was captured at Akashi by Kagetoki and Tekuni. Taira Michimori, third rank and governor of Echizen, was killed near Minato River by Sasaki Toshitsuna. In addition the governor of Satsuma Taira Tada-nori, the governor of Wakasa Taira Tsunetoshi, the governor of Musashi Taira Tomoakira, the fifth rank Taira Atsumori, Taira Narimori, and the former official of Etchū Taira Moritoshi were overcome and captured by the men under Noriyori and Yoshitsune. The former official of Kashima Taira Tsunemasa, the governor of Noto Noritsune, and the governor of Bitchū Moromori were captured by the governor of Tōtomi Yasuda Yoshisada.

8th day. *The Genji send a report of the victory to the ex-sovereign.*

The two commanders of Kanto have despatched a courier to Kyoto to report on the taking of nine heads of Taira leaders and the killing of more than one thousand of their followers in the battle at Ichinotani of the previous day.

9th day. *Yoshitsune returns to Kyoto.*

Shortly after Yoshitsune and his escorts made their entry into the capital, his army also entered the city. Yoshitsune had preceded his army to notify the throne that the heads of the Heiji taken in battle would be borne through the main street of the capital.

11th day. *The court deliberates on whether to permit the Genji to bring the decapitated heads of the Heiji into the capital via the main thoroughfare.*

The matter of deciding on the court's reply to the request of the Genji commanders to bring the heads of the Heiji into the city through the main thoroughfare was given over to a council of the regent and civil dictator, the chancellor and his ministers of the

Left and Right, and the major councilor Horikawa Tadachika. The question was whether the court should make a reply sympathetic to the Heike, who had served the court for so long, or accede to the reasonable request of the Genji, even if the request is in pursuit of their private objectives. The ex-sovereign, hard pressed to choose between these points of view, instructed the officials to deliberate carefully on the matter. Although the opinions were varied, it was decided to accede to the persistent demands of the two Genji commanders. The imperial messenger who made several trips between the Genji commanders and the court was the provisional assistant captain of the Right Outer Palace Guards Sadanaga.

13th day. *The heads of Taira commanders are exposed to public view.*

The heads of the Heiji, namely, those of Michimori, Tadanori, Tsunemasa, Noritsune, Atsumori, Moromori, Tomoakira, Tsunetoshi, Narimori, and Moritoshi were first assembled at Yoshitsune's residence at Rokujō-Muromachi; then they were taken to Hachijō-Kawara and presented to the fifth rank and secretary Nakayori and his subordinates. Each head was placed on a long halberd with a red identification tag. Then they were exposed on the trees facing the prison. The throngs of people who came to view the heads made the area a virtual market place.

14th day. *Taira Shigehira is interrogated by Doi Sanehira; Yoritomo returns control of lands to retainers of Taira Hirotsune.*

Clear. The provisional assistant captain of the Right Outer Palace Guards, having received an imperial assent to interrogate the Middle Captain, third rank, Taira Shigehira, has gone to the residence of the late Middle Councilor Nakamikado Ienari at Hachijō-Horikawa, where Shigehira had been brought for questioning by Doi Sanehira. The interrogation, which was taken down in writing, took place on the patio.

Today His Lordship has issued a directive returning control of lands to many immediate vassals of Kazusa. Their lands had been seized last year on the charge of complicity in the designs of Taira Hirotsune.

15th day. *Messengers of Noriyori and Yoshitsune bring a report of the battle of Ichinotani to Kamakura.*

At 7 A.M. couriers of Noriyori and Yoshitsune arrived at Kamakura from Settsu. They presented His Lordship with a record of the battle at Ichinotani. The gist of the report is as follows: "In the battle which took place on the 7th the Heike suffered many casualties. Taira Munemori and his followers took ship for Shikoku, but Taira Shigehira was captured. Taira Michimori, Tadanori, and Tsunetoshi were slain by Noriyori. Taira Tsunemasa, Moromori, and Noritsune were killed by Yasuda Yoshisada. Taira Atsumori, Tomoakira, Norimori, and Moritoshi were slain by Yoshitsune. In addition more than one thousand of the enemy were beheaded. On the whole, the warriors of Musashi, Sagami, and Shimotsuke performed meritoriously. Thus submitted."

16th day. *Taira Shigehira is interrogated again.*

18th day. *Yoritomo sends instructions to Kajiwara Kagetoki and Doi Sanehira regarding the defense of the capital and the protection of five western provinces.*

Yoritomo has despatched an emissary to Kyoto with instructions regarding the defense and protection of the capital. He has also instructed Kagetoki and Sanehira to provide protection through special deputies appointed by them for the five provinces of Harima, Mimasaka, Bizen, Bitchū, and Bingo.

20th day. *Taira Munemori replies from Shikoku regarding the restoration of Emperor Antoku and the imperial regalia requested by the ex-sovereign.*

21st day. *A former retainer of Yoshinaka brings a grievance to Yoritomo.*

Otō Tomonori, a follower of Yoshinaka until recently, has come to Kamakura to express a grievance. Permitted by Yoritomo to explain the purpose of his visit, Tomonori requested the right to control Nakano Mimaki in Shinano, and Tanaka and Ikeda Manors in Kii Province. When asked on what evidence he based his claims, Tomonori replied: "Since the days of Hidesato, my ancestor, these

lands have remained in the family. But during the Heiji Disturbance, when Minamoto Yoshitomo suffered great reverses, we were
deprived of these lands. I pleaded with Yoshinaka regarding this
matter during the Eighth Month of the past year, and he assured
me of my rights to these manors with a written order." Saying thus,
he produced the order for His Lordship's examination. Yoritomo
thereupon gave instructions to assure Tomonori control of the said
manors.

23rd day. *Partisans of Kiso Yoshinaka are captured in Kyoto and
turned over to the imperial police.*

25th day. *Yoritomo addresses a memorial to the ex-sovereign explaining his policies.*
  Yoritomo has despatched a memorandum containing his policies
regarding the administration of the imperial government to the
ason Takashina Yasutsune. The memorandum reads:
Respectfully submitted, the following:
  Item: On Imperial administration
It is desirable that the court administer a virtuous government according
to precedent. It is especially desirable that His Majesty give his mature
reflection to the administration of provincial offices. Although we are
now in the midst of subjugating rebels in the east and the north, it is
expected that, beginning this spring, order will be gradually restored.
Thus, by the fall of next year, provincial governors may be appointed.
  Item: On the subjugation of the Heike
It is desirable that in the home provinces and the nearby provinces,
all who bear arms, whether they be of the Genji or of the Heiji, shall
be assigned to Yoshitsune's command. Although a naval attack is no
easy matter, it is desirable that His Majesty order Yoshitsune to take
to the field immediately. As for rewards for meritorious services, it is
desirable that His Majesty withhold them until submission of a
memorial from Yoritomo.
  Item: On shrines
As ours is the land of the gods, the lands held by the shrines since
ancient times should be confirmed as a matter of course. Again, it would
be permissible for shrines to acquire new lands. In particular, the
Kashima Shrine has rendered exceedingly great service . . . toward the
elimination of many rebels. Again, it is desirable that, if there be shrines
which sustained damages, His Majesty order the repair of such shrines,
and that there be no neglect in the performance of religious practices
according to time-honored regulations.

Item: On Buddhist temples

It is desirable that the lands of the temples and monasteries be restored as before. In recent years there have been among the monks some who have aspired to military valor to the neglect of Buddhist Law. This it is desirable to stop with the sternest of measures. As a measure to be taken hereafter, it is desirable that weapons maintained by monks be turned over to government troops engaged in subjugating enemies of the nation.

The foregoing items respectfully submitted

Juei 3:2   Minamoto Yoritomo

27th day. *Yoritomo rejects a request for recognition of meritorious service.*

Sasaki Moritsuna, a local lord of Ōmi Province, has come to Kamakura to request an award for his son Toshitsuna for his capture of third rank Taira Michimori in the Ichinotani Battle. His Lordship has replied that, while he has been impressed by Toshitsuna's exploits, he doubts the sincerity of a man who had treated the Minamoto with disrespect and who would come to pay homage only after the flight of the Heike from Kyoto.

30th day. *Yoritomo restores a manor to a member of the court.*

His Lordship has restored the land stewardship of Karita Township, a part of the Tōjō Manor in Shinano Province, to the fifth rank Toshimasa of the Ministry of Ceremonial. Toshimasa had complained that until its confiscation the township had belonged to him.

THIRD MONTH

1st day. *Yoritomo urges local lords of Kyushu and Shikoku to oppose the Heike.*

Yoritomo has sent a directive to the local lords of the nine provinces of Kyushu, urging them to oppose the Heike. Although His Lordship has been able to rally troops for his cause elsewhere in the country, he has been unsuccessful in Kyushu, where support for the Heike is strong. His directive reads:

ORDERED TO: The local lords of the nine provinces of Kyushu

Regarding the prompt enrollment as immediate vassals and the confirmation of original holdings of those who would join in the chastisement of the Heike rebels

On the basis of an edict of the ex-sovereign we urge the men of the aforementioned nine provinces to join us in the chastisement of the enemies of the imperial court. Because of the insurrection of the Heike, the deputies of the Lord of Kamakura—the governor of Tōtomi Yasuda Yoshisada in the Tōkai circuit, and the director of the Left Horse Bureau Kiso Yoshinaka in the Hokuriku circuit—went to the capital last year. Consequently, Yoshinaka himself has entered the conspiracy by coming to terms with the Heike. Thus, not only on the authority of an edict of the ex-sovereign, but also upon my own initiative, to punish enemies of the court, we have pursued and chastised the said Yoshinaka. Meanwhile, the Heike have been active in Shikoku, at times even sending their boats to ports in the nearby provinces and seizing provisions from the people. Their depredations have not ceased. Now we are despatching government troops by land and by sea, and we shall, in short order, chastise the Heike. Take note that we shall confirm the present holdings of local lords of the nine provinces of Kyushu if they will rally the government troops of their respective province and join our cause. We shall, with absolute certainty and in due time, reward those who perform meritoriously. Thus ordered.

Juei 3:3,1   Former Assistant
                Captain of the Middle Palace Guards, Right Division

Some of the more influential warriors of Shikoku, which is also strongly pro-Taira, have come to the side of the Genji. Therefore His Lordship has instructed Lord Hōjō to communicate with them. Lord Hōjō's letter reads:

ORDERED TO: Kuninobu, Kunimoto, and the lay priest Sukemitsu, the Great Lords[8] of Tosa
    Regarding the prompt enrollment as vassals of those who are sympathetic to the Genji cause and who would participate in the chastisement of the Heike

Upon instructions from the Lord of Kamakura, who has received an edict from the ex-sovereign, the great lords and others in the above-mentioned provinces who are favorably disposed toward His Lordship are hereby informed that they may come to pay homage to His Lordship and to participate jointly in the subjugation of the Heike. I am about to despatch the immediate vassal Nobutsune to Shikoku to assure confirmation of your present holdings and to see to it that there are no outrages committed. Take note that all great lords and warriors who would participate in our cause are entitled to the provisions stated herein. Carry out this order without fail. Thus ordered.

Juei 3:3,1   Taira[9]

[8] *Daimyō*, one of the few times that this term appears in the early chapters of the *Azuma kagami*.

[9] Hōjō Tokimasa was of Taira descent, and frequently signed his letters thus.

2nd day. *Doi Sanehira transfers custody of Taira Shigehira to Yoshitsune.*

5th day. *Yoritomo awards recognition to a son of a warrior slain in battle.*

Last month at Ichinotani in Settsu Province, on the day of the defeat of the Taira, Fujita Saburō Yukiyasu had charged into the enemy ranks and had been killed. As a reward His Lordship today granted to his son, Yoshikuni, the right to succeed to his late father's estate. . . .

6th day. *Noriyori is returned to Yoritomo's good graces.*

9th day. *The ex-sovereign complains of excesses of warriors.*

A decree of the ex-sovereign, dated the 18th of the past month, has arrived at Kamakura. It declares that of late warriors, on the excuse of pursuing enemies of the imperial court, have been interfering with the annual tributes of the manors in the various provinces, as well as with the property of the people. It is not known whether these men are spurred to commit such acts on the growing prestige of Kanto, but it has been difficult to punish them, according to letters from the nobles. Yoritomo, receiving this news, has declared that he will remedy this situation immediately and has ordered subordinate officials to desist from oppressing the people.

A decree of the ex-sovereign

Of late, warriors have become unmindful of imperial law and have been exerting their authority, willfully and freely, in the various provinces of the seven circuits. They have forcibly seized tributes bound for shrines. They have seized provisions destined for temples. Indeed, they have violated lands of the ex-sovereign, the sovereign, the provincial officials, and the people, arousing the wrath of Heaven, which has always shown great sympathy for the people. There shall be no recurrence of such acts hereafter. If documentary evidence by the warriors is offered, the third rank Minamoto Yoritomo shall examine such evidence carefully, and he shall report to the ex-sovereign through the officials that there shall be no recurrence of violence. If, however, violence continues, the violators of the laws shall be punished without mercy.

Juei 3:2,18   Fujiwara Mitsumasa,
                               Director of the Sovereign's Private Office,
                               Controller, and
                               Assistant Master of the Empress's Household

10th day. *Taira Shigehira is ordered to Kamakura; Osada Sanetsune of Inaba Province is honored by Yoritomo.*

The third rank Minor Captain Taira Shigehira, escorted by Kajiwara Kagetoki, has departed from the capital today for Kanto upon His Lordship's summons.

Today His Lordship has summoned the lieutenant of the guards Osada Sanetsune, a local lord of Inaba Province. . . . In a letter from Yoritomo it is stated that "although the aforementioned person should be punished for his support of the Heike, it will not be forgotten for generations to come that his father, Suketsune, who was known as Takaniwa-no-suke, sent Tō Shichi Sukeie to Izu to serve me. Therefore, there shall be no change in the control of Sanetsune's present fief." In the Eireki era [1160] during His Lordship's journey to exile, some of his hereditary vassals had died, others had entertained a change of heart, and none would stand at his side, for His Lordship had been degraded. But Suketsune had despatched Sukeie, a member of his own household, to serve him, an act of loyalty which His Lordship has not forgotten.

13th day. *Hara Takaharu, a brother-in-law of Taira Hirotsune, is honored by Yoritomo.*

Hara Takaharu, fifth rank, and a local lord of Owari Province, has come to pay homage to His Lordship at the latter's command. He is a brother-in-law of the late governor of Kazusa Hirotsune. But Takaharu, as father-in-law of the governor of Satsuma Taira Tadanori, had felt kindly toward the Heiji. However, through his friendship with Hirotsune, he had turned against the chancellor Taira Kiyomori, and he had been entirely loyal to the Genji since his arrival in Kanto in Jishō 4 [1180]. But when Hirotsune was assassinated last year, Takaharu had secluded himself out of fear for his life. Now that His Lordship regrets the death of Hirotsune, who had given his life for an offense of which he was entirely innocent, and has been granting pardons to close members of Hirotsune's family, Takaharu has been cited for his distinguished service to the Genji and his control of his original holdings has been restored to him. His Lordship exhorted Takaharu to continue to render loyal service to the Genji.

14th day. *Yoritomo restores control of Miyakoda mikuri in Tōtomi Province to an agent of the Ise Shrine.*

17th day. *Yoritomo rejects Itagaki Kanenobu's charges against Doi Sanehira.*

A messenger of Itagaki Kanenobu arrvied at Kamakura last evening and, today, the purpose of his visit was divulged to His Lordship by the secretary Kunimichi. Kanenobu charges . . . that Doi Sanehira, claiming special authority from Yoritomo, has been acting arbitrarily, refusing to admit Kanenobu or others into discussion on all matters, whether pertaining to the division of troops or to any of the varied duties connected with the campaign in the west. Kanenobu is of the opinion that, if such conduct is permitted, it would lower the morale of the troops. Therefore, he requests the honor of being designated a superior official to Sanehira on all matters. His Lordship has refused to acknowledge Kanenobu's charges, declaring . . . that Sanehira's commission as deputy shall remain in force and that he shall be entrusted with all matters pertaining to the campaign in the west. His Lordship has added that men like Kanenobu should be concerned only with the giving of their lives on the battlefield for the cause. . . . Therefore, Kanenobu's charges were declared unwarranted, and his messenger departed from Kamakura empty handed.

18th day. *Yoritomo goes on a deer hunt to Izu Province.*

20th day. *Yoritomo names Ōuchi Koreyoshi as constable of Iga Province.*

22nd day. *Ōi Saneharu is reported in Ise on a special mission for the Heike.*

25th day. *Local officials of Bitchū are restored to office by Yoritomo.*

Doi Jirō Sanehira has been granted authority by Yoritomo to administer the province of Bitchū. Sanehira has restored to the provincial office the Scattered Rank Fujiwara Sukechika and his subordinates who had been dismissed earlier by the Heike.

27th day. *The prisoner, Taira Shigehira, reaches Izu Province.*

28th day. *Taira Shigehira has an audience with Yoritomo.*

Yoritomo invited the third rank Minor Captain Taira Shigehira to an audience and, addressing him, said: "I am greatly honored by your presence. This meeting was arranged so that you may, on the one hand, allay the ruler's anger, and on the other, absolve your father's shame, by offering to put down the insurrection begun by the Heiji at the Battle of Ishibashi Mountain. . . ." Shigehira replied: "The country has been protected for long by the Minamoto and the Taira. Of late it was the Taira alone who protected the imperial court, and the latter, in recognition of this service, has given promotions to more than eighty members of our family. The glory of the Taira has lasted for more than twenty years, but now fate decrees otherwise. Coming before you in the circumstances of a prisoner, I have no choice except to say that for a warrior it is not humiliating to be taken prisoner by the enemy. I ask immediate punishment by death." This conversation, devoid of trifles, moved all who witnessed it. His Lordship has remanded Shigehira to the custody of the vice governor Karino.

Today, His Lordship has declared that the problem of military men raised by the ex-sovereign in his letter should be settled without further delay. He has decided that questions of justice involving members of military houses should be brought to the attention of the throne.

FOURTH MONTH

1st day. *Yoritomo is feted at a banquet upon his return from Izu.*

On the occasion of the return of His Lordship to Kamakura from Hōjō, Izu Province, Tō Kurō Morinaga gave a banquet this evening in the north room of the headquarters. During the banquet His Lordship called Yukihira, Masayoshi, Tadatsune, Suetaka, and Kuninobu before him and presented each with deerskin. These skins are probably those which he had obtained from the recent hunt in Izu.

3rd day. *Yoritomo honors Ōya Yasusuke of Owari Province.*

For his services to His Lordship, Ōya Chūsaburō Yasusuke, a

local lord of Owari Province, has been granted control of his original holdings. . . . The award was made because Yasusuke, who is a son-in-law of Wada Yoshimori, remained loyal to the Genji in a province where most of the warriors had espoused the cause of the Taira.

4th day. *Yoritomo enjoys the cherry blossoms.*

The cherry blossoms in the garden of His Lordship's residence have bloomed. So brilliant was the bloom that His Lordship invited the *ason* and assistant master of the office of the empress's household Ichijō Yoshiyasu to enjoy the blossoms with him until the end of the day. The former Minor Captain Taira Tokiie also joined the party which, in addition to flower-viewing, enjoyed orchestral music and poetry-reading.

6th day. *Yoritomo returns thirty-four manors to Taira Yorimori.*

The holdings of the former major counselor Taira Yorimori[10] and those of his wife, which had been included in the list of confiscated Heiji lands submitted by the Kyoto court, have been ordered returned by Yoritomo. His Lordship, in order . . . to repay the debt of kindness he owes to the late Ike-no-Zenni, wife of Taira Yorimori, has restored Yorimori's control of thirty-four manors. This action, taken yesterday, was documented today. . . .

8th day. *Taira Shigehira arrives at Kamakura.*

Taira Shigehira has arrived at Kamakura from Izu. His Lordship has designated a house within the headquarters compound as Shigehira's temporary residence. Karino Sukeichi has been ordered to provide ten guards nightly from among his followers to stand watch at the residence.

10th day. *Yoritomo's court rank is raised; his bid for the office of shogun is rejected.*

Yoshitsune's messenger has arrived from Kyoto with the information that His Lordship has been raised to senior fourth rank, lower

---

[10] Yorimori is a brother of Kiyomori. Yorimori's wife had pleaded for Yoritomo's pardon after the Heiji Disturbance of 1160. The names of the thirty-four manors, here deleted, are given and identified by province in the entry.

grade, according to the list of promotions announced at the court on the 27th of the past month. This is in recognition of Yoritomo's subjugation of Yoshinaka. In a separate note Yoshitsune conveyed to Yoritomo the remarks he had heard regarding the promotion: namely, that Yoritomo's advancement from junior fifth rank to senior fourth rank was the first since Tenkei 3:3,9 [940] when the *ason* Fujiwara Hidesato was promoted from the sixth to the junior fourth rank. Also, on the precedent established by the minister of civil affairs Fujiwara Tadabumi,[11] inquiries had been tendered to the court regarding the appointment of Yoritomo to the office of Barbarian-Conquering-Great-General. However, upon deliberation of the ministers, it was announced that while there were precedents for the skipping of ranks, there was none for the granting of the office of shogun to Yoritomo at this time. It was pointed out that the conferment of the office of shogun can be made only after the recipient is first named as regimental commander[12] and divisional commander,[13] and upon acceptance of the Sword of Office from the emperor. To have conferred the office of shogun on Yoritomo on the present list would have created a new precedent which the ex-sovereign's government found difficult to justify. Thus only the promotion in rank was made at this time.

11th day. *Ichijō Yoshiyasu has an audience with Yoritomo.*

Clear skies. Ichijō Yoshiyasu, the new director of the Left Horse Bureau, who was appointed on the 27th of the past month, visited the Tsurugaoka Hachiman Shrine to offer salutations; then he repaired to His Lordship's residence for an audience.

14th day. *Minamoto Mitsuyuki seeks Yoritomo's pardon; Miyoshi Yasunobu arrives from Kyoto.*

Minamoto Mitsuyuki and Miyoshi Yasunobu have arrived at Kamakura. Mitsuyuki has come to seek His Lordship's clemency, for he had served the former official of Buzen Mitsusue, a member of the Heike. Miyoshi Yasunobu has always been a supporter of Kanto, a matter of gratification to His Lordship.

---

[11] Fujiwara Tadabumi was commissioned shogun in 940 and sent against Taira Masakado in the Tenkei Disturbance.

[12] *Gunso,* or regimental commander of the Ezo-Pacifying headquarters.

[13] *Gungen,* another official of the Ezo-Pacifying headquarters.

15th day. *Miyoshi Yasunobu vows to assist Yoritomo.*

Following the presentation of offerings at Tsurugaoka, His Lordship met with the clerk-lay priest Yasunobu in the corridor of the shrine. Yasunobu vowed that he would reside in Kamakura and assist Yoritomo in the administration of affairs of the military families. His Lordship has remarked in private that Yasunobu is an extremely placid man who had espoused the Minamoto cause with true sincerity.

16th day. *The era designation is changed from Juei 3 to Genreki 1.*

GENREKI 1 [1184]

18th day. *Yoritomo orders Tamehisa to make a painting.*

Because of a special vow he had made, Yoritomo has ordered the provisional governor of Shimōsa Tamehisa to make a painting of an image of the Kwannon. Tamehisa, having observed one hundred days of abstinence to purify himself, undertook the work today, wearing an ancient ceremonial court robe. Yoritomo himself has been reading the chapters on the Kwannon to purify himself.

20th day. *Yoritomo provides entertainment for Taira Shigehira.*

Rain fell unceasingly through the day. With Yoritomo's permission, Taira Shigehira indulged in a bath. In the evening His Lordship ordered Fujiwara Kunimichi, Kudō Ichirō Suketsune, and a lady in waiting to visit with Shigehira to cheer him in his leisure moments. In addition, His Lordship sent wine and fruit, for which Shigehira was extremely grateful. The party passed the evening in amusement. Suketsune, playing the drum, sang an *imayō*[14] to the accompaniment of a lute, strummed by the lady in waiting, and the transverse flute played by Shigehira. . . . At midnight, when the lady in waiting wished to take her leave, Shigehira detained her, proffering her more wine and singing more verses. . . . Later they appeared before Yoritomo, who inquired about the party, saying: "I did not attend the affair for fear of unfriendly rumors." Then he ordered the lady in waiting to present Shigehira with a set of night clothes and bedding, an honor for a woman of so remote a place. His Lordship has also issued instructions to her and to

[14] *Imayō,* ballads consisting of lines of twelve syllables.

Suketsune to attend Shigehira as long as he resides in Kamakura. Suketsune has always thought kindly of Shigehira, having served his brother Shigemori for many years in the past. In the course of his service he had seen Shigehira many times.

21st day. *Yoritomo orders his son-in-law killed.*

Last night in the palace quarters there occurred a disturbance involving the young lord Shimizu Yoshitaka. Yoshitaka is a son-in-law of Yoritomo but, as the son of a man who had suffered degradation and who had been killed, he has been an object of suspicion to His Lordship. When Yoritomo had made his decision to kill Yoshitaka and had secretly ordered a close attendant to do so, a lady in waiting learned of it and informed Yoshitaka's wife. Plans were made for his escape. Dressed in the robes of a lady in waiting and in the company of ladies, Yoshitaka made his way out of the quarters to his horse, which he had hidden for this purpose. He had also wrapped the horse's hooves in cloth, so that he could ride away in silence. Moreover, Unno Shōtarō Yukiuji, who was of the same age as Yoshitaka and who was his constant companion, took Yoshitaka's place in the curtained dais, lying under the covers and exposing only his hair. During the day he appeared at places where Yoshitada would normally be and even played *sugoroku*.[15] Yukiuji had always been a partner to Yoshitaka, who had loved this game and had played it from morning to night. No one in the palace suspected this impersonation, but at night it became known. Yoritomo was greatly angered. He summoned Yukiuji and reprimanded him. Then he ordered Hori Tōji Chikaie to send out his men to the various highways to intercept Yoshitaka's flight. Meanwhile, Yoshitaka's wife, who is Yoritomo's daughter, is languishing in grief.

22nd day. *Yoritomo pardons Minamoto Mitsuyuki for his support of the Heike.*

23rd day. *Yoritomo requests relief from taxes for a vassal.*

Shimokōbe Shirō Masayoshi has been conspicuously loyal to His Lordship, both on the battlefield and at the palace. Yoritomo had been especially pleased with Masayoshi's conduct during the re-

---

[15] *Sugoroku* is a game played with dice.

bellion of Shida Yoshihiro. . . . Therefore, at the time of the rebellion, Yoritomo had awarded him the Minami District in Hitachi
Province. However, during the past two years, Masayoshi had not
been able to meet the obligations owed by his fief, and thus His
Lordship, out of commiseration for him, has instructed the provisional governor of Chikugo Toshikane to write a letter in Masayoshi's behalf to the acting governor of Hitachi Province. The letter
reads:

Regarding the provincial affairs of Hitachi: At the time of the rebellion
of Shida Yoshihiro, the Minami District of Hitachi was assigned by
His Lordship to Shimokōbe Masayoshi, but, because of his services at
the capital, where he has distinguished himself in the past year or two,
he has not been able to meet the obligations of his district, including
shares owed to the land steward and the sending of the steward's agents
through the province. This is regrettable, but His Lordship, who thinks
kindly of Masayoshi, instructs that due consideration be given to him
in all matters excepting fixed obligations owed to the court and the
customary taxes on one's person, which shall be met without neglect.
As for shares owed to the land steward, this is a loss which any fellow-
warrior should bear. This is the instruction from the Lord of Kamakura,
which I pass on to you. Thus transmitted.
Fourth Month, 23rd day   Toshikane
Respectfully submitted to: Acting Governor of Hitachi

24th day. *Yoritomo takes steps to check outrages of warriors on
forty-one holdings of the Kamo Shrine in compliance with a directive from the ex-sovereign.*

26th day. *Tōnai Mitsuzumi kills Shimizu Yoshitaka.*

Tōnai Mitsuzumi, a follower of Hori Tōji Chikaie, returned to
Kamakura and reported that he had killed the young lord Shimizu
at Irima Kawara. Although it was intended to keep the matter secret,
His Lordship's daughter, the wife of Shimizu, soon learned of it.
So great was her grief that she refused to take her food. But perhaps
this is her fate. Her Ladyship Masako and many of the men and
women of the palace mourned her fate.

28th day. *The Heiji are reported in Kyushu; Yoritomo makes a grant
of land to Hirota Shrine of Awaji.*

It has been reported that the Heiji are in Kyushu. Thus His Lordship is sending troops thereto.

That his campaign may be successful, Yoritomo has made a grant of the Hirota Manor in Awaji Province to the Hirota Shrine. The document was sent to the head of the department of Shinto, Prince Nakasuke, in the care of the former assistant director of the office of the high priestess Chikayoshi, who is leaving for the capital. . . .

29th day. *Yoritomo's deputies depart for the west.*

The former assistant director of the office of the high priestess Chikayoshi has departed for the capital as His Lordship's emissary. He is to serve as a commissioner in connection with the campaign against the Heike in Kyushu.

Doi Jirō Sanehira and Kajiwara Kagetoki have also taken leave of Kamakura, with instructions to look into the matter of boats for troops and to launch the battle in the coming Sixth Month when the seas turn calm.

FIFTH MONTH

1st day. *Yoritomo makes plans to subdue a Genji revolt in Kai and Shinano.*

Upon receipt of rumors that followers of the late Shimizu Yoshitaka, who have been hiding out in Kai and Shinano, were planning to rebel against Kamakura, His Lordship has decided to despatch troops to subdue them. He has ordered the young lord Ashikaga Yoshikane and Ogasawara Jirō Nagakiyo to take an army of retainers to Kai. He has also ordered Koyama, Utsunomiya, Hiki, Kawagoe, Toyoshima, Adachi, Azuma, and Kobayashi to proceed with their followers to Shinano and ferret out the rebels. In addition, he has instructed Yoshimori and Yoshikazu to rally the immediate vassals of Sagami, Izu, Suruga, Awa, and Kazusa, and has set the date of departure for the 10th of this month.

2nd day. *Genji vassals begin to gather at Kamakura.*

Immediate vassals from the various provinces have been arriving at Kamakura in connection with the forthcoming expedition against the followers of the young lord Shimizu. Most of the men have been assembled.

3rd day. *Yoritomo makes a grant of two villages to Ise Shrine.*

12th day. *Yoritomo inquires after the health of the head priest of Onjō-ji.*

15th day. *Shida Yoshihiro is slain in Ise Province.*
     A special messenger has arrived from Ise Province to report that on the 4th, in the Hatori Mountain in Ise, the retainers of Hatano Saburō, the military guard Ōi Jirō Saneharu, Takiguchi Saburō, and the lieutenant of the Right Outer Palace Guards Ōuchi Koreyoshi battled with Shida Yoshihiro for nearly the entire day. Yoshihiro was finally overcome and his head taken. Yoshihiro had long harbored treasonable intentions. Two years ago, as he approached Kamakura at the head of a military force, he was intercepted and turned back by Koyama Tomomasa. Fleeing from the scene, he joined with Yoshinaka. When Yoshinaka met his death, Yoshihiro fled again. Yoritomo could not allay his anguish so long as Yoshihiro lived. Now His Lordship is greatly cheered by this report.

19th day. *Yoritomo enjoys an outing.*
     Yoritomo invited Taira Yorimori, who has been in Kamakura for several days, and the secretary of the Right Horse Bureau Ichijō Yoshiyasu to accompany him on an outing to the bay. They boarded the boat at Yui and disembarked at Morito. His Lordship's retainers had decorated the boat, and on the way they vied with one another to take the oar. . . . At Morito the party observed the *ogasagake*.[16] This is a custom of the warrior, which His Lordship insisted on observing before going on with the sightseeing. The guests entered into the spirit of the occasion.

21st day. *Yoritomo requests appointments for Taira Yorimori, his son, and three Genji.*
     Yoritomo has written a letter to the *ason* Takashina Yasutsune,

---

[16] See Part One, Chapter IV, note 35.

requesting restoration of office to the former major councilor Taira
Yorimori and his son. Yoritomo added that the attention of the
throne should be brought to the matter of assigning provincial
offices to Minamoto Noriyori, Fujiwara Hirotsuna, and Ōuchi
Yoshinobu from among the members of the Genji. The letter was
drafted by the clerk-lay priest Miyoshi Yasunobu and borne by the
servant Tsurutarō.

24th day. *A former Heike is made land steward.*

The lieutenant of the Left Outer Palace Guards Fujiwara Tomotsuna has been granted the land stewardship of Mibuno Township
in Iga Province. Formerly in the service of the Heike, he had
secretly left the capital and had come to pay homage to Yoritomo.
Thus the award. His Lordship also assured the present holder of
the shrine office of Utsunomiya that there will be no change regarding his tenure.

SIXTH MONTH

1st day. *Yoritomo gives a farewell party for Taira Yorimori; he inquires after Yahei Munekiyo.*

His Lordship was host at a farewell party for the former major
councilor Taira Yorimori, who is leaving for the capital shortly.
His Lordship, the secretary of the Right Horse Bureau Yoshiyasu,
and the former Minor Captain Tokiie exchanged the customary
three cups of wine with the guest. This was repeated several times,
after which they engaged in conversation. Attending the guest on
the matting before him were men who were familiar with Kyoto,
such as Koyama Tomomasa, Miura Yoshizumi, Yui Tomomitsu,
Shimokōbe Yukihira, Hatakeyama Shigetada, Tachibana Kiminaga,
Adachi Tōmoto, Yata Tomoie, and Gotō Motokiyo.

Then gifts were presented to the guest. The first presentation,
a gold-ornamented sword, was made by Tokiie. Then a package
of gold dust was given, the presentation being made by the vice
governor of Aki Ōe Hiromoto. Then ten saddled horses were
brought in and presented, after which His Lordship summoned the
attendants of the guest and presented them with gifts.

His Lordship then called for the lieutenant of the Left Outer
Palace Guards Yahei Munekiyo, the son of Suemune and a mem-

ber of the Heike, about whom he had inquired of the former major councilor when he first arrived at Kamakura. At the time, the major councilor had replied that illness had delayed Munekiyo's departure from the capital. When His Lordship inquired whether he was expected at Kamakura, the major councilor replied that he had not yet arrived. Munekiyo had been an attendant of Ike-no-Zenni, and during the Heiji Disturbance he had espoused the Genji. Therefore, Yoritomo, wishing to repay him, had summoned him to Kamakura. When the major councilor, on the day of his departure from the capital, had conveyed the message to Munekiyo, the latter had replied: "If I were being summoned to take my place on the field of battle, I would go immediately. But I have reflected on this matter seriously and have come to the conclusion that for me to go to Kamakura to accept a reward for my past loyalty to the Genji after the Heike have quit the capital is not an honorable act." So saying, Munekiyo has gone to Yashima to serve the former Great Minister of the Center Taira Munemori.

4th day. *Ishikawa Yoshisuke comes to serve Yoritomo.*

The military guard and secretary Ishikawa Yoshisuke has come to Kanto determined to serve His Lordship day and night. Being a member of the Genji of Kawachi, he had been captured by the Heike in 1181. More recently he had suffered much because of the attacks of Yoshinaka. However, through Yoritomo's intercession in his behalf, he has been restored by the ex-sovereign to his former office of lieutenant of the Military Guards, Right Division.

5th day. *Taira Yorimori departs for Kyoto.*

The former major councilor has departed for the capital. His Lordship has not only returned manors to him, but has also provided him with wine of proven quality every day while he sojourned here. Moreover, there were gifts of gold and silver and embroidered silk of many colors.

16th day. *Ichijō Tadayoshi is executed.*

His Lordship had long suspected the truth of the rumors that Ichijō Jirō Tadayoshi has been acting in contempt of his authority. Therefore today he was executed at the headquarters. This evening

Yoritomo summoned him to the West Room. Following the drinking of the ceremonial wine in the presence of His Lordship and his elder vassals, Tadayoshi was despatched quickly by Amano Tōkage, who had come forward with a long sword to the victim's left. Immediately after the execution Yoritomo opened the sliding screen behind him and retired to his inner chambers. When Tadayori's attendants—Shimpeita, Butō Yoichi, who is Tadayori's son-in-law, and Yamamura Shōtarō—saw the prostrate body of their master from the ground below, they dashed into the West Room with their long swords and attacked His Lordship's attendants. As they approached His Lordship's sleeping quarters, they were confronted by Shigenari, Shigetomo, and Yui Tomomitsu. Shimpeita and Yoichi were overcome and captured as Yamamura battled with Tōkage. Finally, Tōkage took a carving board and flung it at Yamamura. As he tumbled down off the porch, Tōkage's follower cut off Yamamura's head.

17th day. *Sameshima Shirō is punished.*

For the offense of having attacked a fellow-vassal during the disturbance of the previous evening, Sameshima Shirō was summoned by His Lordship and a finger on his right hand cut as punishment.

18th day. *A singer of ballads is ordered to serve at Kamakura.*

Because of his reputation as a singer of ballads, Kai Shōshirō Akiie, a retainer of the late Ichijō Tadayori, was summoned by His Lordship. His Lordship asked him in a friendly way to serve at Kamakura.

20th day. *The announcement of appointments arrives at Kamakura.*

On the 5th of this month the list of appointments was issued at Kyoto. That announcement has arrived at Kamakura today. The recommendations which His Lordship had made have been honored without change. These include the major councilor Taira Yorimori, the chamberlain Taira Mitsumori, governor of Kawachi Taira Yasunari, governor of Sanuki Fujiwara Yoshiyasu, governor of Mikawa Minamoto Noriyori, governor of Suruga Minamoto Hirotsuna, and governor of Musashi Minamoto Yoshinobu.

21st day. *The new appointees are overjoyed; Yoshitsune is displeased.*

Yoritomo assembled Noriyori, Yoshinobu, and Hirotsuna to inform them of their appointments and to toast them. They were overjoyed. However, Yoshitsune, who had persistently sought His Lordship's recommendation for an official appointment, but who had been rejected in favor of Noriyori, was greatly displeased.

23rd day. *Yoritomo restores control of a township in Shinano to Katagiri Tameyasu.*

Katagiri Tarō Tameyasu has been summoned from Shinano Province. Yoritomo has always regarded him cordially, for Tameyasu's father, Shōhachirō, had served Yoshitomo during the Heiji Disturbance. But because of this relationship, the Taira had confiscated the Katagiri Township, and for more than twenty years the family had remained empty-handed. Today, His Lordship restored control to Tameyasu.

27th day. *Yoritomo orders an execution to allay Masako's anger.*

To allay Her Ladyship's anger, a follower of Hori Tōji Chikaie has been decapitated. It was he who had killed the young lord Shimizu during the Fourth Month upon instructions from His Lordship. Following the killing of Shimizu, his wife, who is Yoritomo's daughter, had taken to bed and had become seriously ill, to the concern of all. Because of Her Ladyship's unreasonable anger over the illness of the princess, which she claims was caused by the action of the said follower—even though the latter was merely carrying out orders—Yoritomo, unable to extricate himself from the dilemma, ordered the follower to be killed.

SEVENTH MONTH

2nd day. *Yoritomo adjudicates a suit between two temples.*

An emissary from the high priest of Buddhism of Jōju-in arrived last night . . . to lodge a suit against the monks of Jakuraku-ji for their encroachment on and commission of lawless acts on Ategawa Manor, an estate of Mount Kōya, in Kii Province. The emissary presented a map of the lands of Mount Kōya, as well as documents with the seal of Kōbō Daishi[17] affixed on them. These documents were read and explained to His Lordship by the provisional governor of Chikugo Toshikane. As His Lordship was convinced that these documents were those of Kōbō Daishi, he has issued a directive ordering the immediate cessation of outrages on the said lands. . . .

3rd day. *Yoritomo requests imperial authorization for Yoshitsune to proceed against Taira Munemori.*

5th day. *Heike activity is reported in Iga Province.*

Ōuchi Koreyoshi has sent a special courier to Kamakura to report that on the 7th of the past month he had been attacked in Iga Province by the Heike. Many of his retainers had been killed in the fray. As a result of this report, many Genji are gathering in Kamakura to go to Koreyoshi's assistance.

10th day. *Inoue Mitsumori, a partisan of the late Ichijō Tadayori, is slain in Suruga.*

Today Inoue Tarō Mitsumori, reported to be sympathetic to Ichijō Tadayori, was killed at Kamahara-eki in Suruga. Knowing that Mitsumori would be returning to his native province from Kyoto where he had been in service, the men of Kikkō and Funakoshi, in accordance with His Lordship's instructions, ambushed him as he was returning from the capital, and killed him.

16th day. *Shibuya Takashige's lands are granted immunity from entry by provincial officials.*

Shibuya Jirō Takashige is a gallant warrior. He is a credit to his ancestors and a source of pride to his father. His Lordship, whose attention has been drawn to him many times, has been so pleased with the youth that he has granted to his lands of Kurokawa Township immunity from entry by officials of the provincial government of Kōzuke. Therefore today His Lordship has despatched the directive in care of Adachi Morinaga.

18th day. *Yoritomo orders his vassals to attack Heike followers in Iga Province.*

[17] Kōbō Daishi, the posthumous name of Kūkai (d. 835), who founded Mount Kōya.

In connection with the battles in Iga Province, His Lordship has despatched the servants, Tomoyuki and Muneshige, with a message to the young lord Ōuchi, the lay priest Katō Kagekazu, his son, and Takiguchi Saburō Tsunetoshi to launch a campaign against Heike followers who had been sent into Iga secretly.

20th day. *Yoritomo attends a ceremony dedicating a branch shrine of Atsuta.*

Today His Lordship attended the ceremonies inviting the spirit of Myōjin of Atsuta to reside in the shrine built recently near the sub-shrine of Tsurugaoka. Attending His Lordship were the governor of Musashi Yoshinobu, the governor of Suruga Hirotsuna, and their respective followers. His Lordship's sword was carried by Yui Shichirō Tomomitsu, and his weapons were borne by Kawawa Saburō Sanemasa. Sanemasa had incurred His Lordship's displeasure last winter when he became involved in an argument with fellow vassals at a river crossing in the battle against Ichijō Tadayori. However, His Lordship had excused him from all blame several weeks later. Today, moreover, he had been given this important assignment, to the surprise of all the spectators. At the conclusion of the ceremony a village in Sagami Province was given as a benefice to the shrine. The village will forward tributes of food provisions to the shrine annually.

25th day. *Followers of the late Inoue Mitsumori submit to Yoritomo.*

Attendants of the late Inoue Tarō Mitsumori—Hoshina Tarō and Ogahara Untō Saburō—have surrendered and have come to pay homage to His Lordship. Tōnai Tomomune has been instructed to notify them that they have been accepted as vassals.

EIGHTH MONTH

2nd day. *Ōuchi Koreyoshi defeats the Heike in Iga; he requests a reward.*

Rain. The young lord Ōuchi has again sent a special messenger who reported that on the 19th, at 5 P.M., he had given battle to the remnants of the Heike and had defeated them. Among the more than ninety killed were four of the initiators of this battle—Tomita

Iesuke, the former lieutenant of the military guards Ieyoshi, the
lay priest Iekiyo, and the lay priest Hirata Tarō Ietsugu. The former
governor of Dewa Nobukane and his son, as well as the master
of Buddhist Law Tadakiyo, fled into the mountains. Sasaki Hideyoshi, who with his son Yoshikiyo, had engaged in the battle, was
taken by the Heike. The messenger ventured the opinion that
Koreyoshi had erased his earlier shame and requested that he be
cited for meritorious service.

3rd day. *Yoritomo rejects Ōuchi Koreyoshi's request.*
    Rain. His Lordship summoned Ōuchi Koreyoshi's messenger
and presented him with a detailed letter to be delivered to his
master. The letter states that, while the attack on the rebels was a
splendid achievement, Yoritomo rejects Ōuchi's request for a reward. His Lordship has pointed out that, when a man is appointed
as a constable for a province, it is his duty to maintain order in his
realm. The attack by the rebels and the death of Genji retainers
was caused by Ōuchi's lack of preparations. The attack, in fact, was
the result of a serious oversight on Koreyoshi's part. Moreover, it was
pointed out to Koreyoshi that the matter of determining awards
and punishments is His Lordship's function.
    Yoritomo has also sent instructions to Yoshitsune in Kyoto to
ferret out and put to death the sons of the governor of Dewa
Nobukane, one of the perpetrators of the recent insurrection in Iga.
These men had eluded encirclement and may be hiding in the
capital. The special messenger is Adachi Shinsaburō, who took his
departure today.

6th day. *Yoritomo toasts his vassals on the eve of their departure
for the west.*
    Yoritomo summoned the governor of Mikawa Noriyori, Ashikaga
Yoshikane, Takeda Ariyoshi, and Chiba Tsunetane to accord them
a farewell party preliminary to their departure for the west on a
campaign against the Heike. When the banqueting was over at the
end of the day, Yoritomo presented each with a horse. Among the
horses presented, the one given to the governor of Mikawa had
been His Lordship's most valued possession. Moreover, His Lordship gave him a set of armor.

8th day. *Noriyori and one thousand warriors depart for the west.*

The governor of Mikawa Noriyori, with a commission from His Lordship to pursue and chastise the Heike, departed from Kamakura at 11 A.M. At the head of the train were a standard-bearer and a quiver bearer walking side by side, followed by the governor of Mikawa. . . . Behind him were some one thousand men and their horses. . . . His Lordship viewed the departure from a box constructed near the Inase River.

13th day. *Kashima Shrine reports interference on its lands.*

Because of interference by rebels in the inland districts of Hitachi Province, the Kashima Shrine has not been able to exercise its rights over the lands which had been granted as benefices to the shrine. Thus today His Lordship has reaffirmed the grants.

17th day. *Yoshitsune's court appointments are reported to Yoritomo.*

Yoshitsune has sent a messenger to Kamakura, who reported to His Lordship thus: "On the 6th Yoshitsune received imperial appointments to the office of junior lieutenant of the Left Outer Palace Guards and the office of imperial police. Although he had not sought these offices, the court could not ignore his several meritorious deeds in its behalf, and thus conferred the honors as a matter of course. Under the circumstances Yoshitsune could not decline them."

This is contrary to Yoritomo's wishes. In the case of Noriyori and Yoshinobu, offices had been conferred on them at Yoritomo's recommendation. But Yoshitsune, whom His Lordship secretly suspects, had sought these offices against Yoritomo's wishes. Furthermore, Yoritomo doubts whether these conferments on Yoshitsune would be the last. As a result, His Lordship has postponed the naming of Yoshitsune as a special deputy in the Heike campaign.

18th day. *Yoritomo grants complete exemption from taxes to a vassal.*

Although he is not one of the more influential local lords of Musashi Province, Amakasu Noji Hirotada has asked to join the western campaign against the Heike. Moved by his enthusiasm to serve, His Lordship has granted his fief complete exemption from taxes.

19th day. *The artist Tamehisa leaves Kamakura for Kyoto.*

The artist Tamehisa, provisional governor of Shimōsa, has left Kamakura for the capital. As a going away present His Lordship has presented him with a horse, saddled.

20th day. *Yoritomo requests a dismissal and an appointment.*

His Lordship has sent a letter to Kyoto requesting the dismissal of the chief of the housekeeping office Abe Suehiro, who had been Kiso Yoshinaka's patron priest, and the appointment of Ōe Hiromoto as vice governor of Aki.

24th day. *A new building is begun for the* kumon-jo.[18]

A new building is to be constructed for the *kumon-jo*. Today the ceremony of the raising of the pillars and beams was held. The commissioners in charge are the lay priest clerk Yasunobu and the secretary of the Bureau of Statistics Yukimasa.

26th day. *Yoshitsune reports on the slaying of the sons of the governor of Dewa.*

The imperial police Minamoto Yoshitsune has sent a special messenger to report that on the 10th he had invited the lieutenant of the Left Outer Palace Guards Kanehira, Jirō Nobuhira, and Saburō Kanetoki, the sons of Nobukane, the governor of Dewa, and had them killed in their sleeping quarters. On the 11th their father, Nobukane, had been deprived of his office by an order of the ex-sovereign.

28th day. *The* kumon-jo *is completed.*

A gate was installed in front of the newly constructed building of the *kumon-jo*. The occasion was observed by a gathering of Ōe Hiromoto, Miyoshi Yasunobu, Adachi Tōmoto, and Koremune Takanao. Ōba Kageyoshi, who had built the gate, proffered wine to the gathering.

[18] *Kumon-jo,* documents office, or archives.

NINTH MONTH

2nd day. *Koyama Tomomasa departs for the west to serve under Noriyori.*

Ordered by Yoritomo to serve under the governor of Mikawa, Koyama Shōshirō Tomomasa has departed for the west. Tomomasa had asked for this assignment.

9th day. *Yoritomo notifies the court regarding the jurisdiction of the lands of the former governor of Dewa and of other Heike partisans in the Kyoto area.*

His Lordship has sent instructions to Kyoto to the effect that the lands of the former official of Dewa Nobukane, as well as those of the Heike, situated in Kyoto should be placed under the control of Minamoto Yoshitsune. His Lordship's letter reads:

Regarding residential lands in the capital seized from the Heike

To date there has been no action taken with regard to residential lands in the capital seized from the Heike. Such lands shall not be assigned to anyone, nor shall any part thereof be taken by any warrior. The disposal of these lands shall await the decision of the ex-sovereign. As for the lands formerly belonging to Nobukane, these shall come under the jurisdiction of Yoshitsune.

Yoritomo [monogram][19]

12th day. *Noriyori's arrival in Kyoto and his receipt of a mandate are reported.*

A special messenger despatched by Noriyori on the 1st arrived at Kamakura with the report that Noriyori had arrived in Kyoto on the 27th of the past month and that on the 29th he had received a mandate of the Council of State to proceed against the Heike. Noriyori had planned to depart for Kyushu on the 1st.

14th day. *At Yoritomo's urging a daughter of Kawagoe Shigeyori is betrothed to Yoshitsune.*

The daughter of Kawagoe Tarō Shigeyori has left for the capital to be married to Yoshitsune. This arrangement had been made a

[19] Signatures which were affixed to documents were usually done in a cursive style. Often a name which might have two or three separate Chinese characters was written in a single abridged form or monogram.

few days ago at Yoritomo's urging. Departing with her were two hereditary retainers and thirty other followers.

17th day. *Yoritomo grants lands to Ōyama Temple of Sagami Province.*

Today His Lordship took measures, according to precedent, to grant to the Ōyama Temple in Sagami Province 5 *chō* of ricelands, which are to be exempt from taxes, and 8 *chō* of dry fields.

19th day. *Yoritomo sends Tachibana Kiminari to Sanuki to secure the support of local lords.*

Following the destruction of the Ichinotani fortification in Settsu Province in the Second Month, members of the Heike have been plundering the various provinces in the west, and Genji troops have been sent into the region to check the Heike. One of the means employed has been the sending of Tachibana Kiminari and his men as an advance column into Sanuki Province to secure the support of the local lords. They have since submitted to the Minamoto, and a roster containing their names has been transmitted to Kamakura. Today, His Lordship has sent instructions to the local lords of Sanuki to take their orders from Kiminari.

[Yoritomo's monogram]
ORDERED TO: Immediate vassals of Sanuki Province
   To submit forthwith to the command of Tachibana Kiminari and
   to join in the Kyushu campaign
At this time when the Heike are plundering your lands, you have indicated your submission to me. A roster of your names has been submitted to me. It is indeed a most loyal act on your part. Submit forthwith to the command of Kiminari and conduct yourselves in a loyal and meritorious manner. Thus ordered.
Genreki 1:9,19

Immediate vassals of Sanuki Province
The following is a roster of immediate vassals of Sanuki, in which province, at Yashima, the Heike are presently established, who have renounced the Heike for the Genji and who are now in service in Kyoto. . . .[20] The aforementioned, having served the Genji in Kyoto, are vassals of the Lord of Kamakura, as indicated.
Genreki 1:5

[20] The names of fourteen local lords of Sanuki are listed here.

20th day. *The ex-sovereign transmits a complaint in behalf of Izumo Shrine of Tamba Province.*

A decree of the ex-sovereign notifying His Lordship of the excesses of Tamai Shirō Sukeshige on the lands of Izumo Shrine, the principal shrine of Tamba Province, reached Kamakura today. His Lordship, greatly concerned, has sent instructions to check these outrages. . . .

28th day. *The ex-sovereign revokes the appointments of Abe Suehiro at Yoritomo's request.*

TENTH MONTH

6th day. *The* kumon-jo *is established.*

. . . At 9 A.M. the ceremony of the first writing for the newly constructed *kumon-jo* was held. The scribes for the occasion were the secretary of the Bureau of Statistics Fujiwara Yukimasa, the secretary of the Right Horse Bureau Adachi Tōmoto, Kai Shirō, Ōnakatomi Akiie, and the secretary Kunimichi. The first document, which was opened before His Lordship by Hiromoto, was written by Kunimichi. Then matters pertaining to shrine lands and to Buddhist temples were attended to, following which a banquet was given by the vice governor Chiba. His Lordship, who attended, presented gifts of horses to the higher officials and swords to the lower officials.

12th day. *Noriyori is deputized to reward local lords in the west.*

At Yoritomo's instructions the governor of Mikawa who is now in Aki Province has made awards to the local lords for meritorious service. Among the local residents, Yamagata Tametsuna has been specially honored for his services.

15th day. *An earthquake occurs; Yoritomo goes to the mountains to view the maples.*

An earthquake occurred at 7 A.M.

Today His Lordship viewed the maples at his mountain villa. Accompanying him was the intendant of the sub-shrine Engyō.

20th day. *The* monchū-jo *is established.*

With the assistance of Toshikane and Moritoki His Lordship attended to rendering decisions on cases brought by various persons. The writing of the decisions was assigned to Miyoshi Yasunobu. Two rooms on the east side of His Lordship's residence have been set aside for this purpose and designated the *monchū-jo.*

24th day. *Yoshitsune is given access to the ex-sovereign's palace.*

The governor of Inaba Ōe Hiromoto, who had been appointed on the 18th of the Ninth Month, reports that on the 18th of the past month Yoshitsune was raised in rank, while retaining his present office. On the 15th of this month Yoshitsune was granted admission to the palace of the ex-sovereign. On that occasion he rode in a cart with a crest of eight lotus leaves, and he was escorted by three attendants from the headquarters of the guards and twenty other attendants, all mounted. In the palace courtyard he performed the ceremony of the dance, and waving the sword and the baton he made his entry into the palace.

27th day. *Kajiwara Kagetoki's men are reported to have violated lands of the Hirota Shrine.*

Prince Nakasuke has informed His Lordship that, although Hirota Manor in Awaji Province had been granted as a benefice to Hirota Shrine by His Lordship a few days ago, the followers of Kajiwara Kagetoki, who are presently in Awaji in connection with the campaign against the Heike, have broken into the manor and have interfered with the annual tributes of the said manor. Thus today His Lordship sent a reply to the prince, promising to order Kegetoki to abide by the terms of the benefice, which is to remain as granted.

28th day. *Yoritomo assures the intendant of Iwashimizu Hachiman Shrine that its claims to the manors of Hōtō-in and Miroku-ji will be honored.*

ELEVENTH MONTH

6th day. *Yoritomo is entertained at the Hachiman Shrine.*

His Lordship attended a performance of the sacred dance at the

Tsurugaoka Hachiman Shrine. Following the performance he went
to the residence of the shrine intendant at the latter's invitation.
The intendant's young son, styled Sōjiō, had arrived from Kyoto
a few days ago, and he is a talented singer of popular ballards. He
served as an intermediary between the host and the guest as wine
was proffered. The young lad played the transverse flute as Kajiwara
Heiji sang the songs. Hatakeyama Jirō sang an *imayō*. His Lordship
enjoyed the entire entertainment. At nightfall His Lordship returned to his residence.

12th day. *Yoritomo makes local lords of Hitachi Province his immediate vassals.*

14th day. *Yoritomo orders Yoshitsune to acknowledge lands in
Western Japan assigned by the lieutenant of the Left Outer Palace
Guards Tomotsuna and the secretary of the minister of justice
Naritsuna.*

21st day. *Yoritomo reprimands Toshikane for his ostentation.*
    This morning His Lordship summoned the provisional governor
of Chikugo Toshikane before him. Seeing that Toshikane, who
has always been addicted to ostentation, was dressed in a most
fashionable manner, wearing ten wadded silk garments and a skirt
of many colors, Yoritomo asked for Toshikane's sword. Yoritomo,
taking the sword in his own hands, cut off Toshikane's skirt, saying:
"You are a very gifted man, but why are you not more thrifty and
simple in your ways? Tsunetane and Sanehira . . . have larger
holdings than you; yet each wears the coarsest of garments, abhorring
ostentation. They have wealth with which they support numerous
followers, who are enjoined to perform acts of loyalty. You do not
realize how wasteful you are of your wealth. It is excessive." Toshikane had nothing to say, and hung his head respectfully. Yoritomo then asked him whether he intended to give up his ostenta-
tious ways, to which Toshikane replied that he would. At the time
Ōe Hiromoto and Fujiwara Kunimichi were nearby, and they were
greatly astonished.

23rd day. *The priests of Onjō-ji address a letter to Yoritomo.*

The master of Buddhist Law and intendant of Onjō-ji has come to Kanto to present a letter from the priests of his temple to His Lordship. Yoritomo permitted him an audience and instructed the governor of Inaba Hiromoto to read the letter.

Onjō-ji addresses in writing the Clan of the Assistant Captain of the Middle Palace Guards, Right Division

Regarding the granting of confiscated Heike lands to this temple to promote the development and the prosperity of Buddhism

The aforementioned temple, built by the grace of Maitreya, has seen great prosperity under Chishō Daishi.[21] The philosophy it seeks is that of the mean.[22] It belongs to the order of Buddhism which the ex-sovereign is a member, and he reveres our temple. It has sought to establish tranquility in the eight corners of the world; it has given assistance to the ruler in his administration of the government; it has, since its location at its present site, prayed for the success and prosperity of Your Lordship's house. Indeed, we know that the people and subjects, relatives and families of those who make light of our Buddhist Law are destroyed. This is a matter of cause and effect about which there is no doubt. But the late lay priest Chancellor Kiyomori defied imperial law, committed crimes willfully, imprisoned the ex-sovereign, and banished important ministers serving Fujiwara Motofusa. Then Kiyomori sought to capture Prince Mochihito and to kill the courtier Yorimasa, but they escaped the lion's mouth and came for refuge to our sanctuary. Our monks, imbued with the will to save, gave them comfort and assistance, and, complying with the pronouncement of the imperial prince, joined the Genji in their secret attempt to protect and preserve the country by offering prayers in earnest for the subjugation of the rebels. As a consequence of this act on our part, the Heike sent a hundred thousand troops to burn and destroy our buildings, idols, and sacred writings, which have gone up in smoke and turned to ashes. Our student monks and practitioners have fallen prostrate on the ground in pools of their own tears. The number of the dead, including students and practitioners, is five hundred, while those, including the old and the young, who have been forced to disperse number more than a thousand. How grievous that the light of Buddhism which had been burning for more than three hundred years should be extinguished for so long because of the Heike! How painful that the house of Buddhist worship for forty-nine ex-sovereigns should be lost in a moment because of these outlaws! It surpasses in barbarity the action of the T'ang Emperor dur-

[21] Posthumous name of Enchin (d. 891).
[22] *Chūdō,* the medial way between two extremes.

ing the Hui Ch'ang era [841–46].[23] It surpasses even that of the minister Mononobe Moriya of our own court.[24]

Then on the 25th of the Seventh Month the general of Hokuriku Kiso Yoshinaka entered the capital and routed the rebels of Rokuhara[25] to the great joy of the entire country. . . . However, Yoshinaka's acts soon exceeded in barbarity those of his predecessors. He burned and razed the ex-sovereign's palace; he slew the heads of the two orders of the Tendai sect—acts of extraordinary and unprecedented violence. Who, we asked, has the power to bring him to submission? We could only look to the gracious powers of the great bodhisattva Maitreya. What human, we asked, could subdue him? We relied entirely on the general Yoritomo. Here was a scion of a noble house distinguished for generations of service to the court, upon whom all the people relied. He planned in terms of a distant campaign which materialized in a quick and sudden victory by the coming of his troops to the capital. In fact, it was within the lands of our temple that Yoshinaka's head was taken.

Now, although we are secure and are making plans to settle down once more, we have been hampered in our plans by the unceasing incursion of warriors on the manors of our branch temples. Our monks can only tarry here or live there for awhile. In the spring there is hardly a bracken in the field when the smoke subsides; in the fall there is scarcely a Judas tree when the storms pass. The raiment of the monks is tattered. Buddhism is on the decline. The deterioration of our buildings is shameful to behold—passers-by shield their eyes behind their sleeves. Only if there be compassion from Your Lordship can we plan to do our work.

And thus, if two or three manors of confiscated Heike lands could be assigned as benefices to this temple, we can raise again the lamp of Buddhism, as we had always hoped to do, and continue to propagate the teachings of Buddhism. Such an act on Your Lordship's part will not be without precedent. When Prince Shōtoku brought Moriya to submission, he converted the latter's residence into a temple and gave to the temple as benefices the latter's rice fields and orchards. Since then the emperor's law has prevailed, and there has been peace and tranquility, and Buddhism has flourished. We urge that this precedent be followed at this time. We urge that this age of ours emulate the traditions of Prince Shōtoku's age.

There is also the precedent established by your august ancestor, the governor of Iyo and lay priest Yoriyoshi, who, upon receipt of an imperial decree to subjugate Abe Sadatō, worshiped at Onjō-ji, and in

---

[23] This is a reference to the great Buddhist persecutions in China.

[24] The Mononobe family had opposed the introduction of Buddhism to Japan.

[25] Rokuhara, the southeast section of Kyoto, where the Taira maintained its principal residences and offices.

particular at the shrine of Shinra.[26] It was the efficacy of Shinra's spirits which made it possible for Yoriyoshi to subjugate the barbarous enemy, to send Sadatō's head to the capital, and to increase his prestige in Kanto. If such is the record of your ancestor, why cannot the same be said for his descendant? Thus it has occurred to us that the fate of the house of Minamoto and that of our temple is mutual and interwoven, as are wind and rain. That being so, the prosperity of our temple is dependent on the assistance of your house; the peace and stability of your house is dependent on the prayers of our temple. Therefore, on the 7th day of each month, we have been calling on all the teachers of the Buddhist hierarchy to conduct mass to Fudō[27] on a hundred altars. The fame of those who have affixed their names to this letter is great and enduring.

In the written words of Chishō Daishi, "It is my principle to abide by our ruler and ministers. Should the ruler and ministers sever their ties with our order, the country will decline, the ruler's law will lose its authority, the heavenly gods will forsake them, the earthly gods will despise them, and there will be chaos at home and abroad, and confusion far and near. At such a time the ruler and his ministers will worship in reverence my Buddhist Law. If they fail to do so, the capital will be visited by chaos. If they return to my teachings, there will be peace throughout the land."

The Heiji have sought to destroy this temple and the families of noble descent. The Genji have revered this temple and have sought to make it prosper. The zeal of the monks is single and undivided. They rely wholly on the divine assistance of the Three Treasures. Until the mountains pile one upon another, and the rivers run dry, and though we are separated by thousands of miles and layers upon layers of evening clouds, we shall pray in the morning and intone chants at night for the coming of a new dawn in our respective localities. Although we are far apart, we are brothers when our minds agree. We request that Your Lordship accede to the contents of this circular. Thus communicated.

Genreki 1:10   Jōga, Master of Buddhist Law and Head of Kodera
Keishun, Provisional *Tsuina*[28] and Great Master of Buddhist Law
Ninkei, Provisional *Tsuina* and Great Master of Buddhist Law
Religious Supervisor and Provisional High Priest of Buddhism, First Rank [seal]
Intendant and Senior Assistant High Priest of Buddhism, First Rank
Head Supervisor of Priests, Third Rank
Director of the Court University, Holy Teacher and Great Master of Buddhist Law
Provisional Head Supervisor of Priests and Ritualist, Senior Fourth Rank

[26] Shinra dai-myōjin, a god revealed to Enchin on his way back from China and introduced by him to Onjō-ji.

[27] Fudō, in Buddhist traditions, is a deity who wards off evil influences.

[28] *Tsuina*, priests in charge of the daily miscellaneous activities of the monks.

26th day. *Yoritomo plans to build a temple in memory of his father.*

It has been His Lordship's cherished wish to build a temple in memory of his father. For this purpose he had found a choice spot to the southeast of headquarters, but it was not until the 25th of the past month, following the purification period of the Great Thanksgiving Festival, that the work of drawing the soil was begun. Today the soil was turned at the site, with the governor of Inaba and the provisional governor of Chikugo in charge. His Lordship attended the ceremonies.

TWELFTH MONTH

1st day. *Yoritomo grants lands to Onjō-ji.*

His Lordship summoned the emissary of Onjō-ji and presented him with two letters. These were grants of two villages to the temple.

Granted to Mii[29] Temple
  A place in Tamaki, Wakasa Province
The aforementioned place, being land confiscated from the Heike, has been held in custody by us. We now make a benefice of this land to the said temple that it may promote the prosperity of Buddhism. However, the right of appointing an administrator for the said land shall be held by us. There shall be no deviation from this order. Thus ordered.
Genreki 1:11,28   Former Assistant Captain, Middle Palace Guards,
                             Right Division, Minamoto *Ason*

Granted as a temple domain, one place
  Because of the activities of the Heike rebels, the aforementioned temple has been destroyed. Since then and to this day the temple has known no resident priests nor has it been able to propagate its cherished teachings. It has been my intention to bring the matter to the attention of the court at my first opportunity, but meanwhile the temple itself has called my attention to it. The matter being of such import, I am about to grant two places—Yokoyama in Ōmi Province and Tamaki in Wakasa Province—to the said temple. Villages which offer the least possibility of interference have been selected. It is my intention to make other grants when peace and order are restored. Thus inscribed.
Twelfth Month, 1st day   Former Assistant Captain
                                           of the Middle Palace Guards

2nd day. *The Genji in the west report a shortage of horses.*

His Lordship has sent one of his horses . . . to Sasaki Saburō Moritsuna. Yoritomo took the trouble to do this . . . because

---

[29] Mii-dera, another name for Onjō-ji.

Moritsuna, now engaged in fighting against the Heike in the west, had written him that he was without a horse.

3rd day. *Yoshitsune in Kyoto is instructed to comply with the wishes of Onjō-ji.*

On the occasion of the departure of the emissary and priest in charge of Onjō-ji, Lord Hōjō presented him with a personal letter to be delivered to Yoshitsune, instructing him to abide by the wishes of the said temple. . . .

7th day. *Sasaki Moritsuna negotiates a sea on horseback to attack the Heike.*

Sasaki Saburō Moritsuna had been assigned the mission of destroying Kojima in Bizen Province, defended by the director of the Left Horse Bureau Taira Yukimori and his five hundred mounted men. But Moritsuna, on the dry sand beach at Fujito, was separated from Yukimori by the sea. Unable to find boats, he and six of his followers rode into the sea on their horses and, reaching the far shore, subdued Yukimori.

16th day. *Kibitsu Shrine of Bizen is assured its rights to tax-free ricelands.*

Bearing a letter from the priest Gyōjitsu, the priest in charge of Kibitsu Shrine has arrived at Kamakura today. The letter was an appeal for the restoration of its tax-free ricelands, which had been taken away from the shrine because of the war now being waged in Kyushu. His Lordship, after looking into the matter, affixed a letter to the petition promising judgment, and despatched the same to Sanehira, who is presently in Bizen Province.

20th day. *Yoshitsune assures Yoritomo that he will enforce recognition of rights to lands granted by Yoritomo.*

25th day. *Yoritomo assures Kashima Shrine of its rights to lands in Hitachi.*

In answer to His Lordship's summons, the priests of Kashima Shrine—Nakatomi Chikahiro and Chikamori—called at headquarters today. They presented gifts of gold and silver objects to

His Lordship. Yoritomo assured them that the lawless conduct of the land steward on fiefs granted to the shrine would cease and that the control of the lands would be returned to the priests of the shrine. His Lordship took this action because he believes that the prayer he had submitted to Kashima Shrine was responsible for the death of Yoshinaka and the defeat of Taira Munemori at Ichinotani and his flight to Shikoku.

26th day. *Yoritomo commends Sasaki Moritsuna.*

His Lordship today acknowledged by letter the feat performed by Sasaki Moritsuna, who had crossed over to Kojima, Bizen Province, on horseback and who had attacked Taira Yukimori. The letter reads:

Although there are many instances since ancient times of fording rivers on horseback, this is the first I have heard of anyone crossing a sea on horseback. Moritsuna's feat is unparalleled and deserves commendation.

29th day. *Yoritomo grants tax exemptions to the holdings of Ryōkei, a priest of Kashima Shrine.*

Chapter IV

GENREKI 2 [1185] [1]

FIRST MONTH

1st day. *Yoritomo worships at Tsurugaoka Shrine.*
6th day. *Lack of food and boats stall the Genji in western Honshu;*
Yoritomo addresses local lords of Kyushu.

It has been reported that the eastern warriors now in the west
on a campaign against the Heike have lost the will to fight because
of lack of boats and food provisions. Therefore His Lordship has
ordered vassals in the east to prepare boats and provisions to be
sent to the west. Noriyori's messenger, who had left the west on
the 14th of the Eleventh Month, has arrived at Kamakura today.
He reports that, because of the shortage of military provisions, the
troops are listless, and more than half of them would welcome the
opportunity to desert for their native provinces. The messenger also
briefed His Lordship on other matters pertaining to the west. For
one, Noriyori expects His Lordship to send horses. . . . His Lordship has sent a letter to his vassals in Kyushu which reads:

ORDERED TO: Local Lords of Kyushu
> With regard to your prompt enrollment as immediate vassals of the
> Lord of Kamakura which, on the one hand, would assure continued
> control of your present holdings, and, on the other, would obligate
> you to place yourself under the command of the governor of Mikawa
> Noriyori in cooperation with whom you shall pursue and chastise the
> Heike who are enemies of the imperial court

There has been an edict of the ex-sovereign urging warriors in the
various provinces of Kyushu to chastise the enemies of the court. Therefore, I have despatched Noriyori to Kyushu and am about to send
Yoshitsune, who has been representing me at the capital, to Shikoku.
I exhort you to join in the chastisement of the Heike, whether in Kyushu
or in Shikoku, in compliance with the edict of the ex-sovereign, and

---

[1] The era name was changed from Genreki to Bunji on the 14th day of the
Eighth Month.

under the command of the governor of Mikawa Noriyori. In this connection, rewards will be made for meritorious services rendered, especially by government troops in Kyushu.

Genreki 2:1   Former Assistant Captain
                                                    of the Middle Palace Guards,
                                                    Right Division, Minamoto *Ason*

12th day. *Noriyori is still stalled in western Honshu.*

Noriyori had gone from Suō Province to Akamagaseki in preparation for the crossing of the channel to Kyushu, but he has been stalled there for several days for lack of boats and military provisions. The warriors are reported to be extremely restless, and many long for their homes. Even Wada Yoshimori has attempted secretly to leave for Kamakura.

However, when Noriyori learned that Usuki Jirō Koretaka and his younger brother Ogata Saburō Koreyoshi, who are local lords of Bungo Province, were supporters of the Genji, it was decided in council to ask them for boats. Therefore today Noriyori and his men returned to Suō to prepare for a crossing to Hakata in Bungo Province.

21st day. *Yoritomo and Masako worship at Kurihama Shrine.*

22nd day. *Yoritomo makes a grant of land in Izumo Province to Kamo Shrine.*

26th day. *Noriyori reaches Kyushu.*

In response to Noriyori's request, Koretaka and Koreyoshi have sent eighty-two boats. Also, Usanagi Kamishichi Tōtaka, a local lord of Suō, has contributed a supply of provisions. Thus Noriyori was able to weigh anchor and to cross over to Bungo Province. . . .[2] Among those accompanying him was Chiba Tsunetane, who made the crossing, disregarding his advanced years. Katō Kagekado, although ill at the time, also made the crossing; while Shimokōbe Yukihira, weak from lack of food, sold his armor for a small boat, so that he might sail at the vanguard of the fleet. When someone asked Yukihira how he expected to serve the commander by going forth to battle without his armor, he replied: "I do not regret losing

---

[2] The names of thirty-seven Genji vassals are listed.

my life. But I expect to serve at the very front in a boat over which
I have control. I shall fight, without armor, on the strength of my
will."

Before Noriyori weighed anchor, he had said to his men: "Suō
Province is our western headquarters. It is close both to Kyoto and
to the east. It is Yoritomo's order that we remain in contact with
both Kyoto and Kanto from Suō. Thus it is necessary that we
maintain a force of picked troops to guard this province. Whom
should I designate for this task?" Chiba Tsunetane replied: "Miura
Yoshizumi is an accomplished warrior and he has a large following.
Order him to assume this task." However, when Yoshizumi was
informed of this decision, he declined, saying: "How can I serve
meritoriously if I remain here idly? I am determined to fight at the
very fore of the army." But after repeated commands from Noriyori
that he should restrain his gallantry, Yoshizumi agreed to remain
in Suō.

SECOND MONTH

1st day. *Noriyori's advance party encounters opposition from Harada
Tanenao.*

Reaching Bungo, Noriyori had sent out Hōjō Shirō, the manorial
official Shimokōbe, the manorial official Shibuya Shigekuni, and
Shinagawa Saburō in advance of the rest of the party. Today, at
Ashiya-ura, the advance party met the challenge of Harada Tanenao,
who is the junior assistant governor-general of the government
headquarters in Kyushu, his son Kama Tanemasu, who is a lieutenant of the military guards, and their following of guards. Yukihira and Shigehira dashed around the enemy and shot their arrows,
but their own men could not engage in the battle because of Shigekuni's position. However, Yukihira was able to kill Mike Saburō
Atsutane.

5th day. *Yoritomo sends Nakahara Hisatsune and Kondō Kunihira
on a special mission to the west.*

The master of the imperial table office Nakahara Hisatsune and
Kondō Kunihira have gone up to the capital on a mission for His
Lordship. Their purpose is to put a stop to the lawless activities of
isolated warriors who have been seizing provisions in the neighbor-

ing provinces on the excuse of the war against the Heike. Their
mission is to restore order first in the eleven provinces of western
Honshu, then in Kyushu and Shikoku. His Lordship has instructed
them to bring all matters to the attention of the throne, to act only
in accordance with decrees issued by the ex-sovereign, and never to
take any action on their own initiative. Although these men are not
prominent local lords, Hisatsune is a talented scribe who also distinguished himself during the time of the late Yoshitomo, while
Kunihira is a brave and loyal warrior. Thus their assignment on
this mission. In accordance with His Lordship's instructions, they
have submitted a written pledge to the imperial court to carry out
their assignment in strict compliance with the laws of the land.

12th day. *Yoritomo visits Izu.*

Yoritomo has departed for Izu to oversee the cutting of timber at
Karino Mountain, normally the source of building timber. This is
for the construction of a temple.

13th day. *Yoritomo orders priests to pray for the success of the
wars; he receives details of Noriyori's difficulties.*

To pray for the success of the campaign against the Heike, all
the monks and priests of Kamakura were assembled at Tsurugaoka
Shrine to intone the *Mahā-prajñāpāramitā Sutra.* Esoteric practices
of Kyoto and twenty other temples were also invoked.

Today a letter written by Izawa Gorō in western Japan reached
Yoritomo at his quarters in Izu. According to the letter, the Genji
in their pursuit of the Heike had entered Nagato Province, but the
prevalence of a famine and the lack of provisions there compelled
them to return to Aki Province. Moreover, the lack of boats precluded advances into Kyushu to attack the Heike. Yoritomo's reply
expressed alarm at the possibility of the Genji encountering the
enemy while withdrawing from Nagato without provisions. Yoritomo also suggested that, if there is no possibility of advancing into
Kyushu, the Genji should cross over to Shikoku to engage the Heike
there.

14th day. *Yoritomo exhorts his troops in the west.*

While Noriyori was still in Suō Province, Yoritomo had instructed him to discuss the Kyushu campaign with Doi Sanehira and Kajiwara Kagetoki. His Lordship had further ordered him to rally what forces he could in Kyushu, but not to invade Kyushu unless there was a definite Genji trend among the local lords there. Otherwise, Noriyori was instructed to avoid battle in Kyushu and instead to cross over to Shikoku to attack the Heike there.

Today a special messenger arrived in Izu, bringing news of the plan of the Genji to withdraw from Nagato to Suō for lack of boats and provisions, and because of the restlessness and the decline in morale of the troops. Therefore His Lordship has written to Noriyori and to other immediate vassals in the field, reminding them that there is no honor in returning to the capital without engaging in battle, and he asked them to forbear until provisions could be sent. He told them that in pulling out of Heike territory and in seeking shelter, they had promoted the morale of the enemy forces. His Lordship further reminded them that they had been commissioned to chastise the enemy, and exhorted them to conduct themselves with the bravery and daring which the mission demands.

18th day. *Yoshitsune embarks at Watanabe for Shikoku.*

Yesterday, as Yoshitsune prepared to embark at Watanabe for Sanuki Province across the sea, a storm broke suddenly and destroyed many of his boats. None of his followers would board their boats. Thereupon, Yoshitsune said to them: "As members of a mission to destroy the enemies of the court, we cannot afford to tarry even for a moment. We should not let the dangers of the sea deter us." Thus saying, he embarked at 1 A.M. and reached Katsura in Awa at 5 A.M. with five boats and one hundred and fifty men. This distance is normally negotiated in three days. Upon landing, he summoned Kondō Chikaie, a local lord of this province, to serve as a guide, and departed for Yashima. En route, at Hashira-ura, he attacked Sakuraniwa Yoshitō, a younger brother of Nariyoshi, scattered rank, who quit his castle and fled.

Yoritomo has returned to Kamakura this evening.

19th day. *The construction of the South Chapel begins; Yoritomo hears a case; Yoshitsune attacks Yashima.*

The ceremony for the construction of the South Chapel was

held today. To observe the ceremony His Lordship, dressed in a perfumed ceremonial robe and mounted on a pale-red horse rode over to his place in a temporary shed which had been built to the south of the chapel site at the foot of the hills. Her Ladyship also took her place in the shed. At 3 P.M. gifts were made to the carpenters, and the sacred horses were led in.

Following the ceremony, the matter of the Gamakata and Chikunoya manors in Mikawa Province belonging to Kumano Shrine was attended to. The original lord of these manors, who had given them as a benefice to Kumano, was the scattered rank Toshinari. The intendant Jinkai, the new lord of the manor, then yielded them to his daughter. The daughter, who was at first the spouse of the assistant high priest of Buddhism Gyōkai, was later betrothed to the former governor of Satsuma Taira Tadanori. When Tadanori was killed at Ichinotani, His Lordship took over control of these lands as confiscated property of the Heike. Thereupon, Jinkai's daughter prevailed upon her former spouse Gyōkai to appeal promptly to Kanto for these manors and to obtain a letter of confirmation for them. With child at the time, she promised Gyōkai that if confirmation was obtained she would yield future rights to the manors to her unborn child who had been fathered by Gyōkai. On this agreement Gyōkai had sent an emissary, the monk Eizō, to plead the case. This Gyōkai is a son of Yukinori and a grandson of the imperial police Rokujō Tameyoshi. Having always maintained a friendly attitude toward the Minamoto, Gyōkai has been regarded highly by His Lordship. Thus the case was decided in his favor without argument. The decision was due also in part to His Lordship's reverence for the priest.

Late last night Yoshitsune crossed Nakayama on the border between Awa and Sanuki and today, at 7 A.M., he reached the bay on the far side of the palace at Yashima. When he set fire to and destroyed the people's homes at Mure and Takamatsu, His Highness the former emperor and the former Great Minister of the Center Taira Munemori and his family immediately boarded their boats. Yoshitsune, the young lord Tashiro Nobutsuna, Kaneko Ietada, Kaneko Chikanori, and Ise Yoshimori faced the Heike at the water's edge. While they exchanged arrows, Satō Tsunanobu, Satō

Tadanobu, Gotō Sanemoto, and Satō Motokiyo set fire to the palace
and the tents of Munemori and his subordinates. The black smoke
rose to the sky, obscuring the sun. Then the Heiji retainers, Etchū
Moritsuna and Kazusa Tadamitsu, who had disembarked from their
boats and had established a position before the palace gates, gave
battle to the Genji and slew Yoshitsune's retainer, Tsugunobu.
Yoshitsune, grief-stricken, found a priest and gave Tsugunobu a
burial in a field of pine stumps. Then Yoshitsune presented a prized
horse to the priest. This was the horse, styled Daibu Kurō, originally
from the ex-sovereign's stables, which the ex-sovereign himself had
used in imperial progresses and which had been presented to Yoshitsune on the eve of his departure for this campaign. This was
indeed an inspiring act.

On the same day the governor of Tsu and the priest of Sumiyoshi
Shrine, Nagamori, arrived at the capital and, permitted an audience
with the ex-sovereign, they declared: "On the 16th, while the customary sacred dance was being performed at the shrine, an arrow
appeared from the worship hall and proceeded in a westerly direction." As His Lordship has offered prayers recently in connection
with the campaign against the Heike, the arrow is a divine revelation of a most remarkable nature.

21st day. *Kōno Michinobu offers thirty boats to Yoshitsune.*

The Heike forces have withdrawn into the grounds of Shido
Temple in Sanuki, where Yoshitsune, in pursuit, arrived with
80 mounted men. A retainer of the Heiji, Taguchi Narinao, surrendered to Yoshitsune. Kōno Shirō Michinobu has also come to
serve Yoshitsune with an offer of thirty boats.

Today it was rumored in the capital that, when Yoshitsune crossed
over to Awa, the intendant of Kumano Jinzō had offered his support to the Genji and that he had made the crossing with Yoshitsune.

22nd day. *Kajiwara Kagetoki reaches Yashima with one hundred
and forty boats.*

27th day. *The sacred dance is performed at Kamo Shrine for the
success of the campaign.*

29th day. *Katō Kagekado's father makes a request for his son.*

The lay priest Katō Gorō called at headquarters and, laying an open letter before His Lordship and weeping for a few moments, said in answer to Yoritomo's inquiry as to the reason of his visit: "My son Kagekado has accompanied the governor of Mikawa Noriyori to Kyushu. But last month, as he prepared to cross over from Suō to Bungo, he was stricken with illness. Despite his stricken body, he boarded a boat and accompanied his commander in the crossing. This is his letter. It has been his intention to serve the ruler and to be counted among the dead in the battlefield. He is now stricken and can scarcely hope to escape death. If this aged father of his cannot lay his eyes on him again, there is nothing worth living for." Yoritomo, wiping away his own tears, scanned Kagekado's letter which said, in effect, that, although it had been His Lordship's strict orders to him to serve at his side, he, Kagekado, had taken it upon himself to join the campaign in the west in view of the gravity of the situation. Now he is gravely ill. It is his desire that, should he lose his life as a result of the illness, His Lordship would regard the death as having occurred in battle with the nation's enemy.

THIRD MONTH

1st day. *Warriors gather at headquarters to hear news of the western campaign from a messenger.*

2nd day. *Yoritomo orders Kagekiyo to cease from interfering on lands of the imperial storehouse.*

Last night's messenger, who had been despatched by Shibuya Shigekuni, reported that when the governor of Mikawa and his party crossed over to Bungo in the First Month, Shigekuni had been with the vanguard of the group and that he had attacked Harada Tanenao.

Today Yoritomo issued an order to Kagekiyo to cease from interfering in the affairs of orchard lands in Yamashiro which he himself had given to the imperial storehouse. Yoritomo reminded him that the control of these lands now rests with Nobuchika, the secretary of the Ministry of Justice.

3rd day. *Fraudulent land claims are made in the name of Kiso Yoshinaka's sister.*

A few days ago Her Ladyship Masako completed arrangements to adopt a younger sister of Kiso Yoshinaka. She had been living in a certain village in Mino before going to the capital to reside. During her stay in the capital men of questionable character had come to serve her, although she herself was of noble character. These men, using old, canceled documents, commended lands to which they held no rights to Yoshinaka's sister. Then, claiming to be her agents, they intruded on private and public lands. When this matter, which had become a source of great concern to the people, reached His Lordship's ears, he issued an order to Kondō Kunihira and to other vassals in the neighboring provinces to put a stop to these outrages and to arrest and send to Kamakura those responsible for such acts. Although His Lordship regards it a disgrace for a member of the family to be involved in such frauds, in the letter which he wrote he referred to Yoshinaka's sister as "the mad woman," inasmuch as the public had come to refer to her thus. However, he regards Yoshinaka's sister cordially and has urged her privately to come to Kanto.

4th day. *Yoritomo reaffirms to the court his policy regarding lawless activities of warriors.*

Although His Lordship has already despatched the secretary of the imperial table Nakahara Hisatsune and Kondō Kunihira as his deputies to restore order in the home provinces, reports of outlawry by warriors in the capital continue to come to Kamakura. Therefore, His Lordship, in order to dispel the sovereign's apprehensions, has sent the following explanatory memorial to the court:

The sending of warriors to the capital has been done with a view toward the subjugation of enemies of the court. Were this not the purpose, I would not permit their entry in the capital. Moreover, will acts of outlawry cease if warriors are prevented from going to the capital? It is imperative that we press first the pursuit of the enemy who are situated at a great distance from us, and, although it is my purpose to correct the situation with respect to the disorderly conduct of marauding warriors on the manors in the provinces at the conclusion of the present military campaign, I have, in the meantime, and so far as the neighboring provinces are concerned, despatched two deputies to remedy this situa-

tion. If such impudent acts continue before the campaign against the Heike can be concluded, the deputies are to take only such action as the ex-sovereign decrees and in the company of the ex-sovereign's representative. If my deputies take any action contrary to these conditions, they will have been deemed to have acted on their own free will. On my honor, I declare that steps are being taken to put a stop to the outrageous acts of warriors, and the instructions noted herein have been transmitted to my deputies. Most humbly and respectfully submitted.
Third Month, 4th day   Yoritomo
Respectfully submitted to: Fujiwara Tsunefusa, Middle Councilor

6th day. *Yoritomo recalls Katō Kagekado from Kyushu.*

His Lordship, greatly concerned about Kagekado's illness, has written to the governor of Mikawa Noriyori to take every measure necessary for Kagekado's recuperation and to order him home immediately upon recovery. His Lordship has also written directly to Kagekado, inquiring after his illness and informing him that he is sending a pale-red horse from his own stables to bring him back. The former governor of Inaba Hiromoto is in charge of this matter.

7th day. *Yoritomo pledges support for the rebuilding of the Tōdai-ji.*

His Lordship has pledged his support toward the repair and reconstruction of the Tōdai-ji. In his letter to the priests of Nara and to Jūgen Shōnin, in charge of raising subscriptions for the project, His Lordship pledged contributions of 10,000 *koku*[3] of rice, 1,000 *ryō*[4] of gold, and 1,000 *hiki*[5] of high quality silk. His Lordship's letter is as follows:

Regarding the Tōdai-ji: The aforementioned temple has been damaged by Heike rebels, and subjected to the trials of a fire. Its images have burned to ashes and its priests and monks have perished. Rarely has a temple seen such trials and tribulations, for which I express my personal grief. I now pledge the repair and reconstruction of this temple to its former likeness that it might continue to offer prayers for the defense and safety of the nation. Although the world is in decline, the benign virtue of the ruler will promote the prosperity of both the imperial government and the Buddhist Law. Surely the ex-sovereign is giving thought to measures he might take to assist the temple. As for myself, barring the occurrence of extraordinary events, I shall exert the utmost

[3] *Koku,* a measure equal to 4.96 bushels.
[4] See Part Two, Chapter II, note 22.
[5] See Part Two, Chapter II, note 14.

effort in matters pertaining to your temple, although I fear that at this time, in view of the campaign against enemies of the court, the assistance may be somewhat delayed. Thus inscribed.

Third Month, 7th Day   Former Assistant Captain
                                        of the Middle Palace Guards,
                                        Right Division, Minamoto *Ason*

8th day. *Yoshitsune's messenger arrives from Shikoku.*

Yoshitsune's messenger arrived from the west and reported thus: "On the 17th of the past month Yoshitsune, braving a storm, departed from Watanabe for Shikoku with a mere 150 men. Reaching Awa Province on the following day at 5 A.M., he battled the Heike, killing some and routing others. On the 19th Yoshitsune departed for Yashima. I left immediately for Kamakura without waiting for the results of the Yashima battle, but as I looked back toward Yashima after I had reached Harima, I saw black smoke rising skyward. The battle must have been over by then and the palace and other buildings of the Heike must have been destroyed."

9th day. *Noriyori pleads to retain his command in Kyushu.*

In a letter from the governor of Mikawa Noriyori it is reported: "In our attempt to reach Bungo so that we might be closer to the Heike positions, all the people of the area fled, leaving us without provisions. Whereupon the Wada brothers, Ōtawa Jirō, Kudō Suketsune, and their several followers, insisted on turning back and returning to Kamakura. I did everything in my power to detain them, and finally forced them to make the crossing to Kyushu. It is suggested that Your Lordship's reprimand to these men be added to mine. Also, it is rumored that Jinzō, the intendant of Kumano, has crossed over into Sanuki with Yoshitsune's blessings to command the campaign there, and that he is expected in Kyushu shortly. Shikoku is within Yoshitsune's jurisdiction as Kyushu is within mine. If it is true that I am to be superseded, I shall lose my honor and shall be regarded as one lacking in bravery. This would be most disgraceful."

11th day. *Yoritomo reassures Noriyori; he commends others fighting for the Genji in Kyushu.*

His Lordship has sent a reply to the governor of Mikawa denying the rumor regarding Jinzō's expedition into Sanuki. He has also expressed his warmest regards for all his immediate vassals whom he had despatched from Kanto, in particular Chiba Tsunetane, who is enduring the rigors of the military campaign despite his advanced age. Yoritomo has said of him, "He has excelled his fellow men, and it is impossible in a lifetime to repay him for his magnificent service." Yoritomo has also sent letters of appreciation to the following twelve vassals, each fighting in the west and performing great deeds: Hōjō Yoshitoki, Koyama Tomomasa, Koyama Munemasa, the assistant head Shinto priest Chikayoshi, Kasai Kiyoshige, Katō Kagekado, Kudō Suketsune, Usami Sukemochi, Amano Tōkage, Nitta Tadatsune, Hiki Tomomune, and Hiki Yoshikazu. His Lordship commended in particular their feat of crossing over to Bungo Province and added that the commendation should be conveyed to all the other vassals of Izu and Suruga Provinces.

12th day. *Boats and provisions are sent from the east.*

Thirty-two boats have been assembled at Kohina-no-oki and at Mera and loaded with provisions to be used in the Heiji expedition. His Lordship has ordered that these boats should be despatched to the west without delay. Toshikane is the commissioner.

13th day. *Yoritomo assures the governor of Tsushima safe passage through the western provinces.*

Today His Lordship has sent instructions to Noriyori to receive Fujiwara Chikamitsu, the governor of Tsushima and a distant relative of His Lordship, who had been attacked by the Heike while serving out his appointment. In addition to the instructions, a passport was prepared and sent to him.

ISSUED TO: Immediate vassals in the Saikai and Sanyō Circuits
    Regarding the prompt and safe arrival of the former official of Tsushima
The aforementioned former official of Tsushima is about to return from his tour of duty in the provinces. Instructions are herewith issued that en route he shall enjoy safe passage through the various provinces. Thus ordered,
Genreki 2:3,13   Former Assistant Captain
                                        of the Middle Palace Guards,
                                        Right Division, Minamoto *Ason*

14th day. *Yoritomo orders Noriyori to return the Treasure of the Sacred Mirror Room.*[6]

Rain. Nagikubo Shōshirō Yukichika has left for Kyushu on a mission for His Lordship. He is taking a letter to Noriyori, in which Yoritomo exhorts Noriyori to give his attention to the further planning and execution of the campaign. Noriyori was also ordered to make every effort to retrieve and return the Treasure of the Sacred Mirror Room.

18th day. *Yoritomo believes that his vow to destroy the Heike accords with the will of Buddha.*

At the South Chapel a carpenter called Kannō slipped and fell from the roof of a hut to the ground. However, to the amazement of all, he was not seriously hurt. His Lordship has remarked repeatedly that the youth avoided death because His Lordship's vow accords with the will of Buddha.

21st day. *The local commissioner in charge of boats contributes crafts to Yoshitsune.*

Due to rain, Yoshitsune has postponed his departure for Dannoura to attack the Heiji. Meanwhile, the local commissioner in charge of boats, Funadokoro Gorō Masatoshi, has contributed several tens of boats to Yoshitsune. Consequently Yoshitsune has recommended him to the Lord of Kamakura for investiture as an immediate vassal.

22nd day. *Yoshitsune departs with his fleet for Dannoura.*

Yoshitsune departed for Dannoura at the head of several tens of boats. He had assembled the crafts and had made the plans for departure yesterday. When Miura Yoshizumi learned of these plans, he came to Ōshima to join Yoshitsune. The latter said to Yoshizumi: "You are familiar with Mojinoseki; you shall be our guide. As such, you will be at the vanguard of the fleet." Yoshizumi accepted the command, and today he led the fleet to the vicinity of Okitsu near Dannoura, about 30 *chō* from the Heike position. When the Heike

[6] *Kashikodokoro,* a room in the palace in which was kept the replica of the Sacred Mirror, one of the three Imperial Regalia.

learned of this, they boarded their boats. They abandoned Hikojima and, by-passing Akamagaseki, they have gone to Ta-no-ura.

24th day. *The Genji defeat the Heiji at Dannoura.*

The fleets of the Genji and the Heiji, their line of boats separated by three *chō* of water, met at Dannoura, Akamagaseki, off Nagato Province. The Heike, dividing their fleet of five hundred boats into three groups with Yamaga Hidetō and his band of Matsuura men in command gave battle to the Genji leaders. By 11 A.M. the Heiji were routed. The imperial second rank Taira Tokiko, widow of Kiyomori, and the Lady Azechi sank to the bottom of the sea, the former clutching the Sacred Sword, and the latter holding tightly the eight-year-old former emperor Antoku. Kenrei Mon-in Taira Tokuko, wearing a purple gown, was rescued from the sea with a rake by the lieutenant of the Right Horse Bureau Gengo, a member of the Watanabe band. The Lady Azechi was likewise rescued. However, the former emperor was not recovered. The young prince Morisada, older brother of the reigning emperor, was saved. The former Middle Councilor Norimori, also known as Monkyō, has drowned. The former councilor Tsunemori left the battle scene for the shore to take the Buddhist vow, then returned to drown himself. The newly appointed middle captain and third rank Sukemori and the former minor captain Arimori were drowned, while the former Great Minister of the Center Munemori and the captain of the Right Outer Palace Guards Kiyomune were taken alive by Ise Saburō Yoshimori. Then the warriors boarded the Imperial ship, and, as one of them sought to open the chest which contained the Sacred Mirror, his eyes were suddenly darkened and his spirits paralyzed. And as Taira Tokitada, the major councilor, restrained the Genji from opening the box, the latter withdrew. The embodiment of the hallowed spirit of the gods had been in the sole possession of the imperial family, and during the reign of Emperor Sujin, the tenth ruler after Emperor Jimmu, it was recast in respectful deference to the august spirits. Later, in the Chōreki era [1037–39], during the reign of Ex-Sovereign Suzaku, its circular form had been slightly impaired by a fire at the palace, but during the Heiji uprising it had remained unharmed in the sleeve of the courtier Moronaka, to which it had been transferred for safekeeping. Thereafter it had been placed in a newly constructed casket and consigned to the care of the minister of civil affairs Sukenaga, who is also the director of the sovereign's private office. Now, in this degenerate age, it has again exhibited its supernatural character. It is to be respected and revered.

27th day. *The priest Rinyū who had buried Mareyoshi calls on Yoritomo.*

The Shōnin Rinyū, resident monk of Hiragi Manor in Tosa Province, has come to Kanto. Rinyū had rendered distinguished service to the Minamoto. In the first year of Juei 1 [1182], when the provisional governor Hasuike Ietsuna attacked and killed Yoritomo's younger brother Mareyoshi, Rinyū, wishing to save the body from exposure, had gathered together his parishioners and had given him a burial. Although there were men among the natives loyal to the Minamoto, they had hesitated to give Mareyoshi a burial for fear of reprisal by the Heike. And since the burial Rinyū has not neglected the grave, which is located in Makita Township. On this occasion he had been granted an audience with Yoritomo through the intercession of the priest Ryōkaku of Sōtō-zan, to whom he had gone, wearing around his neck a braid of hair which he had taken from the departed Mareyoshi. Yoritomo welcomed him with words of praise and appreciation, saying that his arrival was tantamount to a visit by the spirit of the dead Mareyoshi.

29th day. *The ex-sovereign urges local lords of Bungo Province to oppose the Heike.*

At Yoritomo's urging, and for the purpose of rallying forces against the Heike, the ex-sovereign's government has issued an edict directed to the local gentry of Bungo Province. This edict, issued a few days ago, has reached Kanto today.

The ex-sovereign's government addresses the principal residents of Bungo
    An exhortation to render meritorious service in the campaign of subjugation, and a promise of rewards
Bands of Heike rebels, returning to the islands off Shikoku, have drawn many people into their cause in defiance of imperial law and with intentions of perpetrating unlawful acts. However, it has been reported that the warriors of Bungo Province, stoutly defending the

imperial law, have refused to join with the rebels and have, instead, come forward in their boats to join with the government troops and to bring the men of Kyushu under their banner. This has been especially heartening to His Majesty, who exhorts you to muster the best troops and to destroy the said rebels. And each of you shall be rewarded upon request and according to your deed. The lords of Bungo are especially directed to take note of this edict and to comply with it. These are His Majesty's instructions. Thus ordered.
Genreki 2:2,2

FOURTH MONTH

4th day. *Yoshitsune's messenger reports to Kyoto on the complete destruction of the Heike.*

Last night Yoshitsune's messenger came in great haste to Kyoto to report the complete destruction of the Heike. Today a roster of names of the dead and the captured was presented to the ex-sovereign by the lieutenant of the Military Guards Minamoto Hirotsuna.

5th day. *An emissary conveys the ex-sovereign's congratulations to Yoshitsune.*

An imperial emissary, the lieutenant Fujiwara Nobumori, fifth rank, has departed for Nagato Province to convey to Yoshitsune His Majesty's expressions of praise and appreciation for his display of military prowess and meritorious service in subjugating the Heike. His Majesty's instructions to return the imperial treasures were also conveyed to Yoshitsune.

11th day. *A record of the Battle of Dannoura is presented to Yoritomo.*

At 9 A.M. His Lordship, while observing the ceremony for the raising of the pillars of the South Chapel, was approached by a special messenger from the west who presented him with a record of the destruction of the Heiji. The messenger presented His Lordship with a scroll, written by Nakahara Nobuyasu. It states that the battle took place on sea on the 24th of the past month at Akamagaseki, Nagato Province, between eight hundred and forty Genji ships and five hundred Heiji ships, and that the rebel groups were defeated and subdued between 11 A.M and 1 P.M. The record continues:

Item: The former emperor has sunk to the bottom of the sea.

Item: Others who lost their lives at sea:

The nun Tokiko, second rank, the middle Councilor Norimori, the chancellor Taira Tsunemori (who took the tonsure), the newly appointed Minor Captain Sukemori, third rank, the Minor Captain Komatsu Arimori, director of the Left Horse Bureau Yukimori.

Item: The prince and Kenrei Mon-in have been safely rescued.

Item: Those taken alive:

The former Great Minister of the Center Munemori, the major councilor Tokitada, the captain of the Outer Palace Guards Kiyomune, the former director of the imperial storehouses Nobumoto (who has sustained an injury), the assistant head official of the Ministry of Military Affairs Koreaki (who is also known as Fukushō-maru, the six-year-old son of Munemori).

Court Ladies

The wife of Tokitada, wet nurse to the former emperor, the wife of the courtier Shigehira, the daughter of Tokiko, Lady Azechi, who had plunged into the sea holding the former emperor.

Priests

The assistant high priest of Buddhism Zenshin, the master of Buddhist Asceticism Chūkai, the teacher Nōen, the teacher Gyōmei, who is also intendant of Kumano.

The above is a roster of the principal personages. Another list of men and women captured will be forwarded later. The Sacred Jewel has been recovered but the Sacred Sword has been lost. It is our intention to retrieve it.

This record was read by the secretary Fujiwara Kunimichi, seated before His Lordship. In attendance on the stone pavement during the reading of the record were the governor of Inaba Toshikane and Chikuzen Saburō. When the reading was over His Lordship personally rolled up the scroll and, holding it in his hands, made obeisance toward Tsurugaoka Shrine, though unable to utter a word. At the conclusion of the ceremony of the raising of the pillars and the beams His Lordship presented emoluments to the carpenters, and returned to the headquarters. Then he summoned the messenger who had brought the record and inquired of him the details of the battles.

12th day. *Policies for the west are formulated at Kamakura.*

Today a council was held to decide on measures to be taken in the west, now that the Heiji have been destroyed. It was decided to order Noriyori to remain in Kyushu for awhile to look into the mat-

ter of confiscated lands, and to order Yoshitsune to take the prisoners
to Kyoto. These instructions were taken to the west by the servants
Tokizawa and Satonaga.

13th day. *Yoritomo orders Koyama Aritaka to return lands belonging to Ikōji Temple of Musashi Province.*

His Lordship had acknowledged the prayers which Chōei, the
priest of Ikōji in Musashi, had offered zealously for the overthrow
of the Heike. However, Koyama Tarō Aritaka had seized the lands
of the temple. Chōei, submitting a document issued to the temple
by Yoritomo in the Ninth Month of the past year, has brought
charges against Koyama. Today judgment was rendered, His Lordship ordering Koyama to restore the lands to the temple. The decree
was drafted by the governor of Inaba Hiromoto. Others who affixed
their signatures to the document were: the secretary of the Bureau
of Statistics Yukimasa, the secretary of the Right Horse Bureau
Tōmoto, Kai Shōshirō Akiie, the secretary Kunimichi, and Chikuzen
Saburō Takanao.

14th day. *The ex-sovereign congratulates Yoritomo.*

A messenger of the minister of finance Yasutsune has arrived in
Kanto, bringing with him a proclamation from the ex-sovereign. The
proclamation declares that seldom has His Majesty been so pleased
as he has been over the success of this campaign. It declares, further,
that the success was due entirely to Yoritomo's skillful military
strategy. His Lordship was greatly pleased.

Today Hatano Shirō Tsuneie, styled Ōtomo, returned to Kamakura from the west. He is the father-in-law of Chikayoshi, the
assistant head Shinto priest. His Lordship summoned him and asked
him many questions about the naval battle in the west.

15th day. *Yoritomo prohibits vassals who had accepted appointments
at the court from returning to the east.*

Many Kanto vassals have sought and received various appointments to the headquarters of the guards without His Lordship's
recommendation and without a record of meritorious service. Distrustful of them, His Lordship has sent to such vassals an order
listing their names and citing their misdeeds.

ORDERED TO: Warriors of the eastern provinces who have received court
   appointments
They shall serve in the capital and are prohibited from returning to
their native provinces.
Attached: A roster of names. . . .[7]

20th day. *Yoritomo makes a grant of land to Mishima Shrine of Izu
Province.*

21st day. *Kajiwara Kagetoki accuses Yoshitsune of harboring personal ambitions.*

Kajiwara Kagetoki has sent one of his relatives as a special
messenger to Kamakura. The letter he presented to His Lordship
contained an account of the military campaign, followed by a complaint against Yoshitsune for his unprincipled behavior.

. . . The secretary of the imperial police Yoshitsune, serving as His
Majesty's deputy and as leader of Your Lordship's vassals who had
been assigned to him, has brought the campaign to a successful conclusion. Although Yoshitsune is of the opinion that the victory was due
to his efforts alone, I ask, was it not the result of the cooperative efforts
of a large force? Every member of this large force had been motivated
by a desire to serve, not Yoshitsune, but the ruler. This was the reason
for the cooperative spirit and the great achievement. However, after the
destruction of the Heike, Yoshitsune's pride has only increased, so
that the very existence of his followers is endangered. He does not
tolerate contrary opinions and refuses to compromise. I, as one close
to Your Lordship, and as one who knows Yoshitsune's inclination toward arbitrariness, have cautioned him, each time that he has acted
in this manner, that such conduct would not be pleasing to Your Lordship. But, instead, these words of counsel have become cause for reprisal, and I may even be punished for them. Now that the war has
been completed, I beg your leave to be recalled to Kamakura and
to terminate my attendance on Yoshitsune.

In general, Wada Yoshimori and Kajiwara Kagetoki are officials of
the *samurai-dokoro*. Thus they had been assigned to look after the
affairs of the troops when Yoritomo's two younger brothers were
despatched as commanders to the west. Yoshimori had been assigned
to Noriyori, while Kagetoki had been assigned to Yoshitsune. But
while the former, and Chiba Tsunetane, were consulted on all
matters large and small by Noriyori, in compliance with His Lord-

---

[7] Twenty-two names are listed.

ship's orders, the latter was ignored by Yoshitsune, who relied entirely on his own judgment and acted arbitrarily, contrary to His Lordship's instructions. Thus hatred of Yoshitsune is not confined to Kagetoki.

24th day. *The Sacred Mirror is returned to Kyoto; Noriyori submits his resignation of the governorship of Mikawa.*

The Sacred Mirror has reached the vicinity of Imazu. As a result, the Middle Captain Michisuke has gone to Imazu. At night the Middle Councilor Tsunefusa, the chancellor and Middle Captain Yasumichi, the provisional Middle Controller of the Right Kane-tada, the Middle Captain Kimitoki, the Minor Captain of the Right Noriyoshi, and the official of the sovereign's private office and provisional assistant captain of the Outer Palace Guards Chikamasa assembled at the Katsura River, and following the performance of the great purification ceremony, the party proceeded with the Sacred Mirror up the Sujaku Highway, past Rokujō and Ōmiya through the gates of the Sacred Mirror Room to the dining hall of the high court nobles via the east gate. During this time Yoshitsune, dressed in armor, was in attendance at the east gate of the palace. Beneath the armor he wore the garment of an imperial police, and he held a torch.

Noriyori, who is in Kyushu, has submitted his resignation from the governorship of Mikawa. This letter of resignation was trans-mitted to Kanto by Chikayoshi today. It has been brought to the attention of the ex-sovereign.

26th day. *Deputies of Doi Sanehira and Kajiwara Kagetoki in the home provinces are accused of abusing their authority; Taira Mune-mori is sentenced.*

There have been incidents of late in which fellow warriors, exer-cising their own private authority, have committed outrages on various manors. Last spring an imperial directive ordered a stop to such outrages. Now His Lordship has issued the following order, commanding warriors to desist from further activities of this nature. Toshikane has been designated the commissioner.

ORDERED TO: Sanehira, constable of the home and near provinces
The immediate cessation of the arbitrary seizure of lands, in com-pliance with an edict of the ex-sovereign

Domains, both private and public, in the aforementioned near provinces have been seized by persons without proper documentary claims to ownership. Warriors residing in the various districts in the capacity of deputies, have been guilty of unprincipled conduct, of disobeying the orders of the legal guardians of the manors, and of disregarding the decrees of the provincial officials. They have seized the annual tribute of the manors and have forcibly taken imperial property. It is hereby ordered that such deputies vacate such lands immediately in accordance with the decree of the ex-sovereign. Those who have cause to remain are ordered to submit their reasons. Thus ordered.
Genreki 2:4,26[8]

. . . .

Today the ex-sovereign secretly stopped his carriage at the Rokujō Palace, so that he might witness the entry into the capital of the former Great Minister of the Center Taira Munemori and other prisoners of war. The arrival occurred at 3 P.M. All were taken to the Rokujō-Muromachi residence of Yoshitsune. On the same day judgment of penalty by death was passed on the former Great Minister of the Center, his sons, and his retainers. The official divination report was submitted by the doctor of law Akisada.

28th day. *Taira Tokuko and Prince Morisada are returned to the capital; a vassal complains of the conduct of Genji warriors.*

Kenrei Mon-in is staying at the abode of the ritualist Jikken in Yoshida. The chamberlain Nobukiyo has been summoned to the capital and ordered to escort Prince Morisada, the older brother of the reigning emperor, to the capital from Funatsu where he has been staying. The prince has been housed at a residence at Shichijō.

Today the governor of Dewa Shigetō has come to Kamakura. His Lordship, friendly to the governor, who is eighty years old and is a hereditary vassal, summoned him to an audience. Accompanied by his younger brother Jūrō and assisted by the priest Rennin, Shigetō appeared before His Lordship and said: "In the more than twenty years since the Heiji wars, I have maintained my traditional friendship for the Genji and have not succumbed to the authority of the Heiji. But since the assumption of authority by Your Lordship, when I had expected my anxieties to diminish, instead my troubles and cares have increased, due to the conduct of Your Lordship's warriors residing in the capital. I have been subjected to their

[8]An almost identical order to Kajiwara Kagetoki follows.

oppressive demands for military levies and guard duty to such an extent that I cannot help but bring a formal complaint. I have not been subjected to such indignities even under the Heiji. When will order be restored in our land?" His Lordship, convinced of the justice of the governor's grievances, immediately rendered a judgment promising him relief and security from such outrages.

29th day. *Vassals in the west are ordered not to serve Yoshitsune; Yoritomo makes a grant of land to a temple in Bitchū.*

The servant Kichie has been sent to the west with a letter from His Lordship to Tashiro Nobutsuna directing him to inform other immediate vassals who intend to remain loyal to Kanto to desist hereafter from serving Yoshitsune. Yoshitsune, it was pointed out, had abused his commission as Kanto's representative in the west and had caused resentment among Kanto's vassals who had been assigned to his command by demanding of them complete subservience to him.

Today His Lordship made a grant of the township of Senoo in Bitchū Province to the Hōka-dō, where the ex-sovereign Sutoku[9] had resided. Yoritomo had resumed control of Senoo as part of the lands confiscated from the Heike. His Lordship has now allotted the township as sustenance land to the said temple as a means of assuring the late ex-sovereign deliverance from all cares.

FIFTH MONTH

1st day. *Yoshinaka's sister arrives in Kamakura; Yoritomo makes an award to Hōka-dō.*

Miyagiku, younger sister of the late governor of Iyo Yoshinaka, has come to Kamakura from Kyoto at the invitation of Yoritomo. Her Ladyship Masako has been especially cordial to her. Miyagiku disclaimed any knowledge of the use of her name by certain unprincipled members of her clan in the cases of land aggrandizement reported a few days ago. She declared that, although her brother Yoshinaka deserved to be punished as an enemy of the court, there is no reason to extend the punishment to her, since she has not

---

[9] The Minamoto had supported the ex-sovereign Sutoku in the succession dispute of 1156 which led to the so-called Hōgen Disturbance.

been delinquent in the discharge of her various obligations. In agreement with her, His Lordship has granted her a village in the manor of Tōyama, Mino Province.

His Lordship has also written to the lady in waiting to the late Ex-sovereign Sutoku in connection with a new grant of land to the Hōka-dō Temple. In it His Lordship explained that, due to difficulties, possession of the Fukuoka Manor in Bizen Province, which had been given to the temple the past year, has been revoked and in its place he is making a grant of Senoo Township. By this grant, and through the intercession of the altar priest in charge at the temple, His Lordship hopes to contribute toward the salvation of the late Ex-sovereign Sutoku. The said lady in waiting and nun is a relative of Yoritomo. She had been a prayer maiden for the late ex-sovereign.

It was reported that Taira Tokuko has entered a Buddhist order.

2nd day. *Rinyū leaves for Tosa; his residence is granted immunity from taxes.*

Rinyū of Tosa has left for his native province. His Lordship had tried to persuade him to remain in Kanto with the offer of the intendancy of a temple, but the priest, pleading that he could not neglect the spiritual care of the grave of the young lord of Tosa Mareyoshi, was finally permitted to go. A farewell banquet was given in his honor by His Lordship. Also, Rinyū's residence at Kera Manor was granted immunity from all taxes. Moreover, as recompense for looking after the late Mareyoshi, His Lordship ordered the local lords of Tosa Province to acknowledge Rinyū's deeds.

3rd day. *Yoritomo orders Komoro Mitsukane of Shinano to provide a stipend for Yoshinaka's sister.*

Yoritomo has instructed Komoro Tarō Mitsukane and his subordinates in Shinano Province to provide a stipend for the sister of Kiso Yoshinaka. His Lordship has declared that Shinano had been Yoshinaka's domain, and that those who would call themselves principal residents of Shinano had been the recipients of Yoshinaka's favors.

4th day. *Kajiwara Kagetoki is relieved of attendance on Yoshitsune; but he is ordered to remain in Kyoto.*

Kajiwara Kagetoki's messenger has returned to the west carrying with him His Lordship's letter rebuking Yoshitsune and ordering Kagetoki not to serve him. Yoritomo added, however, that, the return of Heiji captives to the capital being a matter of great importance, Kagetoki and other Kamakura vassals should remain at and provide protection for the capital. His Lordship has ordered that no vassal should be permitted to return home on his own initiative.

5th day. *Yoritomo sends further instructions to vassals in Kyushu; Yoshitsune is accused of trying to rule Kyushu.*

His Lordship has sent a special messenger to Noriyori, instructing him to make every effort to retrieve the Sacred Sword, and to remain in Kyushu until the winter in order to administer the area and to restore order. The messenger was also ordered to take a letter of commendation to Shibuya Shigekuni for his slaying of Kama Tanemasu in Bungo during the recent battles. Also, Yoritomo ordered his vassals assigned to Noriyori's command to refrain from censuring Noriyori, even if there were some among them who are resentful of him, and to lodge a complaint with Kanto first. Last year Noriyori and Yoshitsune, the two younger brothers of Yoritomo, had received imperial mandates to proceed against the enemy. And, since Noriyori had invaded Kyushu, it was decided a few days later that he should administer Kyushu. Similarly, since Yoshitsune had invaded Shikoku, that area was to be under his control. However, since the successful conclusion of the Battle of Dannoura, Yoshitsune had assumed control of Kyushu as well. He would not tolerate even the most inconsequential faults among his followers, nor would he communicate with Yoritomo on the details of such affairs. He has relied entirely on his own judgment and has thus invited severe criticism. Such an offense cannot be excused, and His Lordship's displeasure continues.

Today Koyama Tomomitsu has returned from the west.

6th day. *Kyoto nobles make offerings to twenty-two shrines to express their gratitude for the success of the war.*

7th day. *Noriyori and Yoshitsune send messengers to Kamakura to explain their positions.*

Kamei Rokurō, an emissary of Yoshitsune, has arrived from Kyoto. He has brought with him a written pledge from Yoshitsune, in which he declares that he holds no treasonable intentions. It is addressed to the former official of Inaba Ōe Hiromoto. On the other hand, Noriyori had been sending a succession of messengers from the west, explaining in detail the reasons why his freedom to act has been curtailed. His Lordship believes in Noriyori and thinks that Yoshitsune is planning to pursue an independent course. For Yoshitsune to declare his loyalty now, having heard of Yoritomo's displeasure with him, leaves no room for pardon. On the contrary, Yoshitsune's action in this instance has only increased Yoritomo's anger with him.

8th day. *Measures to be carried out in the west are adopted at Kamakura.*

A meeting was held to decide on measures to be taken in Kyushu. It was attended by Inaba Hiromoto, Nakahara Chikayoshi, Fujiwara Toshikane, Nikaidō Yukimasa, and Koremune Takanao. The drafting of the document, which enjoins that these measures should be promptly executed, was assigned to Toshikane. The measures are:

Item: The official Kimifusa in charge of the Great Shrine of Usa shall resume administration of the shrine. Although he has offered prayers in behalf of the Heike, he is deserving of this consideration because of his religious devotion.

Item: By His Lordship's grace the assistant to the head official of the same shrine shall be restored to office.

Item: Due to the wars of the past year, the worship hall of the said shrine has been damaged. His Lordship pledges that he will make special efforts to rebuild it.

Item: In addition to the lands already confiscated from the Heike, the fiefs rumored to be held, with the approval of the lords of the manors, by Taira Sadayoshi and the master of Buddhist Law Taira Morikuni shall be marked for confiscation.

Item: The high official of the ministry of finance Mike, having impugned the governor of Mikawa, shall be summoned to Kamakura.

Item: Among the immediate vassals assigned to Kyushu, Shionoya Gorō and many of his followers have returned to the east. His lordship is sending an emissary to the west to put a stop to such a practice and to administer and restore order in that region.

Item: A roster of immediate vassals enrolled in the west shall be prepared by Wada Yoshimori, who will submit same to Kamakura.

9th day. *Yoritomo objects to the actions of Shibuya Shigesuke and his father.*

Action was taken today to cancel the appointment to office of Shibuya Shigesuke, which had been made without the recommendation of Kanto. Although His Lordship had once forgiven Shigesuke for having opposed his own father Shigekuni in the Ishibashi Battle, Shigesuke had again sided with the Heike and had frequently ignored His Lordship's summons. However, on the day of the abandonment of the capital by the Heike, he had remained in Kyoto and had offered his services to Yoshinaka. Following Yoshinaka's death Shigesuke became a devoted follower of Yoshitsune and, being an excellent warrior, his various faults were forgotten and in the end he was given an appointment. The action taken today by His Lordship objects to his appointment.

His Lordship has also expressed his objection to Shibuya Shigekuni's preceding Noriyori to the capital, even though Shigekuni had distinguished himself by being in the vanguard of the invasion of Bungo. Also, instructions were sent to Noriyori to divide and allot the Harada fief to deserving vassals.

10th day. *The vice governor of Kazusa Taira Tadakiyo is captured.*

It has been reported that followers of Katō Mitsukazu have captured a retainer of the Heiji, the master of Buddhist Law and vice governor of Kazusa Taira Tadakiyo, at Azabu-ura in Shima Province and have sent him to the capital.

11th day. *Yoritomo is raised to the second rank.*

As a reward for the capture and return to Kyoto of the former Great Minister of the Center Taira Munemori, His Lordship was raised to junior second rank on the 27th of the past month. The writ of appointment has arrived today. It will be formally transmitted and served to His Lordship by Ichijō Yoshiyasu, who is expected at Kamakura shortly.

12th day. *A messenger is sent to Noriyori in Kyushu with further instructions.*

The servant Tsunemichi has departed for Kyushu on an official mission for His Lordship. He has been entrusted with directives concerning various matters in the western provinces. He is to deliver them to the governor of Mikawa Noriyori.

15th day. *Yoritomo decides on measures to be taken regarding Yoshitsune.*

A messenger sent by Yoshitsune has arrived at Kamakura. He reports that Yoshitsune, escorting Taira Munemori and his son, left the capital on the 7th and that he hopes to reach Sakamaga-eki this evening and Kamakura tomorrow. His Lordship has assigned Lord Hōjō to meet Yoshitsune's party at the inn and to receive the prisoners. He will be accompanied on this mission by the guardsman Munechika and Kudō Yukimitsu. His Lordship has also despatched Koyama Tomomitsu to instruct Yoshitsune to remain in the vicinity and to refrain from entering Kamakura.

16th day. *Taira Tadakiyo is reported executed; Taira Munemori and other prisoners are delivered to Kamakura.*

It has been reported that the master of Buddhist Law Tadakiyo has been executed and his head exposed to public view at Rokujō-Kawara.

Today onlookers lined the streets like a fence as the former Great Minister of the Center and his retainers were delivered to Kamakura. Munemori was transported in a cart, while Kiyomune, Norikiyo, the lay priest Morikuni, Minamoto Suesada, Morisumi, Tsunekage, Gotō Nobuyasu, and Iemura were mounted. They were led down the main street toward the sub-shrine and were halted at the intersection of the main roads as Munemitsu reported the arrival of the party to His Lordship. Then the party was admitted to the headquarters and the West Room was designated as quarters for Munemori and his son. At night upon orders from Yoritomo, the governor of Inaba Hiromoto personally served Munemori with food, but the latter refused the food, so great is his grief. This matter of the delivery of Munemori, his son, and other

members of the Heike had been referred to the court through the
courtier Yoshida Tsunefusa, and its approval obtained, not only
for their delivery to Kamakura but also for their execution. The
death penalty for Taira Tokitada has been commuted because of
his role in retrieving and returning the Sacred Mirror.

17th day. *Ichijō Yoshiyasu arrives at Kamakura; a scuffle is reported between Yoshiyasu's men and Yoshitsune's men.*

Ichijō Yoshiyasu, who had departed from Kyoto on the 7th,
the same day on which Yoshitsune made his departure, arrived at
Kamakura at 5 A.M. and reported directly to headquarters. He
explained his delay as due to high fever and the fear of a stroke
which he suffered yesterday. It has come to Yoritomo's attention
that a scuffle occurred yesterday between the servants of Gotō
Motokiyo, an attendant of Yoshiyasu, and those of Ise Yoshimori,
an attendant of Yoshitsune. The incident began when Motokiyo,
who was mounted, and his servants, who were afoot and carrying
baggage, were passing before the inn at which Yoshimori was
staying and where his horses were being fed. As the party of
servants was passing the inn, Yoshimori's caparisoned horse
trampled on the feet of Motokiyo's servants. One of the servants
cut the crupper on Yoshimori's horse with a sword and ran off.
When Yoshimori was apprised of the incident, he took a stick and
lashed Motokiyo's servants. Whereupon Motokiyo challenged Yoshimori to a duel. Ichijō Yoshiyasu then attempted to restrain
Motokiyo by sending a messenger to Yoshitsune to inform him
of the incident, but Yoshitsune refused to take a hand. Although
Yoshiyasu had refrained from bringing the matter to Yoritomo's
attention, the incident has reached Yoritomo's ears through other
sources. His Lordship is greatly displeased at the arrogance of
Yoshimori and his servants.

19th day. *Bands of robbers are reported in the capital; the Genji
in Tōtomi are reported to be seizing lands.*

Today His Lordship decided on measures to be taken to put
down the outbreak of bands of robbers in the capital and its
environs. So far they have been difficult to suppress. The perpetra-

tors are members of the Heike who have deserted their army and who, now deprived of their original holdings, have forcibly seized ricelands and other fields, and who, moreover, have been preying on the capital and its vicinity, engaging in robbery and attacks.

Another matter which was attended to concerns the recent conduct of immediate vassals residing in Tōtomi Province. On the basis of their military prowess they have been making secret representations to the throne and receiving writs from the ex-sovereign. They have also seized deeds from provincial officials and lords of manors, and they have robbed cultivators of their agricultural yield. It was also reported that the young lord of Izu Aritsuna, son of the governor of Izu Nakatsuna and son-in-law of Yoshitsune, had seized numerous private and public lands in the near provinces. His Lordship has ordered that the matter be brought to the attention of the throne and every effort made to remedy this situation.

21st day. *The sculptor of Buddhist images Jōchō arrives at Kamakura at the invitation of Yoritomo.*

Rain and thunder, followed by clearing. In the evening, which turned very cool, Yoritomo, accompanied by Yoshiyasu, made a tour of the site where the South Chapel is being constructed. The two discussed the matter of the location of the various buildings.

The sculptor of Buddhist images Jōchō has arrived at Kamakura at the invitation of Yoritomo. He will make the images for the chapel.

23rd day. *The governor of Tsushima is reported to be in Korea.*

In compliance with His Lordship's instructions the governor of Mikawa Noriyori had despatched a boat to Tsushima to pick up the governor Chikamitsu. However, it was learned that Chikamitsu, in order to escape the attacks of the Heiji, had gone to Korea on the 4th of the Third Month. Thereupon the local officials were ordered to go to Korea to fetch him. Accordingly the messengers were despatched today. At the same time the constable of Yashima Kawachi Yoshinaga sent a letter to Chikamitsu, informing him that the Heike had been destroyed and that he might return safely.

24th day. *Yoshitsune pleads his case from Koshigoe.*

Minamoto Yoshitsune, who had subdued the enemies of the court as was expected of him, and who had, moreover, delivered the former Great Minister of the Center to Kamakura, had expected with certainty to be rewarded for his efforts. However, by his unprincipled conduct, he had incurred the displeasure of His Lordship and had been barred from entry into Kamakura. Spending his days idly at Koshigoe and feeling extremely depressed, Yoshitsune had addressed a letter to Ōe Hiromoto, stating his case. Although it was opened and read, His Lordship gave no definite instructions regarding the plea. Action is expected later. The letter reads:

Minamoto Yoshitsune, Junior Lieutenant, Left Division, of the Outer Palace Guards, most humbly addresses you. Whereas I have overthrown the enemy of the court as one of your deputies and as the bearer of an imperial mandate; and whereas I have demonstrated the skill of generations of military training and have cleansed the family of its past disgrace and should, hence, be singled out for honors; instead, my prodigious deeds, because of unexpectedly vicious slander, have been ignored. While I have done no wrong, I have been reproached. I have committed no mistakes and I am deserving; yet I have incurred your displeasure, and I weep crimson tears in vain. In thinking over the meaning of this affair, it has occurred to me that good medicine is bitter to the taste and true words are harsh to the ear. This is why I have not been permitted to prove the falsehood of the slanders, and why I am not permitted to enter Kamakura and speak my mind, and why I am spending my days in vain. At such a time, if I do not gaze upon my brother's kind face, there is no meaning in the bond of kindred brotherhood. Is this the fate decreed for me by my former existence? Is it the effect of karma of a previous existence? How sad! If there is no rebirth of the spirit of our late father, to whom might I declare my grievances? Who will bestow sympathy on me? I say this again, though it may be an effusion of my sentiments. This body of mine, a heritage of my parents, became an orphan ere many seasons had passed, when my late lord and father passed on to another world. Clasped to the bosom of my mother, I was taken to Ryūmon-no-maki, Uda Township, Yamato Province, and since that day I have not known a moment free from worry and danger. It was an aimless existence. Rebellions in the capital prohibited travel there; thus I drifted about in the provinces. I hid here and there, making remote places my home, and heeding orders of farmers and natives. However, there was good fortune at last. I entered Kyoto in order to pursue the Heike and, after I had punished Kiso Yoshinaka, in my desire to overthrow the Heike, I often spurred my horse over precipitous boulders, giving no thought for my own life. At other times I have borne the perils of wind and wave on the wide expanse of the sea, submerging to the depths of the seas and clinging to the gills of whales. My harness has been my pillow, and fighting is my profession. I have no other ambition than to allay the anguish of my father's departed soul and to achieve my long-cherished wish. Moreover, as for my appointment as lieutenant of the fifth rank, I regard it as an honor to the house of Minamoto and a position of singular importance, and I can say no more. However, my grief is profound, my sorrow is bitter. If there be no assistance from Buddha and the native deities, how can my appeals be fulfilled? Accordingly, I have called upon the native deities, great and small, and on the invisible way of the Buddha, by disavowing all base motives. I have so vowed in writing on the reverse side of a talisman, marked with the holy seal of the Sacred Ox and distributed to various shrines and temples. And although I have made several vows, I have not yet been pardoned. Our country is a country of the gods. Deities do not accept impropriety. There is no other on whom I can rely. I look up solely to your great generosity. Find an expedient way to convey the message above. Use your excellent discretion and acquaint my brother with the fact that I have committed no wrong. If I receive His Lordship's pardon, the blessings will be extended to my descendants. I shall be relieved of this burden of long standing, and I shall obtain peace in this lifetime. Although I have not exhausted my humble words, I shall close here. I desire that you give this your wise judgment. Humbly and respectfully submitted.

Genreki 2:5 — Minamoto Yoshitsune, Junior Lieutenant of the Outer Palace Guards, Left Division

Submitted to: the Former Official of Inaba Ōe Hiromoto

25th day. Yoritomo warns his emissaries in the west against acceptance of bribes.

Yoritomo has despatched six servants to be assigned, three each, to Hisatsune and Kunihira, who are adjudicating cases in the home provinces. His Lordship has also sent in care of the servants an itemized letter on various matters to be attended to in the capital and nearby provinces. His Lordship has counseled Hisatsune against acceptance of material support from others, and he has warned Kunihira against the showing of any bias in the execution of his duties.

27th day. *A thief who stole the Sword-Beside-the-Sovereign's-Day-time-Throne*[10] *is captured.*

Minamoto Yorikane reported that on the 18th a thief broke into the imperial palace and stole the Sword-Beside-the-Sovereign's-Daytime-Throne. The theft was ascertained immediately by Yorikane and women officials of the palace, who became greatly excited. The capture was made by the guardsman Hisazane, who pursued the robber outside the headquarters of the Left Outer Palace Guards, and the sword has been returned to its place. It is reported that the condition of the culprit is critical, for he had attempted to kill himself as he was being bound. His Lordship, saying that a warrior such as Hisazane should be commended, has entrusted Yorikane with a sword to be presented to Hisazane. He will be highly elated.

SIXTH MONTH

2nd day. *Nine former Heike are ordered to be exiled.*

The Council of State has issued a decree on the 20th of the past month, listing the names of those to be exiled. The Middle Councilor Minamoto Michichika, reporting to the council, received the order from the director of the sovereign's private office Mitsumasa. The list arrived at Kamakura today. It reads:

To be exiled
The former Major Councilor Taira Tokitada to Noto
The former director of the imperial storehouse Taira Nobumoto to Bingo
The former Middle Captain of the Left Taira Tokizane to Suō
The former provisional junior assistant minister of the Ministry of Military Affairs Koreaki to Izumo
The senior assistant high priest of Buddhism Ryōkō to Awa
The provisional junior assistant high priest of Buddhism Zenshin to Aki
The provisional master of Buddhist Asceticism Chūkai to Izu
The teacher Nōen to Bitchū
The teacher Gyōmei to Hitachi

5th day. *Yoritomo makes a vassal of a craftsman who fledges arrows; Iwashimizu Hachiman Shrine receives a grant of land.*

Among the sons of the former imperial police Suesada, now

[10] *Hi-no-omashi-no-goken.*

prisoner of war, is one who is called Genta Munesue. Of late he has changed his name to Munenaga, following his adoption by the young lord Hayami Mitsunaga, and he is reported to have come to Kanto secretly to determine whether or not his father Suesada was still alive. Now this Munesue is extremely adept at archery and horsemanship, and in particular in fledging arrows, an art which he had learned by oral instruction from Yano Kichinai. When by chance His Lordship heard of his reputation from Chūzenji Okujirō Hironaga, an intimate friend and principal resident of Kazusa, in connection with the matter of Obu Manor, a hereditary domain in Yoritomo's mother's line which is situated in the same province, he notified Munesue that he should like to see samples of his work. Munesue submitted a hunting arrow which he had fledged. His Lordship was so pleased with it that he has ordered Munesue enrolled as an immediate vassal.

An addition to the domains of Iwashimizu Shrine was made today by His Lordship. The grant reads:

GRANTED: A domain to Hachiman Shrine
Situated at Minota, Awa Province
The aforementioned *hō*[11] is hereby granted to the said shrine. Its control shall be assumed immediately by the junior intendant Ninken, who will administer its affairs and who may use the products of the said place for prayer offerings and for expenses of the religious activities of the shrine. The grant is thus made.
Genreki 2:6,5   Former Assistant Captain of the Military
                                                          Guards, Minamoto Yoritomo

7th day. *Yoritomo is advised against a personal meeting with Taira Munemori.*

His Lordship discussed with Ōe Hiromoto the question of whether to grant an audience to the former Great Minister of the Center Munemori, who is expected to return to the capital shortly. Although Yoritomo had permitted a meeting with the Middle Captain Shigehira when the latter was in Kamakura, Hiromoto had a different opinion to offer in this case. Said Hiromoto to Yoritomo: "The former case does not provide a precedent for this instance. Your Lordship has restored the country to peace and you have been raised to imperial second rank. Munemori is an enemy of the

---

[11] A *hō* was a group of five households.

nation, and he is a prisoner who has been deprived of his court rank. Should Your Lordship permit an audience with him, you might, on the contrary, invite contemptuous criticism from him." His Lordship thus dropped his plan of meeting Munemori and agreed to observe him from behind a curtain.

Shortly after the men assembled Munemori, wearing a plain white ceremonial robe and an unfolded cap, stepped out of the west room just beyond the sliding doors where the governor of Musashi, Lord Hōjō, the governor of Suruga, the young lord Ashikaga, Ōe Hiromoto, the provisional governor of Chikugo, and the lieutenant of the Right Horse Bureau Adachi were waiting in attendance. His Lordship then ordered Hiki Yoshikazu to convey the following statement to Munemori: "I do not hold a deep enmity toward your family but, as long as I have been commanded by an imperial decision, I have had to pursue and attack you. It is regrettable that you have had to make this long journey to this remote place, but it has been my desire to accord you the treatment due a warrior." When Yoshikazu, bowing respectfully before Munemori, conveyed His Lordship's message to him, he offered his seat to Yoshikazu and otherwise appeared to be extremely accommodating. But Munemori's reply was vague except for his wish to be permitted to maintain a bare existence, to take the tonsure, and to lead the life of a Buddhist. Here is a descendant in the fourth generation of a shogun. He has received the heritage of a brave and gallant family. He is the second son of the chancellor Kiyomori. He has been the recipient of any office or emolument he desired. Now he spurns the dignity of the life of a warrior, and he shows no respect for office and rank. Why should he show such disrespect for Yoshikazu? There is no cause to commute the sentence of death for him. Those who witnessed the scene regarded Munemori's conduct as contemptuous.

9th day. *Yoshitsune is ordered to escort Taira Munemori to Kyoto; the priests of Nara demand the head of Taira Shigehira.*[12]

Today Yoshitsune, who had been staying at Sakamagari, received Munemori for delivery to the capital. His Lordship has ordered Tachibana Kiminaga, Asaba Munenobu, Usami Sane-

---

[12] Shigehira had burned the Nara temples during the early months of the war.

masa, and their following of warriors to join Yoshitsune's party and to assist in escorting Munemori. Yoshitsune, who had expected to be honored for his great feat of subjugating the Heiji upon his return to Kanto, has found the situation quite the contrary and has now turned back to the capital without even the privilege of an audience with Yoritomo. His resentment is greater than ever.

As for the courtier Shigehira, who had been in the custody of Kanō Munemochi since last year, he has been handed over to Minamoto Yorikane. He too has been sent off for delivery to Nara at the request of the monks of the southern capital.

13th day. *Yoshitsune is dispossessed of his lands.*

Twenty-four places of former Heike lands which had been assigned to Yoshitsune have been taken away from him. In charge of this matter are Ōe Hiromoto and the provisional governor of Chikugo Toshikane. Yoshitsune was able to accomplish his military feats only as a deputy of His Lordship and only with His Lordship's vassals who had been assigned to him. He could not have turned back the rebels with divine assistance only. However, it has been his boast that he alone was responsible for the great victory and, upon his return to the capital, he had even dared to say that those who harbor resentment toward Kanto should flock to his command. Even if he turns against His Lordship, how can he avoid reprisal? His Lordship has taken this step of dispossessing Yoshitsune because he is extremely angry at his brother and suspicious of his ambitions.

14th day. *The Genji send men to Korea to rescue Chikamitsu.*

Minamoto Noriyori and Kawachi Yoshinaga have sent escorts to Korea and have brought back the governor of Tsushima Chikamitsu to Tsushima, in compliance with His Lordship's wishes. Two years ago, as Chikamitsu prepared to go to the capital, he had been forced to return to Tsushima because of the retreat of the Heike to the west. The Heike controlled the land and sea routes between Tsushima and Kyoto. Moreover, with the arrival of Taira Tomomori at Yashima in Shikoku, and with the commissioning of Tanenao as junior assistant governor general of Kyushu, these two regions had gone over to the Heike camp. However, Chika-mitsu refused to yield to the Heike, who then sent three expeditions against him. Two of these were under Kō Jirō Tsunenao, a heredi-tary retainer of Tanenao, and one under Munefusa, a follower of Tanemasu. Constantly the Heike sent their men to Tsushima to attack Chikamitsu or to administer the island. When it became dangerous for him to live in Tsushima he braved the sea and crossed over to Korea on the 4th of the Third Month of the past year. His wife, who was with child, accompanied him. She gave birth to the child in a temporary hut built by Chikamitsu on a desolate field. At the time of the birth wild tigers approached the hut, but Chikamitsu's followers killed them. The king of Korea, who had heard of him, made him a grant of three provinces. Just when Chikamitsu had become a subject of Korea, Yoritomo's mis-sion arrived to fetch him home. The king, regretful to see him leave, presented him with three tribute boats laden with valuable presents.

16th day. *Yoritomo is pleased with the work of Hisatsune and Kunihira in adjudicating cases brought by the people in the home provinces.*

Hisatsune and Kunihira have been making an inspection tour of the home provinces as representatives of Kanto, and with the sanction of the ex-sovereign they have been adjudicating cases brought by the people in that region. So far they have been con-ducting themselves most properly, for which His Lordship is greatly pleased. Recently one Tamanoi Sukeshige of Owari Prov-ince, who has been terrorizing the people, was reported to have disobeyed an imperial edict. Accordingly the two commissioners had been instructed by His Lordship to serve Tamanoi with a summons, which he has ignored. In fact, he has spoken disdain-fully of His Lordship. As this matter has been reported at the time to His Lordship, Yoritomo today ordered Toshikane to issue an order which states that anyone who violates an imperial command will be barred from the capital, and anyone who makes light of Kanto will be barred from Kamakura. Tamanoi should be ap-prehended immediately.

18th day. *Taira Yorimori takes the tonsure.*

A few days ago Taira Yorimori sent a messenger to His Lordship to inform him that on the 29th of the past month he had taken the tonsure in accordance with a long-cherished desire. He took the step near the Tōdai-ji. He has taken the priestly name of Jūren.

20th day. *An earthquake is recorded; Kashii Shrine of Chikuzen Province lodges a complaint with Yoritomo.*

Cloudy skies. In the middle of the night there occurred a great earthquake. There were several tremors in the course of an hour.

Kimitomo, a former official of Kashii Shrine of Chikuzen Province, is reported to have committed abuses against the shrine and has stopped the transfer and rebuilding of the shrine. Moreover, because of his former position, he has seized the administration of the shrine. A complaint and a request that he be punished have been filed at Kamakura by shrine officials. Consequently His Lordship has instructed Toshikane to draft an order commanding Kimitomo to withdraw and to permit the resumption of the transfer of the shrine. It was added that, if he refused to do so, a special commissioner would be despatched and the matter adjudicated at law.

21st day. *Taira Munemori and his son Kiyomune are executed; Taira Shigehira is returned to Kyoto from Nara.*

When Yoshitsune's party arrived at the inn at Shinohara, Ōmi Province, he ordered Tachibana Kiminaga to execute Taira Munemori. Munemori's son Kiyomune was killed by Hori Kagemitsu when Yoshitsune's party arrived at Nojiguchi. Throughout the journey the priest Honsei of Ōhara had attended the father and son as their religious teacher, and the two had given themselves over to his guidance. They had, as a result, renounced their enmity and had vowed to be reborn in Paradise.

It was reported that Shigehira had again returned to the capital. As for Munemori, he was a man of noble birth on his mother's side who rose to the position of Great Minister of the Center. But his crime of being an enemy of the imperial court could not be mitigated. . . .

22nd day. *At the request of the monks of Nara Taira Shigehira is again delivered to the Tōdai-ji.*

23rd day. *The heads of Munemori and Kiyomune are delivered to Kyoto; Shigehira is beheaded at Nara.*

The heads of Munemori and Kiyomune were delivered to Rokujō-Kawara by Yoshitsune's retainers. Coming forward to receive the heads were the imperial police Tomoyasu, the lieutenant, sixth rank, Akisada, Nobumori, Kimitomo, the clerk Akimoto, Fushō Tsunehiro, and Kaneyasu. The heads were hung on the trees before the prison upon the orders of the head official of the Controlling Board of the Right Mitsumasa. Mitsumasa's orders were received by the intendant Iemichi, who transmitted them to the director of the sovereign's private office. The latter then transmitted them to the clerk Takamochi, who in turn transmitted them to the imperial police Tomoyasu.

Today Taira Shigehira was beheaded at Nara. The monks of Nara had persistently demanded his head for his part in the burning and destruction of the temples.

25th day. *Yoritomo reverses his decision on Sasaki Naritsuna.*

During the period of Heike rule Sasaki Naritsuna had turned against the Minamoto. When the Heike fled the capital, Naritsuna had followed and served them. However, in the Battle of Ichinotani, Naritsuna's son had served the Genji and had slain Taira Michimori, for which Naritsuna had sought recognition. But Yoritomo would not forgive his past errors and had not approved the request. Whereupon Naritsuna had attached himself to the chamberlain Kimisuke and had appealed to him. As a result Yoritomo has arranged to have Naritsuna resume control of his original fief in recognition of his son's deeds.[13]

SEVENTH MONTH

2nd day. *The details of Taira Munemori's execution are reported to Yoritomo.*

[13] For Yoritomo's earlier decision regarding Naritsuna's request, see Juei 3:2,27. There Naritsuna's name appears as "Moritsuna."

7th day. *The former governor of Chikugo Taira Sadayoshi is pardoned by Yoritomo.*

The former governor of Chikugo Sadayoshi is a member of the Heike and he was a close friend of the late chancellor Kiyomori. However, before the defeat of the Heike in the west, Sadayoshi had absconded from the Heike ranks and had vanished. Recently his whereabouts was disclosed when he appeared without warning before Utsunomiya Tomotsuna to plead for a pardon from Kanto. He explained that when he realized that the Heike was doomed, he had taken the tonsure to avoid misfortune, and that he had since been living in seclusion in the mountains, concerned only with the salvation of his soul. He explained further that he could not hope to continue to lead even such an existence without Kanto's amnesty, and that it was his sincere request to be placed in Tomotsuna's custody. When Tomotsuna brought the matter to Yoritomo's attention, the latter refused to grant an amnesty on the grounds that Sadayoshi was a close relative of the Heiji and that his act of surrendering to the Genji at this time was cause for suspicion. But Tomotsuna persisted in requesting permission to assume custody of Sadayoshi, saying that Sadayoshi, although a Heike and while still residing in the capital, had sought to join the Genji when Yoritomo first called for troops. He had been prevented from joining the Genji by Taira Munemori, but he had persuaded Hatakeyama Shigeyoshi and Oyamada Arishige to do so. These men subsequently joined with His Lordship and participated in battles against the hated enemy. Sadayoshi could not have been thinking of his personal advantage when he took these steps, which were, in fact, highly commendable acts. Tomotsuna declared that if Sadayoshi should later be guilty of treachery, His Lordship had his permission to destroy Tomotsuna's family. Because of this plea an amnesty was granted to Sadayoshi and he was remanded to the custody of Tomotsuna.

12th day. *Yoritomo orders Kunihira and Hisatsuna to Kyushu; he permits Noriyori to return to Kyoto.*

His Lordship has instructed Nakahara Hisatsune and Kondō Kunihira to proceed to Kyushu on an inspection tour, after obtaining the sanction of the ex-sovereign. They have been charged with the mission of checking the unrestrained outlawry of warriors and of remedying the confused situation with regard to manors which are to be restored to their original owners, whether provincial officials or lords of manors, so that payment of annual tributes might be resumed.

Although Yoshitsune had returned to the capital following the conquest of the Heike, in accordance with His Lordship's orders, Noriyori had remained in Kyushu. In the meantime, because of numerous complaints of outlawry on government lands in the home provinces, the court had summoned Noriyori to Kyoto. However, because of the lawless activities of Heike partisans in Kyushu, such as the seizure of lands by Kikuchi and Harada, His Lordship had requested the court to rescind the order recalling Noriyori to Kyoto. Whereupon the ex-sovereign had advised Noriyori that he might have cause for regret if he should come up to the capital while interference on shrine and temple lands in Kyushu remained unchecked.

Today His Lordship despatched a note to Noriyori, assuring him that now he might return to the capital without anxiety, provided he took steps to post land stewards on the confiscated Heike lands and on the lands of Tanenao, Tanetō, Hidetō, Harada, Sakai, and Yamaga.

15th day. *The priest Mongaku is reported to be using questionable methods to obtain land.*

Through a flattering recommendation of Kanto, the priest Mongaku of Shingo-ji had gained access to the ex-sovereign and had obtained His Majesty's seal to a document outlining the history of his temple. It is dated the 25th of the First Month. It has been rumored, to His Lordship's astonishment, that Mongaku had caused distress among holders of manors in the near provinces by his attempts to obtain donations of land from them by the use of this document. Yoritomo is amazed that a Buddhist priest could display such depravity, and he has ordered Toshikane to draft a directive prohibiting such an outrageous practice.

19th day. *An earthquake in Kyoto is reported; Yoshitsune's residence is reported to be undamaged.*

Earthquakes have been rare of late, but on the 19th, at 11 A.M., a severe earthquake shook Kyoto. Such Buddhist structures as the Tokuchōju-in, Rengeō-in, and the Saishōkō-in were upset or damaged. Also, the ridge of the roof of the Fujiwara residential palace was broken, and buildings in the kitchen quarters were over-turned. The divination report which enjoins caution is not being regarded lightly. The strangest phenomenon concerns Yoshitsune's residence at Rokujō-Muromachi which—from its gates and fence to the buildings themselves—was not damaged at all.

22nd day. Yoritomo sends directives to Genji vassals in Kyushu to desist from harming Tōyama Jirō of Hiuga and his followers, who have been made vassals.

23rd day. The vice governor of Yamashiro Hisakane, an accomplished musician, arrives at Kamakura at Yoritomo's invitation.

26th day. The ritualist Chūkai, a member of the Taira, is exiled to Izu.

29th day. Takashina Yasutsune reports that the recent earthquake was a consequence of the banishment of the former Heike; he inquires whether pardons are forthcoming for those banished.

EIGHTH MONTH

4th day. Yoritomo orders his vassals to seek out and kill Yukiie.
    The former governor of Bizen Yukiie is His Lordship's uncle. Although he had been sent against Heiji positions from time to time, he had failed to be effective. Consequently Yoritomo had staunchly refused to reward him. Yukiie himself has not taken the initiative to come to Yoritomo to pay homage. Presently in semi-seclusion in the west, he is using his close associates in Kanto to harass the people. Moreover, it has come to light that Yukiie plans to rebel against Yoritomo. Therefore today His Lordship has written to Sasaki Sadatsuna to rally immediate vassals in the home provinces and to seek out and kill Yukiie.

13th day. Nakahara Hisatsune and Kondō Kunihira receive court sanction for their mission to Kyushu.

A messenger sent by Hisatsune and Kunihira has arrived from Kyoto to report that the two have received a mandate from the ex-sovereign's government and have departed for Kyushu. A copy of the mandate was also brought by the messenger and submitted to Toshikane. It reads:

The ex-sovereign's government orders to: The government headquarters in Kyushu and to officials of local government centers in the provinces under its jurisdiction
That the interference of warriors on lands cease forthwith in accordance with the judgments rendered by Nakahara Hisatsune and Kondō Kunihira, the representatives of Minamoto Yoritomo, junior second rank, and that the provinces and manors be returned to the control of provincial officials and lords of manors

It has been our purpose, upon completion of the war of chastisement, to return control of domains to provincial officials and lords of manors according to precedent. However, the arbitrary seizure of lands by warriors has made the administration of justice impossible. Thus, during the Sixth Month, it has been decreed by the ex-sovereign's government that provincial affairs are to be administered by provincial officials, that manorial affairs are to be administered by owners of manors, that new developments are to be ruled out forever, and that former precedents are to be adhered to. We are despatching Hisatsune and Kunihira, together with a letter from the Lord Minamoto, to check outlawry and to restore government offices and private manors to the provincial officials and lords of manors who held them before. The government headquarters and all officials at local government offices in the provinces under its jurisdiction are enjoined to take special heed of this decree and to act in strict accordance thereunto. Thus decreed.

Genreki 2:7,28   The *Ason* Ōe, Clerk of the Ex-Sovereign's Office, Chief of the Weaving Office and concurrently Senior Clerk of the Office of the Empress's Household
The *Ason* Fujiwara Sanefusa, Intendant, Major Councilor and concurrently Master of the Office of the Empress's Household
The *Ason* Fujiwara Chikatsune, Secretary, Provisional Junior Assistant Minister of the Ministry of the Imperial Household
The *Ason* Fujiwara Narinori, Minister of the Ministry of Civil Affairs
The *Ason* Fujiwara Sadatsune, Assistant Head Official of the Investigators of Records of Outgoing Officials, and concurrently Provisional Senior Secretary of the Office of the Empress's Household
The *Ason* Fujiwara, Provisional Middle Councilor
The *Ason* Fujiwara Sadanaga, Minor Controller of the Right
The *Ason* Taira Chikamune, Imperial Adviser and Provisional Governor of Sanuki
The *Ason* Fujiwara Chikamasa, Provisional Assistant Captain

of the Outer Palace Guards, Left Division, and concurrently
Senior Secretary of the Office of the Empress's Household

The *Ason* Takashina Yasutsune, Minister of the Treasury and
concurrently Provisional Governor of Bingo

The *Ason* Taira Motochika, Minor Controller of the Left

The *Ason* Fujiwara Mitsumasa, Head Official of the Controlling
Board of the Right of the Great Council of State, and con-
currently Assistant Master of the Office of the Empress's
Household

The *Ason* Fujiwara Norisue, Director of the Bureau of Car-
pentry

The *Ason* Takashina Tsunenaka, Director of the Bureau of
Horses, Right Division

14th day. *The era name is changed from Genreki 2 to Bunji 1.*

BUNJI 1 [1185]

20th day. *The priest Senkō-bō of Izu arrives at Kamakura.*

21st day. *Kashima Shrine complains to Yoritomo regarding the
conduct of the land steward Shimokōbe Yoshimasa.*

23rd day. *The artist Tamehisa returns to Kamakura to paint pic-
tures for the new chapel.*

24th day. *Shimokōbe Yukihira returns from the west and recounts
details of the late war.*

27th day. *Ōba Kageyoshi reports a strange phenomenon at a
shrine; Yoritomo orders offerings to be made and the sacred
dance performed.*

At 11 A.M. the shrine dedicated to Minamoto Kagemasa[14]
rumbled, as if an earthquake had occurred. Because of strange
happenings earlier at this shrine, Kageyoshi was alarmed and reported the matter to Yoritomo. Thereupon His Lordship visited
the shrine and discovered that the doors on both sides of the
altar had collapsed. To dispel the evil spirits His Lordship, in
addition to offering a written prayer to the shrine, presented 2 *tan*
of indigo-dyed cloth to the vestal virgins and ordered them to

[14] A member of the Minamoto clan, also known as Kamakura Gongorō, famed
for his bravery and fighting prowess. He flourished in the 11th century.

perform the sacred dance. After the performance His Lordship
returned to his quarters.

28th day. *Yoritomo replies to the ex-sovereign regarding two
manors in Yamato Province.*

29th day. *Six Genji vassals are given provincial posts.*

A report on the appointments which were made on the 16th
has arrived at Kamakura today. Many Genji have received imperial favor. The Genji appointed are: Yamana Yoshinori, governor
of Izu; Ōuchi Koreyoshi, governor of Sagami; Ashikaga Yoshikane,
vice governor of Kazusa; Kagami Tōmitsu, governor of Shinano;
Yasuda Yoshisuke, governor of Echigo; and Minamoto Yoshitsune,
governor of Iyo. Regarding Yoshitsune's appointment, His Lordship had secretly communicated his personal feelings on the matter
to Yasutsune during the Fourth Month. Yoritomo had expressed
his disapproval of Yoshitsune because of his unprincipled behavior, but Yasutsune reported that he has been unable to stop
the appointment and that it has been left entirely to the ex-
sovereign's discretion.

It was also reported that the ex-sovereign is about to announce
the appointments for five other provinces now under the control
of Kanto. The considerations which will govern the appointments
are that the appointees will serve the court loyally on the one
hand and that they will enhance Yoritomo's position on the other.

30th day. *The remains of Yoritomo's father are transferred to
Kamakura.*

In accordance with a long-cherished ambition, His Lordship
has tried to show the greatest devotion to his ancestors, but to date
he has not been able to fully achieve his aim. Since the death of
his father in the Heiji Disturbance, Yoritomo has not failed to
read the *Lotus Sutra* daily and to pray for the salvation of his
father's departed soul. Also, in order to show the fullest respect and
reverence for his father, Yoritomo has planned to build a temple
in his honor, and he has secretly sought the ex-sovereign's sanction to have his father's remains transferred to this temple. On the
12th the ex-sovereign ordered Yoshitomo's remains near the East

Prison in Kyoto to be exhumed and, together with the head of Kamada Jirō Masakiyo, to be delivered to Kamakura. The special emissary for this occasion is the secretary Ōe Kintomo, who arrived from the capital today. His Lordship has gone to Kosegawa to receive the remains. Monks from Shingo-ji, the temple in the care of the priest Mongaku, carried the remains in containers hung from their necks. His Lordship, changing from the usual ceremonial robe of bright silk to a plain white robe, received the remains and returned to Kamakura.

His Lordship has shown an unusual devotion to the Shosha-zan Temple in Harima Province, which has been associated with the reading of the *Lotus Sutra* and wherein are deposited the remains of Jōkū Shōnin. For this reason His Lordship had earlier urged the *ason* Yasutsune to restore and promote this temple to its former greatness. Today His Lordship again reminded the court of this matter.

Chapter V

NINTH MONTH

1st day. *The imperial emissary, Ōe Kintomo, calls on Yoritomo.*

An imperial emissary, the imperial police Ōe Kintomo, called at headquarters. He was pleased to have an audience with His Lordship, who proffered him wine, but the emissary took his leave after a few cups. On the occasion a gift of 10 *ryō* of gold dust, and one horse, saddled, was made to the envoy. Moreover, with the secretary Kunimichi as bearer, 20 *hiki* of glossed silk and 30 *tan* of indigo silk were sent to his lodgings, said to be the residence of Hiki Yoshikazu at Higashimikado.

2nd day. *Yoritomo sends a special mission to Kyoto.*

Kajiwara Kagesue and Gishō-bō Jōjin have departed for the capital on a mission. They have been commissioned to attend to the matter of gifts for the officiating priest at the dedication ceremonies of the South Chapel and to that of decorative objects for the chapel, for the most part already procured and stored in Kyoto. Also, regarding the Heike partisans who have not yet proceeded to their place of exile, the mission is to inquire whether prompt imperial action is to be taken against them. His Lordship has no objection to their remaining at their present domiciles if they have obtained, or will subsequently obtain, imperial pardons.

The mission has also been charged with the task of calling on Yoshitsune, in Yoritomo's name, to inquire into the whereabouts of Yukiie, and to suggest to Yoshitsune that he slay Yukiie. Kagesue was also instructed to watch Yoshitsune's movements.

On the 20th of the Fifth Month the former major councilor Taira Tokitada and others of lesser rank had been ordered exiled by a decree of the Council of State, but, as they have continued to reside in Kyoto to this day, His Lordship is highly indignant. Because of the intimate relationship of the major councilor to Yoshitsune, who is the former's son-in-law, Tokitada has been detained. This action was taken, moreover, because of the prevalence of rumors that Yukiie might be induced to join Tokitada and Yoshitsune in a movement to defy Kanto.

3rd day. *Yoshitomo's remains are interred in the grounds of the South Chapel.*

At 11 P.M. the remains of the late director of the Horse Bureau, Left Division, Yoshitomo, together with the head of Kamada Masakiyo, were interred in the grounds of the South Chapel. On the road a palanquin was used. The arrangements were in charge of Keigan-bō and Senkō-bō. The procession was in the order of the governor of Musashi Ōuchi Yoshinobu, the young lord of Mutsu Mori Yoritaka, and Ōuchi Koreyoshi. During the Heiji insurrection Yoshinobu, who was known then as the young lord of Hiraga, had been an ally of His Lordship's deceased father. Yoritaka's father, the young lord of Mori Yoshitaka, had given his life for Yoritomo's late father. It was for reasons of such past friendship that these men were specially selected.

4th day. *Ōe Kintomo leaves for Kyoto.*

Ōe Kintomo, the imperial emissary, returned to the capital, bearing with him the most cordial farewell presents from Yoritomo. His sojourn here had been prolonged because of a cold. The emissary was to convey to Kyoto, on the one hand, Yoritomo's personal solicitations and prayers regarding the great earthquake of the Seventh Month and, on the other hand, His Lordship's plans for the declaration of a country-wide moratorium.[1] The emissary was also asked to pay special homage to the departed soul of the Ex-Sovereign Sutoku. These requests were made because of Yoritomo's sincere concern for the prosperity of the Kyoto court.

[1] *Tokusei,* literally, "benevolent government," the summary cancellation of debts and mortgages. From the context, however, it is doubtful whether a sweeping *tokusei,* such as those resorted to by the shogunate in the thirteenth century following the Mongol invasions to protect the debt-ridden warrior class, is meant here. It was probably a modified *tokusei,* implying the virtuous, considerate application of laws in view of the emergency.

5th day. *Ikōji Temple of Musashi complains of interference on its lands by Koyama Aritaka.*

As the result of an official communication from a priest of Ikōji, charging that Koyama Tarō Aritaka had interfered with the estates of the temple, an order to cease the interference and to grant the temple fiscal immunity according to precedents was issued. The priest was instructed to submit in person to the Mandokoro documentary evidence, if there be any, and the details. In charge of this matter were Koremune, Takanao, the secretary Tachibana Korehiro, and the secretary Fujiwara Kunimichi. Affixed to the order were the monograms of the ex-governor of Inaba Hiromoto, the secretary of the Bureau of Statistics Nikaidō Yukimasa, Ōnakatomi Akiie, and the secretary of the Right Horse Bureau Adachi Tōmoto. Shindōji Toshinaga and Konakada Mitsuie will, as official envoys, call on Aritaka.

10th day. *The Bishop of Onjō-ji is invited to Kamakura to officiate at the forthcoming chapel dedication ceremonies.*

As officiating priest for the dedication ceremonies of the chapel, the Bishop Kugen of Hongaku-in, Onjō-ji, has been invited. Today his letter of acceptance has arrived. Thus the various details of lodging connected with the priest's journey from the capital have been assigned today to various immediate vassals. In charge of this matter are the former official of Inaba Hiromoto and the assistant director of the office of the high priestess of the Kamo Shrine Nakahara Chikayoshi. The various details of the day of departure will be attended to by Sasaki Sadatsune.

12th day. *Kagesue and Jōjin arrive in Kyoto.*

Kagesue and Jōjin have arrived at the capital to present to the court the matter of the exiled individuals.

18th day. *The Middle Councilor Yoshida Tsunefusa seeks Yoritomo's friendship.*

The Middle Councilor Yoshida Tsunefusa is an upright and faithful minister. Therefore he has been permitted to communicate at all times with Yoritomo. Now they share each other's good and bad fortunes. Thus, when Tsunefusa secretly communicated his desire for a promotion, Yoritomo offered to recommend him.

21st day. *Noriyori's messenger arrives in Kamakura.*

A messenger of the governor of Mikawa Noriyori has arrived at Kamakura. He reports that Noriyori had earlier left Kyushu and is now en route to the capital, where he is expected to arrive this month. Although he had received strict orders to report to the capital during the Eighth Month, he has expressed his regrets that his arrival there had been delayed by a storm. It was to convey these reasons for the delay that the messenger had come from Kyoto. It is His Lordship's opinion that Noriyori is an obedient vassal and respectful of his lord's authority.

23rd day. *Taira Tokitada departs for his place of exile.*

It was reported that the courtier and ex-Major Councilor Tokitada has departed for Noto, his place of exile.

29th day. *The floor of the South Chapel is planed and the artisans are rewarded.*

The planing of the board floor of the South Chapel adytum was completed, and His Lordship was pleased to inspect it. In appreciation the artisans were each rewarded with a *hiki* of glossed silk. Deputized to make the awards for His Lordship were the provisional governor of Chikugo Toshikane and the secretary of the Bureau of Statistics Yukimasa.

TENTH MONTH

3rd day. *Jōjin returns from Kyoto with robes and ceremonial equipment for Yoritomo.*

Gifts for the officiating priest and guest priests of the dedication ceremonies of the South Chapel, as well as presents from all quarters, were examined by His Lordship, and instructions regarding them were discussed with the director of the Left Horse Bureau Ichijō Yoshiyasu. Also, robes and twenty implements for His Lordship and offerings collectors had been brought down from Kyoto last night by Jōjin, who had been assigned to fetch them. These implements will be distributed today to the people assigned to the various duties of the exercises under the supervision of Ōe Hiromoto and the provisional governor of Chikugo Toshikane.

6th day. *Kagesue reports on his mission.*

Returning from Kyoto, Kajiwara Kagesue reported to Yoritomo as follows: "When I called at Yoshitsune's residence and announced my mission, he pleaded illness and would not see me. As this confidential matter could not be transmitted to him through a messenger, I returned to my lodgings at Rokujō-Aburakōji. When I called on him again a few days later, he met me, leaning on an armrest. He looked extremely emaciated and showed scars from self-inflicted burns. As a test of his loyalty, I suggested that he slay Yukiie, to which he replied that it was his intention to look into the matter without delay and to rectify the situation. He indicated that he would do so even were the culprit a mere thief—which he is not, but a member of the Minamoto, as Yoshitsune himself is. Yoshitsune added that Yukiie was no ordinary warrior who could be coerced into submission by the mere despatch of retainers, and that he himself would carry out the suggestion as soon as he could seek medical attention and recover from his present illness." Yoritomo remarked: "The fact that he endorses Yukiie is evident in the illness which he has feigned." Kagetoki concurred, saying, "He refused a meeting the first day but consented to one a few days later. From this fact it may be inferred that if one were to deny himself food for a day and sleep for a night, he would look emaciated. As for scars from burns, there were several, but they could be applied in a brief moment— not to mention several days. If this is true, Yoshitsune has contrived such a deception in the period of a day or two. There is not the slightest doubt that he is acting in concert with Yukiie and making preparations."

9th day. *Tosa-bō Shōshun is sent to kill Yoshitsune.*

The deliberations of the past several days have been concerned with the subject of the slaying of Yoshitsune. Now Tosa-bō Shōshun is to be sent for this purpose. As Shōshun had **volunteered** for the mission when many others had excused themselves, he received the special acknowledgment of His Lordship. When the time for his departure arrived, he appeared before His Lordship and requested sympathetic consideration for his aged mother and children who are living in Shimotsuke. Yoritomo was pleased to consent, and accordingly, made a grant to him of the Nakaizumi Manor in Shimotsuke. Shōshun has mustered a force of eighty-three mounted men, including Mikami Iesue, who is a younger brother of Shōshun, Nishigori Saburō, Kodama Tarō, and Shiozawa Jirō. It is estimated that the journey will take nine days.

11th day. *A mural is completed at the chapel.*

The application of colors to the mural behind the image of Buddha in the chapel has been completed. It depicts auspicious symbols of paradise and the figures of twenty-five bodhisattvas. Upon examination of the mural, His Lordship noted that in the section depicting paradise the crescent moon blocked the view of its own shadow, and that the painting in its present form was not in conformity with the original text. The artist, unable to correct the defect, removed it by scraping.

It was decided today to remand to Sasaki Saburō Naritsuna, who formerly used different Chinese characters for his name, his former tax-lands, but with the provision that they remain under the general supervision of Sasaki Tarō Sadatsuna. The reason is that while Naritsuna and Sadatsuna do not belong to the same family, the latter's family has been the imperial gendarme of the Sasaki manors, and the former's lands lie within the region of Sadatsuna's general supervision.

13th day. *Yoshitsune seeks the support of the ex-sovereign.*

On the 11th of the past month and again today Yoshitsune secretly called at the ex-sovereign's palace and is said to have addressed him thus: "Yukiie is planning to stage a revolt against Kanto because Yoritomo had issued orders to kill him. Yukiie is indignant that he, Yoritomo's uncle, who has not been guilty of any offense or neglect, should be ordered to be killed. Although I have tried repeatedly to restrain him, Yukiie would not listen. As for myself, I have subdued the Heike and restored peace. Was

not this a meritorious deed? Yet, Yoritomo has shown no appreciation. He has completely revoked what lands he had allotted to me.
Moreover, there are rumors that he plans to kill me. To meet that
danger I have taken up Yukiie's cause. For these reasons I seek
a warrant of the Council of State to proceed against Yoritomo. If
imperial sanction is not forthcoming, we two would prefer to kill
ourselves." It has been reported that the imperial response was
sympathetic to Yukiie.

14th day. *The ex-sovereign orders a vassal of Yoritomo to report
to Kyoto.*

A directive of the ex-sovereign, ordering Yasuda Yoshisada to
report to Kyoto, has arrived at Kamakura. It declares that Yoshisada
has violated imperial commands and urges Yoritomo to add his
reprimand. The ex-sovereign's order, which has been attended
to, reads:

Regarding Kosugi *mikuri* of the Ise Shrine, an imperial decree ascertain-
ing its ownership by the shrine has been issued earlier. However, there
has been a protest by the shrine that the provincial official continues to
interfere in the administration of the land. This is a deplorable development. It is hereby ordered and transmitted that the said land be restored immediately to its original status in accordance with an earlier
directive of the ex-sovereign.

9:24   Director of the Horse Bureau,
                                                    Right Division
                                                    per order [monogram]
To: The Governor of Tōtomi

15th day. *The ex-sovereign requests remittance of expenses for
the high priestess of the Ise Shrine.*

A directive of the ex-sovereign has arrived at Kamakura, ordering
the remittance of expenses for the high priestess of the Ise Shrine,
and for the investigation and the execution of justice regarding the
seizure of lands belonging to the Ise Shrine by groups of warriors
living on isolated estates of the shrine, such as Izawa-kambe,
Suzumo-no-mikuri, Numata-no-mimaki, Imbe-kambe, and Takō-
mikuri. These two orders were issued separately.

16th day. *Usuki Koretaka and Ogata Koreyoshi receive imperial
pardons.*

In the course of a battle last year Usuki Koretaka and Ogata Koreyoshi, local lords of Bungo, had destroyed the sanctuary of the Usa Shrine and had usurped its sacred treasures. Consequently a writ of banishment had been issued against them by the Council of State, but on the 4th of the past month an extraordinary pardon was granted to them.

17th day. *Shōshun attacks Yoshitsune, but is repulsed.*

Tosa-bō Shōshun, in compliance with Yoritomo's orders of a few days ago, attacked the Rokujō-Muromachi residence of Yoshitsune with the support of more than sixty mounted men under Mionoya Jōrō. Yoshitsune's warriors being absent on an excursion to Nishikōbe at the time, there was only a handful of retainers. However, with the support of Satō Tadanobu and others, Yoshitsune threw open the gates of his residence and emerged to fight a pitched battle. Meanwhile, word of the battle reached Yukiie, who joined the fray from the rear. Consequently, Shōshun was forced to beat a hasty retreat. Yoshitsune's retainers scattered and gave chase. Yoshitsune then hastened to the ex-sovereign's palace to report on his safety.

18th day. *An imperial mandate is issued to Yoshitsune and Yukiie to proceed against Yoritomo.*

Deliberations regarding Yoshitsune's request for imperial authorization to proceed against Yoritomo were held at the ex-sovereign's palace yesterday. As there is no warrior besides Yoshitsune to protect the court in the event of a disturbance at the capital, it was decided to authorize Yoshitsune's request. The deliberators were of the opinion that, if the reasons for the granting of the mandate were subsequently explained to Kamakura, Yoritomo would not be seriously provoked. The presiding officer was the Great Minister of the Left Tsunemune.

Imperial Dictate
Minamoto Yoritomo, junior second rank, in his zeal to enhance his military prestige, has become unmindful of imperial law. Therefore, this mandate to proceed against him is hereby granted to the ex-governor of Bizen Minamoto Yukiie and to the junior lieutenant of the Outer Palace Guards, Left Division, Minamoto Yoshitsune.

Bunji 1:10,18   Fujiwara Mitsumasa, Director of the Sovereign's
                       Private Office, Head Official of the Controlling
                       Board of the Right, and, concurrently, Assistant
                       Director of the Office of the Empress's Household

19th day. *An esteemed sword of the ex-sovereign is recovered.*

An esteemed sword which had been in the custody of the ex-
sovereign was lost a year ago. However, it was recently recovered
and returned to the ex-sovereign by Ōe Kintomo. As this sword,
which is finished in gold lacquer and named Hoemaru, had been
presented to the throne by Yoritomo's father, His Lordship has
written a note of appreciation to Kintomo. This act was taken
because it was thought auspicious that his late father's treasure
has again been placed in the custody of the imperial house.

20th day. *The bishop Kugen and his retinue of twenty prelates
arrive at Kamakura; Noriyori also arrives and reports on his past
activities.*

The Bishop Kugen of Hongaku-in, the officiating priest for the
dedication services of the chapel, arrived at Kamakura with a
retinue of twenty prelates. Accompanying the party was the
governor of Mikawa Noriyori, who presented himself at His
Lordship's residence this evening to report on past affairs. He
had arrived at the capital from Kyushu on the 27th of the past
month and, having retrieved the sword Unomaru, one of two
esteemed treasures of the ex-sovereign's palace, he took advantage
of his return to Kyoto to present it to the throne. In 1183, at the
time of the flight of the Taira from the capital, Kiyotsune had taken
the two esteemed swords to the west. Noriyori reported also that
he had presented to the ex-sovereign 10 *tan* of Chinese brocade,
110 *tan* of Chinese damask and silk, some gauze, 30 pieces of silver,
10 Chinese ink-sticks, 20 tea bowls, 50 Chinese mats, 1,000 *koku*
of rice, and 10 head of cattle. He then presented separate mementos
to His Lordship and Her Ladyship, as well as gifts of Chinese
brocade, Chinese damask, Chinese silk, 50 pieces of silver, armor,
bows, rice and soy beans.

21st day. *An image of Amida Buddha is installed in the chapel;
Hisazane yields his awards to his son; the written prayer to be read
at the chapel dedication arrives in Kamakura.*

An image of Amida Buddha six jō² in height and finished entirely in gold color by the image caster Jōchō, was installed in the South Chapel under the supervision of Miyoshi Yasunobu, the governor of Yamato Yamada Shigehira, and the secretary of the Bureau of Statistics Nikaidō Yukimasa. Today Minamoto Yorikane arrived from Kyoto. He reports that the retainer Hisazane was elevated on the 11th of the past month to the junior fifth rank, upper grade, in recognition of his capture of the thief who had stolen the Sword-of-the-Sovereign's-Daytime-Throne. He also received the military rank of lieutenant of the Middle Palace Guards. However, Hisazane yielded these awards to his son, Hisanaga.

A copy of the prayer to be read at the chapel dedication has arrived. The draft is by Fujiwara Mitsunori of the Ministry of Ceremonial, and the clear copy is by the Minor Controller of the Right Sadanaga. It was read for His Lordship by the governor of Inaba Ōe Hiromoto.

24th day. *The South Chapel, renamed Shōchōju-in, is dedicated; Yoritomo plans to go to Kyoto.*

Weather clear, winds tranquil. Today the dedication of the South Chapel, named Shōchōju-in, was held. At 3 A.M. the more stalwart of the warriors, specially selected from among the immediate vassals, were posted as guards at every crossroad. The senior assistant minister of the imperial household Fujiwara Shigeyori was in charge of the assembly hall. Temporary shelters had been built to both sides of the chapel, from which the proceedings could be viewed. The shelter on the left was reserved for His Lordship, and the one on the right was used by Her Ladyship and members of the household of Ichijō Yoshiyasu, the director of the Left Horse Bureau. The balcony in front of the chapel was designated the station for the twenty offerings-receivers. Along the foot of the hills were located the seats for Lord Hōjō's wife and for the wives of other qualified immediate vassals. His Lordship made his entrance in full court dress at 9 A.M. The order of the procession was as follows:

First, guards of honor, fourteen men, followed by holders of the fifth and sixth ranks, thirty-two men; next, guards of honor,

² See Part Two, Chapter Two, note 30.

sixteen men, followed by sixty guards of honor selected for their skill in the martial arts.[3]

His Lordship's entrance into the chapel was attended by Yoshimori and Kagetoki, who posted themselves outside to the left and right of the gate. In the chapel Taneyori came forward to take His Lordship's shoes. Sasaki Takatsuna, wearing His Lordship's helmet, attended him in the forecourt. The spectators, seeing Takatsuna place the helmet-badge over the helmet, expressed disapproval. When a young page of Takatsuna communicated the remark to his master, he was greatly provoked, saying: "When one is clad in his lord's armor and an emergency should arise, he serves his lord first by removing the helmet-badge. Those who object strenuously do not know the ancient procedures of the warrior." Then the director of the Horse Bureau, Left Division, Ichijō Yoshiyasu, attired in a ceremonial robe and attended by an official of the fifth rank and a guard; the ex-Minor Captain Taira Tokiie, the chamberlain Sanjō Kinsuke, Mitsumori, the ex-vice governor of Kōzuke Fujiwara Norinobu, the ex-governor of Tsushima Fujiwara Chikamitsu, and the senior assistant minister of the imperial household Shigeyori seated themselves at the front of the hall. The governor of Musashi and his followers took their places beside them. Then the officiating priest and twenty attending priests conducted the dedication rites. Upon the conclusion of the rites, offerings were received. This was in charge of Hiki Tōnai Tomomune and the lieutenant of the Imperial Bodyguards, Right Division, Iekage. Earlier the offerings had been deposited in a long chest which had been placed on the stone pavement of the hall. This had been done under the supervision of Toshikane and Yukimasa. Tokiie, Kinsuke, Mitsumori, Yorikane, Norinobu, Chikamitsu, Shigeyori, Nakayori, Hirotsuna, Yoshinori, Yoshisuke, Shigemasa, Motoshige, Yoshikane, Takashige, and Kunimichi in turn removed the gifts from the chest. The officiating priest's share of the gifts was: 5 suits of robes in silk brocade, 500 suits of robes in damask, 200 *tan* of damask, 200 *hiki* of glossed silk, 200 *tan* of dyed silks, 200 *tan* of blue dyed cloth, 200 *tan* of dark-blue cloth, 200 *ryō* of gold dust, 200 *ryō* of silver, 1 set of sacerdotal

---

[3] The names of all participants, from the first group of fourteen honor guards to the last group of sixty guards, are listed in the text.

robes with a sash of silk brocade, 20 sets of garments for young maids of honor, 30 horses, placed in charge of the guard of the ex-sovereign's palace Munechika. The latter is serving as Lord Hōjō's deputy. Of the horses presented, 10 were saddled and drawn by immediate vassals, the remainder being escorted by stable attendants. . . .[4]

Additional gifts to the officiating priest were: 1 sword, ornamented with gold; robes; rosaries; 1 set of silk garments in a pine pattern which had been given by the court ladies. The above were accepted for the priest by the director of the Horse Bureau, Left Division. Also, 500 *koku* of rice were sent to his lodgings.

Each guest priest received as his share of the gifts the following: 30 suits of various kinds of garments, 50 *hiki* of silk, 50 *tan* of dyed silk, 100 *tan* of unbleached hemp, and 3 horses, one of them saddled. Each item was unexcelled in beauty. The giving of such gifts is a deed which occurs but once in a lifetime.

At the conclusion of the ceremony, upon his return to headquarters, Yoritomo summoned Wada Yoshimori and Kajiwara Kagetoki to inform them that he was leaving for the capital the next morning. He ordered them to assemble their warriors and to submit a roster of those who plan to accompany him to the capital. When more than half of the assembled immediate vassals were asked, it was found that of the two thousand nine hundred and sixteen principal warriors, including Chiba Tsunetane, there were sixty-eight, including Koyama Tomomasa and Tomomitsu, who signified their intention of going to the capital.

25th day. *Yoritomo sends out troops to kill Yukiie and Yoshitsune.*

This morning at dawn the gallant warriors whose names had been listed on the acceptance roll were called out and despatched to Kyoto. Their instructions were: first, to order the inhabitants in Owari and Mino to fortify the ferry crossings below Ajika and Sunomata, and, second, to go to Kyoto and kill Yukiie and Yoshitsune. They were ordered to make no concessions. If these two are not in the capital at the time, the troops are to await Yoritomo's arrival. When the instructions were thus transmitted, each warrior raised his whip as a gesture of acceptance of the assignment.

[4] The names of twenty vassals, two to a horse, have been deleted.

26th day. *Tosa-bō Shōshun is killed in the Kurama Mountains by Yoshitsune's retainers.*

Tosa-bō Shōshun and three of his followers were sought out and captured in the mountain fastness of Kurama by Yoshitsune's retainers. Today their pilloried heads were exposed at Rokujō-Kawara.

27th day. *Yoritomo makes offerings of horses to Izu and Hakone Shrines.*

His Lordship despatched special emissaries with offerings to the Buddha Incarnate shrines at Izu and Hakone. Nitta Shirō Tada-tsune was sent to Izu and Kudō Kagemitsu to Hakone, each presenting a horse. The vice governor of Chikuzen Kaneyoshi has departed for Kyoto as His Lordship's emissary.

28th day. *Kataoka Tsuneharu is dispossessed of his lands.*

Kataoka Hachirō Tsuneharu, having conspired to stage a revolt with Satake Tarō, Tsuneharu's father-in-law, was deprived of his holdings at Misaki in Shimōsa. The confiscated lands were awarded today to the vice governor of Chiba Tsunetane in recognition of his loyal service.

29th day. *Yoritomo leaves Kamakura to direct the campaign against Yukiie and Yoshitsune.*

To crush the revolt of Yoshitsune and Yukiie His Lordship has this day departed for the capital. All able-bodied warriors of the eastern provinces were ordered to join him immediately. Yoritomo circulated an order directing his men of the mountain and northern provinces to assemble at points in Ōmi via the mountain routes.

Concerning Hara Sōsaburō Munefusa of Sagami, a warrior of unexcelled bravery, who had sided with Kagechika against His Lordship in the Hayakawa Battles and who, fearing punishment, had fled to Mino where he is presently living, His Lordship ordered his immediate vassals in Mino to search out Hara and have him join the Genji forces immediately and proceed to the vicinity of Sunomata to pay homage to His Lordship.

His Lordship departed at 9 A.M. Doi Sanehira took his place in the front column, and the vice governor of Chiba Tsunetane in the rear column. Tonight they will encamp at the Nakamura Manor in Sagami Province. All the immediate vassals of Sagami are gathering there.

ELEVENTH MONTH

1st day. *Yoritomo arrives at Kisegawa-eki in Suruga; he awaits word from Kyoto.*

Upon arrival at Kisegawa-eki in Suruga Province His Lordship announced to his immediate vassals that he would remain at this place for awhile to await word regarding the situation in Kyoto. He ordered that meanwhile each warrior should be prepared with regard to mounts, travel provisions, and other matters.

2nd day. *Yoshitsune is reported to be arranging for boats to flee to western Honshu.*

Planning to leave Kyoto for western Honshu, Yoshitsune had despatched the secretary Tomozane to arrange for boats. Along the way Tomozane met one Shōshirō, a former retainer of Yoshitsune but now no longer a follower. When Shōshirō inquired of Tomozane the purpose of his mission, the latter replied truthfully. Not realizing the falsity of Shōshirō's assertion that he was still a follower of Yoshitsune, Tomozane offered to speak to Yoshitsune about this chance meeting and, in fact, permitted Shōshirō to accompany him on his mission. Thereupon an imperial police appeared and slew Shōshirō.

The aforementioned Tomozane is a member of the Saitō family of Echizen Province. He served at Ninna-ji Temple during his adolescence. Upon attaining manhood he served with the Heike. Later he turned against the Heike to serve Kiso Yoshinaka, and about the time when Yoshinaka was being pursued by the Genji he became a retainer of Yoshitsune. While thus serving as Yoshitsune's follower, he had the encounter described above.

3rd day. *Yukiie and Yoshitsune leave Kyoto for the west.*

The ex-governor of Bizen Yukiie, clad in armor with lacings in the pattern of cherry blossoms, and the governor of Iyo Yoshitsune, wearing a robe of red brocade and light-green body armor, have departed for the west. They sent a messenger to the ex-sovereign's palace to explain that they were proceeding to western Honshu to escape the accusations and punitive measures of Kamakura, and that although they should present themselves personally before the ex-sovereign to pay their last respects, they begged to be excused as they were not dressed in proper ceremonial attire. Among those who are accompanying the two are: Taira Tokizane, the chamberlain Yoshinari, who is a younger brother of Yoshitsune's mother and a son of Ichijō Naganari, Izu Aritsuna, Hori Kagemitsu, Satō Tadanobu, Ise Yoshimori, Kataoka Hirotsune, and the master of Buddhist Law Benkei. It is said that their force numbers about two hundred mounted men.

5th day. *The Genji enter Kyoto; Yoshitsune breaks through a Genji line at Kawajiri, but his forces suffer many casualties.*

His Lordship's immediate vassals who had been despatched from Kanto have made their entry into the capital. That His Lordship is indignant at the recent turn of events was, first of all, communicated to the Great Minister of the Left.

Today, as Yoshitsune arrived at Kawajiri, Settsu Province, his advance was intercepted by Tada Yukitsune and the young lord of Toyoshima of the Settsu clan of the Minamoto, who shot a few arrows and stones. However, as Yoshitsune chose to ride through the Genji lines, it was impossible to challenge him to an open battle. Nevertheless, his forces suffered many casualties, only a handful escaping.

6th day. *A storm prevents Yoshitsune from sailing and reduces his party to four; the ex-sovereign orders a search for Yukiie and Yoshitsune.*

When Yukiie and Yoshitsune were embarking at Daimotsu in Settsu, there arose a violent storm and their boats were overturned. Because of this unexpected occurrence, they abandoned their crossing. Their followers scattered, and Yoshitsune was left with only four of his party—the lieutenant of the Left Outer Palace Guards Minamoto Aritsuna, Hori Yatarō, Musashi-bō Benkei, and the concubine Shizuka. It is reported that the party plans to encamp somewhere near Tennō-ji, from which place they will continue their flight. The ex-sovereign has issued a directive today to the provinces to search for Yukiie and Yoshitsune.

7th day. *Yoritomo is angered at the court's approval of Yoshitsune; he is pleased with the position taken by the Great Minister of the Right.*

While Yoritomo was staying at Kisegawa in order to mobilize troops and to await word regarding the situation in Kyoto, it was reported that Yukiie and Yoshitsune had left for the west on the 3rd. It was reported, moreover, that Yukiie and Yoshitsune had been granted a warrant from the ex-sovereign's government, directing the local lords of Shikoku and Kyushu to obey the bearers' commands. It designates Yukiie as steward of Shikoku and Yoshitsune as steward of Kyushu. Yoritomo is extremely provoked, for this turn of events ignores the meritorious services which he himself has rendered to the court from time to time. However, Yoritomo was greatly pleased over the report that the Great Minister of the Right Fujiwara Kanezane had consistently supported Kanto when the question of whether to authorize such a mandate was being deliberated.

Today Yoshitsune was deprived of his present posts of governor of Iyo and imperial police.

8th day. *Yoritomo sends emissaries to Kyoto to express his indignation at the court's approval of Yoshitsune; he cancels his plans to go to Kyoto.*

The governor of Yamato Yamada Shigehiro and Ippon-bō Shōkan have departed for the capital from Kisegawa to communicate to the court His Lordship's indignation regarding the matter of Yukiie and Yoshitsune. But, as Yukiie and Yoshitsune have since left the capital, His Lordship has canceled his earlier plan of going to the capital himself, and has this day returned to Kamakura.

10th day. *Details regarding the grant of a warrant to Yoshitsune are reported to Yoritomo.*

Upon his return to Kamakura, His Lordship was told by the director of the Left Horse Bureau that, according to the latest word of a Kyoto resident, the question of whether to issue an imperial mandate against Yoshitsune for inciting a revolt had been turned over for deliberation to the Great Ministers of the Left, Right, and Center, and to the councilor and governor-general Yoshida Tsunefusa. The views of the Great Minister of the Right, which are always fair and just, were not mere words of partisanship for Kamakura. The Great Minister of the Center offered no positive views for or against, while the Great Minister of the Left insisted on an early decree. Tsunefusa made several attempts to sway him. Again, it is said that in their choice the minister of justice Yoritsune and the provisional director of the Left Horse Bureau Naritada are inclined toward Yoshitsune. The same is true of the imperial police Tomoyasu.

11th day. *The court reverses its position regarding Yoshitsune and Yukiie.*

An imperial dictate in compliance with the request of the treacherous Yoshitsune and others had been handed down a few days ago. However, following this move, the ex-sovereign has been trying to placate Kanto, and because of His Lordship's strong complaints and indignation there has been a change in the attitude of the court in the past few days. Meanwhile there has been a rumor that Yoshitsune and Yukiie, while proceeding to western Honshu to stage a revolt, had drowned at Daimotsu, but there is little reason to believe this. Now the ex-sovereign has issued a directive to the governors of the inner and neighboring provinces to order all who are armed to comb the mountains and the forests to apprehend them. This instrument reads:

A dictate of the ex-sovereign decrees: Whereas Minamoto Yoshitsune and Minamoto Yukiie, while en route to western Honshu to stage a revolt, have suddenly met with adverse winds at Daimotsu on the 6th, and whereas there have been rumors that they have drowned, there is no positive proof of their death. Order forthwith the gallant warriors to search the mountains and forests, rivers and marshes, and to deliver up their bodies at an early date. If the apprehension takes place in a public domain within your province, act in accordance with the instructions contained herein; if it occurs on a manor, submit the matter to the domainial lord to be attended to. These are strict orders. Do not be remiss in carrying them out. The ex-sovereign decrees thus. Make

every effort to carry out the terms of this decree. Respectfully transmitted.

To: The respective governors   Provisional Governor-General of the
                                      Government Headquarters of Kyushu

12th day. *Yoritomo alerts vassals west of Suruga; he punishes
vassals associated with Yoshitsune; Ōe Hiromoto proposes the
posting of constables and stewards.*

Yoritomo addressed letters to his immediate vassals residing
west of Suruga and instructed them to be in readiness to comply
with forthcoming orders regarding Yoshitsune, even though His
Lordship's visit to Kyoto has been postponed. Although it was thus
announced, the provisional governor Okabe Yasutsuna of Suruga,
who had been afflicted with illness and who, as a result, had not
been able to attend the chapel dedication exercises nor come to
pay his respects to His Lordship on his recent trip to Kisegawa,
has lately recovered from his illness and, hearing of His Lordship's proposed visit to the capital, has sent word that in spite of
his weakened condition he would come to Kamakura to offer his
services. He was notified that he need not report, now that the
Kyoto visit has been canceled. Moreover, as Yasutsuna is obese,
and may not have a horse he could mount, he was told to make
preparations and to be ready to comply with the future wishes of
His Lordship.

Today the lands of Kawagoe Shigeyori were confiscated because
of his complicity with Yoshitsune. Of these lands, five districts in
Katori, Ise, were awarded to Ōi Saneharu, and the remaining lands
were given in trust to Shigeyori's aged mother. Also, the holdings
of Shimokōbe Masayoshi were seized, he being Shigeyori's son-
in-law.

Because of the seriousness to Kanto of the present developments,
and because the constant attention which these developments require is a source of great inconvenience, the ex-official of Inaba Ōe
Hiromoto has addressed Yoritomo as follows: "The country has
fallen into decadence. Men possessed of the devil run rampant.
There are rebels in our land whom it has not been possible to
destroy. But in the eastern provinces peace and order have been
achieved because of Your Lordship's presence. Elsewhere, however,
violence is apt to occur. It would be a detriment to the people and

an expense to the provinces if, in each instance, soldiers from the east must be sent out to restore order. Accordingly, if, on this occasion, Your Lordship could take action in the provinces and appoint constables and stewards for each provincial office and manor, there would be nothing to fear. Such a request should be made immediately to the throne." Yoritomo was greatly pleased, and it was decided to pursue this proposal. This wise counsel has strengthened the bond between His Lordship and his minister.

15th day. *The Minister of the Treasury explains his role in the granting of a warrant to Yoshitsune.*

The minister of the Treasury Takashina Yasutsune has sent a messenger to Kamakura. He did not report directly to head-quarters, perhaps out of fear of reprisal, but instead proceeded to the residence of the director of the Left Horse Bureau and in-formed him that he has been entrusted with a letter to the Lord of Kamakura. In a separate letter to the director of the Left Horse Bureau, Yasutsune explained: "I deny any part in the granting of a mandate to Yoshitsune. It was only out of fear of Yoshitsune's military prowess that I transmitted his request to the ex-sovereign. I do not know what the rumors are in these distant places, but I request that you will persuade Yoritomo not to make a hasty decision regarding me on the basis of prevailing rumors."

Then the director accompanied the messenger to headquarters to transmit Yasutsune's letter to Yoritomo. The minister's letter was opened and read by Fujiwara Toshikane. It said: "Regarding the conspiracy of Yukiie and Yoshitsune, it was undoubtedly the work of the devil. The two had addressed the throne to the effect that if imperial sanction was not forthcoming, they would appear at the palace and kill themselves. And although imperial sanction was granted, it was done to avoid this predicament, and it was never His Majesty's will to grant it." His Lordship remarked: "Is this really the imperial attitude? It is ridiculous to ascribe the conspiracy of Yukiie and Yoshitsune to the devil. The devil im-pedes Buddhism and causes suffering to humanity. I have sub-dued the enemies of the court and I have not interfered with the administrative powers of the sovereign. Why then, if it is not His Majesty's wish, should he turn suddenly to the side of the rebels and issue them a mandate? So long as the throne does not authorize the seizure of Yukiie and Yoshitsune, there will be chaos in the provinces and the people will be destroyed. Thus the greatest devil in Japan must be some other devil than the one mentioned."

17th day. *Yoshitsune's mistress surrenders herself.*

As it had been rumored that Yoshitsune was hiding in the Yoshino Mountains in Yamato, a temple secretary at the head of a party of armed monks has been combing the forest lately, but without success. Tonight, at 9 P.M., Yoshitsune's concubine, Shizuka, came down from Fujiosaka in the aforementioned mountains and appeared at the Zōō-dō. She seemed strange and eerie. The monks were suspicious and took her to the temple secretary's abode, where she was questioned in detail. Shizuka replied, "I am the mistress of Yoshitsune, the governor of Iyo. Yoshitsune had come to these mountains from Daimotsu and, after tarrying for five days, he disguised himself as a hermit monk and fled because of a report that monks of temples in the area were searching for him. At the time he gave me many pieces of gold and silver and assigned several male servants to escort me to the capital, but these servants robbed me of my valuables and abandoned me in the snows of the mountain. Thus it is that I have lost my way."

18th day. *The monks of the Yoshino area search the hills and valleys for Yoshitsune.*

As a result of Shizuka's story the monks of Yoshino have been sent out again to search the hills and valleys for Yoshitsune. The temple secretary, out of compassion for Shizuka, has announced that after comforting her he will deliver her to Kamakura.

19th day. *Doi Sanehira and his followers return to Kamakura.*

Doi Jirō Sanehira, at the head of his band, has arrived at the capital from Kanto. This is a very special contingent selected from among the picked troops of the new provinces he now oversees.

20th day. *A report is received on Taira Tokizane.*

Although it had been rumored that Yoshitsune and Yukiie had boarded boats on the 6th at Daimotsu after leaving Koyoto, and that they had been drowned in a storm while weighing anchor, the young lord of Yashima Tokikiyo, returning to the capital on the 8th of the same month, has reported to the throne that the two men are still alive.

It was also reported that Taira Tokizane of Sanuki had been secretly residing in the capital, although ordered into exile, and had on this occasion joined with Yoshitsune to go to western Honshu. When the party was dispersed, following its failure to weigh anchor, and as Tokizane was returning to the capital, he was captured by the master of Buddhist meditation Tsunekore, the younger brother of the assistant director of the Right Horse Bureau. These two matters have been brought to the attention of the throne.

22nd day. *Yoshitsune is reported to be in the vicinity of Nara; the priest Jūji-bō befriends him.*

Enduring the deep snows of the Yoshino Mountains, Yoshitsune has stealthily made his way to Tōnomine to offer prayers for help to the image of Kamatari, the founder of the Fujiwara family. He has arrived at Fujimuro, situated on the lands of the Southern Palace.[5] The head priest of Fujimuro is an armed monk, Jūji-bō, who admires Yoshitsune.

24th day. *Yoritomo sends prayers and offerings to Ise Shrine and to fifteen temples and eleven shrines in Sagami Province.*

Supplications for the nation's peace will be made by His Lordship to various shrines. The duty of presenting the invocation to the Ise Shrine has been assigned to the head Shinto priest Naritomo. In addition, prayers will be sent to the principal Shinto shrines in the neighboring provinces. In Sagami Province fifteen temples and eleven shrines will each receive offerings.

25th day. *The throne approves a warrant against Yukiie and Yoshitsune.*

Hōjō Tokimasa arrived at the capital today and made a strong representation to the throne through the intercession of Yoshida

---

[5] Nan'in, the name of the place where offerings to the graves of emperors were prepared.

Bungo: Requested that it be awarded to Yoritomo, the reason being
that both the provincial officials and the more distinguished resident
warriors of the province have been sympathetic to Yoshitsune's rebellion. Therefore, in order to apprehend and deal with these partisans, it is desirable that His Lordship shall hold and administer this
province.
Item: Vacancies.
Men of ability shall be selected to fill these posts.
Twelfth Month, 6th day   Yoritomo [monogram]

   Item: Dismissals.
Imperial adviser Chikamune
Minister of the Treasury Yasutsune
Head official of the Controlling Board of the Right Mitsumasa
Minister of Justice Yoritsune
Director of the Horse Bureau, Right Division, Tsunenaka
Provisional director of the Horse Bureau, Right Division, Naritada
Senior Recorder of the Left Takamoto
Junior lieutenant of the Outer Palace Guards, Left Division, Tomoyasu
Nobumori
Nobuzane
Tokinari
Director of the Military Storehouse Akitsuna
These are the pernicious ministers who endorsed Yukiie and Yoshitsune,
and who hoped to throw the land into confusion. They shall forthwith
be deprived of their present offices and discharged. Moreover, the degree
of complicity of those retainers of Yukiie and Yoshitsune who acceded
to or encouraged the revolt shall be determined, and each, in the case
of holders of rank, shall be deprived of his rank and office. Furthermore,
as it has been reported that there are monks who are masters of divination among Yoshitsune's partisans, they too shall be sought out and
removed.
Twelfth Month, 6th day   Yoritomo [monogram]

   His Lordship's letter to Fujiwara Kanezane, the Great Minister
of the Right, reads:

Respectfully submitted,
   A statement of reasons:
   To submit an explanation for the recommendations given above
would, I fear, involve details of great length. That the Heike betrayed
the sovereign and that it bore malice toward the throne and schemed
with a singleness of mind to create confusion is common knowledge,
and it cannot be said that this is my first memorial to the court regarding the Heike. During my exile in Izu I drew up a plan to chastise His
Majesty's enemies, although I had received no specific instructions from
the throne. Because the plan succeeded, and because fate willed it,

meritorious deeds have been many and the enemy has suffered constant defeats and has been reduced to submission. The country has been restored to His Majesty, consistent with my long-cherished wish, and all, in both public and private life, have rejoiced.

Without awaiting the final subjugation of the Heike I have despatched two deputies, Hisatsune and Kunihira, to the capital to put a halt to the outrages of warriors in the eleven provinces near the capital. Moreover, as it would be improper for me to issue my own private commands, I instructed them to request the sanction of the ex-sovereign for every act of justice they performed. In consequence thereof, when the outrages in these provinces were generally suppressed, the aforesaid deputies, through a separate order from me, were assigned to the western provinces whence they have proceeded, again only after requesting the approval of the ex-sovereign. Accordingly, even as to the domains of Tanenao, Takanao, Tanetō, and Hidetō, which are confiscated estates whereon supervisory officials should be stationed in pursuance of precedents, I have taken no action. But while, on the one hand, I have been constantly aware of the need to rely on the mandates of the ex-sovereign to suppress lawlessness, as in the case of the neighboring provinces, on the other, there has been an unaccountable development. The appointments of Yoshitsune as steward of Kyushu and Yukiie as steward of Shikoku are inconsistent with the principle that should be followed. These men, acting in collusion, have schemed to stage a shameful revolt. In the course of their flight from the capital, though no perceivable enemy approached them, they could not escape the wrath of heaven. When they were weighing anchor, their boats plunged into the sea or were sent adrift on the waves, and their followers and kinsmen perished. This was indeed not the work of man but that of the gods. However, even now the persons of these two rebels have not been produced. They have absconded, covering their tracks. In searching for them in every province, manor, household, mountain, and temple, there may be some confusion but if they are seized, order will certainly ensue. Now measures have been taken to place stewards uniformly on the manors of the various provinces. I declare that it was not for reasons of personal advantage that this measure was taken. Natives who harbor evil designs may be exposed to these rebels and may be drawn into their ranks, or they may come under the control of bands of warriors in other localities and give rise to some untoward event. If precautionary measures are not taken against such a likelihood, conditions hereafter may become chaotic. If these stewards become negligent, or resist the remittance of the customary fixed dues and irregular services or sundry dues owed to lords of manors, they shall be admonished sternly and commanded to perform their duties without interference and in accordance with the law as has been done in Iyo

Province, where stewards to administer justice on all the lands, public or private, have been posted. I respectfully submit, on the one hand, this letter to inform you of these aims, and on the other, the letter on which I have with due respect noted my humble opinions regarding matters which should be acted upon by His Majesty. One copy, which is to be presented to the ex-sovereign, I am entrusting to the courtier governor general Middle Councilor. In these times of confusion it is imperative that we examine the source of things. I strongly urge that you speak for the prosecution of these aims. It is the will of heaven, and you need have no anxieties. This letter, containing information which I am pleased to convey to the Lord Great Minister of the Right, I respectfully submit thus.

Twelfth Month, 6th day   Yoritomo [monogram]
Respectfully transmitted to the
Middle Controller of the Right

7th day. A messenger is despatched to Kyoto with the letters to the court and to the Minister of the Right; Yoritomo makes a change in his request for dismissals.

The servant Hamashirō has departed for the capital as His Lordship's messenger, bearing with him the affidavit to be submitted to the ex-sovereign, as well as the letter to be presented to the Great Minister of the Right. Kurobōshi-maru, a servant of the director of the Left Horse Bureau, was assigned to accompany him and to serve as a guide for him in Kyoto. In discussing details regarding court attendants sympathetic to Yoshitsune, it was learned that the courtier Narinori, minister of civil affairs, is a blood relation of the Great Minister of the Right Kanezane. Therefore his name was stricken off the list of dismissals.

The details regarding the developments of the past few days and the measures to be taken in Kyoto are to be brought to the attention of the director of the Horse Bureau, Left Division, and the chamberlain Kinsuke before they are carried out. Kinsuke, a son of a daughter of Hokkyō Zenjō, is a grandson of Lord Hōjō, His Lordship's father-in-law. Besides this close relationship, he is of an extremely calm disposition and has not turned against His Lordship. Therefore he was recommended on this occasion to be elevated to provisional director of the Horse Bureau, Right Division.

8th day. *Shizuka is removed to Lord Hōjō's residence in Kyoto.*

The temple secretary of Yoshino has removed Shizuka to Lord Hōjō's residence. In this connection it was reported that troops are to be despatched to the Yoshino Mountains to hunt for Yoshitsune.

11th day. *Yoritomo's son is stricken with illness.*

The young lord, son of Yoritomo, was suddenly stricken with illness. There was much commotion at the headquarters, as a multitude of people called to inquire after his condition. The intendant Engyō of the sub-shrine performed incantations to cure him.

15th day. *Hōjō Tokimasa reports on developments in Kyoto; Yoritomo's son recovers.*

A special courier sent by Hōjō Tokimasa has arrived at Kamakura to report on particulars in the capital. First, the houses of the rebels have been seized, and measures have been taken to prevent the flight of those whose sympathies for or complicity with Yoshitsune are known. This matter was duly reported to the Middle Councilor Tsunefusa. Next, Yoshitsune's concubine, who has been sent to Kyoto, was questioned. She replied that she had accompanied Yoshitsune out of the capital on the morning of his departure for the west, but while they were attempting to cross the sea from Daimotsu, their boats overturned and the crossing was thwarted. The party was completely dispersed. That night they encamped at Tennō-ji, after which Yoshitsune took flight. At the time he made a promise, saying that she should remain at Tennō-ji for a day or two, and that he would send someone to meet her. But if the appointed day should pass without word from him, she should flee. However, someone came to her with a horse which she mounted without knowledge of where she was going. After three days on the road she arrived at Yoshino Mountain and rejoined Yoshitsune. There she remained for five days. Then she parted with him. Not knowing his whereabouts, she endured the snows of the mountain until, miraculously, she came upon Zōō-dō, where she was made captive by the temple secretary. Such was the nature of the communication from Lord Hōjō, who also inquired as to the measures he should take regarding Yoshitsune's mistress.

His Lordship's son has recovered from his illness.

16th day. *The messenger Hamashirō is taken ill; Lord Hōjō is ordered to send Shizuka to Kamakura.*

Kurobōshi-maru, who had accompanied the ambassadors to the capital on the past 7th, has left the party and returned in great haste. He reported that the servant Hamashirō was suddenly stricken ill when the party arrived at the inn at Okabe, and that it appeared that Hamashirō had lost his mind. Although the party waited a few days for his recovery, he was still unable to leave his bed, to say nothing of making a long journey. Consequently His Lordship has decided to send the servant Tsurujirō and Ikuzawa Gorō in Hamashirō's place. Kurobōshi-maru will again accompany them. A reply was also despatched to Lord Hōjō directing him to send Shizuka to Kamakura.

17th day. *The sons of Taira Munemori are beheaded; the son of Taira Koremori is given a temporary stay.*

The chamberlain Tadafusa of Tango, son of the Great Minister of the Center Taira Shigemori, was placed in the custody of Gotō Motokiyo. Also, in compliance with the orders of Kanto, Lord Hōjō arrested the two young sons of Taira Munemori, the former Great Minister of the Center, and one of the sons of the courtier Michimori of Echizen. Rokudai, the eldest son of Taira Koremori, was captured at Henshō-ji, north of Daikaku-ji, in Shōbuzawa, Saga Province. As he was being removed to Noji in a palanquin, the priest Mongaku of Shingo-ji declared that Rokudai had been a member of his parish and that an appeal on the boy's behalf should be made to Lord Hōjō and to Kamakura. The fact that the ex-governor of Tosa Munezane, son of Taira Shigemori, is now the adopted son of the Great Minister of the Left Tsunemune was also communicated to Yoritomo. It has been recommended to Kamakura that Munezane and Rokudai be granted a temporary stay. But as for the sons of Munemori, they have been beheaded.

21st day. *Yoritomo elaborates on the role of stewards.*

It has been declared that private domains in the various provinces shall come entirely under the control of Kanto. Previously those who called themselves stewards were probably retainers of the Heike who had assumed the role without imperial approval. Or they had been given this title by the Heike and were stationed on the lands of the Heike. Also, civil governors and lords of manors have been known to station stewards on their lands as a personal favor to their retainers. As a result the domainial lords and lords of manors who had dispensed private favors are now empty handed and dismayed. Now that the control of manors is uniform throughout the provinces, there need be no anxiety among lords of manors and legal guardians of manors.

23rd day. *The ex-sovereign plans to send an embassy to Kamakura; Yoritomo recommends the ex-governor of Tsushima for office.*

The report has reached Kamakura today that the governor general of the government headquarters of Kyushu and Middle Councilor Yoshida Tsunefusa is to be sent here on a mission. It is said that His Majesty has since approved the mission. Is he being sent for the purpose of tendering His Majesty's replies to the various representations made to him regarding the Yukiie-Yoshitsune incident? This is highly irregular and embarrassing to His Lordship. His Lordship has remarked that envoys and letters are used to address the throne, and His Majesty makes known his wishes by means of directives. One must exercise scruples in sending nobles and ministers as emissaries on such a long and difficult journey.

The ex-governor of Tsushima, notwithstanding the distinguished service he has rendered for the noble houses and the military houses, has been removed from his provincial post against his wishes. Because of repeated appeals from Chikamitsu, Yoritomo has requested of the court that he be reinstated.

24th day. *Mongaku sends a pupil to plead for Rokudai.*

A pupil of the priest Mongaku has come before His Lordship to make the following plea: "Prince Rokudai, the eldest son of the late Koremori, is a pupil of Mongaku's parish. It is the intention of Kamakura to behead him soon. Every member of his band has been hunted down. What harm is there in freeing such a young man? His grandfather, the Great Minister of the Center Shigemori, was very generous toward Your Lordship. Partly because of his deeds, and partly as a favor to Mongaku, may Rokudai be left in Mongaku's custody." Rokudai is the legitimate heir of the Taira generals.

Although a young man, it is certain he will be a man. It is most difficult to fathom his mind but, again, the priest's plea cannot be ignored. His Lordship was in an extreme dilemma. After the messenger had pleaded earnestly several times, Yoritomo decided to send a note to Lord Hōjō, instructing him to leave Rokudai in Mongaku's custody for the time being.

26th day. *Taira Tokizane is delivered to Kamakura; the Minister of the Left pleads for Taira Munezane.*

Taira Tokizane, who had sided with Yoshitsune, was captured while fleeing toward the west. Today he was delivered here in the custody of the ex-sovereign's guard Munechika. Another letter from the Great Minister of the Left Tsunemune has arrived concerning the ex-governor of Tosa Munezane, the youngest son by adoption of the late Great Minister of the Center Shigemori. There is a rumor that sentence is to be passed on him as he is, after all, a surviving member of the family. The Great Minister of the Left wishes to have him placed in his custody. His Lordship has sent a reply to the effect that he understands the request.

28th day. *Strange happenings and dreams are related to Yoritomo; he orders the priest Engyō to offer prayers for the safety of the land.*

Shōshijirō, a native of Amanawa, died suddenly last night while standing on the threshold of his house. Crowds of people came out to see him. A member of the household related the following story to the throng which had gathered. "Someone rapped at the door after midnight and called out the boy's name. The boy answered and opened the door; then I heard nothing more. After some time had elapsed, I became suspicious and, taking a torch, I went to look for him. Whereupon I found him dead."

Again, recently, a lowly monk in service at the intendant's abode at the sub-shrine, suddenly ceased to exist while traveling at night. After a brief moment he returned to life and related the following story. "I chanced upon several great masters of Buddhist Law and I thought I should like to embrace them and tarry with them." That monk still looks as if he is not himself.

Again, Lady Shimotsuke, a lady in waiting to Her Ladyship Masako, dreamed that an old man, called Kagemasa, appeared and addressed His Lordship thus: "The Ex-sovereign Sutoku has cast a curse upon the world. Though I have tried to curb it, I have not been able to do so. I wish you to report this to the intendant of the sub-shrine." At this point the dream came to an end. When the dream was related the following morning, no instructions were given. But meanwhile it was said that the dream was an act of the devil. As a result the intendant Hōgen-bō of the sub-shrine was ordered to offer prayers for the safety of the land. Moreover, wadded silk garments and glossed silk cloth were given to the shrine attendants and functionaries. The secretary Kunimichi was in charge.

29th day. *The court honors Yoritomo's request for the dismissal of officials sympathetic to Yoshitsune.*

A messenger of Lord Hōjō arrived with the report that on the 17th an imperial directive regarding dismissals from office had been issued. This has been transmitted to Kamakura by the senior secretary of the Council of State Moronao. A copy has now been submitted to His Lordship.

Minister of the Treasury and, concurrently, Provisional Governor of
   Bingo Takashina Yasutsune
Director of the Horse Bureau, Right Division, Takashina Tsunenaka
Chamberlain Fujiwara Yoshinari
Governor of Echizen Takashina Takatsune
Junior private secretary of the Ministry of Central Affairs Nakahara
   Yasunobu

The Great Minister of the Left Tsunemune announces, upon orders of His Majesty, that the aforementioned persons shall be removed from their present positions.
Bunji 1:12,17   Senior Secretary Nakahara Moronao
                                            per order

30th day. *A district in Tosa Province is awarded to a shrine.*

In connection with the granting of the posts of stewards in the various provinces, the district of Agawa in Tosa was awarded to the sub-shrine of Rokujō. The said shrine, located on the vacated estate of the late Minamoto Tameyoshi at Rokujō in Kyoto, has been dedicated as a branch shrine of the Iwashimizu Hachiman Shrine. Ōe Hiromoto's younger brother, the teacher Kigon, has been appointed intendant of the shrine.

Selected Bibliography

JAPANESE SOURCES AND TEXTS

Primary sources, specialized dictionaries, chronologies, and other reference works are listed under their titles; all others are listed under the authors.

Azuma kagami, ed. by Katsumi Kuroita. Vol. 1. Tokyo, Kokushi taikei kankō-kai, 1932.

Azuma kagami, ed. by Hirotani kokusho kankō-kai. Vol. 1. Tokyo, Hirotani kokusho kankō-kai, 1929.

Azuma kagami, Kikkawa-bon, ed. by Kokusho kankō-kai. Vol. 1. Tokyo, Kokusho kankō-kai, 1915.

Azuma kagami, ed. by Susumu Ryō. Vol. 1. Tokyo, Iwanami shoten, 1939.

Azuma kagami, ed. by Hiroshi Yosano and others. Vol. 1. Tokyo, Nihon koten zenshū kankō-kai, 1926.

Azuma kagami hyōchū, ed. by Shōzō Hotta. Vol. 1. Tokyo, Tōyō-dō, 1943.

Buke myōmoku-shō, ed. by Zōtei kojitsu sōsho henshū-bu. 8 vols. Tokyo, Yoshikawa kōbun-kan, 1928–31.

Bunka dai-nempyō, comp. by Shōichi Heki. Vol. 1. Tokyo Ōkura shuppan kabushiki kaisha, 1955.

Dai-bukan, ed. by Hiroshi Hashimoto. 12 vols. Tokyo, Daikō-sha, 1935–36.

Dai-Nihon chimei jisho, ed. by Tōgo Yoshida. 7 vols. Tokyo, Fuzambō, 1911–13.

Dai-Nihon dokushi chizu, ed. by Tōgo Yoshida. Tokyo, Fuzambō, 1935.

Dai-Nihon jiin sōran, comp. by Yoshizō Hori. Tokyo, Meiji shuppan-sha, 1916.

Dai-Nihon jimmei jisho, comp. by Dai-Nihon jimmei jisho kankō-kai. 5 vols. Tokyo, Dai-Nihon jimmei jisho kankō-ka, 1937.

Dai-Nihon nempyō, comp. by Zennosuke Tsuji. Tokyo, Dai-Nihon shuppan kabushiki kaisha, 1943.

Dokushi biyō, comp. by Tokyo teikoku daigaku shiryō hensan-jo. Tokyo, Naigai shoseki kabushiki kaisha, 1933.

Gyokuyō, comp. by Kokusho kankō-kai. 3 vols. Tokyo, Kokusho kankō-kai, 1906–07.

Hara, Katsurō. *Nihon chūsei-shi no kenkyū.* Tokyo, Dōbun-kan, 1929.

Hashimoto, Minoru. *Nihon bushidō-shi.* Tokyo, Chijin shokan, 1942.

Heike monogatari, ed. by Yoshio Yamada. Tokyo, Hōbun-kan, 1933.

Imai, Rintarō. *Nihon shōen-sei-ron.* Tokyo, Mikasa shobō, 1940.

Ishii, Ryōsuke. *Nihon hōsei-shi gaisetsu.* Tokyo, Kōbun-dō, 1948.

Ishimota, Shō. *Chūsei-teki sekai no keisei.* Tokyo, Itō shoten, 1947.

Itō, Tasaburō. *Nihon hōken seido-shi.* Tokyo, Ōyashima shuppan kabushiki kaisha, 1948.

Izu, Kimio, and Yoshio Matsushita. *Nihon gunji hattatsu-shi.* Tokyo, Mikasa shobō, 1938.

Jinja taikan, comp. by Hoshirō Mitsunaga. Tokyo, Nihon dempō tsushin-sha, 1940.

Kanshoku yōkai, ed. by Hidematsu Wada. Tokyo, Meiji shoin, 1926.

Koji ruien, comp. by Junjirō Hosokawa and others. 60 vols. Tokyo, Koji ruien kankō-kai, 1931–36.

Kokushi dai-jiten, ed. by Kuniji Yashiro and others. 6 vols. Tokyo, Yoshikawa kōbun-kan, 1927.

Kokushi dai-nempyō, comp. by Shōichi Heki. Vol. 1. Tokyo, Heibon-sha, 1935.

Kokushi dai-zukan, ed. by Kokushi dai-zukan henshū-jo. Vol. 2. Tokyo, Yoshikawa Kōbun-kan, 1932.

Kokushi jiten, comp. by Fuzambō kokushi jiten hensan-bu. 4 vols. Tokyo, Fuzambō, 1940–43.

Kōtei kokushi kenkyū nempyō, ed. by Katsumi Kuroita. Tokyo, Iwanami shoten, 1936.

Maki, Kenji. *Nihon hōken seido seiritsu-shi.* Tokyo, Kōbun-dō, 1941.

Miura, Shūkō. *Nihon hōsei-shi.* Tokyo, Sōgen-sha, 1943.

Nakada, Kaoru. *Hōsei-shi ronshū.* 3 vols. Tokyo, Iwanami shoten, 1926–43.

Nakamura, Naokatsu. *Shōen no kenkyū.* Tokyo, Hoshino shoten, 1939.

Nihon bukke jimmei jisho, comp. by Junkei Washio. Tokyo, Kōyū-kan, 1903.

Nihon chiri fūzoku taikei, ed. by Teruhisa Nakama. Tokyo, Shinkō-sha, 1929–32.

Nihon rekishi-chiri gakkai, comp. *Kamakura jidai shiron.* Tokyo, Katsurai-sha, 1931.

Nihon shaji taikan, ed. by Kōzaburō Fujimoto and others. 2 vols. Kyoto, Hinode shimbun-sha, 1933.

Ōmori, Kingorō. *Buke jidai no kenkyū.* 2 vols. Tokyo, Fuzambō, 1927–29.

Ono, Takeo. *Nihon shōen shiron.* Tokyo, Yūhi-kaku, 1943.

Ryō, Susumu. *Kamakura jidai no kenkyū.* Tokyo, Shunju-sha shōhaku-kan, 1944.

Satō, Shin'ichi. *Bakufu-ron.* Tokyo, Chūō kōro-sha, 1955.

Seishi kakei dai-jiten, ed. by Akira Ōta and Sanji Mikami. 3 vols. Tokyo, Seishi kakei dai-jiten kankō-kai, 1934–36.

Shigaku chiri-gaku dōkō-kai, comp. *Kamakura jidai no kenkyū.* Tokyo, Hoshino shoten, 1925.

Shiryō sōran, comp. by Tokyo teikoku daigaku bungaku-bu shiryō hen-san gakari. Vols. 1–4. Tokyo, Chōyō-kai, 1925–27.

Shoku-Nihon-gi, ed. by Jirō Mochizuki. Kokushi taikei, vol. II. Tokyo, Shuei-sha, 1897.

Takigawa, Seijirō. *Nihon dorei keizai-shi.* Tokyo, Tōkō shoin, 1930.

Takimoto, Seiichi. *Nihon hōken keizai-shi.* Tokyo, Maruzen, 1930.

Tsuji, Zennosuke. *Jimbutsu ronsō.* Tokyo, Yūzan-kaku, 1925.

――― *Nihon bunka-shi, Kamakura jidai.* Tokyo, Shunju-sha, 1950.

Wada, Hidematsu. *Kokushi setsuen.* Tokyo, Meiji shoin, 1939.

Wakamori, Tarō. *Chūsei kyōdō-tai no kenkyū.* Tokyo, Kōbun-dō, 1950.

Watanabe, Tamotsu. *Gempei kōsō-shi.* Tokyo, Hakuyō-sha, 1940.

――― *Genji to Heishi.* Tokyo, Shibun-dō, 1955.

Yashiro, Kuniji. *Azuma kagami no kenkyū.* Tokyo, Yoshikawa kōbun-kan, 1913.

Yūsoku kojitsu jiten, ed. by Teijirō Katō. 3d rev. ed. Tokyo, Rimpei shoten, 1936.

Yūzan-kaku henshū-kyoku, comp. *Isetsu Nihon-shi, Jimbutsu-hen.* Vol. 3. Tokyo, Yūzan-kaku, 1931.

――― *Isetsu Nihon-shi, Sensō-hen.* Vol. 1. Tokyo, Yūzan-kaku, 1932.

OTHER SOURCES

Asakawa, Kanji. *The Documents of Iriki, Illustrative of the Development of the Feudal Institutions of Japan.* New Haven, Yale Univ. Press, 1929.

――― *The Early Institutional Life of Japan: A Study in the Reform of 645 A.D.* Tokyo, Shuei-sha, 1903.

――― "The Founding of the Shogunate by Minamoto No Yoritomo," *Seminarium Kondakovianum* (Prague, Institut Kondakov), VI (1933), 109–29.

――― "The Life of a Monastic Sho in Medieval Japan," *Annual Report of the American Historical Association for 1916,* I (1919), 311–46.

――― "Some Aspects of Japanese Feudal Institutions," *Transactions of the Asiatic Society of Japan,* Series 1, XLVI (1918), 76–102.

Brinkley, Frank. *A History of the Japanese People from the Earliest Times to the End of the Meiji Era.* New York, Encyclopedia Britannica, 1915.

Coates, Harper Havelock, and Ryūgaku Ishizuka. *Honen, the Buddhist Saint, His Life and Teachings.* Kyoto, Chionin, 1925.

Coulborn, Rushton, ed. *Feudalism in History.* Princeton, Princeton Univ. Press, 1956.

Ishii, Ryōsuke. "On Japanese Possession of Real Property—A Study of *chigyō* in the Middle Ages," *Japan Annual of Law and Politics,* No. 1 (1952), pp. 149–62.

Jouon des Longrais, Frédéric. *Age de Kamakura, sources* (1150–1333), *archives, chartes, japonaises* (*monjo*). Paris and Tokyo, Maison Franco-japonaise, 1950.

Murdoch, James. *A History of Japan*. Vol. 1. 2nd ed. London, Kegan Paul, 1925.

Reischauer, Edwin O., and Joseph K. Yamagiwa. *Translations from Early Japanese Literature*. Cambridge, Harvard University Press, 1951.

Reischauer, Robert Karl. *Early Japanese History*, Parts A and B. 2 vols. Princeton, Princeton Univ. Press, 1937.

Sadler, Arthur Lindsay. "Heike monogatari," *Transactions of the Asiatic Society of Japan*, Series 1, XLVI (1918), i–xiv, 1–278; XLIX (1921), i–ii, 1–354.

Sansom, George B. "Early Japanese Law and Administration," *Transactions of the Asiatic Society of Japan*, Series 2, IX (1932), 67–109; XI (1934), 117–49.

—— *Japan; A Short Cultural History*. Rev. ed. New York, Appleton Century, 1944.

Tarring, C. J. "Land Provisions of the Taiho Ryo," *Transactions of the Asiatic Society of Japan*, Series 1, VIII (1880), 145–55.

Yanaga, Chitoshi. "Source Materials in Japanese History: The Kamakura Period, 1192–1333," *Journal of the American Oriental Society*, LIX (1939), 38–55.

Index